PELICAN

THE PELICAN

NEW TESTAMENT COMMENTARIES

EDITED BY D. E. NINEHAM

THE GOSPEL OF ST MATTHEW

John Fenton, the son of a Liverpool vicar, was born in 1921 and educated at St Edward's School and the Queen's College, Oxford, where he read theology and was a pupil of R. H. Lightfoot. He went on to Lincoln Theological College and, on ordination in 1944, worked as a curate in the outskirts of Wigan until he returned to Lincoln Theological College in 1947, first as Chaplain and later as Sub-Warden. In 1954 he was appointed vicar of Wentworth in Yorkshire, where he remained for four years. He had already started his commentary on St Matthew's Gospel when, in 1958, he was appointed Principal of Lichfield Theological College. He became Principal of St Chad's College, University of Durham, in 1965.

THE PELICAN
NEW TESTAMENT COMMENTARIES

The Gospel of St Matthew

J. C. FENTON

PENGUIN BOOKS

Penguin Books Ltd, Harmondsworth, Middlesex, England
Penguin Books Inc., 7110 Ambassador Road, Baltimore, Maryland 21207, U.S.A.
Penguin Books Australia Ltd, Ringwood, Victoria, Australia

—

First published 1963
Reprinted 1966, 1968, 1971, 1973

—

—

Made and printed in Great Britain
by Cox & Wyman Ltd,
London, Reading and Fakenham
Set in Monotype Bembo

The Bible text in this publication is from the *Revised
Standard Version of the Bible*, copyright 1946 and 1952
by the Division of Christian Education, National Council
of Churches, and used by permission

Contents

Editorial Foreword

Biblical commentaries are of various kinds. Some are intended solely for the specialist; others are devotional commentaries meant simply to help the Christian believer in his prayer and meditation. The commentaries in this series belong to neither class. Though they are based on full scholarly study and deal with technical points wherever necessary, the aim throughout has been to bring out the meaning the Evangelists intended to convey to their original readers. Since that meaning was religious, it is hoped that the commentaries, while being of interest to readers of any religious persuasion or none, and giving a fair indication of the current position in Gospel study, will help Christian readers to a deeper and more informed appreciation of the Gospels.

Technical terms have been avoided wherever possible; where used they have been fully explained in the Introductions, and readers are advised to read the Introduction to each volume before beginning on the commentary proper. The extended introduction to the volume on Mark is in some degree intended as an Introduction to the series as a whole.

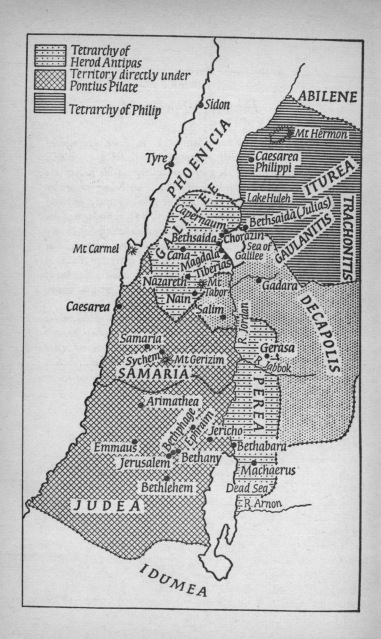

Tetrarchy of
Herod Antipas

Territory directly under
Pontius Pilate

Tetrarchy of Philip

ABILENE

Sidon

PHOENICIA

Mt Hermon

Tyre

Caesarea
Philippi

ITUREA

GALILEE

Lake Huleh

TRACHONITIS

Capernaum

Bethsaida (Julias)

Mt Carmel

Bethsaida

Chorazin

Cana

Magdala

Sea of
Galilee

GAULANITIS

Tiberias

Nazareth

Mt
Tabor

Gadara

Nain

DECAPOLIS

Caesarea

Salim

R. Jordan

Samaria

Gerasa

Sychem

Mt Gerizim

R. Jabbok

SAMARIA

PEREA

Arimathea

Bethphage

Ephraim

Jericho

Emmaus

Bethany

Bethabara

Jerusalem

Machaerus

Bethlehem

Dead Sea

R. Arnon

JUDEA

IDUMEA

Introduction

The reader for whom this commentary is intended is not a specialist in the study of the Bible, but one who would like to understand one of the books of the New Testament and has very little previous knowledge of the work that has been going on in this field during the last century.

Such a reader will almost certainly find here many attitudes and statements which will surprise him, and possibly even offend him. The purpose of the Introduction is to explain the point of view from which the commentary is written, in the hope that the reader and the author of this book may see eye to eye.

WHAT IS A GOSPEL?

First of all it may be assumed that because this is a commentary on a book of the Bible, every statement in the biblical text will be true in every sense. The reader may have heard, and he may believe, that 'The Bible is true', and 'The Bible is History'. And even if he has heard that there is legend and myth in the Old Testament, he may well believe that since we are here dealing with a Gospel, there will not be anything unhistorical here; one of the current meanings of the word 'Gospel' is 'thing that may safely be believed'. The reader may come to the Gospel according to Matthew expecting to find here an accurate historical account of the life of Jesus. If he does so, he will be disappointed. We must therefore begin by finding out what a Gospel is, in order to understand how to read it and to know what to look for in it.

Immediately we run into this difficulty: we have no means of finding out what a Gospel is, except from the Gospels themselves. No writer from the time when the Gospels were written has left us any information that would enable us to answer the question, What is a Gospel? Our investigation into the nature and purpose of a Gospel is therefore confined to a study of the Gospels. We shall have to ask, What do the Gospels show us about themselves? And in particular, What does this Gospel according to Matthew disclose concerning itself?

We shall begin to be able to answer this question if we can discover the approximate date of its writing. If it was written very soon after the events which it describes, then it may contain accurate history; but if it was written long after the events, unless it is based on contemporary sources, it may well contain non-historical elements. We have examples of these two kinds of writing in the Old Testament; the books of Samuel and Kings are much nearer in date to the time of the events recorded in them than are the two books of Chronicles which partly cover the same period, but include writing of a non-historical nature. The date of writing of Matthew may therefore help us to some extent to see what kind of book it is: history, or something else.

A further method of discovering the Gospel writer's aims may be shown by the case of Chronicles and Kings. The writer of Chronicles had a copy of Kings as a source; and so the reader of Chronicles can see how the author used his source, by turning up the appropriate passage in Kings. If we could do this in the case of Matthew's Gospel we should have some guide to what he was doing when he wrote his book, and fortunately we can do this: the Gospel according to Mark was one of Matthew's sources – his chief source in fact – and it lies before us in the New Testament much as it lay before Matthew when he wrote. A comparison of Mark with Matthew will be one of our chief methods for understanding Matthew.

Another key to the intention of an author is the way in which he arranges the material of his book. If his primary purpose is to write history, he will arrange his material chronologically – or, if he is not doing so, he will usually tell his readers that he is departing from the strict order of events. If, however, his principal purpose is something other than the writing of history, he may arrange his material according to any other plan that he thinks appropriate – for example, he may collect his material according to topics, rather than according to the sequence in which the events happened. Matthew, we shall see, has certainly made some of his arrangements according to topic; he has, in fact, paid a great deal of attention to arrangement in producing his Gospel, but this arrangement is not chronological. From this, also, we shall be able to form some idea of what his Gospel is.

We shall begin, therefore, with an examination of (i) the probable date of the writing of this Gospel; (ii) the use of sources; and (iii) the arrangement of the material in the book.

(i) The date of the writing of Matthew's Gospel

The earliest surviving writings which quote this Gospel are probably the letters of Ignatius, the Bishop of Antioch, who, while being taken as a prisoner from the East to Rome about A.D. 110, wrote to various churches in Asia Minor and to the church at Rome. Ignatius refers to the star which appeared at the time of the birth of Jesus, the answer of Jesus to John the Baptist when he was baptized, and several sayings of Jesus which are recorded only in this Gospel (12^{33}, 15^{13}, 19^{12}). It seems almost certain therefore that Ignatius, and possibly the recipients of his letters also, knew this Gospel, and thus that it was written before A.D. 110. But how long before?

Here we cannot be so certain. But it is possible that we can find evidence that Matthew was writing after the war between the Romans and the Jews which ended in the destruction of the temple at Jerusalem in A.D. 70. See, for example, 22^7: *The king was angry, and he sent his troops and destroyed those murderers and burned their city*; and compare also 21^{41}, 27^{25}. Similarly, Matthew's Gospel contains a strongly anti-Jewish note running through it, from the teaching not to do *as the hypocrites do* in Chapter 6, to the Woes on the *scribes and Pharisees* in Chapter 23; and this may point to a date after *c.* A.D. 85 when the Christians were excluded from the Jewish synagogues. It is worth noticing here that Matthew often speaks of *their synagogues* (4^{23}, 9^{35}, 10^{17}, 12^9, 13^{54}), as if to distinguish Christian meetings and meeting-places from those of the Jews, from which the Christians had now been turned out.

If this is the case, then we should have to conclude that Matthew's Gospel was written between about A.D. 85 and 105; perhaps, however, the most we can say so far is that it was written in the last quarter of the first century, or in the early years of the second.

This by itself will not give us the information that we are looking for concerning the nature of this Gospel. It tells us that the book might have been written not more than forty or fifty years after the crucifixion: it could, therefore, have been written by an eyewitness of the events which it records, a contemporary of Jesus, in his old age. But an investigation of the sources used in this Gospel will show that this cannot have been the case.

(ii) *The sources used in Matthew's Gospel*

In the following chapters of Matthew, the reader will find verses which are almost exactly the same as verses in Mark's Gospel: 3, 8, 9, 12–17, 19–22, 24, 26–28. (There are also Marcan elements in other chapters of Matthew.) These parallels between Matthew and Mark call for some explanation. It used to be thought, and is still maintained by a few writers, that Mark took these passages from Matthew, and that Matthew's Gospel is earlier than Mark's. But since 1835, when it was first put forward, the view has become very widely accepted that Matthew drew upon Mark, and that Mark's is the earlier Gospel. This is the opinion which will be accepted in the commentary which follows. It is not capable of a simple demonstration: the reader must read through the two Gospels side by side, note the differences between them, especially in the passages which are common to both, and ask, Which is more likely: that Mark was adapting Matthew's words, or Matthew Mark's?

If, as we believe, Matthew was making use of Mark's Gospel; and if, as will follow from this, Matthew was to a very considerable extent dependent on Mark, especially for the narrative sections of the Gospel, then another important conclusion for our present purpose will follow.

It is usually thought that Mark's Gospel was written about A.D. 65; and that the author of it was neither one of the apostles nor an eyewitness of the majority of events recorded in his Gospel. Matthew was therefore dependent upon the writing of such a man for the production of his book. What Matthew has done, in fact, is to produce a second and enlarged edition of Mark. Moreover, the changes which he makes in Mark's way of telling the story are not the corrections which an eyewitness might make in the account of one who was not an eyewitness. Thus, whereas in Mark's Gospel we may be only one remove from eyewitnesses, in Matthew's Gospel we are one remove further still.

We must, at this point, turn aside from the main argument for a moment to consider another question: Have we any evidence of written sources used by Matthew, other than Mark's Gospel? Unfortunately, we cannot be as certain about the answer to this question as we can be about Matthew's use of Mark. There are about 200 verses in Matthew which are very similar to Luke but have no parallel in Mark, and in some cases the similarity is so close that there must have been a written source. A good example of this is the account of the temptations of Jesus in Matthew 4$^{1-11}$ and Luke 4$^{1-13}$; but the greater part of this material consists of sayings of Jesus. Three explanations of these agreements between Matthew and Luke in non-Marcan passages are possible: Matthew copied from Luke; Luke copied from Matthew; or both Matthew and Luke drew upon a common written source or common sources. The last explanation, the lost second source of Matthew and Luke, has been the most popular hypothesis since the beginning of the century. (This source is sometimes referred to as Q.) But the suggestion that Luke copied from Matthew (which has always had its upholders) has recently been revived.

If there was a written document or series of documents containing these verses, then we should say that Matthew used Mark and Q, and both were in writing before him. But if Luke took this material from Matthew, then we cannot say for certain that these 200 'Q' verses stood before Matthew in a written form: they may have come to him orally; or he may have composed them himself; or some may have been written, some oral, and some composed by Matthew.

Fortunately it is not essential to decide this question for the study of Matthew's Gospel; it is much more important in the study of Luke, since it would add considerably to our knowledge of Luke if we could be sure that he had the whole of Matthew, and rejected or ignored or corrected certain statements in it. The only way in which the problem of Q is important for the study of Matthew's Gospel is as follows: if there was a common source, used independently by both Matthew and Luke, then it may be that at some points Luke has reproduced it in a more original form than Matthew. It would then be possible to trace Matthew's editorial work on a Q passage by comparing the Lucan parallel, just as we can trace Matthew's adaptations of Mark by turning up the Marcan original.

The Marcan and Q material do not account for the whole of Matthew's Gospel. There is still a remainder, when these two kinds of material have been subtracted from Matthew. Some of this material consists of sayings of Jesus (e.g. some of the Beatitudes in Chapter 5, and the final parable in Chapter 25); some of it is narrative (e.g. the account of the birth of Jesus and the coming of the Magi in Chapters 1 and 2, and the final scene in Galilee in Chapter 28). It is almost impossible to say whether this material came to Matthew in a written form or orally, or whether Matthew himself composed it; probably something of all three. (The letter M has often been used to designate either all the material found only in Matthew, or that part of it which is thought to have been written before it was incorporated in this Gospel.)

Let us now return to the main investigation. We are trying to find out what kind of a book Matthew's Gospel is; and we have seen that it may have been written between A.D. 85 and 105. We now know that the author used, as the main source of his book, an earlier Gospel (Mark), and possibly other written sources, or oral traditions. Moreover, a study of Matthew's use of his sources does not show us a man correcting one source from first-hand knowledge of events. In the author of this Gospel, we have an editor, an arranger of material, rather than someone who is revising in the light of accurate historical information. We shall now look at the way in which Matthew has arranged and ordered his material.

(iii) *The arrangement of the material in Matthew*

Of all the Evangelists, Matthew has most obviously paid attention to arrangement; the plan and structure of his book are plain for all to see. This is most clear in his five collections of sayings of Jesus, each of which is marked at its conclusion by the use of a formula: e.g. 7^{28} *And when Jesus finished these sayings* . . . Cf. 11^1, 13^{53}, 19^1, 26^1.

The five collections of sayings of Jesus which are marked off at their conclusions in this way are as follows:

1 Chapters 5–7 ('The Sermon on the Mount'), the way of life which must be followed by those who want to enter the kingdom of heaven.

II Chapter 10, directions for those who are to proclaim the kingdom to others.

III Chapter 13, the coming of the kingdom described in parables and in the explanation of parables.

IV Chapter 18, how disciples are to treat one another.

V Chapters 23–25 (or 24 and 25, but reasons for including Chapter 23 will be given later), the coming of the kingdom of heaven, and the way to enter it.

The rest of the Gospel is mainly (though by no means entirely) narrative; and in some cases the narrative leads up to and introduces the teaching section which follows it. The whole Gospel may therefore be divided as follows:

1–4 Introduction.
5–7 The first section of teaching.
8, 9 Jesus' miracles of healing.
10 The second section of teaching.
11, 12 The rejection of John the Baptist and Jesus by the Jews.
13 The third section of teaching.
14–17 Further miracles, controversy with the Pharisees, Peter's confession, and the transfiguration of Jesus.
18 The fourth section of teaching.
19–22 The journey of Jesus and his disciples to Jerusalem and the teaching in the temple there.
23–25 The fifth section of teaching.
26–28 The last days of Jesus in or near Jerusalem; his arrest, trials, crucifixion, resurrection, and final appearance in Galilee.

Matthew has used this structure or scaffolding to express the main theme of the whole of his book; Jesus proclaimed the coming of the kingdom of heaven to the Jews by words and deeds, and invited them to repent – but they refused. However, there were those who paid attention and followed Jesus, and they are the beginning of the new Israel, which will grow (specially from among the Gentiles) and enter into the kingdom when God brings this age to its end.

It may, however, be possible to go further into Matthew's plan and arrangement of his material. We shall notice, on a number of occasions, Matthew's fondness for arranging items in the order a, b:b, a – the technical term for which is chiasmus. A good example of this is in his quotation from Isaiah 6⁹ᶠ· in 13¹⁵ where we have the order *heart, ears, eyes: eyes, ears, heart*. It may be that Matthew has ordered the whole of his Gospel so that it forms one great chiasmus. The evidence for this is as follows:

If we take the five collections of sayings of Jesus, which are spread out through the Gospel, as guides, then the middle point of the Gospel will be the middle of the central collection. This collection is unlike the two which come before it, in that here Jesus first teaches the crowds, and then leaves the crowds and goes into a house, where he explains his parables to his disciples. There is thus a break in this middle teaching section – a turning away from the crowds, and a concentration upon the disciples. It may be that Matthew saw this point as the central point both in his theme and in the structure of his book, and arranged the material symmetrically around it.

Certainly the first teaching section (5–7) and the last (23–25) are similar, both in length and subject-matter (entry into the kingdom); similarly the second (10) and the fourth (18) are of much the same length, and whereas the former describes the sending-out of apostles, the latter describes the receiving of people who have been sent in Christ's name. In the same way, the beginning of the whole Gospel matches the end of it: the birth of Jesus (1) and his resurrection or rebirth (28); the first quotation from the Old Testament, *God with us*, and the last words of Jesus, *I am with you always*; his baptism (3), and his death, which he speaks of as his baptism in Mark 10³⁸ (27); the temptations, with the twice-repeated *If you are the Son of God* (4), and his trials before Caiaphas and Pilate, and temptation to come down from the cross *If you are the Son of God* (27).

We cannot indeed be certain that Matthew planned his work in this way, but whether he did so or not, we can be certain that he paid careful attention to the arrangement of his material; and from a comparison of his Gospel with Mark's we can see that he re-arranged the paragraphs of that Gospel, although we may not always be certain of his reason for doing so.

We asked, at the beginning of this Introduction, What is a Gospel? and it may be that we are now in a position to give some kind of an answer to that question, at least in the case of Matthew's Gospel. To our author, a Gospel seems to have been an arrangement of the material describing the words and deeds of Jesus in such a way that certain doctrines held by the author might be expressed through the pattern of the whole book. Therefore, as we read this Gospel, we must be on the watch for suggestions and ideas conveyed through arrangement, sequence, and contrast, and look for the author's meaning by asking, Why did he put this here?

SOME DIFFICULTIES IN MATTHEW'S GOSPEL

So far, we have been mainly concerned with the form of the Gospel: and it may have come as a surprise to some readers to find that a Gospel is not simply an account of the life of Jesus, arranged chronologically. But there are other difficulties which will present themselves to a twentieth-century reader of Matthew's Gospel – difficulties connected with subject-matter rather than with form – and to these we must now turn.

(i) The fulfilment of the Scriptures

Ten times in his Gospel, Matthew uses a formula to introduce a quotation from the Old Testament: the formula is *this took place to fulfil what the Lord had spoken by the prophet* . . . (see 1^{22}, $2^{15, 17, 23}$, 4^{14}, 8^{17}, 12^{17}, 13^{35}, 21^4, 27^9). These quotations introduced by a formula are additions which Matthew has made to his source, Mark, and are one of the characteristic features of this Gospel. But there are also many other places in the book where we can be almost certain that Matthew has an Old Testament passage in mind, although he does not explicitly refer to it: see, for example, 27^{34}, *they offered him wine to drink, mingled with gall*; with which compare Psalm 69^{21}, *They gave me poison* [Greek, *gall*] *for food, and for my thirst they gave me vinegar to drink*; and contrast the Marcan parallel, *they offered him wine mingled with myrrh* (Mark 15^{23}). Many other examples of allusions to the Old Testament will be found throughout the commentary.

Matthew believed that the events which he was describing had been foretold by God, many years before they happened, in the Old Testament. There, through the prophets (and by 'the prophets' Matthew would understand not only the authors of the books which we call prophetic, but all the Old Testament writers), God had announced beforehand what he would do in the last days; now, with the coming of Jesus, these last days had come, and the events of his life were the events about which the Old Testament writers had been speaking.

It is probable, moreover, that Matthew conceived part of his task as an Evangelist to be that of making clear the correspondence between prophecy in the Old Testament and the life of Jesus; and when he records a saying of Jesus, that *every scribe who has been trained for the kingdom of heaven is like a householder who brings out of his treasure what is new and what is old* (13^{52}), he may have understood by *what is new* the words and deeds of Jesus, and by *what is old* the prophecy of this in the Old Testament. His work, therefore, was to match event with prophecy.

Moreover, so sure was Matthew of the truth of this relationship between the Old Testament and the life of Jesus that he would sometimes change the details of an event as they were recorded in his source, in order to bring out more clearly the correspondence to a prophecy; as in the example given above, where he changed Mark's *myrrh* to *gall*, to make clear the fulfilment of the Greek version of Ps. 69^{21}.

Modern study of the Old Testament does not support Matthew's understanding of it, nor the use he made of it when he was writing his Gospel. It is now seen that the Old Testament was not a collection of detailed foretellings of future events, which could only be understood centuries later: the Old Testament writers were in fact writing for their contemporaries in a way which could be understood by them, and describing things that would happen more or less in their own lifetime. Thus Matthew's use of the Old Testament, though it was no doubt of first-rate importance to Matthew's original readers, and continued to be helpful until modern historical study enabled us to see the Old Testament in a new way, is now a stumbling-block to the twentieth-century reader of his Gospel.

We must, however, try to see what Matthew was saying by means of these fulfilments; because it may be that what he was saying is still capable of being understood and accepted, although his way of saying it is no longer valid. And we should notice here that Matthew is not alone in using the Old Testament in this way: from the first, the Christians had preached the death and resurrection of Jesus as events which happened *in accordance with the scriptures*, see 1 Cor. 15³ff.; and it may be that Jesus himself interpreted his life and death as the fulfilment of prophecy: see, for example, Mark 14²⁷, where Jesus quotes Zech. 13⁷, *You will all fall away; for it is written, 'I will strike the shepherd, and the sheep will be scattered'* as a prophecy of his death and his disciples' flight.

Matthew and the other Christians who used this fulfilment-method were saying by means of it: Jesus is not just an ordinary man, but a special person, the one for whom the Jews have been waiting, the one sent by God to Israel. What he did, and what the Jews did to him, might lead you to doubt this. But although the Jews themselves did not believe it, Jesus *was* the one whom God had sent: the fact is proved by the correspondence between his life and the Old Testament prophecies.

That is to say, the fulfilment of the Old Testament is a first-century method of bearing witness to Jesus as the one who is to be believed and obeyed. We would not use it if we were asked to write a Gospel today: at least, we would not use it in the way that Matthew used it, sometimes even reading into the prophecy the event which he finds fulfilled in the life of Jesus, as in 2¹⁵ where he quotes Hosea's saying concerning the Exodus as a prophecy of the return of Jesus from Egypt. We might show how Jesus fulfilled other laws – moral and psychological laws, for example; Matthew did not do so, because Matthew lived in the first century. But it is still possible for us to believe what Matthew believed about Jesus, without expressing it in the way that Matthew expressed it.

(ii) *The miracles*

Matthew believed that Jesus miraculously healed people of diseases, raised the dead to life, fed and satisfied crowds by means of a small quantity of food, commanded a storm to stop, walked on water and enabled Peter to do so; and that Jesus had been miraculously conceived, that he possessed foreknowledge of events, and was raised from the dead on the second day after his death and burial.

The present-day reader of Matthew's Gospel may take up any one of a number of different positions in relation to these statements. He may, for example, argue that since God can, if he wishes, intervene in the world which he has created, and since this occasion warranted such intervention, we should expect miracles to have happened, and should not be surprised if they did.

With regard to this position there is one point which must be made. Just as Matthew can sometimes change a detail in the narrative from the way in which it was recorded in Mark in order to bring out a fulfilment of the Old Testament, so he can add to a narrative which he has received from his source in order to increase the number of miracles in his Gospel. Examples of this Matthean extension of the miraculous are: Peter's walking on the water ($14^{28ff.}$), the resurrection of the dead after the death of Jesus ($27^{52f.}$), and the earthquake before the women came to the tomb (28^2). In each of these cases, it is almost certain that Matthew had no written source other than Mark, who did not record the particular miracle that Matthew mentions; and that Matthew has in fact increased the frequency of miraculous events in his Gospel, without having historical evidence for them.

Some might therefore want to extend this argument backwards, beyond Mark's Gospel, and argue that if we could get to a time earlier than Mark or his sources we should not find any miracles at all; or that the events which were thought to be miracles (e.g. the casting out of demons and some of the cases of healing) were in fact performed by non-miraculous means (suggestion and faith-healing). Against this it must be said that the earliest strata that we can recover (i.e. the first preaching of the apostles) include the miracle of the resurrection. There is no recoverable presentation of Christianity that is wholly without this miraculous element. Nevertheless, it can and must be admitted that as the tradition was handed on, the number and magnitude of the miracles increased.

Again, our best method is to ask what Matthew and the other Christian writers who recorded the miracles of Jesus were saying when they said that he performed miracles, and that he was himself the subject of supernatural activity (his conception and his resurrection). They believed that Jesus was the one upon whom God's Spirit had come (3^{16}), and that it was through this Spirit that he was able to do miraculous acts (12^{28}). This Spirit, they believed, would renew the whole of creation when this age came to an end. Jesus was therefore the one who was sent by God to declare the coming of the new age, and to demonstrate it by means of miracles. He was the bringer of the complete, full, and indestructible life – the life of the age to come.

Here again we see that Matthew writes in the way he does because he belongs to the first century; and that this is not the way we should write today. Nevertheless, it is possible for us today to believe what Matthew believed about Jesus as miracle-worker (i.e. that Jesus offers a full and indestructible way of living), without necessarily believing in the historicity of the miracles which Matthew records.

(iii) *The imminent end of the world*

Matthew believed that the present history of the world, involving as it does sin and sickness and death, would come to an end soon. Jesus would come in glory, and everyone would be allotted to one or another of two classes, 'the blessed' and 'the cursed', and be sent either to *eternal life* or to *eternal punishment* (25[31ff.]). Matthew believed that this would happen soon: before the apostles would have had time to preach in all the towns of Israel (10[23]); before some of Jesus' contemporaries had died (16[28]); before that generation had passed away (24[34]). And it is clear that it did not happen as Matthew expected.

Although Matthew's Gospel is one of the places in the New Testament where this expectation of the imminent end of the world is most clearly expressed, in fact almost all the New Testament writers expressly state this belief; and in the opinion of a very large number of scholars, Jesus himself looked forward to his coming to the earth in glory soon after his death.

The idea that God would intervene soon, and reveal himself as King over the world by abolishing everything that was against his will, was not confined to Christians: we find it in the Jewish writers of books called 'apocalypses' (e.g. Daniel), and it may be that the Jewish sect which produced the Dead Sea Scrolls also thought in this way. We know from Jewish sources that people claiming to be Messiah, i.e. God's king, sent to rule at the end of this age, had appeared in Palestine at the time when Jesus was alive, and had succeeded in persuading people to follow them and accept their claims. So belief that the end of this age was near was in the air in the first century, and Christians breathed it just as much as their Jewish contemporaries.

We cannot take Matthew's statements about the end literally: history has proved them wrong. But we can try to understand what the first Christians meant when they used end-of-the-world language about Jesus. They were using a current way of thinking, in order to express one of their beliefs about Jesus – and they only had current ways of thinking for this purpose. They were saying at least this: the way into eternal life depends on your attitude to Jesus; he is the judge, and he will judge people according to their obedience to his teaching. To them, the most important question was, Shall I go to eternal life or to eternal punishment? And they believed that the answer to this question was bound up with the answer to a question which Jesus had asked, *who do you say that I am?* (16¹⁵). The imminence of the end (as they thought) made it all the more urgent for them to answer this question, and to live out the answer in a life of obedience to the teaching of Jesus.

We do not find it natural to think like this about the end of the world – because we cannot today revive the belief that history is coming to an end soon, in the way that the first-century Jews believed that it was. Instead of thinking of an imminent judgement, we find it more natural to think in terms of an integrated life, a wholeness. Our urgent need is for a way of living that really is living. And this is one way in which we can interpret Matthew's statements about the imminent end of the world.

(iv) 'Who do you say that I am?'

The three difficulties in Matthew that we have looked at so far (fulfilment of scripture, miracles, expectation of the end) have, in each case, turned out on inspection to be ways by which the first-century Christians expressed their faith in Jesus and proclaimed it to others. So we must go on now to look at two more questions: What did Matthew believe about Jesus? and, What can we believe about him?

Matthew believed that Jesus was miraculously conceived by the Holy Spirit in fulfilment of Old Testament prophecy; that the Holy Spirit descended upon him at his baptism, and enabled him to perform miracles; that he offered himself to God as a sacrifice for the world, through which God would make a new covenant with men; that he was raised up from the dead, and given authority from God to rule over the universe; and that he would soon come to exercise this authority in the last judgement. Matthew, following the earlier Christians, therefore used certain titles which were available in the Old Testament and in later Jewish writing: *The Son of Abraham, The Son of David, The Christ, The King of Israel, The Son of man, The Son of God, The Lord.* But what did Matthew mean when he used these titles?

Jesus is presented in this Gospel as one who calls people to *follow* him; and following him involves living by the faith by which he lived, and according to his teaching. Matthew emphasizes the work of Jesus as *teacher*; he gives us a large number of his sayings, and he closes his book with the words, *teaching them to observe all that I have commanded you* (28²⁰). This teaching can be summarized (as it was summarized by Paul) as *faith* in Jesus (i.e. obedience to him), *hope* in God (i.e. the abandonment of security in the expectation of salvation from God), and *love* towards other men (i.e. the giving up of claims against them, and the organization of one's life for them).

In Matthew's Gospel, Jesus is put before the reader as the one who makes the most complete claim upon a man that it is possible to make – the demand for his life – and as the one who promises, to those who answer this demand with obedience, the gift of *eternal life*. Obedience, as Matthew saw it, is more important than correct belief about Jesus; notice, for example, 7²¹: *Not every one who says to me, 'Lord, Lord,' shall enter the kingdom of heaven, but he who does the will of my Father who is in heaven.* Although Matthew uses many titles of Jesus, he is much more concerned that his readers should obey Jesus, by living in faith, hope, and love, than that they should be correct in their understanding of who Jesus is.

(v) Faith and unbelief

If this is true, and Jesus is above all the one to be followed and obeyed, then another difficulty will arise: Why should he be believed and followed? What are his credentials?

No doubt Matthew would have said that the fulfilment of scripture and the miracles were evidence that answered that question. But, although Matthew believed this to be true, this is not his final position. And this is fortunate for us, because we have already seen some reason to doubt both the validity of the argument for the fulfilment of scripture, and the historicity of some, at least, of the miracles.

Matthew was well aware of the unbelief of the majority of the Jews – even of those who had seen the miracles and witnessed the fulfilment of prophecy. The answer which he gives to the question, Why do some believe and not others? is, *To you it has been given* [i.e. by God] *to know the secrets of the kingdom of heaven, but to them it has not been given* (13¹¹); and, *Blessed are you, Simon Bar-Jona! For flesh and blood has not revealed this to you, but my Father who is in heaven* (16¹⁷).

This is the final mystery and it cannot be dispelled: some people do believe, and some do not. Those who do, know that their faith is a gift given to them, and not a result of their own effort. And the gift is given through the preaching of Jesus as the Christ: *faith comes from what is heard, and what is heard comes by the preaching of Christ* (Rom. 10¹⁷). Matthew himself had become a Christian through the preaching of others: and he wrote his Gospel in order that those who read it – both Christians and those who were not yet Christians – might, by this means, have faith in Jesus, and obey his teaching, and enter *eternal life* in the *kingdom of heaven*.

(vi) Rewards and punishments

There is one other feature of this Gospel which the reader may well find difficult, but it is of a rather different kind from those which we have been considering. Throughout the book there are repeated references to rewards and punishments; and even in the limited space available, something must be said on this point.

The theme begins in the words of the Baptist, when he says of Jesus that he will *gather his wheat into the granary, but the chaff he will burn with unquenchable fire* (3¹²). The *wheat* here is a symbol of the *blessed*, who will enter *the kingdom of heaven*, and the *chaff* means the *cursed* who will depart into *the eternal fire prepared for the devil and his angels* (25³⁴, ⁴¹).

The difficulty, however, is not so much the either/or of salvation/damnation in itself, as that this either/or seems at times to be used as the motive for action. This is particularly the case in Chapter 6, where Jesus instructs his disciples to give alms, pray, and fast *in secret* in order that they may be rewarded by God; and the section concludes with this saying, *lay up for yourselves treasures in heaven, where neither moth nor rust consumes and where thieves do not break in and steal,*

For where your treasure is, there will your heart be also (6²⁰f.). Notice also the promises of reward in each of the Beatitudes at the beginning of Chapter 5 (vv. 3–10); the saying *your reward is great in heaven* (5¹²); and, on the other hand, the threat of punishment contained for example in the formula *there men will weep and gnash their teeth* (8¹², 13⁴², ⁵⁰, 22¹³, 24⁵¹, 25³⁰). The last words of Jesus in this Gospel before the account of the Passion and resurrection are concerned with this subject: *they* [i.e. the cursed] *will go away into eternal punishment, but the righteous into eternal life* (25⁴⁶).

The difficulty about this is that hope of reward is usually thought to be a wrong motive for action; and similarly that avoidance of punishment is regarded as an inferior aim. Surely, it is said, we should act without considering such extrinsic matters as reward or punishment. And yet there is no denying that both are frequently mentioned in Matthew's Gospel, and indeed throughout the New Testament. Indeed, we might contrast the New Testament unfavourably, in this respect, with one of the Jewish rabbis, who said, 'Be not like servants who serve their lord on condition of receiving a reward; but rather be like servants who serve their lord under no condition of receiving reward' (Pirqe Aboth 1³).

A solution of this problem may be as follows: First, disinterestedness is not a mark of Christianity or of the New Testament. Christianity is about salvation and it offers salvation to people as something that is to their advantage. Matthew and the other New Testament writers are quite unashamed on this point: *seek first his* [God's] *kingdom and his righteousness, and all these things* [food, drink, clothing] *shall be yours as well* (6³³); *Enter by the narrow gate* (7¹³); *every one who has left houses or brothers or sisters or father or mother or children or lands, for my name's sake, will receive a hundredfold, and inherit eternal life* (19²⁹).

That is to say, the point of view of Christianity is that men are not in a position to speak of disinterestedness and 'pure love'; they cannot afford to. They are in a state of need, and they must receive something from God, or else be destroyed.

But, secondly, Matthew and the other New Testament writers believe that God's rewards are always greater than men's deserts, that everyone is in the position of the labourers in the parable who receive a full day's wage for one hour's work (20¹ff.). The experience of Christians is therefore that God is a giver of gifts, rather than one who rewards merit, because his gifts exceed any possible estimate of a man's labour.

And, thirdly, that the particular kind of life for which rewards are promised is a life of self-forgetfulness and abandonment to God, which ceases to look for rewards. Jesus 'promises reward precisely to those who obey not for the sake of reward' (Bultmann).

Finally, perhaps it is necessary to say something further about the threats of hell: e.g. *Every tree . . . that does not bear good fruit is cut down and thrown into the fire* (3¹⁰); *the gate is wide and the way is easy, that leads to destruction, and those who enter by it are many* (7¹³).

However difficult we find it to reconcile the infinite love of God with the etrnal damnation of some of his creatures, we can be certain of two things. First, that Jesus used first-century Jewish ideas about hell to warn his contemporaries of judgement and condemnation. Secondly, that a way of life that departs from his teaching – particularly his teaching about *love* – is a way of life that leads to destruction; that is to say, that the man who does not love is already half-dead; he may have gained *the whole world*, but he has forfeited his life (16²⁶). Thus the promises of reward and the warnings of destruction are at least descriptions of what may be, to a great extent, put to the test in the present; *whoever would save his life will lose it, and whoever loses his life for my sake will find it* (16²⁵).

MATTHEW'S PURPOSE

Let us consider Matthew's intention when he wrote his Gospel, and see what he was doing for his readers by writing it.

He took Mark's Gospel, and enlarged it by the addition of a few narratives, mainly at the beginning and at the end, and by the addition of the teaching of Jesus which was available from other sources. He revised Mark, sometimes making small alterations in the text, sometimes adding Old Testament references, sometimes re-arranging the order of events. But both in his enlargement of Mark, and in his revision of it, his purpose was to make clearer to his readers the claim of Jesus to be believed and to be obeyed.

Matthew was not attempting to write an account of the life of Jesus which would be historically more accurate than Mark's Gospel – perhaps there was not the material to do so by that time; but in any case he has not done so. He was rather bringing out further, by his additions and revisions, the meaning, as he understood it, of Mark's Gospel, and of Jesus' life and teaching.

The reader of this Gospel, if he is to use it as Matthew intended it to be used, is to ask, above all, the question: What does this mean for me in terms of faith and obedience? If he comes to Matthew's Gospel with this in mind, he will neither be disappointed with what he finds there, nor misuse what he is given.

Author's Note

A number of points in the first edition (1963) were corrected in the 1966 reprint, and four books published after the commentary was written were added to the list of *Suggestions for Further Reading*.

For the 1968 reprint, further misprints and a few other errors were corrected; the page references to the revised edition (1963) of J. Jeremias' *The Parables of Jesus* were inserted, and a revised list of books published since the commentary was written was added.

Further additions are made to this list for the 1971 reprint.

G. Bornkamm, G. Barth and H. J. Held, *Tradition and Interpretation in Matthew* (S.C.M., 1963)

W. D. Davies, *The Setting of the Sermon on the Mount* (Cambridge, 1964), *The Sermon on the Mount* (Cambridge, 1966)

C. F. Evans, *The Lord's Prayer* (S.P.C.K., 1963)

Austin Farrer, *The Triple Victory* (Faith Press, 1965)

R. H. Fuller, *Interpreting the Miracles* (S.C.M., 1963)

B. Gerhardsson, *The Testing of God's Son* (Gleerup, 1966)

D. R. A. Hare, *The Theme of Jewish Persecution of Christians in the Gospel according to St Matthew* (Cambridge, 1967)

J. Jeremias, *The Prayers of Jesus* (S.C.M., 1967)

J. D. Kingsbury, *The Parables of Jesus in Matthew 13* (S.P.C.K., 1969)

E. Linnemann, *Parables of Jesus* (S.P.C.K., 1966)

J. Lowe, *The Lord's Prayer* (Oxford, 1962)

E. Lohmeyer, *The Lord's Prayer* (Collins, 1965)

Suggestions for Further Reading

(i) Introduction

J. H. Ropes, *The Synoptic Gospels* (Oxford University Press, 1960)

F. C. Grant, *The Gospels* (Faber, 1959)

G. D. Kilpatrick, *The Origins of the Gospel according to St Matthew* (Oxford, 1946)

B. C. Butler, *The Originality of St Matthew* (Cambridge, 1951)

(ii) Commentaries

B. T. D. Smith, *The Gospel according to St Matthew* in the *Cambridge Greek Testament* (Cambridge, 1927)

F. W. Green, *The Gospel according to Saint Matthew* in *The Clarendon Bible* (Oxford, 1936)

G. E. P. Cox, *The Gospel according to St Matthew* in the *Torch Bible Commentaries* (S.C.M., 1952)

F. V. Filson, *A Commentary on the Gospel according to St Matthew* in *Black's New Testament Commentaries* (Black, 1960)

(iii) Other Studies

Austin Farrer, *St Matthew and St Mark* (Dacre, 1966)

T. W. Manson, *The Sayings of Jesus* (S.C.M., 1949)

J. Jeremias, *The Parables of Jesus* (S.C.M., Revised edition, 1963)

D. Bonhoeffer, *The Cost of Discipleship* (S.C.M., 1948)

The abbreviation *Lexicon* in the commentary refers to W. F. Arndt and F. W. Gingrich, *A Greek-English Lexicon of the New Testament and Other Early Christian Literature* (Cambridge University Press, 1957).

The abbreviation LXX refers to the Greek translation of the Old Testament called the *Septuagint*, and the edition used is that of A. Rahlfs, *Septuaginta* (Stuttgart, 3rd edition, 1949).

Matthew 1¹-4¹⁷

Matthew's Introduction

Ancient writers did not divide their books up with chapter numbers or headings to sections; therefore any division of Matthew's Gospel is bound to be hypothetical. We shall take 1^1–4^{17} as the introduction to the Gospel as a whole; and then we shall find a short setting of the scene for the first section of teaching – i.e. 4^{18}–5^2 sets the scene, and 5^3–7^{27} is the first section of teaching.

The purpose of Matthew's introduction is to put the reader in the picture at the beginning of the book. This introduction is in two parts: (i) Chapters 1 and 2 give the genealogy of Jesus and an account of his birth and his early years; (ii) 3^1–4^{17} tells us about John the Baptist, the baptism of Jesus and his temptations in the wilderness, and the beginning of his preaching in Galilee.

For this second section, 3^1–4^{17}, Matthew had the introduction to Mark's Gospel as his source, to which he added material of his own. But for the genealogy, birth, and early years in Chapters 1 and 2 there was nothing in Mark.

1, 2: The Genealogy, Birth, and Early Years

This section divides into four parts: (i) the title, 1^1; (ii) the genealogy, 1^{2-17}; (iii) the birth of Jesus, 1^{18-25}; (iv) the Magi, King Herod, the flight into Egypt, and the return to Nazareth, 2. Throughout these two chapters, Matthew is primarily concerned to tell the reader who Jesus is: he is *the Christ*, that is the anointed one, the king whom God will send to rule over the world; he is *the son of David*, descended from David through the royal line; and he is *the son of Abraham*, in whom God's promise that he would bless *all the families of the earth* is to be fulfilled (Gen. 12^3); he was miraculously conceived by the power of the Holy Spirit, fulfilling God's promise by the prophet; and though his own people, the Jews, reject him, he is worshipped by the Gentiles.

Matthew appears to be writing about things that happened: but we must ask how accurate a historian he is in these chapters. We must ask this, because ancient writers of history had not the same standards or methods as modern historians. We have already seen, for example, that Matthew changed details in Mark, in order to bring out fulfilments of the Old Testament; and that he added accounts of miracles for which he had no evidence in Mark, nor, as far as we know, elsewhere. How historical are Matthew's first two chapters?

One view is that they are not based on the evidence of those who were present at the time, or of those who had heard accounts of what happened from others. There are three reasons for this view: first, in the remaining part of the Gospel Matthew was completely dependent on Mark for the deeds of Jesus. He had independent access to the sayings of Jesus, but apparently he had no information about what Jesus had done, other than the Gospel of Mark. (The only exception is the story of the healing of the centurion's servant in 8^{5-13}.) Matthew does indeed add narrative – incidents in his account of the Passion and resurrection, but they are legendary rather than historical; and they are written in Matthew's own style and vocabulary (e.g. the death of Judas, Pilate's wife's dream, Pilate washing his hands, the opening of the tombs and the resurrection of the dead saints, the guard at the tomb). These incidents have been added by Matthew to bring out the meaning of what he is describing. If Matthew was unable to add historical narratives at the end of his Gospel, it is unlikely that he would have been able to add them at the beginning of it, since the events connected with the death and resurrection of Jesus were the central core of the preaching of the first Christians; and since there would have been more witnesses of the things which happened c. A.D. 30 than of those which happened when Jesus was born. Secondly, when we examine Matthew 1, 2 we shall find that they are very largely made up out of reflections upon certain Old Testament passages read in the light of Jewish expectations and Christian faith. That is to say, there is nothing here which can only have come to Matthew from historical tradition. Thirdly, there is what one might call a different atmosphere about these chapters from what we find in the rest of the Gospel: there, with a few exceptions, no one knows who Jesus is, and the veil which hides him is seldom drawn aside; here, on the other hand, dreams, an angel, and a star reveal him as the king. This is the atmosphere of legend, not of history.

Against this we must set two points: first, there are birth-stories in Luke, which to some extent corroborate the birth-stories in Matthew; e.g. the virgin birth, the birth at Bethlehem, the revelation of Jesus to shepherds (instead of to the Magi), the early life of Jesus at Nazareth. Second, Would Matthew have been as free as we have suggested that he was, in the composition of what appears to be history, if he had no historical evidence?

We are not yet in a position to answer the first point for certain; it may be that Luke used Matthew's birth-stories in writing Luke 1, 2 (see p. 13). Or it may be that Matthew and Luke both knew traditions of the virgin birth (though there is no other certain evidence for it from early Christian literature), the birth at Bethlehem, and the early years at Nazareth.

With regard to the second point, the question, Would Matthew have composed these chapters without historical evidence? we must realize that this question would not have meant anything to him as stated in this way; he would have said that the historical evidence for these two chapters lay in the Old Testament, and that he was describing what *must* have happened, because this is what the prophets had said would happen.

If this view of Matthew 1 and 2 is accepted (and many scholars do not accept it), then we should read these chapters to find out what Matthew believed about Jesus, rather than for information concerning the early life of Jesus. And though this may seem to be a loss and deprivation, in fact it is not so: Matthew's intention was to put the reader in the picture, by telling him who Jesus really is; and this can be done by means of non-historical narratives as well as by means of those which are historical.

I *The book of the genealogy of Jesus Christ, the son of David, the son of Abraham.*

The title which Matthew has put at the beginning of his book is ambiguous – and perhaps intentionally so. It contains a word (*genesis*) which can mean *genealogy*, or *birth*, and is the title of the first book in the Old Testament, Genesis, and it includes an expression taken from Genesis, *the book of the generations* (Gen. 2[4], 5[1]). The title is therefore telescopic: it can be extended to include more and more of what Matthew is beginning to write about. First, it can cover *the genealogy* which immediately follows it; then, it can refer to the account of *the birth* of Jesus (the same word is translated *birth* in 1[18]); thirdly, it can mean 'history', or 'life-story'; and finally, it can refer to the whole new creation which begins at the conception of Jesus and will be completed at his second coming. Matthew adds these titles to the personal name, *Jesus: Christ, the son of David, the son of Abraham.*

Although Matthew is not using Mark until Matt. 3[1ff.] (= Mark 1[2ff.]), it is possible that Mark 1[1] may have suggested to him the use of the phrase from Genesis *The book of the genealogy*. Mark began his Gospel with these words: *The beginning of the gospel of Jesus Christ, the Son of God*; the word *beginning* (*archē*) is used in the first sentence of Genesis, *In the beginning God created the heavens and the earth*: and there are other allusions to Genesis in Mark 1[1ff.].

ראש

Jesus: The Greek form of the Hebrew name Joshua, and a common name among the Jews. On its meaning see 1[21].

Christ is simply the Greek (*Christos*) for the Hebrew word Messiah, meaning 'anointed'. *Christ* was originally a title, not a personal name, and though Gentile Christians used it as a name, in Matthew it is still a title, and should be translated here, The Christ. The Jews had used it for the anointed king who would be sent by God in the last days; e.g. 'And he shall be a righteous king, taught of God, over them, and there shall be no unrighteousness in his days in their midst, for all shall be holy and their king the anointed of the Lord' (*Psalms of Solomon* 17[32]).

the son of David: This title is used frequently in this Gospel (9[27], 12[23], 15[22], 20[30, 31], 21[9, 15], 22[42, 45]) and it goes back to passages in the Old Testament where God promises a son to David, e.g. *When your days are fulfilled and you lie down with your fathers, I will raise up your son after you, who shall come forth from your body, and I will establish his kingdom* (2 Sam. 7[12]). The title had also been used by the Jews of the Messiah, e.g. 'Behold, O Lord, and raise up unto them their king, the son of David, at the time in which Thou seest, O God, that he may reign over Israel Thy servant' (*Psalms of Solomon* 17²³).

the son of Abraham: For God's promises to Abraham, see Gen. 12ff., and notice the use which is made of these words in Gal. 3¹⁶: *Now the promises were made to Abraham and to his offspring. It does not say, And to offsprings, referring to many; but, referring to one, And to your offspring, which is Christ.* Thus the title *son of Abraham* refers back to God's words to Abraham, *In you all the families of the earth will be blessed* (Gen. 12³, margin), and forward to the preaching to the Gentiles (28¹⁹).

I²⁻¹⁷ *The Genealogy*

Matthew has used in his title the three names *Christ, David,* and *Abraham*; he now begins, in his characteristic way, with the last of these (*Abraham*), and writes the genealogy, through *David,* to *Christ.* He then divides the genealogy into three equal ages: (i) *Abraham to David,* (ii) *David to the deportation,* and (iii) *the deportation . . . to the Christ* (1¹⁷).

I²⁻⁶ᵃ   FROM ABRAHAM TO DAVID   Luke 3³¹⁻³⁴

²*Abraham was the father of Isaac, and Isaac the father of Jacob, and Jacob the father of Judah and his brothers,* ³*and Judah the father of Perez and Zerah by Tamar, and Perez the father of Hezron, and Hezron the father of Ram,*ᵃ ⁴*and Ram*ᵃ *the father of Ammin' adab, and Ammin' adab the father of Nahshon, and Nahshon the father of Salmon,* ⁵*and Salmon the father of Bo' az by Rahab, and Bo' az the father of Obed by Ruth, and Obed the father of Jesse,* ⁶*and Jesse the father of David the king.*

a Greek *Aram*

The first age is the fourteen generations from Abraham, to whom God made promises, to David, in whom promises were fulfilled, since he reigned as king, and to whom a promise of another king was made. This first age is the age of waiting. Three women are named in it: in each case there is something remarkable about the woman herself, and the presence of their names in the genealogy may be in order to draw attention to the strange ways in which divine providence works.

ॐ

Matthew's source here is almost certainly 1 Chron. 1³⁴, 2¹⁻¹⁵, but he has added *Rahab* and *Ruth* in v. 5; for the latter, he may have used Ruth 4¹⁸. Luke 3³¹⁻³⁴ agrees with Matthew in this part of the genealogy, though Luke writes it in the reverse order; but between *Hezron* and *Amminadab* Luke has *Arni* and *Admin*, instead of Matthew's *Ram*.

3
Tamar is the first of the five women who are mentioned in the genealogy. She was the daughter-in-law of *Judah*, by whom she conceived twins, *Perez and Zerah*, through deceiving Judah as to her identity; see Gen. 38.

5
Rahab, the second woman named in the list, is presumably the harlot at Jericho, though there is no evidence apart from this verse that she was the wife of *Salmon* and the mother of *Boaz*; see Joshua 2, 6²²⁻²⁵.

Ruth, the third woman in the genealogy, was a Moabitess and not a descendant of Abraham; see Ruth 1⁴, 4¹⁰.

6
David the king: The addition of the title, *the king*, marks the end of this period of waiting, and points forward to Jesus, *the son of David, the Christ, the King of the Jews.*

I^{6b-11}   FROM DAVID TO THE DEPORTATION

And David was the father of Solomon by the wife of Uri'ah, ⁷*and Solomon the father of Rehobo'am, and Rehobo'am the father of Abi'jah, and Abi'jah the father of Asa*^a, ⁸*and Asa*^a *the father of Jehosh'aphat, and Jehosh'aphat the father of Joram, and Joram the father of Uzzi'ah,* ⁹*and Uzzi'ah the father of Jotham, and Jotham the father of Ahaz, and Ahaz the father of Hezeki'ah,* ¹⁰*and Hezeki'ah the father of Manas'seh, and Manas'seh the father of Amos,*^b *and Amos*^b *the father of Josi'ah,* ¹¹*and Josi'ah the father of Jechoni'ah and his brothers, at the time of the deportation to Babylon.*

a Greek *Asaph*
b Other authorities read *Amon*

The second period is the age of the kings, from *David*, the first king to reign in Jerusalem, to *Jechoniah*, the last king of Judah before the exile. Whereas the previous age reached a climax with the first king, this age is a period of decline to *the deportation to Babylon*. One woman is mentioned by name: *the wife of Uriah*, i.e. Bathsheba, whose husband David murdered.

ﱞ

Matthew has probably continued to draw upon 1 Chron. (3^5, $^{10-16}$), but he has omitted three generations between *Joram* and *Jotham*, and omitted *Jehoiakim* after *Josiah*. Luke's genealogy is traced through another son of David, namely *Nathan* (Luke 3^{31}; 1 Chron. 3^5).

6

the wife of Uriah: Matthew's expression here emphasizes the sin of David; but in fact Uriah was dead, through David's orders, before *Solomon* was conceived; see 2 Samuel 11, 12.

11

at the time of the deportation to Babylon marks the next turning point in Israel's history.

I$^{12-16}$ FROM THE DEPORTATION TO
THE CHRIST

^{12}*And after the deportation to Babylon: Jechoni'ah was the father of She-al'ti-el,^{a} and She-al'ti-el^a the father of Zerub'babel, ^{13}and Zerub'babel the father of Abi'ud, and Abi'ud the father of Eli'akim, and Eli'akim the father of Azor, ^{14}and Azor the father of Zadok, and Zadok the father of Achim, and Achim the father of Eli'ud, ^{15}and Eli'ud the father of Elea'zar, and Elea'zar the father of Matthan, and Matthan the father of Jacob, ^{16}and Jacob the father of Joseph the husband of Mary, of whom Jesus was born, who is called Christ.*

a Greek *Salathiel*

The third period begins *after the deportation to Babylon*, and it is another period of waiting. It brings us back to the climax from which the second period began – to the king, the *Christ, the son of David*. But it is a new and better beginning, which is marked by a new conception. This is only hinted at here, in the words *Joseph the husband of Mary, of whom Jesus was born*. *Mary* is the fifth woman to be mentioned in the list: the reason why she is included, and included in this way, will be explained in Matthew's next paragraph but one.

เจๅ

Matthew was able to take the first three names, *Jechoniah, Shealtiel*, and *Zerubbabel*, from 1 Chron. 3^{16ff}; but for the remainder of the list Matthew had, as far as we know, no written source. Luke also has *Shealtiel* and *Zerubbabel* in his genealogy, but none of the others (Luke 3^{27}).

16

Joseph the husband of Mary, of whom (feminine, i.e. of Mary) *Jesus was born:* This is probably the original text of Matthew, although there are a number of variants in the ancient manuscripts and versions. Matthew believed that Jesus was both descended from David, and conceived by the Holy Spirit. He therefore shows that Joseph, who married Mary, was the *son of David* (1^{20}); and that Jesus was conceived *before they came together* (1^{18}). Joseph thus became the legal father of Jesus, and Jesus was in this way both *the son of David* and miraculously conceived.

I^{17} THE CONCLUSION TO THE GENEALOGY

^{17}*So all the generations from Abraham to David were fourteen generations, and from David to the deportation to Babylon fourteen generations, and from the deportation to Babylon to the Christ fourteen generations.*

Matthew now looks back over the genealogy, and points out that in each of the three ages there were *fourteen generations* (though in fact he has only thirteen names in the last period, 1$^{12-16}$). This can be interpreted in two ways: (*a*) On the analogy of the waxing and waning of the moon; just as there are fourteen days from new moon to

full moon, and fourteen days from full moon to the end of the
month, so Abraham is a beginning, David is a climax, the exile is an
end and a new beginning, and the final climax is the birth of Christ.
(b) We know from Dan. 9$^{2, 24}$ that the Jews sometimes reckoned
seven years, or *weeks of years*, as a unit; so on the analogy of the week,
each of Matthew's three periods is two weeks of generations, and the
whole time is six weeks of generations. Therefore, as God created the
world in six days (Gen. 2$^{1ff.}$), Matthew may have thought it appropriate that history, from Abraham to Christ, should be six weeks of
generations; and the time after Christ was to be the eternal sabbath of
the age to come, because *this generation will not pass away till all these
things take place*, 24^{34}. (For the idea of eternal life as the sabbath,
see Hebrews 3, 4; and for the arrangement of history in six periods of
weeks, see Revelation, and Dr Austin Farrer's study of it, *A Rebirth of
Images*, 1949. But cf. his *The Revelation of St John the Divine*, Oxford,
1964.)

ॐ

The dates of *David* (c. 1000 B.C.) and the deportation (586 B.C.) show that
Matthew's reckoning is rough and ready, and this is borne out by his
omission of some of the names in the second period. He seems to have
been more interested in ideas than in facts; and sometimes to have
been prepared to arrange the facts so as to fit the ideas.

I$^{18-25}$ THE BIRTH OF JESUS   Luke I$^{26-38}$

^{18}*Now the birth of Jesus Christ^a took place in this way. When his mother
Mary had been betrothed to Joseph, before they came together she was found
to be with child of the Holy Spirit;* ^{19}*and her husband Joseph, being a just
man and unwilling to put her to shame, resolved to divorce her quietly.* ^{20}*But
as he considered this, behold an angel of the Lord appeared to him in a
dream, saying, 'Joseph, son of David, do not fear to take Mary your wife,
for that which is conceived in her is of the Holy Spirit;* ^{21}*she will bear a son,
and you shall call his name Jesus, for he will save his people from their
sins.'* ^{22}*All this took place to fulfil what the Lord had spoken by the prophet:*

^{23}*'Behold, a virgin shall conceive and bear a son,
and his name shall be called Emman'u-el'*

(*which means, God with us*). ^{24}*When Joseph woke from sleep, he did as the*

41

angel of the Lord commanded him; he took his wife, ²⁵but knew her not until she had borne a son; and he called his name Jesus.

a Other ancient authorities read *of the Christ*

Matthew has led the reader to expect an unusual birth-story, and now he tells him how it happened: Mary was found to be pregnant before her marriage to Joseph, and the child had been conceived by the Holy Spirit. But Joseph did not understand this until he was told by an angel, who also foretells the name and work of the son who is to be born. Matthew sees in this the fulfilment of a prophecy in Isaiah.

❧

In the Lucan account, the angel appears to *Mary* (not to *Joseph*), and tells her that she will bear a son through the Holy Spirit, that his name will be *Jesus*, and that *the Lord God will give to him the throne of his father David.*

18

the birth (*hē genesis*): The same word as *genealogy* in 1¹.

of Jesus Christ: There are only three places where Matthew appears to write *Jesus Christ*, 1¹, 16²¹, and here. 1¹ may be translated 'Jesus the Christ'; in 16²¹ the text is uncertain (see note); and here also the manuscripts have different readings: probably Matthew wrote either *of the Christ* (margin), or 'of Jesus'. For *the Christ* compare 1¹⁷, 2⁴, 11², 16¹⁶, ²⁰, 22⁴², 23¹⁰, 24⁵, ²³.

betrothed: According to Deut. 22²³ff., a betrothed virgin who willingly commits fornication with a man other than her future husband is to be stoned, along with the man; and she is referred to in this passage in Deuteronomy as *his neighbour's wife* – which shows that, to the Jews, betrothal was a more important step than engagement is with us; compare v. 20, where Mary is called *your wife*, although they are not yet married.

before they came together: The word implies both living together in one house and intercourse: 'domestic and marital relations are combined' (*Lexicon*).

she was found to be with child of the Holy Spirit: Matthew's explanation for the reader anticipates what Joseph himself understood at this time. For *the Holy Spirit* as the agent in the birth of Jesus, compare the Spirit as the creative power of God in Gen. 1², *the Spirit of God was moving over the face of the waters.*

19

Joseph, not knowing that the child is miraculously conceived, and not wishing to make the matter public, decides to *divorce* Mary *quietly* (i.e. before two witnesses). He would be bound to do this according to the law, and he was *a just man* – i.e. one who kept the law.

20

Joseph's obedience to the law does not, by itself, reveal to him who the child is; he needs the revelation of God to understand this; compare 11²⁷, *no one knows the Son except the Father;* and 16¹⁷, *flesh and blood has not revealed this to you, but my Father who is in heaven.* For other examples of revelation through angels and dreams in this Gospel, see 2¹², ¹³, ¹⁹, ²², 27¹⁹.

do not fear to take Mary your wife: i.e. take her into your home.

21

Jesus, for he will save his people from their sins: The Hebrew name means 'God is salvation', so, as Matthew points out, it is applicable to Jesus who will save *his people*, Israel, *from their sins*. There may be an echo here of Ps. 130⁸, *he will redeem Israel from all his iniquities.*

The word *people* (*laos*) is characteristic of Matthew who uses it fourteen times (Mark had used it twice) of the Jews, the people of God.

22

This is the first use in Matthew of his formula for the fulfilment of an Old Testament passage (see also 2¹⁵, ¹⁷, ²³, 4¹⁴, 8¹⁷, 12¹⁷, 13³⁵, 21⁴, 27⁹); and the passages which are quoted after it are usually given in a form which is different from the Greek translation of the Old Testament.

23

The quotation is from Isa. 7¹⁴, but in the original Hebrew the word translated here as *virgin* means *young woman.*

Emmanuel . . . God with us: The name of the child in the prophecy meant Prosperity, because God would be favourable to his people, *with* them and not *against* them (for this contrast compare 12³⁰, *He who is not with me is against me*). Notice the last words of Jesus in this Gospel, which match the first fulfilment of the Old Testament, *I am with you always, to the close of the age,* 28²⁰.

24

he took his wife: See note on v. 20.

25

but knew her not until she had borne a son: This need not necessarily imply that he did know her after she had borne her son; but the references to Jesus' *brothers* and *sisters* (12^{46}ff., 13^{55}f.) without further explanation suggest that he did.

he called his name Jesus: Jewish boys were given their names on the eighth day after birth, when they were circumcised; see Luke 2^{21}.

2 *The Magi, King Herod, the Flight into Egypt, and the Return to Nazareth*

In this chapter, Matthew introduces the major theme of his Gospel: the Jews have rejected the offer of salvation, but the Gentiles will accept it. Herod, his son Archelaus, and the people of Jerusalem are the representatives of the Jews; and the wise men (Magi) from the East are the representatives of the Gentiles. The Gentiles will be brought into the place which the Jews had forfeited by their unbelief, and the Church will be the Israel of the last days, destined to share in the joys of the age to come.

The Jews looked back to the Exodus from Egypt as the beginning of their history, and looked forward to a new Exodus, under a new Moses, at the end of the world. So the Christians said that Jesus was the new Moses; and in this chapter we shall find a number of places where there are references back to Exodus, and to the birth and early history of Moses.

The R.S.V. divides the chapter into five paragraphs: (*a*) the Magi at Jerusalem, (*b*) the Magi at Bethlehem, (*c*) the flight into Egypt, (*d*) the murder of the children at Bethlehem, (*e*) the return to Israel and settlement at Nazareth.

There are no parallels to this chapter in the other Gospels: Matthew has probably composed it himself (it is full of his characteristic expressions), and we cannot discover what basis, if any, it had in history.

2 *Now when Jesus was born in Bethlehem of Judea in the days of Herod the king, behold, wise men from the East came to Jerusalem, saying,* ²'*Where is he who has been born king of the Jews? For we have seen his star in the East, and have come to worship him.*' ³*When Herod the king heard this, he was troubled, and all Jerusalem with him;* ⁴*and assembling all the chief priests and scribes of the people, he inquired of them where the Christ was to be born.* ⁵*They told him, 'In Bethlehem of Judea; for so it is written by the prophet:*

> ⁶"*And you, O Bethlehem, in the land of Judah,*
> *are by no means least among the rulers of Judah,*
> *for from you shall come a ruler*
> *who will govern my people Israel.*"'

At this point Matthew tells us the place and date of the birth of Jesus: it was at Bethlehem, which had been David's home; and it was the time of King Herod (whom Matthew will portray as a second Pharaoh, the symbol of unbelief and hard-heartedness in the Old Testament). Magi come from the East, inquiring where the king of the Jews is born, because they have seen his star and have come to worship him. Their inquiry causes confusion in Jerusalem; Herod assembles the Sanhedrin, and they say that Bethlehem has been foretold as the place of the king's birth.

※

Bethlehem of Judea: See Luke 2^{1-7} for the Lucan account of how Jesus came to be born at Bethlehem although he was brought up at Nazareth. For Bethlehem as David's home, see e.g. 1 Sam. 16. The place is called *Bethlehem of Judea*, because there was another Bethlehem in Zebulun (Joshua 19^{15}).

in the days of Herod the king: Herod was king from 37–4 B.C.

wise men (magoi): The word could be used in either of two senses: wise man or magician. The only other magus in the New Testament is

45

Elymas, in Acts 13⁶ff., and he is clearly a magician. Possibly Matthew also meant the word to be understood in this sense, and this is certainly how Ignatius of Antioch understood the passage: 'From that time [i.e. the appearance of the star] all sorcery [*mageia*] and every evil spell began to lose their power; the ignorance of wickedness began to vanish away; the overthrow of the ancient dominion was being brought to pass, since God was appearing in human form unto newness of life eternal' (Letter to the Ephesians, 19).

2

The Magi ask for the *king of the Jews*, because they themselves are Gentiles, and Jews did not call themselves Jews; Jews would say, either *the Christ*, as in v. 4; or the *King of Israel*, as in 27⁴². For a *star* as the sign of a king, see Num. 24¹⁷, *a star shall come forth out of Jacob, and a sceptre shall rise out of Israel*. The planet Jupiter apparently crossed the paths of Venus and Saturn in 7 B.C., and there may be some reference to this in Matthew.

3

Herod the king and *all Jerusalem* do not rejoice at the news, but are *troubled* – the word is used again at 14²⁶ of the terror of the disciples; and in both places it is the fear which comes from unbelief.

4

assembling all the chief priests and scribes of the people, i.e. the Sanhedrin, the supreme council of the Jews. There may be a reference here to Ps. 2², as in 22³⁴, 26³,⁵⁷; see the notes on these verses.

5f.

The prophecy is from Mic. 5², but it is not given in the LXX translation, nor is it an exact rendering of the Hebrew text, 2 Sam. 5² may have been combined with the Micah prophecy; combining of similiar Old Testament passages was a regular feature of rabbinic study of the scriptures.

2^{7-12} THE MAGIC AT JERUSALEM

⁷*Then Herod summoned the wise men secretly and ascertained from them what time the star appeared;* ⁸*and sent them to Bethlehem, saying, 'Go and search diligently for the child, and when you have found him bring me word, that I too may come and worship him.'* ⁹*When they had heard the king they*

went their way; and lo, the star which they had seen in the East went before them, till it came to rest over the place where the child was. ¹⁰*When they saw the star, they rejoiced exceedingly with great joy;* ¹¹*and going into the house they saw the child with Mary his mother, and they fell down and worshipped him. Then, opening their treasures, they offered him gifts, gold and frankincense and myrrh.* ¹²*And being warned in a dream not to return to Herod, they departed to their own country by another way.*

Herod sends the Magi to Bethlehem, and tells them to return to him, so that he too can worship the king; and he inquires the date of the appearance of the star. The reader is not told why Herod is doing this – but is kept in suspense until the next paragraph. The star leads the Magi to the child and his mother, and they present their gifts to him; but they do not return to Herod, because of a warning in a dream.

৩৫

7
From v. 16 it seems that the star had appeared two years earlier.

10
With the *great joy* of the magi, compare the *great joy* of the women in 28⁸.

11
they fell down and worshipped him: Worship of Jesus is a feature of this Gospel, in contrast to Mark's; see note on 8ª.

gold and frankincense and myrrh: Detailed symbolic meanings have been found in these three gifts; but they may all be gifts suitable for presentation to a *king* – see Ps. 72¹⁵ (*gold*), Isaiah 60⁶ (*gold* and *frankincense*), Ps. 45⁸ (anointing a king with *myrrh*), Song of Songs 3⁶, etc. (*frankincense* and *myrrh*); or they may be the materials used by magicians: by offering them to Jesus, they are declaring the end of their practices.

2¹³⁻¹⁵   THE FLIGHT INTO EGYPT

¹³*Now when they had departed, behold an angel of the Lord appeared to Joseph in a dream and said, 'Rise, take the child and his mother, and flee to*

Egypt, and remain there till I tell you; for Herod is about to search for the child, to destroy him.' ¹⁴*And he rose and took the child and his mother by night, and departed to Egypt,* ¹⁵*and remained there until the death of Herod. This was to fulfil what the Lord had spoken by the prophet, 'Out of Egypt have I called my son.'*

Matthew now explains why the Magi had been warned not to return to Herod: an angel tells Joseph that Herod is about to kill Jesus, and so Joseph must take him to Egypt. Matthew sees in this a repetition of the events which happened before the Exodus: once more a king is killing Jewish children; but just as Moses had been hidden and saved, so now Jesus is to be saved by flight; and God's purpose will be fulfilled, because he will call his son out of Egypt.

છ૭

13

Contrast the words of Herod in v. 8, *search diligently for the child . . . that I too may come and worship him*, with his real motive, *Herod is about to search for the child, to destroy him.*

14

departed to Egypt: The word translated depart (*anachōrein*) is characteristic of Matthew's style and thought; for similar passages, in which Jesus departs from one place to another because of unbelief, see 2²², 4¹², 12¹⁵, 14¹³, 15²¹.

Anachōrein has an interesting history. In later Christian times it became the technical term for monasticism – i.e. withdrawal from the world – hence 'anchorite'. Before that, it had been used of withdrawal from public life; of withdrawal into oneself in contemplation; and, in Egypt, of withdrawal into the desert by peasants who were oppressed by taxation – a kind of strike-action (see A.-J. Festugière, *Personal Religion among the Greeks*, Chapter IV). Matthew's use of it, however, was probably suggested to him by the first occurrence of the word in LXX: *Moses fled (anechōrēsen) from Pharaoh, and stayed in the land of Midian*, Exod. 2¹⁵.

15

The quotation is from Hos. 11¹; it is a translation of the Hebrew text, and is not taken from the LXX version. It referred originally to God's calling Israel, his *son*, from Egypt at the time of the Exodus.

THE DEATH OF THE CHILDREN
AT BETHLEHEM

[16] *Then Herod, when he saw that he had been tricked by the wise men, was in a furious rage, and he sent and killed all the male children in Bethlehem and in all that region who were two years old or under, according to the time which he had ascertained from the wise men.* [17] *Then was fulfilled what was spoken by the prophet Jeremiah:*

> [18] *'A voice was heard in Ramah,*
> *wailing and loud lamentation,*
> *Rachel weeping for her children;*
> *she refused to be consoled,*
> *because they were no more.'*

The angel's warning is now fulfilled, and Herod kills the children in Bethlehem. But Matthew can see the foreknowledge of God here, in the prophecy of Jeremiah; and can see also a repetition of Pharaoh's slaughter of Israelite children before the Exodus (Exod. 1^{15-22}).

ಐಐ

16
See v. 7

17.
The quotation is from Jer. 31^{15}, where the prophet sees *Rachel*, the mother of Joseph and Benjamin, weeping over *her children* (i.e. the exiles) as they are taken into captivity in Babylon. There was a connexion with Bethlehem, in that Rachel's grave was believed to have been there (Gen. 35^{19}). *Ramah* was about six miles north of Jerusalem, on the road which the exiles would take. (Bethlehem is about the same distance south of Jerusalem; see map, p. 8.)

THE RETURN TO ISRAEL AND
SETTLEMENT AT NAZARETH

19But when Herod died, behold, an angel of the Lord appeared in a dream to Joseph in Egypt, saying, 20'Rise, take the child and his mother, and go to the land of Israel, for those who sought the child's life are dead.' 21And he rose and took the child and his mother, and went to the land of Israel. 22But when he heard that Archela'us reigned over Judea in place of his father Herod, he was afraid to go there, and being warned in a dream he withdrew to the district of Galilee. 23And he went and dwelt in a city called Nazareth, that what was spoken by the prophets might be fulfilled, 'He shall be called a Nazarene.'

Just as, when Pharaoh died, Moses was told to return to Egypt, so now that Herod is dead, Joseph is told to bring Jesus back to Israel; but not to Judea, because one of Herod's sons is king there; he goes to Galilee, to Nazareth; and here again prophecy is fulfilled.

ᔕᔕ

19

See v. 15; Herod died in 4 B.C. (The system of dating events A.D. was worked out by Dionysius Exiguus, *c.* A.D. 500–50, who wrongly accepted the year 753 after the founding of Rome as the date of the incarnation.)

20

for those who sought the child's life are dead is a free quotation from Exod. 4^19, where God says to Moses, *Go back to Egypt; for all the men who were seeking your life are dead.* (The plural in Matthew, *those who sought,* is only explicable because this is a quotation.) Notice the contrast between the Old Testament and the New: in Exodus, the king of Egypt is the enemy of Israel; here, a king of Jerusalem is the enemy. In Exodus, Moses flees for safety out of Egypt and then returns; here, Jesus is taken into Egypt for safety and then returns. In the Old Testament, Egypt and Pharaoh are the symbols for unbelief and hardness of heart; in the New Testament, Jerusalem and Herod fulfil this role.

22

Archelaus reigned over Judea from 4 B.C. to A.D. 6, and Herod Antipas
(who is mentioned later in the Gospel, 14¹⁻¹²) over Galilee from 4 B.C.
to A.D. 39. It is not made clear here why Joseph is to go to the district
of Herod Antipas instead of that of Archelaus: the only explanation is
the prophecy which is given in the next verse; and see also the prophecy
of *Galilee of the Gentiles* in 4¹²⁻¹⁶. On *he withdrew (anachōrein)* see note
on 2¹⁴: once more, there is a withdrawal from unbelief, to a place
where there will be faith, *Galilee of the Gentiles.*

23

The source of this prophecy is not known, but Isa. 11¹ has been suggested: *There shall come forth a shoot from the stump of Jesse, and a branch
(nēitzer) shall grow out of his roots.*

3¹–4¹⁷ John the Baptist; the Baptism and Temptations of Jesus, and his Preaching at Capernaum

Matthew goes straight on to describe John the Baptist who was
preaching in the wilderness that the kingdom was coming; he shows
how John fulfilled prophecy, demanded repentance, and pointed
forward to the coming judge; how Jesus was baptized by John, and
declared to be God's Son by a voice from heaven; how he was
tempted in the wilderness; and finally how, after the arrest of the
Baptist, he began to preach that the kingdom was coming, and did
this in Capernaum in Galilee, to fulfil prophecy.

This section begins and ends with the same words: at the beginning
the Baptist says, *Repent, for the kingdom of heaven is at hand*; and at
the end of it, Jesus says, *Repent, for the kingdom of heaven is at hand.*
There are other examples in this Gospel of a paragraph or section
having the same words at the beginning and at the end, and the
technical term for this is *inclusio.*

Matthew had used Mark 1¹, *The beginning of the gospel of Jesus
Christ, the Son of God,* for his first two chapters: they were an exposition of the titles The Christ and The Son of God, by means of a
genealogy, birth-story, and the story of the Magi. Matthew now

returns to Mark 1^2, and this section, Matt. 3^1-4^{17}, is his revision of Mark 1^{2-15}.

Matthew has made a number of additions to Mark here: the account of John's preaching, the conversation between John and Jesus, the longer account of the temptations, the note on the preaching in Capernaum. The section as a whole, with these additions, brings out four ideas which are typical of Matthew:

(i) The fulfilment of the Old Testament: e.g. John is the man whom Isaiah had foretold; Capernaum is in the district where Isaiah had said that light would dawn. Moreover, the baptism of Jesus and his temptations correspond to the Israelites' crossing of the Red Sea in the Old Testament, and their temptations in the wilderness.

(ii) The coming of judgement: this follows on from the fact that the scriptures are being fulfilled; because, if the scriptures are being fulfilled, that means that the kingdom is coming; and before the kingdom comes there must be the judgement, when men will be divided into those who will enter the kingdom, and those who will not. The Baptist warns the Pharisees and Sadducees of this coming separation of men, and the theme is repeated again and again in the Gospel: notice particularly the last three parables in Chapter 25.

(iii) The demand for good works: the way to enter the kingdom is by repentance and good works, so the Baptist exhorts the Jewish leaders to *bear good fruit*. This will also be repeated throughout the Gospel, but notice again the last parable, 25^{31}ff., in which men are divided according to whether they have or have not given food to the hungry, drink to the thirsty, etc.

(iv) The question, Who is Jesus?: John points away from himself to Jesus, *who is ... mightier than I*, and says to him *I need to be baptized by you*; the voice from heaven says, *This is my beloved Son;* and the devil says, *If you are the Son of God.* Matthew is here preparing the reader for the teaching which he will begin to give in Chapters 5–7, and is showing him that this teaching has the authority of one who is greater even than the Baptist.

3¹⁻⁶ JOHN THE BAPTIST IN THE WILDERNESS Mark 1²⁻⁶

3 *In those days came John the Baptist, preaching in the wilderness of Judea,* ²'*Repent, for the kingdom of heaven is at hand.*' ³*For this is he who was spoken of by the prophet Isaiah when he said,*

> '*The voice of one crying in the wilderness:*
> *Prepare the way of the Lord,*
> *make his paths straight.*'

⁴*Now John wore a garment of camel's hair, and a leather girdle around his waist; and his food was locusts and wild honey.* ⁵*Then went out to him Jerusalem and all Judea and all the region about the Jordan,* ⁶*and they were baptized by him in the river of Jordan, confessing their sins.*

Matthew introduces us to a new character, John the Baptist, who is the herald of the king, and the one who announces the nearness of the kingdom. He fulfils the prophecy of Isaiah, preaching *in the wilderness*, and preparing *the way of the Lord*; and he is dressed like Elijah, whom the Jews expected to return before the Messiah. John demands repentance and baptism, and the Jews come to him, are baptized, and confess their sins.

༄༅

The greater part of this paragraph is from Mark 1²⁻⁶, but Matthew has made certain changes in it. The words of John in v. 2 are a Matthean addition, possibly based on Mark's account of the preaching of Jesus (Mark 1¹⁵). Matthew has omitted the quotation from Mal. 3¹ in Mark 1², which he will use later (11¹⁰). The description of John, which came at the end of Mark's paragraph (1⁶), Matthew has brought forward to v. 4.

1
In those days: Possibly Matthew has taken these words from Mark 1⁹; they are vague and must refer to a time between twenty and thirty years after the events described in Chapter 2. Matthew's interests were less chronological than theological: John was the fulfilment of prophecy; therefore the beginning of the Gospel is dated from him; cf. 11¹³ *all the prophets and the law prophesied until John.*

John the Baptist: 'John, who was called the Baptist' is mentioned by the Jewish historian Josephus (*c.* A.D. 90) in his *Antiquities of the Jews,* XVIII, 5, 2. Josephus says that Herod was afraid of John, because of John's influence over the people; and that he put him to death in order that he should not raise a rebellion. Josephus does not mention any messianic prophecies of John, but it is probable that they were known to him, and that he intentionally omitted them in order to avoid giving offence to the Romans. There are some similarities between the teaching of the Baptist, and that of the sect responsible for the Dead Sea Scrolls; in particular, the insistence on ritual washing.

preaching in the wilderness of Judea: The place of John's preaching – *in the wilderness* – agrees with the prophecy quoted in v. 3, which see.

2

Repent, for the kingdom of heaven is at hand: Matthew has substituted these words for Mark's *preaching a baptism of repentance for the forgiveness of sins* (Mark 1⁴), perhaps because he wanted to insist on the forgiveness of sins through Jesus (he adds *for the forgiveness of sins* at 26²⁸, in the words over the cup at the last supper). To *repent* is to change one's mind, and is always used in the New Testament in the religious sense of turning from evil ways to the commandments and love of God. *The kingdom of heaven* is here mentioned for the first time in Matthew; on the meaning of the term, and on the belief that it was *at hand,* see Introduction, pp. 21f., and D. E. Nineham's *The Gospel of St Mark,* pp. 43f.

3

The quotation is from Isa. 40³, and agrees with the LXX translation, except that Mark and Matthew both have *his paths* instead of the Septuagint *the paths of God:* the change of text may have been made in order to apply the quotation to Jesus, *the Lord.* (Jesus is seldom spoken of as 'God' in the New Testament.) Notice that the Hebrew is differently punctuated:

> *A voice cries:*
> *In the wilderness prepare the way of the Lord,*
> *make straight in the desert a highway for our God.*

The fact that in the Septuagint the voice cries *in the wilderness* may account for the Evangelists' statement that John was *preaching in the wilderness* (Mark 1⁴, Matt. 3¹).

4

This verse is parallel to Mark 1⁶, but the words *and a leather girdle around his waist* may not be part of the original text of Mark (they are omitted in some of the authorities for the Marcan text); Matthew may have added them from 2 Kings 1⁸, the description of Elijah, and they may have been copied into Mark by a scribe. Matthew believed that John the Baptist was Elijah returned from heaven (see 17¹⁰⁻¹³) in accordance with Jewish expectation (Mal. 4⁵. Ecclus 48¹⁰). *Locusts* are 'even today commonly eaten by the poorer people of Arabia, Africa, and Syria' (*Lexicon*).

5f.
The popularity of John is attested by Josephus, and by the Jewish leaders who say later in this Gospel *all hold that John was a prophet* (21²⁶; cf. 11⁷ff.); nevertheless, the use of *all* here (*all Judea and all the region about the Jordan*) is no doubt an exaggeration – cf. 2³ *all Jerusalem*, 21¹⁰ *all the city*, 27²⁵ *all the people*.

3⁷⁻¹⁰   JOHN WARNS THE PHARISEES   Luke 3⁷⁻⁹
AND SADDUCEES

⁷*But when he saw many of the Pharisees and Sad'ducees coming for baptism, he said to them, 'You brood of vipers! Who warned you to flee from the wrath to come?* ⁸*Bear fruit that befits repentance,* ⁹*and do not presume to say to yourselves, "We have Abraham as our father"; for I tell you, God is able from these stones to raise up children to Abraham.* ¹⁰*Even now the axe is laid to the root of the trees; every tree therefore that does not bear good fruit is cut down and thrown into the fire.'*

John demanded repentance and baptism: baptism without repentance would not be enough. Among the crowds he saw *Pharisees and Sadducees*, people who in this Gospel always represent unbelief and impenitence. He therefore warns them that they must do the good works which will necessarily follow from a change of mind; if they do not, they will have no place in the coming kingdom of heaven: their descent from Abraham will not by itself ensure their salvation.

ॐ

These four verses have no parallel in Mark, but they are almost word for word identical with Luke 3^{7-9}, where, however, it is *the multitudes* which are addressed, not *the Pharisees and the Sadducees*. This is therefore the first Q passage in Matthew (see Introduction, pp. 12f.).

7

The *Pharisees* were a sect of the Jews who recognized the authority of later, unwritten traditions, as well as the authority of the written law in the Old Testament; the *Sadducees*, on the other hand, accepted only the written law (see Acts 23^8; Josephus, *Antiquities*, XIII, 10, 6). The latter would be found mainly in and around Jerusalem.

You brood of vipers! See 12^{34}, 23^{33} for the same words in the mouth of Jesus; the contexts of these two passages show that viper is used as a metaphor for wickedness and murder. The serpent as an image of the devil goes back to Gen. $3^{1ff.}$; and Christians believed that the Jewish leaders were possessed by the devil; cf. John 8^{44}, *You are of your father the devil, and your will is to do your father's desires.*

The question *Who warned you to flee from the wrath to come?* is probably to be taken as ironical: they come to John as if they were repenting in order to escape the coming wrath; but in fact they have not repented, and are therefore not doing the good works which will follow repentance.

8

Fruit is a metaphor for deeds: *good fruit* stands for good deeds, and *evil fruit* for evil deeds (cf. 7^{15-20}). (In Greek, the word translated *bear*, *poiein*, also means 'do'.) The *fruit that befits repentance* is the new life which will follow from the new mind of the repentant.

9

The Pharisees and Sadducees are not to rely on their descent from Abraham; the coming judgement will cut across the descendants of Abraham and divide them; and God will call in the Gentiles to take the place of the Jews as his new people (see $8^{11f.}$). In Aramaic the words *children* and *stones* are almost identical.

10

The judgement is near – the time for cutting down fruitless trees has come. For *fire* as a metaphor for God's condemnation, see 3^{12}, 5^{22}, 7^{19}, $13^{40, 42}$, 18^8, 25^{41}.

^{11}'*I baptize you with water for repentance, but he who is coming after me is mightier than I, whose sandals I am not worthy to carry; he will baptize you with the Holy Spirit and with fire.* ^{12}*His winnowing fork is in his hand, and he will clear his threshing floor and gather his wheat into the granary, but the chaff he will burn with unquenchable fire.*'

John has foretold the approaching kingdom (3^2) and the judgement which must precede the kingdom (3$^{7-10}$); now he bears witness to the King who is also the judge, one who is greater than John himself, and who will bring greater gifts, and divide men finally into the blessed and the cursed.

ॐ

Matthew has altered and expanded the messianic preaching of John as it was recorded in Mark 1$^{7, 8}$, inserting *for repentance* and *and with fire;* changing Mark's *the thong of whose sandals I am not worthy to stoop down and untie*; and adding v. 12 which is parallel to Luke 3^{17}.

11

The addition of the words *for repentance* may have been made in order to emphasize the inferiority of John's baptism to Christian baptism, which brings the receiver of it into the sphere of *the Holy Spirit*. (See also below 3$^{13-15}$ for the inferiority of John to Jesus.) For the expectation of the gift of the Spirit, see, for example, Joel 2^{28}:

> *And it shall come to pass afterward,*
> *   that I will pour out my spirit on all flesh.*

John foretells this gift from the coming *mightier* one, and associates it with baptism: *he will baptize you with the Holy Spirit*. To the Christian reader, this baptism will be the baptism which Jesus commanded *in the name of the Father and of the Son and of the Holy Spirit* (28^{19}). Matthew adds, *and with fire* (so also Luke 3^{16}): this may refer to the *tongues as of fire* described in Acts 2^3, or, more likely, to the judgement which either purifies or destroys; cf. 1 Cor. 3^{13}, *the Day . . . will be revealed with fire, and the fire will test what sort of work each one has done.*

12

Just as in threshing *wheat* is divided from *chaff*, so the judge will divide the wicked from the righteous. Compare, with these last public words of John in this Gospel, the last words in the public teaching of Jesus: *And they* (the wicked) *will go away into eternal punishment, but the righteous into eternal life* (25⁴⁶).

3^{13-17} JESUS IS BAPTIZED BY JOHN   Mark 1⁹⁻¹¹

¹³ *Then Jesus came from Galilee to the Jordan to John, to be baptized by him.* ¹⁴ *John would have prevented him, saying, 'I need to be baptized by you, and do you come to me?'* ¹⁵ *But Jesus answered him, 'Let it be so now; for thus it is fitting for us to fulfil all righteousness.' Then he consented.* ¹⁶ *And when Jesus was baptized, he went up immediately from the water, and behold, the heavens were opened*ᵃ *and he saw the Spirit of God descending like a dove, and alighting on him;* ¹⁷ *and lo, a voice from heaven, saying, 'This is my beloved Son,*ᵇ *with whom I am well pleased.'*

    a Other ancient authorities add *to him*
    b Or *my Son my* (or *the*) *Beloved*

The first three paragraphs of this chapter described John the Baptist, the fulfilment of Isaiah's prophecy of the one who prepares the way of the Lord, his demand for repentance, his warning of judgement, and his announcement of the coming of one who is mightier than himself. Now, for the first and only time, John and Jesus meet, *the Voice* and *the Lord*, the one who baptizes *with water for repentance*, and the one who baptizes *with the Holy Spirit and fire*.

We saw, in Chapters 1 and 2, that Matthew is comparing the beginning of the Gospel narrative with the early parts of the Old Testament, and in particular, the life of Jesus with the life of Moses; N.B. *Out of Egypt have I called my son* (2¹⁵) and *those who sought the child's life are dead* (2²⁰, quoting Exod. 4¹⁹). Israel came out of Egypt to the Red Sea where, to quote Paul, they were *all baptized into Moses in the cloud and in the sea* (1 Cor. 10²). Jesus coming now to John to be baptized by him in the Jordan fulfils the pattern of events foreshadowed in the history of Israel.

ᏸᎯᏬ

$3^{13, 16, 17}$ are taken from Mark 1^{9-11} with a few alterations, of which the most important are, first, Mark's *he saw the heavens opened* is changed to *and behold, the heavens were opened*; second, Mark's *Thou art my beloved Son, with thee I am well pleased* becomes *This is my beloved Son, with whom I am well pleased*. The effect of these changes is to make the event more public than it had been in Mark – the voice of God speaks to the world in Matthew, but only to Jesus in Mark.

The conversation between John and Jesus in $3^{14, 15}$ has no parallel in Mark or Luke. It may have been added in order to answer certain questions which the Marcan narrative raised, e.g. Why had Jesus to be baptized? did his baptism imply his sinfulness and his need of repentance (cf. $3^{2, 6, 11}$)? did it point to the inferiority of Jesus to John? Part of Matthew's purpose in writing his Gospel was to overcome difficulties which had been raised by the work of his predecessor, and the addition of these verses seems to be an explanation of this kind.

13
Jesus came from Galilee where he had been last mentioned, in 2^{22f}.

14
I need to be baptized by you: Cf. above 3^{11} *he who is coming after me is mightier than I, whose sandals I am not worthy to carry.*

15
It is fitting for us to fulfil all righteousness is difficult; *righteousness (dikaiosyne)* seems to be used here in the sense of the divine commandments; and because these are contained in the Old Testament, *to fulfil all righteousness* is almost equivalent to 'to fulfil the scriptures' – i.e. the baptism in the Red Sea is repeated in the baptism by John in the Jordan.

16
The *dove*, to which the spirit is likened, may refer to a rabbinic interpretation of Gen. 1^2. *The Spirit of God was moving over the face of the waters:* '. . . like a dove which broods over her young but does not touch them'. If this is the case, then the meaning of it may be that as at the creation of the world the Spirit of God was at work, bringing order out of chaos, so now, in the new creation, the Spirit of God is at work again, first on Jesus (cf. $1^{18, 20}$), then upon his disciples (3^{11}, 10^{20}, 28^{19}).

17

The *voice from heaven* declares, *This is my beloved Son* (*ho huios mou ho agapētos*), *with whom I am well pleased*; it speaks in words from the Old Testament, but the reference is not to any one passage in the Old Testament; see Gen. 22², *Take your son, your only son* (*ton huion sou ton agapēton*), *Isaac.*

Ps. 2⁷

> I will tell of the decree of the Lord:
> He said to me, You are my son,

and Isa. 42¹

> Behold my servant, whom I uphold,
> my chosen, in whom my soul delights;
> I have put my spirit upon him,
> he will bring forth justice to the nations.

(quoted in 12¹⁸)

Matthew has taken over the account of the baptism of Jesus from Mark. In the earlier Gospel it formed part of the introduction to the Gospel, and the purpose of the story was, at least in part, to give the reader a right understanding of the person of Jesus, at the beginning of the book. In Matthew, on the other hand, the birth-stories have already done this to some extent. Nevertheless, the account of the baptism in Matthew increases the reader's understanding of Jesus. He sees now the fulfilment of the crossing of the Red Sea, which he might have expected from 2¹⁵ (*Out of Egypt have I called my son*); the word *beloved* or 'only' (*agapētos*) may remind him of Gen. 22 and recall that Jesus is to be the sacrifice which God will accept, as he is also *the son of Abraham* (cf. 1¹); the *dove* and the *water* may remind him of Gen. 1² and recall that Jesus is the new man, the last Adam (Rom. 5¹⁴; 1 Cor. 15⁴⁵), *the beginning of God's creation* (Rev. 3¹⁴).

It has sometimes been held that the baptism was the occasion when Jesus first became conscious of himself as the Son of God. Whether this was so or not (and we are now not in possession of material for proving such a theory), it is clear that the story was not told by Matthew as an account of how Jesus became aware of his office. The changes which he has made in 3¹⁶, ¹⁷, as we have seen already, tend in the opposite direction, and make the event and the announcement more public than they were in Mark.

4 *Then Jesus was led up by the Spirit into the wilderness to be tempted by the devil.* ²*And he fasted forty days and forty nights, and afterward he was hungry.* ³*And the tempter came and said to him, 'If you are the Son of God, command these stones to become loaves of bread.'* ⁴*But he answered, 'It is written,*

> *"Man shall not live by bread alone,*
> *but by every word that proceeds from the mouth of God."'*

⁵*Then the devil took him to the holy city, and set him on the pinnacle of the temple,* ⁶*and said to him, 'If you are the Son of God, throw yourself down; for it is written,*
> *"He will give his angels charge of you,"*

and
> *"On their hands they will bear you up,*
> *lest you strike your foot against a stone."'*

⁷*Jesus said to him, 'Again it is written, "You shall not tempt the Lord your God."'* ⁸*Again, the devil took him to a very high mountain, and showed him all the kingdoms of the world and the glory of them;* ⁹*and he said to him, 'All these I will give you, if you will fall down and worship me.'* ¹⁰*Then Jesus said to him, 'Begone, Satan! for it is written,*

> *"You shall worship the Lord your God*
> *and him only shall you serve."'*

¹¹*Then the devil left him, and behold, angels came and ministered to him.*

The only saying of Jesus which Matthew has so far recorded is 3$^{\text{15}}$, *Let it be so now; for thus it is fitting for us to fulfil all righteousness*; and we saw then that the meaning of this may be, We must fulfil the scriptures. In this paragraph, 4$^{\text{I-II}}$, Jesus speaks three times (4$^{\text{4, 7, 10}}$) and in each case he uses the phrase *it is written* (i.e. in the Old Testament). That is to say, he answers the suggestions of the devil by means of references to the scriptures which he has come to fulfil.

We may therefore say that the words of Jesus in this paragraph provide the reader with some explanation of his words in the previous paragraph, that he must *fulfil all righteousness*. Similarly, the first two sayings of the devil in this paragraph begin, *If you are the Son of God . . .* (4$^{3, 6}$), thus also linking back the voice from heaven 3^{17}, *This is my beloved Son*.

The three answers of Jesus to the devil include quotations which are all from the same book in the Old Testament, Deuteronomy. They refer to the testing of Israel in the wilderness, after the crossing of the Red Sea. If therefore Matthew had that crossing in mind when he wrote 3$^{13-17}$, he may also have had these events in the wilderness which Deuteronomy describes in mind when he wrote 4$^{1-11}$.

There is one particular passage in Deuteronomy which we should notice at this point, because of its general similarity to 4$^{1, 2}$ and to the situation described there. Moses is addressing Israel and he says: *And you shall remember all the way which the Lord your God has led you these forty years in the wilderness, that he might humble you, testing you to know what was in your heart, whether you would keep his commandments, or not* (Deut. 8^{2}). Similarly Jesus *was led up by the Spirit, into the wilderness, to be tempted* (cf. *testing you*, same word in the Greek), *and he fasted forty days and forty nights*. It may therefore be that we are to see here that Jesus fulfils the role of Israel, passing through similar temptations or testings; but where Israel had failed, Jesus is triumphant.

৩৫

Matthew is still following the Marcan sequence, though now he expands it considerably. In Mark, after the baptism of Jesus, there was a bare statement that Jesus was driven by the Spirit into the wilderness, where he was tempted forty days by Satan, *and he was with the wild beasts; and the angels ministered to him* (Mark 1$^{12, 13}$). Matthew omits only the reference to the wild beasts; apart from that, he is following his usual procedure of adding suitable material to Mark at appropriate points in the narrative.

The material which Matthew has added here is found also in Luke 4$^{1-13}$, and may therefore come from a common source. On the other hand, notice here the remarkable suitability of the material for this point in Matthew's sequence of events, between the baptism and the sermon on the mount (i.e. the fulfilment of the crossing of the Red Sea and of the giving of the law on Sinai); this suitability may lead us to think that these verses were composed by Matthew himself, to fit in here, and were not part of an earlier document, Q (see pp. 12f.). The fact that the Old Testament quotations in this passage agree with the Septuagint supports the possibility that Matthew composed it.

1

The Spirit leads Jesus *into the wilderness*, which was believed to be the home of the evil spirits, in order that there he may be *tempted by the devil, the prince of the demons* (12²⁴); he is therefore taken directly to the headquarters of evil.

2

Mark had not explicitly mentioned fasting; by means of it, Matthew introduces the first temptation, to satisfy hunger.

3

If you are the Son of God looks back to the voice from heaven in 3¹⁷ (cf. 2¹⁵) and see note on v. 10; and the suggestion that the Son of God can command the *stones to become loaves of bread* may recall the warning of the Baptist that *God is able from these stones to raise up children to Abraham* (3⁹); if he can raise up children from stones, then he can certainly make stones into loaves.

4

The answer of Jesus refers to the next verse in Deut. 8 to that quoted above (p. 62); Moses reminds Israel that God *humbled you and let you hunger and fed you with manna, which you did not know, nor did your fathers know; that he might make you know that man does not live by bread alone, but that man lives by everything that proceeds out of the mouth of the Lord* (Deut. 8³). The temptation is therefore similar to that of Israel described in Exod. 16¹ff., the temptation to doubt the power of God to provide; cf. 6²⁵, *Do not be anxious about your life, what you shall eat.* Jesus overcomes the temptation to anxiety by his faith in the care of God for his creatures.

5, 6

The second temptation by the devil arises out of the answer of Jesus to the first. If God cares for those who are his, then they will come to no harm whatever they do. Therefore let him throw himself down from the pinnacle of the temple, and prove the truth of the promise made in Ps. 91¹¹⁻¹².

The holy city is Jerusalem; for this title in Matthew, see also 27⁵³.

If you are the Son of God: Cf. v. 3, and note on v. 10.

7

The answer to the second temptation is from Deut. 6^{16}; *You shall not put the Lord your God to the test, as you tested him at Massah.* Massah means 'proof' or 'testing', and the incident which Moses is here recalling is described in Exod. 17$^{1-7}$: *Moses . . . called the name of the place Massah . . . because they put the Lord to the proof by saying, Is the Lord among us or not?* When Jesus says *It is written, You shall not tempt the Lord your God,* the title *the Lord your God* does not refer to himself, but to the Father. He refuses to test God by calling for angelic aid; we may compare 26$^{53f.}$: *Do you think that I cannot appeal to my Father, and he will at once send me more than twelve legions of angels? But how then should the scriptures be fulfilled, that it must be so?*

8, 9

The third temptation is to receive authority over the world and the possession of it by worshipping the devil. For the idea of the devil as the ruler or god of this world, cf. John 12^{31}, 16^{11}, 2 Cor. 4^4, 1 John 5^{19}.

10

The answer to the third temptation is from Deut. 6^{13}, but notice the whole passage: *You shall fear the Lord your God; you shall serve him, and swear by his name. You shall not go after other gods, of the gods of the people who are round about you; for the Lord your God in the midst of you is a jealous God; lest the anger of the Lord your God be kindled against you, and he destroy you from off the face of the earth* (Deut. 6$^{13-15}$).

The reference may be to the sin of Israel in making the molten calf: the incident is described in Exod. 32, and notice the wrath of God (Exod. 32^{10}) which would have destroyed Israel if Moses had not interceded. Jesus does not commit the sin of Israel, in worshipping *other gods*; and he therefore receives what the devil had (falsely) promised him, and more: *All authority in heaven and on earth has been given to me* (28^{18}).

Before the answer to this third temptation, Jesus says, *Begone, Satan!* These words are found also in Mark 8^{33} = Matt. 16^{23}, where they are addressed to Peter, who had tempted Jesus to avoid the crucifixion at Jerusalem. There may be more than a verbal link between these passages: the temptations of the devil here are temptations to live in a way different from that of faith in God and obedience to his commandments. Jesus rejects both the tempter here and Peter in Chapter 16; he goes to Jerusalem, and suffers, and dies, and is raised from the dead, and is rewarded with *all authority* (cf. Phil. 2$^{5-11}$).

Notice also how the temptations here are linked with the account of the crucifixion by the repetition there of the title *Son of God*; i.e. 27^{40}

If you are the Son of God, come down from the cross; 27^{43} *He trusts in God; let God deliver him now, if he desires him; for he said, I am the Son of God.*

11

The *Begone, Satan!* of v. 10 is effective, and the devil goes. The service of the angels may indicate Jesus' authority as the Lord – compare Heb. 1^6: *when he* [God] *brings the first-born into the world, he says, Let all God's angels worship him.* He has been victorious over the devil, and therefore he is exalted to a place above the angels.

4$^{12-17}$	JESUS GOES TO GALILEE	Mark 1$^{14, 15}$
	AND PREACHES THERE	Luke 4^{16}

^{12}*Now when he heard that John had been arrested, he withdrew into Galilee;* ^{13}*and leaving Nazareth he went and dwelt in Caper'na-um by the sea, in the territory of Zeb'ulun and Naph'tali,* ^{14}*that what was spoken by the prophet Isaiah might be fulfilled:*

> ^{15}'*The land of Zeb'ulun and the land of Naph'tali,*
> *toward the sea, across the Jordan,*
> *Galilee of the Gentiles –*
> ^{16}*the people who sat in darkness*
> *have seen a great light,*
> *and for those who sat in the region and shadow of death*
> *light has dawned.*'

^{17}*From that time Jesus began to preach, saying,* '*Repent, for the kingdom of heaven is at hand.*'

When Jesus hears of the handing-over of John the Baptist (to imprisonment), he leaves the wilderness of Judea (3^1, 4^1) and goes to Galilee; not, however, to Nazareth, where he had been brought up (2^{23}), but to Capernaum by the Sea of Galilee, in the district where the tribes of Zebulun and Naphtali had lived before the exile, but which was now populated with Gentiles. Isaiah's prophecy of the light to lighten the Gentiles is therefore fulfilled when Jesus begins to preach here.

Matthew has made use here of Mark $1^{14, 15}$ with some alterations and considerable additions. He has added, in v. 12, that Jesus heard that the Baptist had been arrested; the whole of vv. 13–16 is additional; and there are abbreviations of Mark's version in v. 17.

12

Notice the change from Mark's *Jesus came into Galilee* to *he withdrew into Galilee*. On Matthew's use of withdraw (*anachōrein*), see notes on $2^{14, 22}$.

Jesus withdraws from Judea, because he has heard of the arrest of John (which is mentioned again in 14^{1-12}), and goes to Galilee, and there, as we shall see, scripture is fulfilled. The meaning of the Evangelist can scarcely be that Jesus is leaving the jurisdiction of Herod Antipas who had seized John, since Herod ruled over Galilee as well as over Transjordan. Perhaps we are to see here, as in other places in Matthew where to *withdraw* is used, that the rejection of God's word in one place leads to the preaching of it in another place; and in particular that the rejection of it by the Jews leads to its offer to the Gentiles (N.B. v. 15, *Galilee of the Gentiles*).

13

The words *and leaving Nazareth* are abrupt and somewhat unexpected. Luke 4^{16-30} describes a visit to Nazareth at this point, and both in this verse in Matthew and in Luke 4^{16} the form of the name in the Greek is *Nazara*, whereas in all the other instances of it in the New Testament it is spelt *Nazareth*. This has led to the suggestion that there was a Q account of preaching in Nazareth, retained by Luke, and only briefly alluded to here by Matthew. On the other hand, it is possible that Matthew has the last mention of Jesus in Galilee in mind (2^{22}f. *he withdrew to the district of Galilee. And he went and dwelt in a city called Nazareth . . . 3^{13} Jesus came from Galilee*), and that he meant that Jesus did not begin his preaching there, but in *Capernaum by the sea*, thus fulfilling Isaiah's words which he quotes in verse 15.

14–16

Matthew's quotation of Isa. $9^{1, 2}$ does not agree with LXX or the Hebrew text. It has been suggested that he has independently translated the Hebrew, though knowing the Septuagint; notice in particular that he uses past tenses – *sat, have seen, has dawned* – thus stressing that the prophecy has now been fulfilled.

17

This verse marks the end of this section and the beginning of a new stage – the public preaching of Jesus. *From that time Jesus began to . . .* is used again to mark another stage in the narrative at 16^{21}, when Jesus begins to speak to his disciples of the necessity of his going to Jerusalem to die and be raised.

Some of the textual authorities have a shorter version of the words of Jesus, viz. *The kingdom of heaven is at hand*. Whether the shorter or the longer version is original, the repetition of the announcement of the coming of the kingdom which John the Baptist had made in 3^2 rounds off the section 3^1-4^{17}. It is probably better to put a break between vv. 17 and 18, than between 4^{22} and ^{23} as in R.S.V.

This section, 3^1-4^{17}, has been as it were a second introduction to the Gospel proper; until the last verse, Jesus has spoken only to John the Baptist (3^{15}) and to the devil ($4^{4, 7, 10}$); from now on, he will speak publicly. This phenomenon of a second introduction is due to Matthew's use of Mark 1^{1-15}, and his addition of the birth narratives in Chapters 1 and 2. The theme which links together 1, 2, and 3^1-4^{17} and the teaching on the mountain in 5–7 is the Exodus pattern of events.

Matthew 4¹⁸-7²⁹

Entry into the Kingdom

In 5^3-7^{27}, Matthew will give us the first of the five sections of teaching in his Gospel; 4^{18}-5^2 is the introduction to this teaching and sets the scene for it. It is made up of three paragraphs: (1) the calling of the two pairs of brothers to be followers or *disciples* of Jesus (4^{18-22}); (2) a summarized account of the teaching, preaching, and healing done by Jesus in Galilean synagogues, as a result of which *great crowds* follow him (4^{23-25}); (3) Jesus sees *the crowds* and goes up *the mountain*, and there teaches his disciples ($5^{1,2}$).

In these paragraphs we are introduced to two groups – *the disciples* and the *crowds*. As we shall see more clearly in the introduction to the second section of teaching (9^{35}-10^4), the *disciples* are to be sent to the *crowds*, as shepherds who are to look after sheep or as labourers who are to bring in a harvest (9^{36-38}). This mission of the disciples is suggested here, in the introduction to the first section of teaching, in two ways: (*a*) Jesus says to the first pair of brothers, *Follow me, and I will make you fishers of men* (4^{19}); (*b*) Jesus addresses the *disciples* in the presence of the *crowds* ($5^{1f.}$, cf. $7^{28f.}$).

Thus the two groups to which we are introduced here, the *disciples* and the *crowds*, stand for the missionaries and the congregations which they will teach; both have their origin in the initiative of Jesus, who calls his disciples to follow him and, by his proclamation of the kingdom through teaching, preaching, and healing, draws crowds also to follow.

4^{18-22} JESUS CALLS FOUR DISCIPLES   Mark 1^{16-20}
                 TO FOLLOW HIM

18As he walked by the Sea of Galilee, he saw two brothers, Simon who is called Peter and Andrew his brother, casting a net into the sea; for they were fishermen. 19And he said to them, 'Follow me, and I will make you fishers of men.' 20Immediately they left their nets and followed him. 21And going on from there he saw two other brothers, James the son of Zeb'edee and John his brother, in the boat with Zeb'edee their father, mending their nets, and he called them. ²²*Immediately they left the boat and their father, and followed him.*

In the previous verse (4¹⁷) Jesus had announced *the kingdom of heaven is at hand*; that is, God is about to rule on the earth, and abolish everything that is against his will. It is an axiom of Christianity that no one is able to enter God's kingdom through his own merit and good works; *all have sinned and fall short of the glory of God* (Rom. 3²³). Therefore the bare announcement of the imminence of the kingdom would not be a *gospel* – that is, good news – but a message of doom. This is why John the Baptist (3²), and Jesus (4¹⁷ if the text is correct), say *Repent.* And this is why God, who is merciful and forgiving, has provided time for repentance and called some who will, by their words and deeds, prepare the world for judgement. Such a time of preparation had been prophesied by Malachi, and the Christians believed that John the Baptist had been the fulfilment of this promise: *Behold, I will send you Elijah the prophet before the great and terrible day of the Lord comes. And he will turn the hearts of the fathers to their children and the hearts of children to their fathers, lest I come and smite the land with a curse* (Mal. 4^{5, 6}). Similarly Jesus, immediately after the announcement of the kingdom, calls disciples whose work will prepare the world for the day of the Lord.

სოცი

Here, Matthew has made use of Mark 1^{16–20} with almost no alterations; though notice that he has added the words *who is called Peter*; in Mark, Simon's new name is first mentioned at Mark 3¹⁶: *Simon whom he surnamed Peter* (cf. Matt. 10²).

18

by the Sea of Galilee looks back to v. 13 *Capernaum by the sea*, and to the prophecy quoted in v. 15.

they were fishermen: The occupation of Simon and Andrew foreshadows their future work.

19

Follow me: Literally 'Come after me' (*deute opisō mou*). The idea of following Jesus as a disciple will be elaborated later on in the Gospel; see for example 10^{38}.

I will make you fishers of men: For the metaphor of fishing, see also $13^{47f.}$, where the kingdom is compared to a net thrown into the sea which gathers fish of every kind. This has been elaborated in Luke 5^{1-11} and John 21^{4-8}, the accounts of great catches of fish, which symbolize the work of the ministry. A prophecy of Ezekiel may lie behind some or all of these passages: *Fishermen will stand beside the sea; from En-gedi to En-eglaim it will be a place for the spreading of nets; its fish will be of very many kinds, like the fish of the Great Sea* (Ezek. 47^{10}).

20

Immediately they left their nets and followed him: One of the points which the Gospels make quite clear is that the disciple or follower of Jesus must give up anything which he might think more important than Jesus; cf. 10^{37}, *He who loves father or mother more than me is not worthy of me; and he who loves son or daughter more than me is not worthy of me*; and 19^{27}, where Peter says, *Lo, we have left everything and followed you.* The leaving of the nets here suggests the complete renunciation which the disciples are to make eventually. Notice that no explanation is given, on the biographical or psychological level, why Simon and Andrew followed Jesus. Matthew does not tell us whether they had met him and heard him preach before this. It is no part of Matthew's purpose to answer every question which his narrative raises: he points to what is to him of most importance – the calling of disciples by Jesus – and he leaves it at that.

21, 22

James and *John*, the sons of Zebedee, are mentioned together again in this Gospel at 20^{20}ff. They leave *the boat and their father*: cf. 19^{29}, *every one who has left houses or brothers or sisters or father or mother or children or lands, for my name's sake, will receive a hundredfold, and inherit eternal life.*

We may perhaps ask whether the Evangelists saw any significance in the statement that James and John were *mending their nets*; if the fishing of Simon and Andrew foreshadowed their future work as *fishers of men*, did James and John *mending their nets* similarly foreshadow anything? Certainly the text does not say that it did, and so we cannot be certain. But it may be worth pointing out that the word used for *mending*, *katartizein*, is used in the epistles for *perfecting* the Church, and this is part of the work of the ministry: see 1 Cor. 1^{10}, 2 Cor. 13^{11}, Gal. 6^{1}, Eph. 4^{12}, 1 Thess. 3^{10}, Heb. 13^{21}, 1 Pet. 5^{10}. If there is anything in this, then *casting a net into the sea* may prefigure the evangelistic aspect of the ministry to those who are outside the Church, and *mending their nets* the pastoral ministry to those within.

4$^{23-25}$ GREAT CROWDS Mark 1$^{28, 39,}$
BEGIN TO FOLLOW JESUS 3$^{7, 8, 10,}$
6^{55}

23*And he went about all Galilee, teaching in their synagogues and preaching the gospel of the kingdom and healing every disease and every infirmity among the people.* 24*So his fame spread throughout all Syria, and they brought him all the sick, those afflicted with various diseases and pains, demoniacs, epileptics, and paralytics, and he healed them.* 25*And great crowds followed him from Galilee and the Decap'olis and Jerusalem and Judea and from beyond the Jordan.*

Matthew now describes in general terms the work of Jesus throughout the whole of Galilee (cf. the prophecy quoted in 4$^{15f.}$); he teaches in the synagogues of the Jews, preaches the good news of the coming of the kingdom, and, as a sign that God is beginning to rule, he heals all kinds of sickness. The result is that sick people are brought to him from the whole of Syria, and that *great crowds* follow him. Matthew's chief interest at this point is in these *crowds*, which he mentions again in 5^{1} and 7^{28}, i.e. immediately before and after the teaching on the mountain. To these *crowds* the disciples, whom he has called, will eventually be sent (9^{36}, 10$^{5ff.}$); they foreshadow the members of the Church whom Jesus will heal and teach through his disciples.

৩৩

Here, for the first time, Matthew has departed from the Marcan order of events. In Mark, the paragraph which follows the calling of the four disciples is the teaching and exorcism in the synagogue at Capernaum (Mark 1$^{21-28}$); Matthew does not reproduce that story in his Gospel, but he makes use of some of the elements in it – e.g. he takes the astonishment of the synagogue congregation at the teaching of Jesus (Mark 1^{22}) and uses it for the conclusion to the teaching on the mountain (7$^{28, 29}$).

That is to say, whereas Mark had given us no idea of the substance of the teaching of Jesus at that point, Matthew, by means of the contents of Chapters 5–7, tells us what the teaching was which astonished people as that of *one who had authority*.

In place of the visit to the Capernaum synagogue, Matthew composes a paragraph out of various sentences scattered through Mark 1–6, and it will be useful to notice these in order to see one of the ways in which Matthew has used his source:

> Matthew 4²³: Cf. Mark 1³⁹ *And he went throughout all Galilee, preaching in their synagogues and casting out demons*
> and Mark 1¹⁴ *preaching the gospel of God*
> Matthew 4²⁴: Cf. Mark 1²⁸ *And at once his fame spread everywhere throughout all the surrounding region of Galilee*
> and Mark 6⁵⁵ ... *began to bring sick people*
> and Mark 3¹⁰ *he had healed many*
> Matthew 4²⁵: Cf. Mark 3⁷ᶠ. *a great multitude from Galilee followed; also from Judea and Jerusalem and Idumea and from beyond the Jordan and from about Tyre and Sidon a great multitude, hearing all that he did, came to him.*

Matthew seems to have searched through Mark for sentences and phrases and words which would suit his purpose, and arranged them in his own way. We can see from this that he must have known Mark extremely well, and that he appears to have preferred, when it was available, a Marcan phrase (*wherever* he had to look for it) to his own composition.

23

all Galilee ... every disease and every infirmity: Cf. *all Syria ... all the sick* (v. 24); and cf. 3⁵ for this exaggerated use of *all* in editorial sections.

teaching ... preaching ... healing: Cf. 9³⁵ for the same three verbs used to describe the activity of Jesus. In due course, Jesus will give authority to his disciples to do what he does: 10¹ *to heal*, 10⁷ *to preach ... saying, The kingdom of heaven is at hand*, 28²⁰ *teaching them to observe all that I have commanded you*. (Notice the inversion of the order in which these activities are delegated to the disciples from that in which they are used to describe the work of Jesus, and see Introduction, pp. 15f., on chiasmus.)

their synagogues: Matthew regularly uses the pronoun *their* with the word *synagogue* (9³⁵, 10¹⁷, 12⁹, 13⁵⁴ [23³⁴]) in order to underline the

distinction between the Christians and the Jews. For the use of the word
'synagogue' of the Christian assembly, see James 2^2.

the people: The word translated *people* (*laos*) is used fourteen times in
Matthew (1^{21}, 2$^{4, 6}$, 4$^{16, 23}$, 13^{15}, 15^8, 21^{23}, 26$^{3, 5, 47}$, 27$^{1, 25, 64}$), and
only twice in Mark (Mark 7^6, 14^2); in most cases it clearly means the
Jews, the people of God. Its use here, of those whom Jesus healed, may
mean that although the ministry of Jesus is in *Galilee of the Gentiles* (4^{15}),
it is at present directed only to the Jews who live there (cf. 10$^{5f.}$, 15$^{21-28}$);
the scope of his activity will not be extended to the Gentiles until the
Jews have finally rejected him (cf. 27^{25}, 28^{19}).

24

Syria is mentioned in the Gospels only here and at Luke 2^2 (*Quirinius
was governor of Syria*). The reference to it here has been used as evidence
for the writing of this Gospel in Syria – e.g. in Antioch.

For healing as one of the signs of the nearness of the kingdom, see
Introduction, pp. 20f.

5$^{1, 2}$ JESUS GOES UP THE MOUNTAIN   Mark 3^{13}
                            TO TEACH

5 *Seeing the crowds, he went up on the mountain, and when he sat down
his disciples came to him.* ^{2}*And he opened his mouth and taught them,
saying:*

Jesus sees *the crowds*, who must be brought into the kingdom. At
present they do not know the way of life which is necessary for those
who wish to enter it, and they must be taught this way of life by
the disciples of Jesus. He therefore goes up the mountain with the
disciples, and teaches them in the presence of the crowds (7$^{28f.}$).
Eventually, when he has been given *all authority* by God, he will
authorize his disciples to teach others *to observe all that I have commanded you* (28$^{18ff.}$).

෴

Matthew probably composed these verses himself, but notice that he
had the words 'he goes up the mountain' (*anabainei eis to oros*) in Mark

3^{13}, and he reproduces them here, changing only the tense from historic-present to past (*anabē eis to oros*).

1

the mountain: The reader is not told which mountain, and he does not need to be, because he has been prepared for this since 2^{20} where he was told that Jesus is the fulfilment of Moses. Just as Moses received the Law from God on the mountain in the Old Testament, so Jesus gives his teaching to the disciples on the mountain. The comparison and contrast between the Law which was given to Moses and the commandments of Jesus runs through much of the following section (5^{17-20}, $21f.$, $27f.$, $31f.$, $33f.$, $38f.$, $43f.$, $7^{28f.}$).

When he had sat down: Jesus sits to teach; this was usual, but is emphasized in this Gospel (see $13^{1, 2}$ [15^{29}] 24^3, 26^{55}).

2

he opened his mouth and taught them saying: An example of 'semitic redundancy'; Matthew may, however, be drawing attention to the beginning of the teaching of Jesus, an aspect of his work to which the Evangelist attached particular importance; N.B. 28^{20} *teaching them to observe all that I have commanded you.*

5^3-7^{27} The Teaching on the Mountain

How did Matthew mean his readers to understand this section of the teaching of Jesus – the first of the five sections which all end with the formula for transition from teaching to narrative (see Introduction, p. 14)?

As we have already pointed out (note on 5^1), he intended them to see in this teaching that which, in the Christian faith, corresponds to the Law in the Old Testament. In Exodus there is a description of the making of the covenant between God and Israel: Moses *took the book of the covenant, and read it in the hearing of the people; and they said, All that the Lord has spoken we will do, and we will be obedient. And Moses took the blood and threw it upon the people, and said, Behold the blood of the covenant which the Lord has made with you in accordance with all these words* (Exod. $24^{7f.}$). Jesus has come to make a new covenant with a new Israel: cf. 26^{28} *this is my blood of the covenant, which is poured out for many for the forgiveness of sins.* His death corresponds to the blood of oxen in Exod. 24; his commandments correspond to the words of the Lord there – i.e. to the Law. Notice the contrast between the Law and the words of Jesus in 5^{17-20}, $^{21f.}$, $^{27f.}$, $^{31f.}$, $^{33f.}$, $^{38f.}$, $^{43f.}$, $7^{28f.}$.

John the Baptist and Jesus have both announced the coming of the *kingdom* (3^2, 4^{17}, ^{23}); and the commandments of Jesus show the way of life which is necessary if one would *enter the kingdom* (5^3, ^{10}, ^{20}, $7^{13f.}$, ^{21}). We have already been told that Jesus is *king* (2^2); it is therefore for him to declare who are his citizens. And just as he himself is only known by the revelation of God to those who have been chosen to receive it (Joseph, $1^{20f.}$; the Magi, 2^2; a larger group, so far undefined, 3^{17}) so the citizens of the kingdom which is to come are designated now by Jesus. God has borne witness to his Son in Chapters 1–3; the Son bears witness to his subjects in 5–7 – they are those who live in this way. And in both cases – that of the king and that of his subjects – the reality is other than one would have expected: the poor, not the rich; the mourners, not those who rejoice, etc.

It has recently been suggested that the eight Beatitudes (5^{3-10}) form as it were the 'text' for the whole section 5^3–7^{27}, or at least for the larger part of it; and that the material from 5^{11} onwards has been arranged according to a pattern set by these Beatitudes.* In $6^{9f.}$, the Lord's Prayer is given, and similarly it may be that the material from 6^{14} to 7^{27} is arranged as an exposition of that prayer. But see the notes which follow.

Whatever the pattern in this block of teaching is, it has almost certainly been contrived by the Evangelist himself, because it is almost certain that Matthew has collected together here sayings of Jesus which were not all spoken on the same occasion. The words and deeds of Jesus seem to have been remembered and preserved in the period before they were written down as isolated small units of not more than a paragraph each; and the arrangement of these paragraphs and sayings was the work of the Evangelists. (See D. E. Nineham, *The Gospel of St Mark*, pp. 21ff.).

What sources did Matthew use for 5^3–7^{27}? There are just over a hundred verses here, and about half of them have parallels in Luke;

---

* Austin Farrer, *St Matthew and St Mark* (1966), Chapter X.

moreover, a quarter of them are found in one section of Luke (6^{20-49}) which is sometimes known as the Sermon on the Plain (see Luke 6^{17}). It has therefore been held that Matthew and Luke used a common source which contained a 'Sermon', a collection of sayings of Jesus, which Matthew has expanded, partly perhaps with other sayings which he found elsewhere in this source, partly with sayings from another source.

Some of the remaining fifty verses or so in 5^3-7^{27} (i.e. those which have no parallel in Luke or Mark) may be assigned to another written source, sometimes designated M (e.g. $5^{19f.}$, $^{21-22}$, $^{27f.}$, $_{33-37}$, $_{38-41}$, 6^{1-8}, $^{16-18}$).

If however Luke used Matthew, and drew those passages which are common to his Gospel and Matthew's from Matthew, we shall not be able to divide the material into two distinct sources. In that case, Luke will have made a selection from Matt. 5^3-7^{27} for his sermon on the plain (Luke 6^{20-49}), used other sayings elsewhere in his Gospel, and omitted the remainder as unsuitable for his purpose.

5^{3-10} JESUS DECLARES WHO ARE   Luke $6^{20, 21}$
                          THE BLESSED

^{3}'Blessed are the poor in spirit, for theirs is the kingdom of heaven.

^{4}'Blessed are those who mourn, for they shall be comforted.

^{5}'Blessed are the meek, for they shall inherit the earth.

^{6}'Blessed are those who hunger and thirst for righteousness, for they shall be satisfied.

^{7}'Blessed are the merciful, for they shall obtain mercy.

^{8}'Blessed are the pure in heart, for they shall see God.

^{9}'Blessed are the peacemakers, for they shall be called sons of God.

^{10}'Blessed are those who are persecuted for righteousness' sake, for theirs is the kingdom of heaven.'

The first eight verses contain eight short sayings ('the Beatitudes'), each in the same form: Blessed are . . . for . . . These sayings declare who is to enter the kingdom which is coming. God will then reverse the positions and judgements which men have made for themselves in this world, and *the last will be first, and the first last* (20^{16}); so it is those who are least like kings and rulers – the least prosperous – who are the blessed. There is thus, running through these sayings, a contrast between present appearances and the future reality.

ಐಐ

The closest parallels in Luke $6^{20f.}$ are *Blessed are you poor, for yours is the kingdom of God*, and *Blessed are you that hunger now, for you shall be satisfied*; whether Luke's form is earlier and more original than Matthew's is much disputed.

Some of the ancient versions of Matthew place v. 5 before v. 4, and there are good grounds for thinking that this is the original order. We should then have: *Blessed are the poor in spirit, for theirs is the kingdom of heaven. Blessed are the meek, for they shall inherit the earth* – thus having *the poor* and *the meek* in parallel, and *the kingdom of heaven* and *the earth* likewise in parallel. The next two Beatitudes would then be: *Blessed are those who mourn, for they shall be comforted. Blessed are those who hunger and thirst for righteousness, for they shall be satisfied* – another couplet, with mourning balancing hungering and thirsting (for mourning and fasting, cf. $9^{14, 15}$), and *be comforted* balancing *be satisfied*. We shall rearrange in this order for the notes which follow.

3

the poor in spirit: *the poor* was a term used of the pious in the Old Testament (e.g. Isa. 61^1, *the Lord has anointed me to bring good tidings to the poor*, alluded to in 11^5, *the poor have good news preached to them*) and seems to have become a self-designation of certain Jews in the period after the Old Testament (e.g. in the *Psalms of Solomon* and the *Dead Sea Scrolls*). *In spirit* may mean 'willingly', 'voluntarily' – i.e. those who have renounced their possessions in order to follow Jesus; see $19^{23ff.}$ To these, Jesus promises the *kingdom of heaven* – that is, the greatest possession of all, to reign over the earth when God begins his rule.

5

the meek is similar in meaning to *the poor*: and for the whole of this saying cf. Ps. 37^{11}, *But the meek shall possess the land* (the Greek version of the Psalm is almost identical with this verse). To *possess the land* explains what is meant in the previous saying by *theirs is the kingdom of heaven* – i.e. to be set over the earth as rulers under God (cf. $25^{21, 23}$, *I will set you over much*).

4

those who mourn . . . comforted: Cf. Isa. 61² *to comfort all who mourn.* The disciples *mourn* because of the disobedience of the world to God; they *shall be comforted* by God when his kingdom comes and his will is done (6¹⁰).

6

Fasting accompanies mourning; and fasting is a form of prayer. Therefore to *hunger and thirst for* something is to pray for it; and what they pray for is *righteousness,* that is, the obedience of the world to the will of God, the coming of his kingdom. *They shall be satisfied* (by God), that is, their prayer will be answered, and they will be filled (cf. the idea of the kingdom as a feast, e.g. 8¹¹).

7

the merciful – i.e. those who forgive others, *shall obtain mercy* from God, in the forgiveness of their own sins (cf. 6¹⁴, 18²¹⁻³⁵).

8

the pure in heart is another phrase used in the Old Testament (Pss. 24⁴, 51¹⁰, 73¹), and in Hebrew psychology the *heart* is the seat of thought and will, rather than of emotion. The promise to them is that *they shall see God,* which was originally a Palestinian way of saying 'appear before God, attend the temple worship, specially that of the great festivals', cf. Ps. 24³ᶠ·:

> *Who shall ascend the hill of the Lord?*
> *And who shall stand in his holy place?*
> *He who has clean hands and a pure heart . . .*

Here it is used of the life of the blessed in the age to come.

9

the peacemakers: That is, those who create peace on the earth; *they shall be called* (by God) *sons of God* – and what God calls anything is what it is; cf. 5⁴⁴ᶠ. *Love your enemies and pray for those who persecute you, so that you may be sons of your Father who is in heaven.* The phrase 'son of . . .' means also 'like . . .' cf. 5⁴⁸ *You, therefore, must be perfect, as your heavenly Father is perfect.*

10

persecuted for righteousness' sake means persecuted because of their obedience to God, which they have learned by the commandments of Jesus. The promise to them, that *theirs is the kingdom of heaven,* rounds off the paragraph by repeating the promise in the first saying (5³) – an example of Matthew's use of *inclusio*, i.e. the marking off of a section by repeating the words from the beginning of it at the end.

These eight sayings at the beginning of the section will be expounded in the teaching which follows. They show who will enter the kingdom and share with God, under God, in the new order which is about to come. And those to whom they point are *the last* in this world, the unhappy and empty, who will eventually be *the first*, blessed and satisfied by God; they were capable of being filled, precisely because they were empty.

5^{11-20} THOSE WHO ARE   Mark 9^{50}, 4^{21}
PERSECUTED FOR   Luke $6^{22f.}$, $14^{34f.}$,
RIGHTEOUSNESS' SAKE 16^{17}

^{11}*'Blessed are you when men revile you and persecute you and utter all kinds of evil against you falsely on my account.* ^{12}*Rejoice and be glad, for your reward is great in heaven, for so men persecuted the prophets who were before you.*

^{13}*'You are the salt of the earth; but if salt has lost its taste, how shall its saltness be restored? It is no longer good for anything except to be thrown out and trodden under foot by men.*

^{14}*'You are the light of the world. A city set on a hill cannot be hid.* ^{15}*Nor do men light a lamp and put it under a bushel, but on a stand, and it gives light to all in the house.* ^{16}*Let your light so shine before men, that they may see your good works and give glory to your Father who is in heaven.*

^{17}*'Think not that I have come to abolish the law and the prophets; I have come not to abolish them but to fulfil them.* ^{18}*For truly, I say to you, till heaven and earth pass away, not an iota, not a dot, will pass from the law until all is accomplished.* ^{19}*Whoever then relaxes one of the least of these commandments and teaches men so, shall be called least in the kingdom of heaven; but he who does them and teaches them shall be called great in the kingdom of heaven.* ^{20}*For I tell you, unless your righteousness exceeds that of the scribes and Pharisees, you will never enter the kingdom of heaven.'*

The last of the Beatitudes promised *the kingdom of heaven* to *those who are persecuted for righteousness' sake* (5^{10}), and it is possible that we should take the four paragraphs in 5¹¹⁻²⁰ as an exposition of this: the first paragraph mentions persecution, and the last is about the *righteousness* which is necessary in order to *enter the kingdom of heaven*. The two middle paragraphs continue the idea of a righteous group in an unrighteous world which persecutes it: the Church is to be *the salt of the earth* and *the light of the world* (5^{13, 14}).

ཉྫ

Verses 13 and 15 have partial parallels in Mark 9⁵⁰ and 4²¹, but we cannot be sure whether Matthew expanded Mark or drew on another source. Similarly vv. 11ff. are similar to Luke 6^{22f.}, v. 13 to Luke 14^{34f.}, v. 18 to Luke 16¹⁷; this may indicate a common source used independently, or Luke's use of Matthew.

11

The new section is linked on to the Beatitudes by its opening word, *Blessed*; but it then departs from the form of the Beatitudes by changing to the second person plural – *are you*. This is the first time that the recipients of Jesus' teaching have been mentioned in the teaching itself; in the first instance, *you* refers to the *disciples* (5¹) as the ministers of the Church, but it is capable of extension to include the whole of the Church.

The word *falsely* is omitted by some of the manuscripts, and is probably a safeguard, introduced by a scribe.

on my account, in Greek, is similar to the expression *for righteousness' sake* in v. 10; the latter is *heneken dikaiosynēs*, the former *heneken emou*. The similarity of expression suggests that in some way Jesus is *righteousness*, and recalls his first words in 3¹⁵, *it is fitting for us to fulfil all righteousness*. He has identified himself with the demands of God, and what is suffered on his account is suffered also for the sake of God.

12

The disciples are to *rejoice and be glad* when they suffer as disciples of Jesus, because they will know by means of their suffering that they are the blessed who will share in the kingdom. This is their *reward* for suffering. *In heaven* means, not that they will 'go to heaven' (an idea which is seldom found in the New Testament), but 'with God', *heaven* being a way of avoiding the use of the word 'God', which was thought by the Jews to be too sacred to be pronounced.

so men persecuted the prophets who were before you: The Church is the successor of the prophets, and as the Jews persecuted them, so they will persecute it; cf. 23$^{29-36}$.

13

Israel had been likened to *salt*; the Church is the new Israel, called because the old Israel had *lost its taste* (cf. 21^{43}). The Church is not to repeat the sin of the Jews. The saying suggests that just as *salt* is useful in cooking, preserving, and as a fertilizer on *the earth*, so the Church has a usefulness to God in making the world acceptable to him, by its sacrifice and intercession.

14

the light was also a metaphor used for Israel and of the Law. Now the Church is to be *the light of the world*, and *the city set on a hill* (perhaps suggesting Jerusalem).

15

God is lighting *a lamp* by means of the teaching which Jesus is giving to his disciples, and the purpose of this *lamp* is to *give light* to the whole world – cf. 4^{16}, *the people who sat in darkness have seen a great light, and for those who sat in the region and shadow of death light has dawned.* This light will be displayed *to all* when Jesus sends the disciples to *all nations* (28^{19}).

16

The light will be seen, however, not in the words of the disciples so much as in their *good works*, i.e. in doing *the will of my Father who is in heaven* (7^{21}).

17

In this paragraph, Matthew returns to the idea of *righteousness* (5^{10}). The *righteousness* of the scribes and Pharisees was based on *the law and the prophets*. Although Jesus has come to found a new Israel, and thus in a sense *abolish* the old Israel, and although he will make serious criticisms of *the law and the prophets,* and of the scribes and Pharisees who are their official exponents, nevertheless he has come *to fulfil.* This may be taken either in the sense that he fulfils the prophecies of the Old Testament (cf. 3^{15}, *it is fitting for us to fulfil all righteousness*), or in the sense that he teaches a righteousness which *exceeds that of the scribes and Pharisees* (v. 20).

18

This is one of the most difficult verses in this Gospel. It may mean that the whole of the Law is binding until the end of the world (cf. 23$^{2f.}$, *The scribes and the Pharisees sit on Moses' seat; so practise and observe what they tell you*); or that the Law would stand in its entirety unless it was fulfilled in Jesus – and because he will fulfil its demands, it will be no longer binding on Christians.

19

There is also a difficulty in this verse: what are *these commandments*? Are they the commandments of *the law* (v. 18), or the commandments of Jesus which follow? Although the second interpretation is tempting, the first is perhaps more likely. The Christians for whom Matthew was writing seem to have been Jews by birth, and to have contrived to keep the Law after their conversion to Christianity. We know from other parts of the New Testament that there were those who adopted this attitude (e.g. Acts 21²⁰ where James says to Paul, *You see, brother, how many thousands there are among the Jews of those who have believed; they are all zealous for the law*). If this is the correct interpretation of this verse, then it raises the question of the authenticity of it – Did Jesus in fact teach his disciples to keep the Law? The late Dr T. W. Manson believed that he did not: 'These sentiments are put into the mouth of Jesus: it is in the last degree unlikely that he thought or said such a thing.' (*The Sayings of Jesus*, p. 154).

shall be called least in the kingdom of heaven means, God shall call him least, and therefore he shall be least. Similarly, *shall be called great in the kingdom of heaven* means shall be great in the kingdom of heaven; compare *they shall be called sons of God* (5⁹). And notice that this verse looks forward to degrees of *reward* (v. 12).

20

How the *righteousness* of the Christians is to exceed *that of the scribes and Pharisees* is to be explained in the following vv. 21–48. *You will never enter the kingdom of heaven* picks up the promise of the eighth Beatitude from which this section started, *theirs is the kingdom of heaven* (5¹⁰).

5^{21-48} *The Old Righteousness and the New Righteousness*

The righteousness *of the scribes and Pharisees* (5²⁰) was based on the Law, and their obedience to it. If therefore Jesus demands a greater righteousness he must teach a more exacting 'law'. (On the sense in which this is a law, see the note after 5⁴⁸.) This is what we have in 5²¹⁻⁴⁸: five paragraphs each beginning *You have heard that it was said* . . .

But I say to you . . . $5^{21f.,\ 27f.,\ 33f.,\ 38f.,\ 43f.}$. (There is another paragraph, beginning It was also said . . . But I say to you . . . which continues the subject of adultery that had been mentioned in the previous paragraph (5^{27-30}); we can therefore treat it as an appendix to that paragraph.) We have here, then, the new 'law' which is binding upon the new Israel, given to the Church by Jesus who is greater than Moses (cf. John 1^{17}, Heb. 3^3). The subjects which are dealt with in this section are: anger, lust, oaths, retaliation, love. It may be that we are to relate them to the sixth and seventh Beatitudes – the pure in heart and the peacemakers ($5^{8,\ 9}$); certainly 5^{25}, Make friends quickly with your accuser, can be likened to making peace, and lust can be thought of as the opposite to purity of heart. Similarly, the promise to be called the son of God is picked up in 5^{45}, so that you may be sons of your Father.

^{21}'You have heard that it was said to the men of old, "You shall not kill; and whoever kills shall be liable to judgement." ^{22}But I say to you that every one who is angry with his brother^a shall be liable to judgement; whoever insults^b his brother shall be liable to the council, and whoever says, "You fool!" shall be liable to the hell^c of fire. ^{23}So if you are offering your gift at the altar, and there remember that your brother has something against you, ^{24}leave your gift there before the altar and go; first be reconciled to your brother, and then come and offer your gift. ^{25}Make friends quickly with your accuser, while you are going with him to court, lest your accuser hand you over to the judge, and the judge to the guard, and you be put in prison; ^{26}truly, I say to you, you will never get out till you have paid the last penny.'

    a Other ancient authorities insert without cause
    b Greek says Raca to (an obscure term of abuse)
    c Greek Gehenna

Matthew takes first the sixth Commandment in the Decalogue You shall not kill, and contrasts that with Jesus' prohibition of anger. Anger is to killing as thought is to deed. Moreover, the disciple is not only to avoid anger in himself: he is also to avoid or remove the anger of others against himself, and thus be a *peacemaker* (5⁹).

๛

Verses 21–24 have no parallel in any of the other Gospels, but vv. 25, 26 are parallel to Luke 12⁵⁷⁻⁵⁹, where they have a different context and interpretation: in Matthew, they are an exhortation to reconciliation; in Luke, they are in the form of a parable of crisis. The latter is usually thought to be more original, and nearer Jesus' meaning. If Luke has taken them from Matthew he has re-applied them in a sense closer to the meaning which they had when they were first spoken by Jesus.

21
to the men of old: i.e. to Israel in the wilderness, who first received from Moses the Law of God.

You shall not kill (Exod. 20¹³, Deut. 5¹⁷): The sixth Commandment. (Although the order of the sixth and seventh Commandments differs in the Hebrew and some manuscripts of the Greek translation, 15¹⁹ and 19¹⁸ show that Matthew followed the order of the Hebrew, which is followed by the R.S.V. in Exodus and Deuteronomy.)

whoever kills shall be liable to judgement is not an exact quotation from the Old Testament, but see Exod. 21¹², Lev. 24¹⁷, Deut. 17⁸⁻¹³; *judgement* may mean the decision of a court, or condemnation.

22
But I say to you contains a double contrast with the previous verse: Moses and Jesus; the old Israel and the new.

Jesus declares that anger, the motive behind killing, is *liable to* the same punishment as that for killing, and is therefore as bad. Compare the saying of Rabbi Eliezer (*c.* A.D. 90): 'He who hates his neighbour, lo he belongs to the shedders of blood.'

The words in the margin, *without cause*, found in some of the manuscripts and versions, are, like the word *falsely* in v. 11, probably not part of the original text, but may have been added by a copyist.

The second half of the verse refers to another type of sin – that of word. *Insults* is literally *says Raca to* (margin), and *Raca* is probably an Aramaic word meaning 'stupid' or 'blockhead'.

the council may mean the Sanhedrin, the supreme court of the Jews, in contrast with the local court (= *judgement*) in vv. 21, 22. In that case, there is an ascending order of punishment – local court, Sanhedrin, hell.

Gehenna (margin) means the place of punishment after death: it received its name from a valley south of Jerusalem; 'there, according to later Jewish popular belief, the last judgement was to take place' (*Lexicon*, p. 152). Matthew uses the word again at $5^{29, 30}$, 10^{28}, 18^9, $23^{15, 33}$.

23f.

The reference to the *gift* and *the altar* may imply that the Christians still take part in the temple services (see note on 5^{19}). The duty of reconciliation is to take precedence even over the duties commanded by God in the temple-worship. But notice that these verses go beyond what is said in vv. 21ff.: there, anger is forbidden; here, the disciples are to seek reconciliation with those whom they have offended – not only with those who have offended them. This is a more difficult task since the disciple, having put himself in the wrong, starts from a weaker position.

25f.

The idea of priority and urgency (*first*, v. 24) links these two verses to the previous verses, and that of being in the wrong (*till you have paid the last penny*). Probably Matthew sees behind this saying the final *court*, at which the Son of man will be *the judge* and the *prison* will be Gehenna cf. 18^{23-35}).

5^{27-32} | ADULTERY | Mark 9^{43-47}, $10^{11, 12}$
 | AND LUST | Luke 16^{18}

^{27}'You have heard that it was said, "You shall not commit adultery." ^{28}But I say to you that every one who looks at a woman lustfully has already committed adultery with her in his heart. ^{29}If your right eye causes you to sin, pluck it out and throw it away; it is better that you lose one of your members than that your whole body be thrown into hell.^{a} ^{30}And if your right hand causes you to sin, cut it off and throw it away; it is better that you lose one of your members than that your whole body go into hell.^{a}

^{31}'It was also said, "Whoever divorces his wife, let him give her a certificate of divorce." ^{32}But I say to you that every one who divorces his wife, except on the ground of unchastity, makes her an adulteress; and whoever marries a divorced woman commits adultery.'

a Greek *Gehenna*

88

Matthew takes next the seventh Commandment, *You shall not commit adultery*; as anger is the motive behind killing, so lust is the motive behind adultery, and Jesus' new righteousness forbids lust, just as it forbids anger. The phrase *looks at a woman lustfully* is used as a link, with a saying about the *eye* causing sin, and this links up with another saying about the *hand* causing sin – i.e. the occasions which lead to the sin of lust are to be avoided, as well as the sin itself. This section has an appendix, on divorce – another contrast between the righteousness of the scribes and Pharisees and the righteousness of the disciples. (It may be that Matthew is collecting material here to illustrate the sixth Beatitude, *Blessed are the pure in heart, for they shall see God* (5⁸), and contrasting lust with purity, and the sinful use of the eye in this world with the vision of God in the age to come.)

ℵℵ

Verses 27, 28 have no parallel in the other Gospels; vv. 29, 30 are similar to Mark 9⁴³⁻⁴⁷ and Matthew may have taken them from there; he has however reproduced that part of Mark in 18⁸⁻⁹, thus creating a duplication in his Gospel. Verse 32 may be from Mark 10¹¹, ¹², which Matthew has used in 19⁹, making another duplication. However, v. 32 is closer to Luke 16¹⁸, and may therefore come from a source other than Mark.

27
The seventh Commandment, Exod. 20¹⁴, Deut. 5¹⁸.

28
As in the previous paragraph, Jesus equates the thought with the deed: cf. the rabbinic saying 'He who looks at a woman with desire is as one who has criminal intercourse with her'.

29ff.
Just as in v. 23, the thought moved from being angry with others to those who are angry with you, here also a further step is taken: in order to avoid lust, the occasions which give rise to the sin must be avoided; and since looking was mentioned in v. 28, the *eye* is placed first, before the *hand* (contrast Mark 9⁴³⁻⁴⁷, hand . . . foot . . . eye). The word *right* in v. 29 is difficult: why should the *right eye* be specified? (Mark does not use the word in 9⁴³⁻⁴⁷.) We can understand the *right hand* in verse 30 – since it is usually the more active (6³, and cf. Song of Solomon 2⁹). The word may have been introduced into v. 30 first, and the saying

in v. 29 may have been assimilated to it later. The sayings in this verse illustrate one of the basic Christian ideas – that the way to the greatest gain in the world to come involves sacrifice and loss in life here and now; compare the blessing on the persecuted, 5¹⁰⁻¹².

31

The reference is to Deut. 24¹⁻⁴, which allows a man to write a bill of divorce if his wife *finds no favour in his eyes because he has found some indecency in her.*

32

No exception to this command is mentioned in Mark 10¹¹f. or in Luke 16¹⁸; only in Matthew (here, and at 19⁹) is the exception allowed *on the ground of unchastity (porneia)*; it is not clear whether *unchastity* refers to fornication before marriage (and discovered after), or (which is more probable) to adultery after marriage. On the presence of the exceptive clause in Matthew, notice 16¹⁹, 18¹⁸, the power to *bind* and *loose* given to the apostles – that is, power to adapt laws and to make exceptions. The permission to allow divorce in certain circumstances seems to be one example of the use of this authority by the early Church; cf. 1 Cor. 7¹²ff., ²⁵ff. where Paul gives his opinions on marriage problems; but notice that he distinguishes clearly and explicitly between his *opinion* and the Lord's *command*; in these verses in Matthew (5³², 19⁹), the distinction between the original command of the Lord and the Church's legislation has been obscured.

5³³⁻³⁷   OATHS AND TRUTHFULNESS   James 5¹²

³³'*Again you have heard that it was said to the men of old, "You shall not swear falsely, but shall perform to the Lord what you have sworn." ³⁴But I say to you, Do not swear at all, either by heaven, for it is the throne of God, ³⁵or by the earth, for it is his footstool, or by Jerusalem, for it is the city of the great King. ³⁶And do not swear by your head, for you cannot make one hair white or black. ³⁷Let what you say be simply "Yes" or "No"; anything more than this comes from evil.'ᵃ*

a Or *the evil one*

The third contrast between the Law and the commandments of

Jesus is on the questions of oaths. The Law forbade the use of oaths when the swearer of the oath was going to lie and commanded oaths in the name of the Lord. Jesus forbids all oaths – in the name of the Lord, or in any other name. The disciples are simply to be truthful.

ཏྩ

There is no parallel to this paragraph in Mark or Luke, but there is some connexion between vv. 34, 35, 37, and James 5¹².

33
to the men of old: See in 5²¹.

You shall not swear falsely is not an exact quotation from the Old Testament, but cf. Exod. 20⁷, Deut. 5¹¹, *You shall not take the name of the Lord your God in vain* (the third Commandment), and Lev. 19¹², *You shall not swear by any name falsely.*

but you shall perform to the Lord what you have sworn probably means 'You shall keep your vows to the Lord'; it probably refers to Ps. 50¹⁴ *Pay your vows to the Most High* (though a different Greek word for *vows* is used in these two passages).

34f.
The disciples are not to swear at all – by God, or *heaven*, or *earth*, or *Jerusalem*, since these belong to God, and thus to swear by them is, in a sense, to swear by God.

36
Similarly, you have no power over your head – e.g. over the colour of your hair; God determines that; therefore to swear by your head (which was done) is to swear by God.

37
The disciples' conversation is to be completely free from oaths – all oaths are from *the evil one*. (The Greek words, *ek tou ponerou*, may be either masculine (*the evil one*) or neuter (*evil*). The same uncertainty is found also at 5³⁹, 6¹³, 13³⁸; in 13¹⁹ it must be masculine.) On the use of oaths by the scribes and Pharisees, see also 23¹⁶⁻²².

[38]'*You have heard that it was said, "An eye for an eye and a tooth for a tooth."* [39]*But I say to you, Do not resist one who is evil. But if any one strikes you on the right cheek, turn to him the other also;* [40]*and if any one would sue you and take your coat, let him have your cloak as well;* [41]*and if any one forces you to go one mile, go with him two miles.* [42]*Give to him who begs from you, and do not refuse him who would borrow from you.*'

The Law allowed a person who had been wronged to take an equivalent from the person who had wronged him. Jesus will not allow retaliation of this kind: evil actions are not to be resisted, demands are to be met with double that which is demanded. The disciples are to have no selfish concern for their property or for themselves, but to be open and liberal.

ĩǾǾ

There is a close parallel to vv. 39b, 40, 42 in Luke $6^{29, 30}$ – either this is the next part of the Q sermon after the Beatitudes; or this is the next part of Matthew's sermon that Luke wanted to include in his Sermon on the Plain.

38
An eye for an eye and a tooth for a tooth: See Exod. 21^{24}, Lev. 24^{20}, Deut. 19^{21}.

39
one who is evil (to pōnērō), cf. 5^{37}: This word may provide the link with the earlier sayings.

right cheek: Luke 6^{29} omits *right*; $5^{29, 30}$ above; here, however, there may be a particular point in mentioning the *right* side of the face, since it may imply a blow with the back of the aggressor's hand which was 'a peculiarly insulting assault and punishable by a specially heavy fine' (Manson, *The Sayings of Jesus*, p. 51).

40
The *coat (chitōn)* is the under-garment; the *cloak (himation)* is the outer-

garment. The former could be demanded as a legal fine or pledge, Exod. 22²⁵ᶠ·, Deut. 24¹³ᶠ·.

41

The Romans, following the practice of the Persians, made use of privately owned horses etc., for the public services, and the word translated *forces* (*angareuein*) is the technical term for such requisitioning; cf. 27³², where Simon of Cyrene was *compelled to carry* Jesus' *cross*. The disciples are not only to be liberal with their possessions – their time also is to be available to all who ask for it.

42

They are to give to beggars and to lend to borrowers. They are to have no anxious care for their property in this world; cf. Heb. 10³⁴, *you joyfully accepted the plundering of your property, since you knew that you yourselves had a better possession and an abiding one.*

5⁴³⁻⁴⁸   HATRED AND LOVE   Luke 6²⁷, ²⁸, ³²⁻³⁶

⁴³'*You have heard that it was said, "You shall love your neighbour and hate your enemy." ⁴⁴But I say to you, Love your enemies and pray for those who persecute you, ⁴⁵so that you may be sons of your Father who is in heaven; for he makes his sun rise on the evil and on the good, and sends rain on the just and on the unjust. ⁴⁶For if you love those who love you, what reward have you? Do not even the tax collectors do the same? ⁴⁷And if you salute only your brethren, what more are you doing than others? Do not even the Gentiles do the same? ⁴⁸You, therefore, must be perfect, as your heavenly Father is perfect.*'

The last of the five paragraphs contrasting the two covenants, and the climax: the old had limited love to love for the *neighbour*; Jesus commands his disciples to love those who are their enemies and persecute them. If the disciples do this, they will be sons of their Father – that is, they will be like him who is indiscriminate in his gifts of sun and rain (cf. the seventh Beatitude . . . *they shall be called sons of God* 5⁹). Love for the loving is no more than the practice of the 'natural', sinful man; but love for enemies and persecutors goes beyond what is 'natural', and thus merits a *reward* (cf. $5^{11, 12}$ the reward for those who are persecuted). The whole of this section which began in 5^{21} is then summarized in the saying *You, therefore, must be perfect, as your heavenly Father is perfect* – this is the righteousness which *exceeds that of the scribes and Pharisees*, without which the disciples *will never enter the kingdom of heaven* (5^{20}).

ۼ

The relationship between vv. 44–48 and Luke $6^{27, 28, 32-36}$ is not at all clear; some have said that Luke preserves the sayings in a more original form; but it may be that Luke has selected and re-arranged from Matthew.

43

You shall love your neighbour is quoted from Lev. 19^{18}, but the words *and hate your enemy* are not found in the Old Testament. The Jews did, however, limit the interpretation of the word *neighbour* (*plēsion*) to members of Israel, and may, in practice, have drawn the conclusion that the Gentiles were to be hated. And sayings have now been found in one of the Dead Sea Scolls which support this possibility; e.g. '(it is the duty of members of the sect) to love everyone, whom he (God) has elected, and to hate everyone, whom he has rejected' (I Q S, i, 4, quoted in *The Scrolls and the New Testament*, ed. K. Stendahl, p. 120).

44

The disciples are to pay no attention to other people's attitudes toward them: they are to be indiscriminate in their love, and *love* those who hate them, and *pray for those who persecute* them. This saying refines what was said about persecution in 5^{10-12}: it is not enough to be persecuted; they must meet their persecutors with love and prayer for them.

45

The indiscriminate goodness of the disciples is a reflection of the goodness of their Father (cf. 5^9).

46

To return love for love is only another form of *an eye for an eye*. It does not involve doing anything more than what those who are outside even the old Israel (*the tax collectors*) do. Therefore it merits no reward.

47

Similarly, to *salute* (*aspazesthai*, 'be fond of, cherish', *Lexicon*, p. 116) *only your brethren* does not earn any reward; *the Gentiles*, who are outside

Israel, *do the same*; but the disciples are to do *more* than, not the Gentiles only, but *the scribes and Pharisees* (5^{20}).

48

With this saying, compare Lev. 19^2, of which it contains an echo: *You shall be holy; for I the Lord your God am holy*. Under the old covenant, holiness had involved separation from those outside Israel; and there is still a sense in which the disciples are to be distinct from the world (cf. 5$^{13f.}$ *the salt of the earth, the light of the world*); but the distinction and separation must not take the form of a refusal to love – their love like their Father's must be indiscriminate. The perfection of the disciples is a perfect love – this is the final truth about the new righteousness, which *exceeds that of the scribes and Pharisees*; and this is the fulfilment of *the law and the prophets* (5^{17}). Cf. Rom. 13$^{9f.}$, *The commandments, You shall not commit adultery, You shall not kill, You shall not steal, You shall not covet, and any other commandment, are summed up in this sentence, You shall love your neighbour as yourself. Love does no wrong to a neighbour; therefore love is the fulfilling of the law*.

We said above (p. 85) that Jesus teaches a more exacting 'law' than that in the Old Testament. In what sense is 5$^{21-48}$ a new law? Not in the sense that Jesus replaces one set of instructions by another set, which is more difficult to keep. His 'law' is impossible, because it puts before us perfection and love which are beyond our capability. And his 'law' is not a set of detailed instructions, but is redudible to one word, love. The 'law' of Jesus is therefore both simpler and more demanding than the Law of the Old Testament, and by it the disciples are made entirely dependent on the mercy of God, because they are put permanently into the position of sinners who must always say *Forgive us our debts* (6^{12}).

6$^{1-21}$ *Three Pious Acts and Their Reward*

The fourth section of the teaching on the mountain, 6$^{1-21}$, is very clearly arranged: there is first an Introduction, warning the disciples not to practise their *piety* in full view of others, so as to be praised for what they are doing; if they do so, they will have *no reward* from God, 6^1; this is followed by three examples: almsgiving, prayer, and fasting, each introduced by the formula, *when you . . .* followed by a command not to do what the hypocrites do (6$^{2, 5, 16}$);

finally, there is a conclusion, contrasting the reward of praise *on earth* with the reward of praise *in heaven*, 6$^{19-21}$. Moreover, there is, in each of the three examples, a repetition of the saying, *Truly, I say to you, they have their reward* (6$^{2, 5, 16}$) and each example concludes with another formula, *your Father who sees in secret will reward you* (6$^{4, 6, 18}$). This section therefore considers *the reward*, which was first explicitly mentioned at 5^{12}, in relation to acts which are directed (or should be directed) solely towards God. Each of the Beatitudes had included the promise of a reward: the disciples are now told how to make sure of that promise. There may also be a link between the first act of piety, almsgiving, and the fifth Beatitude, *Blessed are the merciful for they shall obtain mercy* (5^{7}): in Greek, *alms* is *eleēmosynē*, *merciful* is *eleēmōn*; and the point which is underlined with regard to prayer, the second act of piety, is forgiveness – *if you forgive men their trespasses, your heavenly Father also will forgive you* (6^{14}). In the same way, the fourth Beatitude, *Blessed are those who hunger and thirst for righteousness, for they shall be satisfied* (5^{6}), can be linked with the third act of piety, fasting (6$^{16-18}$).

6¹   INTRODUCTION

6 '*Beware of practising your piety before men in order to be seen by them; for then you will have no reward from your Father who is in heaven.*'

The previous paragraphs taught a righteousness which was more demanding than that of the Old Testament Law; those which now follow, in 6$^{2-18}$, are more concerned with the manner than the matter; the disciples are to *beware* lest they practise their piety in the wrong way, with the wrong motive: taking a short-term view and collecting their reward now, from *men*, rather than at the last judgement, from their Father in *heaven*. Notice how this expounds the future tenses in all the Beatitudes from the second to the seventh (5$^{4-9}$ *they shall . . .*).

ॐ

They had been told in 5^{16}, *Let your light so shine before men, that they may see your good works and give glory to your Father who is in heaven.* Here, however, they are told not to do their good works of piety in *order to be seen by* men. How is this contradiction to be resolved? One way would be to divide good works into two kinds – those which may be seen, and those which must be kept secret (e.g. love of man may be seen by others, love of God must be kept secret). However, it is more likely that the resolution does not lie in this external division, but in a consideration of motives: is the motive of the action that men may give glory to God, or is it that they may give glory to the one who is performing the action? The disciples must indeed be *the light of the world* (5¹⁴), and this light will only shine through their *good works* (5¹⁶); but in order that it may give *light to all in the house* (5¹⁵) they must be free from any desire to let it illuminate themselves. This would be to act *in order to be seen* by men. And this would destroy the real nature of the action, which is directed (or should be) towards God and the world, and would therefore disqualify the disciples from receiving a *reward* from God.

²'*Thus, when you give alms, sound no trumpet before you, as the hypocrites do in the synagogues and in the streets, that they may be praised by men. Truly, I say to you, they have their reward.* ³*But when you give alms, do not let your left hand know what your right hand is doing,* ⁴*so that your alms may be in secret; and your Father who sees in secret will reward you.*'

The first example of hidden piety is almsgiving: the disciples are not to give alms in order to be praised, but so to hide their actions that only God sees what they are doing; then they will be rewarded by him in the kingdom. This hiddenness of the disciples is contrasted with the ostentation of *the hypocrites* – i.e. *the scribes and Pharisees* (5²⁰, cf. 23¹³, ¹⁵, ²³, ²⁵, ²⁷, ²⁹ where Matthew repeats the formula *Woe to you, scribes and Pharisees, hypocrites!*).

༄

2

alms (eleēmosynē): The word is derived from *mercy* (5⁷); see above p. 96.

The *trumpets* are probably metaphorical, and refer to ostentation – though ram's horn trumpets were sounded during the autumn fasts for rain, and almsgiving was expected at that time.

the hypocrites (the word is used thirteen times by Matthew, once by Mark, three times by Luke): The original meaning is 'play-actor', but it could also mean 'godless', 'profane'.

that they may be praised by men: The word translated *praised* (*doxazein*) is used elsewhere in Matthew always of praising or giving glory to God (5^{16}, 9^8, 15^{31}). The *hypocrites* have robbed God of what should be given to him.

they have their reward (*apechousin ton misthon autōn*): Cf. 6^5, ^{16}; not in the sense of a future reward from God, or even of a reward now in the present from him, but in the opposite sense: the praise of men is their full payment, and the account is closed: they have nothing owing to them from God in the age to come (*apechein* is a technical term in commerce, to 'receive a sum in full and give a receipt for it', *Lexicon*, p. 84).

3

you is emphatic and contrasts the disciples with *the hypocrites* (cf. 5^{21}ff. in which Jesus contrasted himself with Moses, and *the men of old* with the disciples).

your right hand is usually the hand which performs actions (cf. 5^{30}); the disciple is so to hide his action that even his *left hand* is unaware of his deeds – i.e. he is neither to seek satisfaction through others' knowledge and praise of him, nor through his own self-knowledge; cf. 1 Cor. 4^4 *I am not aware of anything against myself, but I am not thereby acquitted. It is the Lord who judges me.*

4

your father . . . will reward you in the kingdom: *reward* (*apodōsei*) is another word from commerce (see on v. 2), and can mean simply 'pay', as in 20^8 *pay them their wages*. The poverty of the disciples (5^3) is to extend to praise: they are to live without it now, in order that they may have it from God then, when God *will repay every man for what he has done* (16^{27}). (For praise from God, see 25$^{21, 23}$, *Well done, good and faithful servant.*) This is a large part of what is meant by 'living in hope' – enduring a present poverty in view of a future wealth.

⁵'*And when you pray, you must not be like the hypocrites; for they love to stand and pray in the synagogues and at the street corners, that they may be seen by men. Truly, I say to you, they have their reward.* ⁶*But when you pray, go into your room and shut the door and pray to your Father who is in secret; and your Father who sees in secret will reward you.*

⁷'*And in praying do not heap up empty phrases as the Gentiles do; for they think that they will be heard for their many words.* ⁸*Do not be like them, for your Father knows what you need before you ask him.* ⁹*Pray then like this:*

> *Our Father who art in heaven,*
> *Hallowed be thy name.*
> ¹⁰*Thy kingdom come,*
> *Thy will be done,*
>   *On earth as it is in heaven.*
> ¹¹*Give us this day our daily bread;ᵃ*
> ¹²*And forgive us our debts,*
>   *As we also have forgiven our debtors;*
> ¹³*And lead us not into temptation,*
>   *But deliver us from evil.ᵇ*

¹⁴*For if you forgive men their trespasses, your heavenly Father also will forgive you;* ¹⁵*but if you do not forgive men their trespasses, neither will your Father forgive your trespasses.*'

   a Or *our bread for the morrow*
   b Or *the evil one*. Other authorities, some ancient, add, in some form,
     For thine is the kingdom and the power and the glory, for ever. Amen

The second example of *piety* is prayer, and it receives much the same treatment as almsgiving: it is to be done secretly, in order that it may be repaid by God in the future. To this second example an appendix is added (cf. the appendix to the second example of the old and new righteousness, 5²⁷⁻³²), which contrasts the disciples with the Gentiles, who *think that they will be heard for their many words*, and this introduces the Lord's Prayer; after the Lord's Prayer, Matthew adds a footnote or elaboration emphasizing one aspect of the Prayer, namely, forgiveness (cf. 5⁷ *the merciful*).

❧

There is another, shorter version of the Lord's Prayer in Luke 11²⁻⁴; and the saying about forgiveness in v. 14 is similar to Mark 11²⁵ (which Matthew omits when he is reproducing Mark 11²⁰ff. in 21¹⁸ff.).

5

See notes on 6². The Jews practised private prayer, as well as the public prayer in the temple and the synagogues. This private prayer is mainly under consideration here and in the next verse; the early Church did not abandon corporate prayer.

6

go into your room and shut the door is a quotation from the Greek version of Isa. 26²⁰: *Come, my people, enter your chambers, and shut your doors behind you*; and cf. 2 Kings 4³³, where Elisha *went in and shut the door upon the two of them, and prayed to the Lord.*

pray to your Father who is in secret: The word translated *who* (*tō*) is omitted in some of the authorities for the text; in that case, the translation will be 'pray in secret to your Father'. See also the notes on 6⁴ above.

7

do not heap up empty phrases (*mē battalogēsēte*): The meaning is uncertain; perhaps 'babble, speak without thinking' (*Lexicon*, p. 137).

8

your Father knows what you need before you ask him: The disciples are not to think that their words supply God with information, without which he cannot answer their prayers. The purpose of words in prayer is to help us, not to inform God.

9

Pray then like this: The rabbis composed prayers for their disciples to use, and according to Luke 11¹ John the Baptist had *taught his disciples* to pray.

Our Father who art in heaven (Luke has simply, *Father*); the longer form in Matthew is probably due to the addition by him of phrases characteristic of his style and of the formal phraseology which is characteristic of Jewish prayers; cf. 6¹ *Your Father who is in heaven.*

Hallowed be thy name means 'May thy name be held in reverence' (*Lexicon*, p. 9), and is probably an instance of the Jewish use of a passive verb to avoid the divine name; therefore the meaning is, 'Make thy name be held in reverence' – i.e. reveal thy kingdom. (Name of a person = person himself.) Cf. Ezek. 36²³. *I will vindicate the holiness* (Greek *hagiasō*, as here in Matthew) *of my great name, which has been profaned among the nations, and which you have profaned among them; and the nations will know that I am the Lord, says the Lord God, when through you I vindicate my holiness (hagiasthēnai me) before their eyes.*

10

Thy kingdom come: Jesus had preached that *the kingdom* was *at hand* (4¹⁷, cf. 4²³); the Beatitudes had described the rewards in the kingdom (5³⁻¹⁰). If the disciples live in hope (see 6⁴), they will pray for the kingdom to come, in order that they may receive their reward, and God's will may be done everywhere.

Thy will be done, On earth as it is in heaven: These words are not in Luke's version of the prayer; and they reflect Matthew's style: he has probably added them as a further explanation of the two previous petitions. *On earth as it is in heaven* should probably be translated 'Both in heaven and on earth'; see 24²⁹.

The first three petitions in the prayer are in a sense synonymous: when God vindicates his holiness, his kingdom has come and his will is done. The disciples are therefore taught to pray first for the coming of the age to come; cf. the Aramaic prayer in 1 Cor. 16²¹, *Maranatha (Our Lord, Come!)*; and Rev. 22²⁰, *Come, Lord Jesus!*

11

Give us this day our daily bread: The word translated *daily (epiousios)* is rare, and its meaning is uncertain, but there is some support for the translation in the margin, *our bread for the morrow*; and it has been suggested that *the morrow* is 'the day of the Lord', *the kingdom*. This in turn may be connected with the story in Exod. 16²²ff. of the gathering of enough manna for two days on the day before the sabbath. (The kingdom was thought of as the eternal sabbath, cf. Hebrews 4¹ff.) If this is right, then this petition will also be a prayer for the coming of the kingdom.

12

And forgive us our debts, As we also have forgiven our debtors: Sin against God and man is described as *debt* in 18²³⁻³⁵, the parable of the unforgiving servant. Notice the saying after the parable: *So also my heavenly Father will do to every one of you, if you do not forgive your brother from your heart* (18³⁵). That is, the last judgement is thought of as a time of reckoning, and the disciples are taught to pray for the remission of their debts with God then, as they have already forgiven those who have sinned against them.

13

And lead us not into temptation (eis peirasmon): The *temptation* or 'testing' is probably the time before the end of this age: cf. Rev. 3^{10}, *I will keep you from the hour of trial (tou peirasmou) which is coming on the whole world, to try those who dwell upon the earth.* The disciples are to ask for the kingdom to come, and thus for the time of testing before the kingdom to be *shortened:* cf. 24^{22}. See further D. E. Nineham, *The Gospel of St Mark*, p. 43f.

But deliver us from evil (not in Luke): Probably another explanatory expansion, synonymous with the previous clause. As in 5^{37}, the Greek may be masculine – *from the evil one* (margin). The Jews believed that his activities would increase in the last days – *the hour of trial.*

The doxology, *For thine is the kingdom . . .* (see margin) is certainly not part of Matthew's text, but had been added by scribes in various forms. This was, we are told, the normal way to end a prayer, and it would have been left to the user of it to fill it in for himself.

14f.

These verses underline the petition for forgiveness, v. 12; cf. 5^7, God will have mercy on those who have mercy on others. Trespasses (*paraptōmata*), 'false steps, sins' – only used in the Gospels here and in the parallel passage Mark 11^{25} (^{26}).

FASTING

^{16}'*And when you fast, do not look dismal, like the hypocrites, for they disfigure their faces that their fasting may be seen by men. Truly, I say to you, they have their reward.* ^{17}*But when you fast, anoint your head and wash your face,* ^{18}*that your fasting may not be seen by men but by your Father who is in secret; and your Father who sees in secret will reward you.*'

The third act of piety is fasting, which the Jews practised as an accompaniment to prayer, in order to strengthen prayer. It is treated in the same way as the two previous acts (6$^{2ff.}$, 5f.) – the disciples are not to lose God's future reward through receiving a reward now from men, and therefore their fasting is to be done in secret. We may perhaps compare the third and fourth Beatitudes ($5^{4, 6}$, see notes on them for the order), on those who *mourn* and those who *hunger and thirst*.

ಜಲ

16

See notes on v. 2. *The hypocrites*, do not wait for reward from God, but draw attention to their fasting by means of their appearance: refraining from washing or anointing themselves, and covering their heads with ashes. They receive their reward here and now, and leave nothing to God in the future.

17f.

The disciples are to hide their fasting from men, so that it will be seen only by God, and thus be rewarded.

anoint your head may be more than a literal command to perform the normal toilet; it may include the metaphorical sense of anointing – viz. repent, be converted, rejoice.

6^{19-21} CONCLUSION   Luke 12$^{33, 34}$

^{19}'*Do not lay up for yourselves treasures on earth, where moth and rust^a consume and where thieves break in and steal,* ^{20}*but lay up for yourselves treasures in heaven, where neither moth nor rust^a consumes and where thieves do not break in and steal.* ^{21}*For where your treasure is, there will your heart be also.*'

  a Or *worm*

These three verses are the conclusion to the section which began at 6^1: to practise *piety* (alms, prayer, and fasting) in order to be seen by men is to *lay up treasures on earth*, in the praise and approval of men; but to practise *piety in secret* is to *lay up treasures in heaven*, with God, and to wait for his praise and approval at the last judgement. The former is uncertain – reputations can be lost in a moment; but the latter is safe and enduring.

ಜಲ

The Lucan parallel is closer in v. 21 than in vv. 19f., but it is uncertain how the two passages are related to each other.

19f.
There is a link-word which joins this paragraph to the preceding paragraph – *consume* in this verse and in v. 20 is the same word in Greek as the word which is translated 'disfigure' there (*aphanizein*).

For *treasures* as rewards, cf. 19^{21}, *sell what you possess and give to the poor, and you will have treasure in heaven.*

  Notice the contrast between *earth* and *heaven* in these verses, which is typical of this Evangelist – cf. 5$^{3, 5}$; 6^{10}.

rust (*brōsis*): The word means primarily 'eating', and there is some evidence that it had been used to translate 'grasshopper' in Mal. 3^{11}; hence the margin *worm*.

21
If their *treasure* is in heaven – i.e. if they are looking to God for their reward – then their *heart* (i.e. plans and purposes) will be directed to him. Compare the sixth Beatitude, on the *pure in heart* (5^8). But if they are looking to men for praise, their lives will be determined by men's desires and wishes. This verse helps to make the transition to the next section of the teaching.

6$^{22-34}$ FAITH   Luke 11$^{34, 35}$, 16^{13},
         OR ANXIETY   12$^{22-31}$

^{22}'*The eye is the lamp of the body. So, if your eye is sound, your whole body will be full of light;* ^{23}*but if your eye is not sound, your whole body will be full of darkness. If then the light in you is darkness, how great is the darkness!*

  ^{24}'*No one can serve two masters; for either he will hate the one and love the other, or he will be devoted to the one and despise the other. You cannot serve God and mammon.*

  ^{25}'*Therefore I tell you, do not be anxious about your life, what you shall eat or what you shall drink, nor about your body, what you shall put on. Is not life more than food, and the body more than clothing?* ^{26}*Look at the birds of the air; they neither sow nor reap nor gather into barns, and yet your heavenly Father feeds them. Are you not of more value than they?* ²⁷*And which of you by being anxious can add one cubit to his span of life.ᵃ* ²⁸*And why are you anxious about clothing? Consider the lilies of the field, how they grow; they neither toil nor spin;* ²⁹*yet I tell you, even Solomon in all his glory was not arrayed like one of these.* ³⁰*But if God so clothes the grass of the field, which today is alive and tomorrow is thrown into the oven, will he not much more clothe you, O men of little faith?* ³¹*Therefore do not be anxious, saying, "What shall we eat?" or "What shall we drink?" or "What shall we wear?"* ³²*For the Gentiles seek all these things; and your heavenly Father knows that you need them all.* ³³*But seek first his kingdom and his righteousness, and all these things shall be yours as well.*

³⁴*'Therefore do not be anxious about tomorrow, for tomorrow will be anxious for itself. Let the day's own trouble be sufficient for the day.'*

a Or to his stature

It is not, at first sight, very obvious how the next four paragraphs hang together or follow on from the previous part of the teaching on the mountain: first there is a short saying about the *sound eye*, and the *eye* which is *not sound*; then another about the impossibility of serving two masters; after that, a much longer paragraph on *anxiety*; and a final short saying on anxiety about tomorrow. The line of thought may be as follows: the word translated *sound* (*haplous*) can mean 'single' or 'simple', and it can also mean 'generous'. The disciple is to be generous in his gifts to God (*piety* 6¹⁻²¹), and he is to have a single-minded devotion to him (unlike the *hypocrites*, who pretend to give to God, but in fact collect their reward from men). Double-mindedness is impossible in practice – like being the slave of two masters. The disciple must be the slave of God alone, and have no care for anything except his will; and if he does this, he need not be afraid for himself, because the God whom he is serving is the God who cares for his creation. He can be trusted today and *tomorrow*.

There is no very obvious verbal echo of the Beatitudes here. We should expect to find some reference to the blessings on *the poor in spirit* and *the meek*, and to the promises of *the kingdom of heaven* and *the earth* (5³, ⁵: see notes on these for the order). The connexion may lie in the subject-matter: the man who lives by faith in God, and is not anxious about his life, will be *poor*. But God will reward him in the age to come, and will feed him and clothe him here and now.

᛭

The parallels to these verses in Matthew are spread out in three different chapters of Luke: $6^{22, 23}$ = Luke $11^{34, 35}$; 6^{24} = Luke 16^{13}; 6^{25-34} = Luke 12^{22-31}.

22f.

We have already been reminded that the lamp *gives light to all in the house* (5^{15}); similarly, the eye gives *light* (in sight) to the *whole body*: whether you are a seeing man or a blind man depends entirely on your eyes. In what sense is Matthew using this parable? *sound* is *haplous*, which as we have seen means both single and generous; *not sound* is *ponēros*, and 'the evil eye' means 'grudging', 'mean', 'stingy' (see 20^{15}, where R.S.V. translates 'Is your eye evil . . . ?' as *do you begrudge . . . ?*). If the disciple is generous towards God, he will be *full of light* (*perfect, as his heavenly Father is perfect* 5^{48}). If he is mean, he will be *full of darkness* (like the devil). The next saying expounds the other sense of *haplous* – single or simple. The disciple must keep his eye on one master, not on two.

24

The man with the eye which is *not sound* is attempting the impossible – to *serve two masters*; the man with the *sound* eye has chosen *God*. *Mammon* is an Aramaic word, meaning 'wealth', 'property'. Devotion to God cannot be combined with devotion to mammon, because, as we have seen already, there will be occasions when the former will demand the sacrifice of the latter ($5^{29, 30, 40}$). A choice is therefore necessary – between God and mammon; or between faith and anxiety (see following verses).

25

The disciple who is told not to serve *mammon* may well reply, But I must have enough to live and to clothe myself. To this, Jesus replies that God who has made *life* and *the body* will certainly look after those things which are less than these – viz. *food* and *clothing*.

26

Moreover, he *feeds* the birds: how much more will he feed men.

27

And anxiety cannot increase a man's *span of life* (or *stature* [margin], *hēlikia* can mean both). Cf. 5^{36} for our inability to control the colour of our hair. These things are in the hands of God.

28–30

The same type of argument as that in v. 26 above is used with regard to anxiety *about clothing*. God clothes *the lilies*, even better than man can clothe himself; the *lilies* are of less value than man: therefore God will take care of man's clothing. To think otherwise is to be *men of little faith* (*oligopistoi*, a rare word, which Matthew uses four times: here and at 8^{26}, 14^{31}, 16^8; the only other occurrence of it in the New Testament is in Luke 12^{28}, the parallel to this passage: did Luke take it from here?).

31

repeats v.25 in order to round off the passage – an example of Matthew's use of *inclusio* (see above, p. 51).

32

The Gentiles (who live without faith in God, cf. 5^{47}) are anxious about these things. The disciples, on the other hand, are to trust God as the Father who knows all their needs before they ask (cf. 6^8).

The prayer which Jesus had taught them did not include petitions for *clothing*, and even the petition for food may have been a petition for the kingdom. That is what the disciples are to pray for, and to trust God to give them *all these things as well*.

34

The final futility is to be *anxious about tomorrow*: *tomorrow* is completely outside our possible control today (cf. 5^{36}, 6^{27}). There is a possible set of verbal links common to vv. 33, 34, and vv. 10, 11 in the Lord's Prayer: *kingdom, righteousness, tomorrow, this day; kingdom,* [God's] *will, this day, tomorrow.*

Mark 4^{24}
JUDGING AND ASKING Luke $6^{37, \ 38, \ 41, \ 42}$,
11^{9-13}, 6^{31}

7 '*Judge not, that you be not judged.* [2]*For with the judgement you pronounce you will be judged, and the measure you give will be the measure you get.* [3]*Why do you see the speck that is in your brother's eye, but do not notice the log that is in your own eye?* [4]*Or how can you say to your brother, "Let me*

take the speck out of your eye," when there is the log in your own eye? 5You hypocrite, first take the log out of your own eye, and then you will see clearly to take the speck out of your brother's eye.

6'Do not give dogs what is holy; and do not throw your pearls before swine, lest they trample them underfoot and turn to attack you.

7'Ask, and it will be given you; seek, and you will find; knock, and it will be opened to you. 8For every one who asks receives, and he who seeks finds, and to him who knocks it will be opened. 9Or what man of you, if his son asks him for a loaf, will give him a stone? 10Or if he asks for a fish, will give him a serpent? 11If you then, who are evil, know how to give good gifts to your children, how much more will your Father who is in heaven give good things to those who ask him? 12So whatever you wish that men would do to you, do so to them; for this is the law and the prophets.'

We saw that in the last two verses (6$^{33, 34}$) there may be a reference back to the prayer for the kingdom, and for tomorrow's bread (6$^{10, 11}$); the next petition in the prayer is for forgiveness *as we also have forgiven our debtors* (6^{12}), and in the three paragraphs which we are to consider now, forgiving and asking are further expounded. Just as the disciples are to forgive one another in order that they may be forgiven by God, so they are not to *judge* one another, in order that they may not be judged by God. They are to begin with themselves, and remember their own *debts* to God, which are so much greater than the debts which they are owed by one another. If they repent, they will be able to ask God for the *good things* which he can give – that is, as the next paragraphs will show, deliverance from destruction and entry into the life of the kingdom (cf. the last petitions of the Lord's Prayer, *And lead us not into temptation, But deliver us from evil* 6^{13}).

The sequence of thought in these paragraphs may therefore be as follows: Do not condemn others, in order that God may not condemn you; repent of your sins, and be merciful to those who have sinned against you. You will receive from God treatment of the same kind as that which you give to others. Just as you do not give holy and valuable things to those who are unworthy of them, neither will God do so. Nevertheless, persist in asking God for what he has to give, because he is your Father, and he will not do less for you than you would do for your children. This forgiveness of others is part of the charity which is the fulfilment of *the law and the prophets*.

ॐ

Verse 2b is the same as Mark 4^{24} (and Matthew omits it in Chapter 13, to avoid duplication). Verses 1–5 are parallel to Luke 6$^{37f.}$, $^{41f.}$; v. 6 has no parallel in Mark or Luke; vv. 7–11 are parallel to Luke 11$^{9-13}$ (though there are interesting differences in Luke); v. 12 is parallel to Luke 6^{31}.

1

Judge (*krinein*) is possibly used here in an unfavourable sense, 'criticize, find fault with, condemn'. *that you be not judged* – i.e. by God at the last judgement.

2

The disciples' *judgement* of others (here favourable or unfavourable) will be used by God of the disciples themselves, at the last judgement. If their *measure* is generous and merciful, God will be merciful to them; if it is mean, God will be mean with them; cf. Ps. 18$^{25f.}$:

> With the loyal thou dost show thyself loyal;
>   with the blameless man thou dost show thyself blameless;
> with the pure thou dost show thyself pure;
>   and with the crooked thou dost show thyself perverse.

3

The eye has been mentioned earlier in Chapters 5–7 at 5$^{29, 38}$, 6$^{22, 23}$ (and cf. 5^8 *they shall see God*); notice in particular the last of these: the eye is compared to a lamp (cf. 5^{15}), and the man whose eyes do not work is in darkness. One of the causes of blindness is the presence of some object in the eye, which prevents the man from seeing. There is a contrast in this saying between a large object in the eye (a *log*) and a small object (a *speck*). We may compare the parable of the two debtors in 18$^{23-35}$, where the large debt is a man's sins against God, and the small debt is his sins against other people. Here, similarly, our sins against God, if we do not repent of them, will blind us (cf. 15^{14}, 23^{16}, where the Jewish leaders are called *blind guides*).

4, 5

The disciple is to repent of his sin against God, and receive forgiveness. This will enable him to *see clearly*, and be merciful to his brother, and forgive him.

    This is the only place in the Gospels where the disciples are called hypocrites: it may be that the saying was originally addressed to the

Pharisees; but Matthew believed that the sins of the Pharisees could be committed by the disciples (cf. Chapter 23 and notes on it).

The saying about the man with a *log* in his *eye* is hyperbolic: for other examples of hyperbole in the teaching of Jesus in this Gospel, see 19²⁴ (*it is easier for a camel to go through the eye of a needle . . .*) and 23²⁴ (*swallowing a camel*).

6

It is difficult to see how this saying fits into the sequence of thought in this part of the teaching. *Dogs* could mean Gentiles, as in 15²⁶, and the *pearl* could be the Gospel of the kingdom (cf. 13⁴⁵), and so the saying could be a command not to preach the Gospel to the Gentiles (cf. 10⁵). At a very early date, it was interpreted as a command not to admit the unbaptized to the Eucharist. Neither of these interpretations fits this context. Possibly the saying is to be understood as a transition between the sayings about judging and measuring (7¹, ²) and the sayings about asking (7⁷ᶠᶠ·). Men do not give *what is holy* to dogs, or *throw pearls before swine*: they discriminate in their giving, according to the character of the receiver of their gifts. God will do the same – giving forgiveness only to the forgiver, and mercy to the merciful. Notice the chiasmic arrangement – *dogs, swine: trample, attack* (or 'tear in pieces with their teeth', *Lexicon*, p. 742); the dogs attack; the swine trample.

7, 8

The subject changes to asking God in prayer: this may be partly because the Lord's Prayer, especially in the second part, is a petition for entry into the kingdom – *Give us . . . forgive us . . . lead us . . . deliver us*; it may be also because the only way that the disciple can *take the log out of* his *own eye* (7⁵) is by asking for forgiveness from God. There is also a verbal link with the previous verse in the word *give*.

it will be given to you means 'God will give to you' cf. v. 11; he will give them *the kingdom*.

seek: cf. 6³³, *seek first his kingdom and his righteousness*.

you will find: cf. v. 14, *those who find it*.

knock and it will be opened: cf. v. 14 and 25¹⁰, *the door was shut*.

it will be opened to you means 'God will open the gate that leads to life in the kingdom'.

9–11

The argument is *a fortiori*: evil men give good gifts to their children who ask for them; God, who is free from evil, will certainly give the kingdom to those who ask him in prayer. Notice that *a loaf* and *a fish* may here stand for the life of the age to come, which in 8^{11}, 22^2, 25^{10} is compared to a feast; and N.B. *loaves* and *fish* in $14^{17ff.}$, $15^{34ff.}$.

12

This saying rounds off the section, by returning to the starting point in 7^1: you wish for mercy from men and from God; therefore show mercy to men; this is *the law and the prophets* which Jesus came to fulfil (5^{17}).

7^{13-27} THE TWO WAYS   Luke $13^{23, 24}$,
$6^{43f., 46}$, $13^{26f.}$, 6^{47-49}

[13]'*Enter by the narrow gate; for the gate is wide and the way is easy,[a] that leads to destruction, and those who enter by it are many.* [14]*For the gate is narrow and the way is hard, that leads to life, and those who find it are few.*

[15]'*Beware of false prophets, who come to you in sheep's clothing but inwardly are ravenous wolves.* [16]*You will know them by their fruits. Are grapes gathered from thorns, or figs from thistles?* [17]*So, every sound tree bears good fruit, but the bad tree bears evil fruit.* [18]*A sound tree cannot bear evil fruit, nor can a bad tree bear good fruit.* [19]*Every tree that does not bear good fruit is cut down and thrown into the fire.* [20]*Thus you will know them by their fruits.*

[21]'*Not every one who says to me, "Lord, Lord," shall enter the kingdom of heaven, but he who does the will of my Father who is in heaven.* [22]*On that day many will say to me, "Lord, Lord, did we not prophesy in your name, and cast out demons in your name, and do many mighty works in your name?"* [23]*And then will I declare to them, "I never knew you; depart from me, you evildoers."*

[24]'*Every one then who hears these words of mine and does them will be like a wise man who built his house upon the rock;* [25]*and the rain fell, and the floods came, and the winds blew and beat upon that house, but it did not fall, because it had been founded on the rock.* [26]*And every one who hears these words of mine and does not do them will be like a foolish man who built his house upon the sand;* [27]*and the rain fell, and the floods came, and the winds blew and beat against that house, and it fell; and great was the fall of it.*'

    a Other ancient authorities read *for the way is wide and easy*

There is one theme running through the last four paragraphs of the teaching on the mountain – the contrast between *the way that leads to destruction* and *the way that leads to life* (7$^{13f.}$). The two gates or ways are two kinds of life, and those who live these lives are thought of as either *wolves* or *sheep* (v. 15), good trees or bad trees (vv. 16–20), those who are all talk and no action, and those who do the will of God (vv. 21–23), those who hear Jesus' words and act on them, and those who only hear (vv. 24–27). There is perhaps a greater emphasis in these paragraphs on the danger of *destruction* than on the promise of *life* and this emphasis may be due to the references to *temptation* and *evil* (or the evil one) in the Lord's Prayer (6^{13}), which may have set the tone for this part of the teaching.

In vv. 7, 8 the figure of knocking at a door in order that it might be opened was introduced, and we suggested above that the door stands for entry into the kingdom of God (see notes on vv. 7, 8). Verses 13, 14 pick up this idea: *Enter by the narrow gate; . . . the gate . . . that leads to life.* There are those within the Church who preach the way of destruction; they must be distinguished from the true disciples, and the test is not what they say, but whether they do the will of God. Therefore let the disciples be men of action, and not only hearers.

১০৫

There is a saying about *the narrow door*, and *few* entering by it, in Luke 13$^{23, 24}$, which may be related in some way to vv. 13, 14 here. In the second paragraph, vv. 16, 18, 20 are similar to Luke 6$^{43, 44}$, but vv. 15, 17, 19 have no parallel in Luke. In the third paragraph, the substance of vv. 21, 22 is given in Luke 6^{46}; v. 23 is similar to Luke 13$^{26-27}$ (both of them quote Ps. 6^8). The fourth and last paragraph is closest to Luke, where it also stands as the conclusion to a section of continuous teaching (the Sermon on the Plain, see pp. 78f.) – Luke 6$^{47-49}$.

13, 14

The idea of two ways is common in the Old Testament (e.g. Deut. 30$^{15ff.}$, *I have set before you this day life and good, death and evil. . . .* Jer. 21^8, *I set before you the way of life and the way of death*). Everyone has the power to choose between the only two possible ways of living – one of which ends in *destruction* and the other in *life* (i.e. *Gehenna*, on which see 5^{22}, and *the kingdom*; cf. 18^9, 25^{46}, where *hell* or *eternal punishment* and *life* are again contrasted). The former way is easier than the latter, and it is taken by *many*. The variants in v. 13 do not affect the sense, though they do upset the symmetry of the two sayings, unless, with the support of a few authorities, we omit the word *gate* in both v. 13 and v. 14.

15

As there are two ways, so there are also two kinds of teacher – the teacher of the *easy way* and the teacher of *the hard way*: and here also there is a parallel in the Old Testament teaching about true prophets and *false prophets* (e.g. Deut. 13$^{1-5}$, 18$^{20-22}$). They seem to be members of the Church (*sheep's clothing*), but in fact they are of the devil (*wolves*: cf. Acts 20^{29} for false teachers as *wolves*: *fierce wolves will come in among you, not sparing the flock*).

Christian *prophets* are mentioned again in this Gospel at 10^{41}, 23^{34}: they were an order in the Church, and were probably much the same as teachers (in Acts 13^{1} we are given a list of *prophets and teachers* at Antioch). For *false prophets*, see 24$^{11, 24}$, where they are foretold as one of the tribulations of the last days, before the return of the Son of man. Compare the situation which lies behind the First Letter of John: *false prophets* had appeared in the Church, and led off a group of disciples; how was the ordinary Christian to know which was the true prophet and which the false prophet? John says that one of the tests is whether the commandment to love is being kept: *He who loves his brother abides in the light* (1 John 2^{10}). Here also, the test is deeds, not words; see next verse, and vv. 21–27, and compare 1 John 3^{18}, *let us not love in word or speech but in deed and in truth*.

16–20

The picture of the *sheep* and the *wolves* is changed for that of the *sound tree* and the *bad tree*; the *fruits* are the only way of determining the usefulness or otherwise of the tree. Love or good works is the test for distinguishing the true from the false teachers. (This passage recalls the words of the Baptist in 3$^{8, 10}$, *Bear fruit that befits repentance . . . every tree therefore that does not bear good fruit is cut down and thrown into the fire.*)

thorns and *thistles*: Cf. Gen. 3^{18}, where they are both mentioned as the plants which grow as the result of the fall of man – i.e. they are useless.

The Greek words translated *bear fruit* in vv. 17, 19 are *karpous poiein*: *poiein* can also mean 'to make' or 'to do'–hence the link between these verses and v. 21 *he who does* (*poiōn*) *the will of my Father*; and see also the contrast in the last paragraph, between the man who *does* the teaching of Jesus, and the man who *does not* (vv. 24, 26). Notice the repetition of the saying in v. 16 in v. 20 also; an example of Matthew's use of *inclusio* (see p. 51).

21–23

fruit is now explained further: fruit is not what a man *says*, but what he *does*. The way of distinguishing the two kinds of prophet is by their deeds; and Jesus, the judge at the last day, will judge by deeds and not by words. (N.B. *prophesy* in v. 22 and cf. *false prophets* in v. 15; for *prophesy in your name* cf. Jer. 14¹⁴.) For Jesus as judge, cf. above, 3¹², *he will clear his threshing floor and gather his wheat into the granary, but the chaff he will burn with unquenchable fire.*

I never knew you: Cf. 25¹², *I do not know you:* knew is here used in the sense of 'acknowledge, recognize'. Jesus says that though they claimed his authority for what they did (*in your name*) he had not commissioned them.

depart from me: Cf. 25⁴¹ *Depart from me, you cursed* (different words for *depart* are used in the Greek). The whole sentence here, *depart from me, you evildoers,* is a quotation from Ps. 6⁸.

24–27

The last paragraph is addressed to *every one who hears* the teaching of Jesus, and it applies the principle of judgement by deeds, which has been expounded in the case of the *false prophets,* to every disciple: they will all be judged by what they have done. The *wise man* builds on *rock* and his house does not fall; the *foolish man* builds on *sand* and his house falls. The *wise man* is the man who *does* Jesus' *words* – i.e. obeys his teaching; and the *foolish man* is the one who disobeys. For *wise* and *foolish* contrasted in this way, cf. 25², *wise* and *foolish maidens.* The last days are compared to the flood at the time of Noah. This is *the temptation* and *evil* from which the disciples are to pray to be delivered (6¹³).

These last few verses of this first section of teaching in Matthew have made us look on to the fifth and last section of teaching, 23–25 and in particular to Chapter 25 – e.g. with the *wise man* and the *foolish man* in vv. 24, 26, cf. the parable of the ten maidens, *wise* and *foolish,* in 25¹⁻¹³. *The door was shut* in that parable, and, though they asked for it to be opened, saying *Lord, Lord* (cf. 7²²) the bridegroom said, *I do not know you* (cf. 7²³). For the whole arrangement of the five sections of teaching, see Introduction, pp. 14ff.

THE ASTONISHMENT OF THE   Mark 1^{22}
                        CROWDS

²⁸*And when Jesus finished these sayings, the crowds were astonished at his teaching,* ²⁹*for he taught them as one who had authority, and not as their scribes.*

We have here the first of the five instances of Matthew's formula for passing from continuous teaching to narrative (the other instances are 11^1, 13^{53}, 19^1, 26^1).

෨෨

The words from *the crowds were astonished* to *scribes* are taken from Mark 1^{22}, with one alteration – Matthew has added *their* to *scribes*.

28

these sayings (*tous logous toutous*): The same words in Greek are translated *these words* in vv. 24, 26. The context of Mark 1^{22} is the first event which Mark describes after the calling of the fishermen (Mark 1^{16-20} = Matthew 4^{18-22}), namely, the teaching in the synagogue at Capernaum, and healing of a man with an unclean spirit in the synagogue on a sabbath (Mark 1^{21-28}). Matthew took this, the first mention of *teaching* in Mark, and made it the occasion for a much fuller statement of his sayings. He has omitted the miracle for the moment (see p. 132), but retained the astonishment of the crowds.

29

The Marcan contrast between Jesus' *teaching* and that of the *scribes* fits well into the new context which Matthew has given to this verse, after such sayings as 5^{21}f. *You have heard that it was said to the men of old … But I say to you …* Scribal teaching was exposition of *the law and the prophets*: Jesus' teaching fufils them; and the *righteousness* which he demands *exceeds* that which they represent.

their scribes: Cf. *their synagogues* 4^{23} and notes there. For Christian scribes, see 13^{52}, 23^{34}.

Matthew 8^1-9^{34}

The Deeds of the Christ

The R.S.V. places a double space before 8^1, and again after 9^{34}, and we are now to consider the section 8^1–9^{34} which is thus marked off as the next division of the Gospel. (The divisions here are almost certainly correct, unlike the division after 4^{22}; see p. 67. $7^{28f.}$ is the formula for the end of a section of teaching, and the transition to narrative; 9^{35}–10^5 is the introduction to the second section of teaching, which is given in 10^{5b-42}; 11^1 is the formula for the end of another section of teaching. Thus 8^1–9^{34} is the narrative section which comes between the end of the first teaching section, and the introduction to the second.)

We shall start by looking at this passage as a whole.

First of all, if we count the paragraphs in 8^1–9^{34} as they are set out in R.S.V. we find that there are thirteen of them. Ten of them have been taken from Mark (i.e. all except $8^{5ff.}$, $8^{18ff.}$, $9^{32ff.}$), but Matthew has not kept them in the order in which he found them in his source; he has re-arranged them, and it may be that he has re-arranged them for some purpose.

Secondly, the ten paragraphs which he has taken from Mark are spread over a fairly wide stretch of that Gospel – from Chapter 1 to Chapter 10. Why has Matthew, at this point, searched through Mark for a particular group of incidents to place together here?

Thirdly, if we compare the Matthean paragraphs with their Marcan originals, we shall find that in two cases ($8^{28f.}$ and $9^{27ff.}$) Matthew describes a pair of people healed – two demoniacs and two blind men; whereas in Mark (5^{1-20} and 10^{46-52}) in each case there is only one sick person.

What is the explanation of these facts?

Nine of the thirteen paragraphs describe acts of power: in one case ($8^{23ff.}$) the power of Jesus is exercised over the sea, in the other eight over people who are sick. These nine acts of power are arranged in three groups of three each; and the groups are divided from one another by passages which are non-miraculous.

The acts of power give the character to the section, and when, after the next section of teaching in Chapter 10, Matthew resumes his narrative, he begins *Now when John heard in prison about the deeds of the Christ* (11^2).

Matthew seems, therefore, to have regarded this section (8^1–9^{34}) as a collection of examples of *the deeds of the Christ*. He had referred to these *deeds* in general in $4^{23f.}$; now he describes them in detail. And to do this, he has looked through the greater part of Mark, to gather together his material. (For the *deeds*, as opposed to the *words* of Jesus, he was almost entirely dependent on Mark; see Introduction, p. 12.)

We saw above (4^{23}) that Matthew describes the ministry of Jesus by means of three verbs, *teaching, preaching, healing*, and that these are repeated in 9^{35}. He has given us an account of the *preaching* of Jesus (4^{17}) and of the *teaching* of Jesus (5^3–7^{27}; N.B. 7^{28}, *the crowds were astonished at his teaching*); now the time has come to give us some detailed account of his *healing*. This will prepare the way for the second section, in which he will say to the twelve: *preach as you go, saying, The kingdom of heaven is at hand. Heal the sick, raise the dead, cleanse lepers, cast out demons* ($10^{7, 8}$). (The command to the disciples to teach is reserved until 28^{20}, the last verse of the Gospel.) *The servant* is to be *like his master* 10^{25}; therefore Jesus himself does first what he will command his servants to do after; cf. John 14^{12}, *He who believes in me will also do the works that I do.* When we come to look at Chapter 10, we shall be able to look back at 8^1–9^{34} to see how the commands to the twelve charge them to do what he has done (see pp. 157, 162).

We have not yet answered the question why the number of persons healed has twice been doubled, nor have we completely satisfied ourselves about the re-arrangement of the Marcan order here. With regard to the first of these questions, we shall see in the notes on $8^{28ff.}$ and $9^{27ff.}$ that Matthew is, in each case, combining two Marcan stories; and thus, by doubling the number of persons healed, he is retaining the same total number of healed people as there were in the similar part of Mark. There may be another point in the arrangement: if we omit the one clear case of the healing of a Gentile in this section (the centurion's servant, $8^{5ff.}$), we are left with two groups of five persons healed, which have a certain similarity to each other:

Leper $8^{1ff.}$ Woman with the haemorrhage $9^{20ff.}$
Peter's mother-in-law $8^{14ff.}$ The ruler's daughter $9^{23ff.}$

Two demoniacs 8^{28}ff.	The two blind men 9^{27}ff.
The paralytic 9^1ff.	The dumb demoniac 9^{32}ff.

Leprosy and haemorrhage are both mentioned in Leviticus as causes of uncleanness (Lev. 14^2ff., 15^{25}ff.); both Peter's mother-in-law and the ruler's daughter rise at the touch of Jesus; in the cure of the demoniacs and that of the blind men, a pair of sufferers is healed on each occasion; the reaction of the crowd to the healing of the paralytic and to the exorcism of the demoniac is mentioned in both cases.

Clearly Matthew has taken some care over the arrangement of the paragraphs in this section, and the numbers of people involved: it may be that he wished to arrange it as two groups involving five people in each.

8^{1-4} **JESUS CLEANSES A LEPER**   Mark 1^{40-45}

8 *When he came down from the mountain, great crowds followed him;* [2]*and behold, a leper came to him and knelt before him, saying, 'Lord, if you will, you can make me clean.'* [3]*And he stretched out his hand and touched him, saying, 'I will; be clean.' And immediately his leprosy was cleansed.* [4]*And Jesus said to him, 'See that you say nothing to any one; but go, show yourself to the priest, and offer the gift that Moses commanded, for a proof to the people.'* [a]

a Greek to them

The incident which Matthew has placed first after the teaching on the mountain is the healing of a leper: the sick man comes and kneels to Jesus, and declares his faith in the power of Jesus to restore him. His disease was not only a sickness of the body, but was regarded in the ancient world as a form of uncleanness which separated a man from his neighbours. This is what the Law said about the leper: *The leper who has the disease shall wear torn clothes and let the hair of his head hang loose, and he shall cover his upper lip and cry, Unclean, unclean. He shall remain unclean as long as he has the disease; he is unclean; he shall dwell alone in a habitation outside the camp* (Lev. $13^{45f.}$)

The Law was not able to cure the leper, but it did lay down the sacrifices to be offered by anyone who was cured (see Lev. 14). So the leper's faith, *Lord, if you will, you can make me clean* (v. 2) is faith that Jesus is able to do what the Law could not do (cf. Rom. 8^3).

Jesus cleanses the leper, and tells him to remain silent (as to who had healed him) but to fulfil the Law of Moses by showing himself to the priest and offering the sacrifices which were laid down in Leviticus. The command of Jesus in this paragraph to fulfil the Law may account for its position here: Matthew may have placed it first, after the teaching on the mountain, to illustrate the saying of Jesus *I have not come to abolish* the Law and the prophets *but to fulfil them* (5^{17}).

Notice also that the leper is a Jew (otherwise Jesus would not have commanded him to keep the Law of Moses), and that the next story describes the healing of a Gentile: in it Jesus compares the faith of a Gentile with the absence of faith in Israel. See notes on 8^{5-13}, and compare Rom. 1^{16} where Paul says that the Gospel *is the power of God for salvation to every one who has faith, to the Jew first and also to the Greek.*

৯৫৪

Matthew has taken the story from Mark 1^{40-45}: he has passed over Mark's account of the healing of Simon's mother-in-law, and of the many sick people in the evening, and the departure of Jesus from Capernaum early in the morning. (Some of this he will go back to use later.) Moreover he has abbreviated Mark, leaving out the statement that Jesus was angry (so the correct text in Mark 1^{41}), and that *he sternly charged him, and sent him away at once*: but he has added the leper's address to Jesus, *Lord* (cf., in the next miracle, the centurion's use of the word, $8^{6, 8}$). There are certain agreements here between Matthew and Luke 5^{12-16}, against Mark.

1

Verse 1 is an editorial addition, to link the teaching on the mountain to the healing of the leper.

2

behold (not in Mark at this point) is a favourite word with Matthew, who uses it forty-five times; whereas Mark had used it seven times.

knelt before him (*prosekynei autō*): The word translated *knelt* is translated *worship* in 2², ⁸, ¹¹, 4⁹, ¹⁰, 14³³, 28⁹, ¹⁷; and *kneel* here, and in 9¹⁸, 15²⁵, 18²⁶, 20²⁰; it is another favourite word with Matthew.

Lord (not in Mark here): Cf. 8⁶, ⁸ where the centurion addresses Jesus as *Lord*; and above 7²¹, ²². The Jew and the Gentile both call upon him as their *Lord*, who is able to give them what they need; cf. Romans 10¹², *There is no distinction between Jew and Greek; the same Lord is Lord of all and bestows his riches upon all who call upon him.*

3
Jesus touches the leper as the method of curing him, and as a sign of his power over the disease. For other instances of cure by touch in this Gospel, see 8¹⁵, 9²⁰f., ²⁹, 14³⁶ [177].

4
See that you say nothing to any one: Commands to silence are frequent in Mark; Matthew retains a few of them (see also 9³⁰, 12¹⁶, 16²⁰, 17⁹) but omits the majority.

show yourself to the priest: An echo of Lev. 13⁴⁹.

8⁵⁻¹³　　JESUS HEALS THE SERVANT　Luke 7¹⁻¹⁰, 13²⁸f.
　　　　　　　　OF A CENTURION

⁵As he entered Caper'na-um, a centurion came forward to him, beseeching him ⁶and saying, 'Lord, my servant is lying paralysed at home, in terrible distress.' ⁷And he said to him, 'I will come and heal him.' ⁸But the centurion answered him, 'Lord, I am not worthy to have you come under my roof; but only say the word, and my servant will be healed. ⁹For I am a man under authority, with soldiers under me; and I say to one, "Go," and he goes, and to another, "Come," and he comes, and to my slave, "Do this," and he does it.' ¹⁰When Jesus heard him, he marvelled, and said to those who followed him, 'Truly, I say to you, not even*ᵃ* in Israel have I found such faith. ¹¹I tell you, many will come from east and west and sit at table with Abraham, Isaac, and Jacob in the kingdom of heaven, ¹²while the sons of the kingdom will be thrown into the outer darkness; there men will weep and gnash their teeth.' ¹³And to the centurion Jesus said, 'Go; be it done for you as you have believed.' And the servant was healed at that very moment.

　a Other ancient authorities read *with no one*

Jesus returns to Capernaum (last mentioned in 4¹³) and a centurion of
the Roman army asks him to heal his servant who is at home. Jesus
says that he will come and heal him, but the centurion answers that
he is not worthy to receive the Lord in his house; and that there is no
need for him to come, because his word, by itself, will be effective;
and he goes on to compare the power of Jesus to heal, with his own
authority over his subordinates: as they obey him, so the paralysis
(from which his servant is suffering) will obey Jesus. Jesus marvels at
the faith of the Gentile, unlike anything he has found among the
Jews; and he foretells the coming of the Gentiles into the kingdom,
and the exclusion of the Jews. He tells the centurion to go: his faith
has been answered. At the same moment, the servant is healed.

The main points to notice in this paragraph are the fact that the
centurion is a Gentile; the contrast between the Gentiles and the Jews;
and the faith of the centurion in the power of Jesus, which is a pointer
to the future, the reversal of the previous positions of Jews and
Gentiles. Cf. for example Rom. 11²⁰; the Jews *were broken off because
of their unbelief, but you* (the Gentiles) *stand fast only through faith.*

༄

The paragraph has no parallel in Mark, but there is a more elaborate
version of the story in Luke 7¹⁻¹⁰, and the sayings in vv. 11, 12 are found
in a slightly different form in Luke 13²⁸f.. If Matthew and Luke took
the miracle from a common source (Q), this is the only miracle story
which they have both drawn from it.

6

The word *Lord* is omitted by some of the authorities in this verse; but
there is no evidence for its omission in v. 8 below. The Greek word
translated *servant* here and in vv. 8 and 13 (*pais*) can also mean 'son',
and it may be that that is the real meaning here – cf. 15²¹f. the Canaanite
woman's *daughter.*

8

The centurion confesses his own unworthiness, and his faith in the
power of Jesus' *word* to heal. Jesus does not in fact go to the house of
the centurion – and it may be that we are to see in this, and in the other
miracle performed at the request of a Gentile on a Gentile (15²¹⁻²⁸
which is also done at a distance), that Jesus will not go to the Gentiles
himself, but will bring them his gifts through the work of his disciples,
and only after his exaltation (cf. 10⁵, *Go nowhere among the Gentiles,*

with 28¹⁹, *Go therefore and make disciples of all nations* [Gentiles], and John 12²⁰ff. the coming of the Greeks to see Jesus, and his saying which foretells his death and resurrection).

9

We should expect the centurion to say, I am a man who has authority; and this is the reading of one of the versions. However, it is certainly an alteration of the text, and what he says is *I am a man under authority*. There may be a mistranslation here of an Aramaic word which, we are told, can mean 'under' or 'in place of' – i.e. the centurion is the representative of the government, just as Jesus is the representative of God. *slave* (*doulos*), a different word from that translated *servant* in vv. 6, 8, 13.

10

he marvelled: Cf. 15²⁸ *O woman, great is your faith!*

The marginal reading, *with no one*, is more probably correct. *Israel:* See note on 2².

11

This saying looks forward to *the kingdom* at the end of the world, which is here pictured as a feast (cf. 5⁶, 22¹⁻¹⁴, 25¹⁰); the Gentiles will enter the kingdom.

12

the sons of the kingdom here means the Jews; the expression is used in 13³⁸ of those who enter the kingdom. As used here, it refers to the Jews as those who were in the privileged position of *children of Abraham*; but as we have already been told by John the Baptist, this privilege does not guarantee their salvation, or exclude the Gentiles (3⁷⁻¹⁰).

the outer darkness: A phrase only used by Matthew (cf. 22¹³, 25³⁰), it refers to *hell* (see note on 5²²).

there men will weep and gnash their teeth is also a favourite Matthean phrase (13⁴², ⁵⁰, 22¹³, 24⁵¹, 25³⁰). It does, however, occur once in Luke (Luke 13²⁸, parallel to this verse); either both Matthew and Luke found it in the common source here, or Luke copied it from Matthew on this occasion, and omitted it thereafter.

13

be it done for you as you have believed: Cf. 9²⁹, 15²⁸, for similar sayings.

at that very moment: Cf. 9²², 15²⁸, 17¹⁸. These Matthean expressions in vv. 12, 13 indicate that Matthew has been responsible for the form in which the ending of the story lies before us now.

JESUS HEALS PETER'S   Mark 1²⁹⁻³⁴
MOTHER-IN-LAW, AND MANY
SICK PEOPLE

¹⁴*And when Jesus entered Peter's house, he saw his mother-in-law lying sick with a fever;* ¹⁵*he touched her hand, and the fever left her, and she rose and served him.* ¹⁶*That evening they brought to him many who were possessed with demons; and he cast out the spirits with a word, and healed all who were sick.* ¹⁷*This was to fulfil what was spoken by the prophet Isaiah, 'He took our infirmities and bore our diseases.'*

For the third act of power in the first group of three (see p. 119) Matthew has used Mark's account of the healing of Peter's mother-in-law and of many other sick people; and has added the prophecy of Isaiah, that the Lord's servant would heal the people. Matthew wants his readers to see in Jesus' work the fulfilment of the promises which God has made through his prophets, the victory of God over the evil spirits, and the nearness of the kingdom of which Jesus had spoken in his preaching (4¹⁷, ²³) and his teaching (5³ etc.).

ಐಐ

Matthew has turned back to the first two paragraphs in the section of Mark which he has so far not used (Mark 1²⁹⁻³⁴, see notes on 8¹⁻⁴), and reproduced them with omissions, and with additions, of his own. Notice in particular Matthew's omission of *at sundown* (Mark 1³²) which Mark had specifically mentioned, because the previous events happened on a sabbath, and the law forbidding work would end at sundown; therefore people could then begin to carry the sick to Jesus. On some of the additions, see the notes below.

14

Mark mentioned the four disciples – *Simon and Andrew, James and John*; he had described their calling by Jesus only a few verses before (Mark 1¹⁶⁻²⁰ = Matt. 4¹⁸⁻²²). Matthew does not mention them, possibly because he has added so much new material since Chapter 4. Peter's wife is mentioned again in the New Testament at 1 Cor. 9⁵: *Do we not have the right to be accompanied by a wife, as the other apostles and the brothers of the Lord and Cephas?*

15

he touched her hand (Mark: *took her by the hand*): Perhaps Matthew wanted to make the method of cure here like that in 8³ (*he stretched out his hand and touched him*).

she rose and served him (Mark . . . *them*): The healing miracles of Jesus express in pictorial form the salvation which he brings to the world. This salvation is likened to life from the dead (e.g. *You have been raised with Christ*, Col. 3¹); and those who have received it are commanded to serve Jesus (e.g. *You are serving the Lord Christ*, Col. 3²⁴). This kind of teaching may have been drawn out of a statement such as this, that Peter's mother-in-law *rose and served* Jesus, or the description of the miracle may have been influenced by the teaching of the Church.

16

he cast out the spirits with a word: Matthew adds *with a word* (*logō*) possibly picking up the phrase of the centurion, *only say the word* (*monon eipe logō*), 8⁸; cf. note on previous verse.

17

The quotation is from Isa. 53⁴ and in this case Matthew follows the Hebrew rather than the Greek translation, which is 'he bears our sins and suffers pain for us', and is less suitable in this context.

8¹⁸⁻²²   JESUS SPEAKS ABOUT   Mark 4³⁵
                         FOLLOWING HIM   Luke 9⁵⁷⁻⁶⁰

¹⁸*Now when Jesus saw great crowds around him, he gave orders to go over to the other side.* ¹⁹*And a scribe came up and said to him, 'Teacher, I will follow you wherever you go.'* ²⁰*And Jesus said to him, 'Foxes have holes, and birds of the air have nests; but the Son of man has nowhere to lay his head.'* ²¹*Another of the disciples said to him, 'Lord, let me first go and bury my father.'* ²²*But Jesus said to him, 'Follow me, and leave the dead to bury their own dead.'*

The next group of three miracles is linked together by a narrative thread, which describes how Jesus got into a boat, crossed the Sea of Galilee, arrived at the other side, was asked to leave that district, and returned to Capernaum (8²³–9¹). Before this crossing of the sea, Matthew places another paragraph, our present five verses, in which

Jesus sets out on this journey. The situation provides Matthew with
the occasion for two sayings of Jesus to people who declare themselves ready to be his 'followers' – with the double sense of following
him from one place to another, and of being his disciples. To each of
the followers, Jesus gives a warning of the suffering which is involved
in discipleship. We saw above that the miracles in these two chapters
prepare for the teaching in Chapter 10; similarly, these sayings about
following Jesus and suffering prepare for the saying in 10³⁷ᶠ· *he who
loves father or mother more than me is not worthy of me ... he who does
not take his cross and follow me is not worthy of me.*

ﻼﻼ

Verse 18 seems to be Matthew's version of Mark 4³⁵. Verses 19–22 are
parallel to Luke 9⁵⁷⁻⁶⁰ with some differences; e.g. Luke has a third
saying in Luke 9⁶¹ᶠ· which Matthew does not record.

Notice the word *follow*, which is a link-word here (vv. 19–22) and
in v. 23 and 9⁹, ²⁷.

19

a scribe: Matthew does not say 'one of their scribes' (see note on 7²⁹);
and in v. 21 he says *Another of the disciples*. It seems, therefore, as though
Matthew means that the *scribe* is a disciple. On the other hand, the *scribe*
addresses Jesus as *Teacher* (*didaskale*), a form of address which is found
also at 12³⁸, 19¹⁶, 22¹⁶, ²⁴, ³⁶ (cf. 23⁸ where Jesus speaks of himself as
teacher). Usually, this title is used by the enemies of Jesus in this Gospel,
and Matthew has omitted those examples of it in the mouth of disciples
which he found in Mark (Mark 4³⁸ [9¹⁷] 9³⁸ [10²⁰] 10³⁵, 13¹). Matthew
seems to have regarded it as an inadequate form of address for those
who were within the fellowship of the disciples of Jesus: not that he
regarded the teaching of Jesus as unimportant; he most clearly did not.
But he regarded Jesus as more than a teacher, just as John was *more
than a prophet* (11⁹).

wherever you go: The word *go* (*aperchē*) is the same as that which is
translated *go over* in the previous verse (*apelthein*).

20

There is some evidence that *foxes* is a term used for Herod (cf. Luke
13³²) and the Herodians, and *birds of the air* for the Gentiles (cf. 13³²).
The saying may originally have meant, 'Everyone else has his place in
Israel, except the true King of Israel, the Son of man.'

the Son of man has nowhere to lay his head: This is the first time in
Matthew that Jesus has used the self-designation *Son of man*; altogether,
it is used twenty-nine times in this Gospel: thirteen times of the coming
of the Son of man at the end of the age; nine times of his death and
resurrection; and seven times of his present ministry – as here.

21

Lord: Perhaps a contrast with *teacher* in v. 19: this is a *disciple*, not a
scribe.

let me first: The word *first* is awkward (contrast Luke 9⁵⁹ where Jesus
calls on the man to follow him, and the man replies, *Lord let me first . . .*);
possibly in Matthew it means 'I will follow you, but let me first . . .'.

go and bury my father: The Jews, like the Greeks, placed the duty of burying the dead high on the list, but Jesus says that following him is still
more important, v. 22.

22

leave the dead to bury their own dead: This has been interpreted in various
ways: (*a*) as a possible mistranslation of an Aramaic original which
meant, 'leave the dead to the burier of dead'; (*b*) 'leave the burying of
the dead completely alone'; (*c*) by taking *the dead* in a metaphorical
sense, of those who are not disciples. The third possibility has some
support from 10⁸ (which see).

The sayings in vv. 19f. show that the disciple is to be *poor*; the sayings
in v. 24 show the urgency of discipleship: it takes precedence over all
other claims.

8²³⁻²⁷   JESUS CALMS THE STORM   Mark 4³⁶⁻⁴¹

²³*And when he got into the boat, his disciples followed him.* ²⁴*And behold,
there arose a great storm on the sea, so that the boat was being swamped by
the waves; but he was asleep.* ²⁵*And they went and woke him, saying, 'Save,
Lord; we are perishing.'* ²⁶*And he said to them, 'Why are you afraid, O
men of little faith?' Then he rose and rebuked the winds and the sea; and
there was a great calm.* ²⁷*And the men marvelled, saying, 'What sort of man
is this, that even winds and sea obey him?'*

This paragraph is the first in the second group of three miracle stories in these chapters: they are linked together by means of a narrative: the boat, crossing the lake, landing on the other side, and returning to Capernaum; and by a new feature which Matthew has introduced here, namely, the reaction of the spectators to the miracle (*the men* 8²⁷, *all the city* 8³⁴, *the crowds* 9⁸). This first miracle shows the power of Jesus over *the winds and the sea*: Matthew and his readers would not think of these, as we do, as impersonal forces; to them, they would be manifestations of the power of demons. Jesus rebukes *the winds and the sea*, and the word 'rebuke' implies the personality of the person rebuked; similarly, they *obey* him – because they are personal beings. Jesus has the power, therefore, to reduce even the demons of the storm to obedience to himself. The Church, like the disciples in the boat, is not to fear the persecution of the world; it will not be destroyed. The Lord is present with his Church, and it must believe in him. (See 10¹⁶ff. and N.B. 10²⁶, *So have no fear*.)

෨෧

Matthew has taken the story from Mark 4³⁶⁻⁴¹; he had used the Marcan introduction to it (Mark 4³⁵) in 8¹⁸. He has omitted some of the details (e.g. Mark says that Jesus was asleep *in the stern, on a cushion*), and made some changes in the wording (see notes below).

23
the boat: Cf. 8¹⁸, *he gave orders to go over to the other side*.

his disciples followed him: Cf. 8¹⁹⁻²², when the word *follow* was also used.

24
but he was asleep recalls Jonah 1⁵, *Jonah . . . was fast asleep*.

25
they went and woke him, saying, Save (sōson), Lord; we are perishing (apollymetha): Cf. Jonah 1⁶, *So the captain came and said to him, What do you mean, you sleeper? Arise, call upon your god! Perhaps the god will give a thought to us* (Greek 'save us' *diasōsē*), *that we do not perish (apolō-metha)*. Matthew has changed the form of address from *Teacher* (Mark 4³⁸) to *Lord* (see note on 8¹⁹); and the words *do you not care if we perish?* to *we are perishing*, perhaps to remove the rebuke of Jesus by the disciples.

26
O men of little faith (Mark 4⁴⁰ *Have you no faith?*): See note on 6³⁰.

rebuked (epetimēsen): cf. 17¹⁸ for Jesus rebuking a boy in whom there was a demon.

27
And the men (hoi de anthrōpoi): These words are added by Matthew – do they refer to the *disciples* (8²³), or the crew of the boat, or men in general as opposed to the demon in v. 24? Or are they another echo of Jonah (1¹⁶) *Then the men (Greek hoi andres) feared the Lord exceedingly*?

What sort of man (potapos): The meaning of the word can be 'how great', 'how wonderful', and the sentence might be an exclamation, not a question.

8²⁸⁻³⁴   JESUS EXORCIZES   Mark 5¹⁻²⁰ (1²¹⁻²⁸)
                      TWO DEMONIACS

²⁸*And when he came to the other side, to the country of the Gadarenes,ᵃ two demoniacs met him, coming out of the tombs, so fierce that no one could pass that way.* ²⁹*And behold, they cried out, 'What have you to do with us, O Son of God? Have you come here to torment us before the time?'* ³⁰*Now a herd of many swine was feeding at some distance from them.* ³¹*And the demons begged him, 'If you cast us out, send us away into the herd of swine.'* ³²*And he said to them, 'Go.' So they came out and went into the swine; and behold, the whole herd rushed down the steep bank into the sea, and perished in the waters.* ³³*The herdsmen fled, and going into the city they told everything, and what had happened to the demoniacs.* ³⁴*And behold, all the city came out to meet Jesus; and when they saw him, they begged him to leave their neighbourhood.*

a Other ancient authorities read *Gergesenes*; some *Gerasenes*

The narrative continues with the arrival of Jesus at the other side of the Sea of Galilee, in the district of Gadara; here he is met by two demoniacs, who are able, by their superior insight, to know the answer to the question (if it was a question) in 8²⁷ – they address him as *Son of God*; cf. 4³, ⁵. They know also that the *Son of God* will send them into the torments of hell when he comes at the end of the world, and they ask whether Jesus has come to Gadara to do this *before the time.* No answer is given to this question; so the demons ask leave to enter a herd of swine which is near by. Jesus sends them into the swine, and the herd rushes in to the sea and is destroyed. The story ends with *all the city* asking Jesus to go away.

A comparison with the Marcan account of this miracle will show that Matthew has abbreviated the story considerably: the emphasis in Mark is, at least partly, on the complete cure of the demoniac (there is only one of them in Mark); whereas in Matthew we are never explicitly told that the two men were restored to health. Possibly Matthew attached more importance to the request of the Gadarenes that he would leave their neighbourhood (cf. 10¹⁴, *if anyone will not receive you or listen to your words, shake off the dust from your feet as you leave that house or town* and 10²³); and the exorcism looks forward to the command in 10⁸, *cast out demons.*

৯৩

In Mark (5¹⁻²⁰) the story is told in twenty verses: in Matthew, in only seven. Matthew has omitted a great deal of the descriptive details, both before and after the exorcism. The reader of both Gospels cannot help feeling that whereas the story was of great importance for Mark, Matthew was less interested in it. But notice that Matthew has increased the number of the demoniacs from one to two. One of his reasons for doing this may have been to make up for the demoniac in Mark 1²¹⁻²⁸ whom Matthew had omitted; and there is evidence that he has Mark 1²⁴ in mind when he writes 8²⁹.

28

the country of the Gadarenes: This is almost certainly the right reading here (see margin for variants). There is the same uncertainty in Mark 5¹, but there *Gerasenes* is probably correct. Gerasa is in the Decapolis, and about thirty miles from the Sea of Galilee: Gadara is about five miles south-east of the sea (see map on p. 8).

the tombs were believed to be the home of demons; for the *uncleanness* of tombs, see 23²⁷.

29

What have you to do with us (Greek *ti hēmin kai soi,* literally, 'What [is there] to us and to you?' – used in the Greek translation of 1 Kings 17¹⁸): The meaning may be 'Why are you meddling with us?' *O Son of God:* cf. 4³, ⁶, where the devil uses the same title; the supernatural powers have supernatural insight; contrast *the men* in v. 27. *Have you come here to torment us before the time?* The demon in Mark 1²⁴ said *Have you come to destroy us?*, and in the parallel to this passage, *do not torment me* (Mark 5⁷). Matthew has changed Mark here, in order to bring the saying of the demoniacs nearer to that in the earlier story in Mark. Many commentators say that Mark 1²⁴ should be read as a statement, not as a question: i.e. 'You have come to destroy us.' Therefore, here also we may translate 'You have come here to torment us before the time.' *Here* may mean *the country of the Gadarenes*, or the earth. *The time* is the last judgement, when, according to Jewish belief, the demons will be punished and thrown into hell: cf. 25⁴¹ *Depart from me, you cursed, into the eternal fire prepared for the devil and his angels.*

30

swine: Their presence shows that this is a non-Jewish district.

31

The demons require somewhere to live; cf. 12⁴³ where a demon who has gone out of a man seeks *rest*.

32

The demons obey the command of Jesus, but can find no rest in the swine, because they are destroyed in the sea.

34

In Mark, the men from the city *saw the demoniac sitting there, clothed and in his right mind;* Matthew has changed this to *they saw* Jesus.

they begged him to leave their neighbourhood: See 10¹⁴ᶠ·.

9¹⁻⁸   JESUS FORGIVES AND HEALS   Mark 2¹⁻¹²
                    A PARALYTIC

9 *And getting into a boat he crossed over and came to his own city.* ²*And behold, they brought to him a paralytic, lying on his bed; and when Jesus saw their faith he said to the paralytic, 'Take heart, my son; your sins are forgiven.'* ³*And behold, some of the scribes said to themselves, 'This man is blaspheming.'* ⁴*But Jesus, knowingᵃ their thoughts, said 'Why do you think evil in your hearts?* ⁵*For which is easier, to say, "Your sins are forgiven", or to say, "Rise and walk"?* ⁶*But that you may know that the Son of man has*

authority on earth to forgive sins' – he then said to the paralytic – 'Rise, take up your bed and go home.' ⁷And he rose and went home. ⁸When the crowds saw it, they were afraid, and they glorified God, who had given such authority to men.

a Other ancient authorities read *seeing*

The last miracle in the second group of three shows Jesus as the Son of man who has power to forgive sins. This aspect of his work had been foretold by the angel to Joseph, *You shall call his name Jesus, for he will save his people from their sins* (1²¹, cf. 26²⁸). Forgiveness is here linked very closely with healing. The Jews believed that sickness was the result of sin; therefore, healing would accompany forgiveness. Jesus heals the man, in order to show *the scribes* that his claim to forgive is true.

ಌ

Matthew has turned back to Mark 2¹⁻¹² for this paragraph, and has shortened it, chiefly by the omission of the account of the difficulty which the bearers of the paralytic had in bringing him to Jesus. The emphasis is thus moved from the faith of the bearers (though this is still mentioned), and placed on the hostility of the scribes, the authority of Jesus, and the comment of the crowds. There are various detailed changes which Matthew has made in Mark, and some of them are shared by Luke (Luke 5¹⁷⁻²⁶).

1

getting into a boat: See above, 8¹⁸, ²³, ²⁸, for the earlier references to *the boat*, which link these paragraphs together; this tying together of stories which were originally separate, or had been linked in other ways, is the work of the Evangelist himself. By comparing Mark at this point (2¹), we can see how Matthew has rewritten the introduction to the story in order to make the sequence of incidents follow on more smoothly.

his own city: Mark had *Capernaum*, but he also said that *it was reported that* [Jesus] *was at home* (Mark 2¹). In Matthew Jesus was born in *Bethlehem*, in fulfilment of prophecy (2¹⁻⁶) and left it because of persecution (2¹³); he returned to *Nazareth*, again to fulfil prophecy (2²³), and left it after the arrest of John (4¹²) to live in *Capernaum*. For other references to Capernaum in Matthew, see 11²⁰⁻²⁴, 17²⁴. In the former passage, we are told that, although *most of his mighty works had been*

done in Capernaum and other cities in that district, *they did not repent.*
Here also we are shown the scribes rejecting him.

2
Jesus pronounces forgiveness, in response to the faith of those who
brought the paralytic to him: the point is clearer in Mark, where the
difficulty which they had in bringing him is more fully described; cf.
8$^{5-13}$ for the healing of the centurion's servant in response to the faith of
the centurion.

The word translated *Take heart (tharsei)* has been added here by Matthew
as also in 9^{22}; in 14^{27} Matthew has it again, and there he copied it from
Mark 6^{50}.

For the relationship between sin and sickness, cf. James 5$^{14f.}$.

3
The good news which Jesus has brought, of the forgiveness of sins,
arouses opposition in the part of *the scribes*, that is, the official exponents
of the Law. Their objection is that Jesus is acting in the name of God,
by declaring the forgiveness of sins.

4
knowing their thoughts (margin, *seeing their thoughts*): The difference in
Greek is very small (*eidōs* or *idōn*); cf. 12^{25} for the same disagreement
among the manuscripts.

Why do you think evil in your hearts? The opposition of the Jews to Jesus,
which is beginning in this paragraph, starts in their *hearts* and *thoughts*,
and will develop into words (e.g. see 9^{11}); cf. 12^{34}, *You brood of vipers!
How can you speak good, when you are evil? For out of the abundance of the
heart the mouth speaks.*

Jesus offers to show his power to forgive sins, by demonstrating his
power to cure the paralytic. The miracle is a sign of the truth of his
teaching; cf. 11$^{4ff.}$, 12^{28}.

the Son of man may be used here in the sense 'I myself'; cf. 8^{20} for its
previous use in this Gospel.

8
the crowds represent a position between that of the disciples (faith) and
that of the scribes (unbelief): they are, as we have already seen (7^{28}), the
foreshadowing of the Church; and their reaction (*they glorified God,
who had given such authority to men*) looks forward to the time when God
will give authority to the apostles to forgive sins.

⁹*As Jesus passed on from there, he saw a man called Matthew sitting at the
tax office; and he said to him, 'Follow me.' And he rose and followed him.*

It is possible that this Gospel was from the first published with the
title *According to Matthew*. The reader will therefore want to know
who this Matthew was, and what authority he had for writing the
Gospel. In this short section the author mentions himself – or rather,
he describes the calling of one who was called Matthew, though, as
we have seen, his identity with this disciple is almost certainly a fiction.
The disciple will be mentioned by name only once more in the book,
at 10³, in the list of the twelve apostles: *Matthew the tax collector*.

§

Matthew has omitted Mark 2¹³ (an editorial verse, describing the teaching of Jesus by the sea), and has here copied out Mark 2¹⁴, with this
important alteration: Mark's *he saw Levi the son of Alphaeus*, he has
changed to *he saw a man called Matthew*. Levi was not mentioned again
in Mark – he was not included in the list of the twelve in Mark 3¹⁶⁻¹⁹,
though *Matthew* was. Why did our Evangelist make this change here?
There is no evidence that *Matthew* was the 'Christian' name of *Levi*.
Possibly (though this is pure conjecture) there was some connexion
between the apostle Matthew and the Church for which this Gospel
was written; and the author of this Gospel attributed his work to the
founder or teacher of the Church who had borne this name. (A similar
situation may lie behind the connexion between the Johannine writings
and the apostle John.) The Evangelist may have used the opportunity
which Mark gave him, for rewriting the call of a disciple, to tie it up
more closely with the list of the twelve; and to tie it up with the
particular one of the twelve whom he venerated as the apostle of the
Church to which he belonged.

As in the case of the call of the first four disciples (4¹⁸ᶠᶠ.), no explanation
is given of the reason why Matthew *followed* Jesus. The Evangelist con-
fines himself to writing a Gospel, and does not attempt to supply

motives, etc., as the modern biographer might do. The point which he wants to bring out here is expressed in the words of Jesus to the apostles in the next chapter: *You received without pay* (10^8): that is to say, they received their calling to be apostles without first giving anything for it. They had no previous good works, by which they had earned or merited their appointment.

Matthew was a *tax collector*, that is one who was classed by the Jews among the sinners (see next verse, *tax collectors and sinners*); his work for the Romans, and the dishonesty of the methods usually adopted, cut him off from Israel. The calling of a tax collector into the company of those who followed Jesus was a sign that the kingdom would be given to those who had put themselves outside the Law.

9^{10-13} JESUS EATS WITH TAX Mark 2^{15-17}
COLLECTORS AND SINNERS

10*And as he sat at table*a *in the house, behold, many tax collectors and sinners came and sat down with Jesus and his disciples.* 11*And when the Pharisees saw this, they said to his disciples, 'Why does your teacher eat with tax collectors and sinners?'* 12*But when he heard it, he said, 'Those who are well have no need of a physician, but those who are sick.* 13*Go and learn what this means, "I desire mercy, and not sacrifice." For I came not to call the righteous, but sinners.'*

  a Greek *reclined*

The calling of a tax collector was a sign of the gospel – that God does not demand righteousness according to the Law, but gives the kingdom to those who have no righteousness of their own. The same lesson is taught in this paragraph: Jesus admits *tax collectors and sinners* to table-fellowship with himself, and defends his action against the complaints of the Pharisees (the upholders of the Law) with the saying about the physician and the sick, and with the prophecy of Hosea. He says that he has come to invite the sinners to the messianic feast; he is vindicating the gospel against the Pharisees' demand for works, and the grace of God against the righteousness which is based on obedience to the Law.

❧

Matthew has here taken the next section from Mark, made some abbreviations, added *your teacher* in v. 11 and the quotation from Hosea in v. 13.

10

Neither Mark nor Matthew makes it clear in whose house the meal is held – Jesus', Levi's (or Matthew's), or another's. In Luke, *Levi made him a great feast in his house* (Luke 5^{29}); but it is possible that Mark and Matthew intended us to understand that Jesus was the host; cf. v. 13.

11

The Pharisees ask the disciples why Jesus eats with people who have put themselves outside the Law: to eat with such people is to identify oneself with them (cf. Gal. 2^{12}, 2 John $^{10f.}$), and thus defile oneself, according to the Pharisees. See note on 8^{19} for *teacher* in the mouth of Jesus' opponents in this Gospel.

12

Jesus implies that he has come to heal the sick: and those who are outside the Law are most patently the sick. Sickness is here used as a symbol for sin, and this may be the meaning of 10^8, in which Jesus sends his disciples to *heal the sick:* that is, to bring forgiveness and life.

13

Go and learn what this means, I desire mercy, and not sacrifice: These words have been added by Matthew: the introductory formula is a typical rabbinic phrase; the quotation is from Hos. 6^6, and Matthew introduces it again at 12^7. Jesus is revealing the *mercy* of God towards the sinners; whereas the Pharisees are demanding *sacrifice* and the works of the Law.

The word *to call* (*kalein*) is used in $22^{3, 4, 8, 9}$, of inviting guests to a feast. This is the sense here also: Jesus' meal with his disciples and the tax collectors and sinners is a sign of the kingdom. Cf. 8^{11} *many will come from east and west and sit at table with Abraham, Isaac, and Jacob in the kingdom of heaven.* By inviting sinners to his meals, Jesus is revealing the generosity of God, and contradicting the Pharisaic teaching about the Law.

¹⁴ *Then the disciples of John came to him, saying, 'Why do we and the Pharisees fast,ᵃ but your disciples do not fast?'* ¹⁵ *And Jesus said to them, 'Can the wedding guests mourn as long as the bridegroom is with them? The days will come, when the bridegroom is taken away from them, and then they will fast.* ¹⁶ *And no one puts a piece of unshrunk cloth on an old garment, for the patch tears away from the garment, and a worse tear is made.* ¹⁷ *Neither is new wine put into old wineskins; if it is, the skins burst, and the wine is spilled, and the skins are destroyed; but new wine is put into fresh wineskins, and so both are preserved.'*

a Other ancient authorities add *much* or *often*

The subject of this paragraph, as of the three previous paragraphs also, is the relationship between the old covenant and the new. The disciples of John the Baptist ask why they and the Pharisees fast, but Jesus' disciples do not fast. Jesus replies that this is a new age – the time of the wedding, the messianic age. It is a time for feasting, not for fasting or mourning. The Law, which had commanded men to fast, is no longer in force; now is the time of the kingdom. To try to keep the Law at this time is like patching an old garment with un-shrunken cloth, or putting new wine into old wineskins. Among these sayings which defend the putting-aside of the Law, there is one, v. 15ᵇ, which looks forward to a time when the bridegroom will be taken away and the disciples will fast. This is probably a separate saying, possibly not original; it looks forward to the Passion, and the Church's practice of fasting.

ᛣᚱᚪ

Matthew has abbreviated Mark 2¹⁸⁻²², and some of his alterations are shared by Luke 5³³⁻³⁹, which perhaps shows Luke's knowledge of Matthew here.

14

In Mark, the questioners were not identified: *people came and said to him, Why do John's disciples and the disciples of the Pharisees fast?* Matthew has rewritten this, so that the questioners are *the disciples of John* themselves, and they belong with *the Pharisees* to the old order; cf. 11^{11-15}, where John is the turning-point between the Law and the prophets, and the kingdom of heaven.

The word *much* or *often* (margin) is added in some of the manuscripts, and may be original. There is evidence that some of the Jews had begun to fast on Mondays and Thursdays (Luke 18^{12}, *Didache* 8).

15

The words of Jesus are a parable: just as wedding-guests do not fast at a wedding-feast, so men should not fast in this new age of the kingdom. The Christians, however, understood the saying as an allegory: Jesus is the bridegroom; the disciples are the guests (cf. 22^{1-14}).

The saying about the taking away of the bridegroom is almost certainly a product of the early Church, which has been put into the mouth of Jesus. The passage in the *Didache* (Chapter 8) which tells us that the Jews fasted on Mondays and Thursdays, commands the Christians to fast on Wednesdays and Fridays. (The *Didache* may belong to about the same date as this Gospel.)

16f.

Two more parables: the patch and the wineskin. Judaism cannot be patched up with the new teaching which Jesus has brought; and the gospel cannot be contained within the framework of the Law. The words *old* (*palaios*) and *fresh* (*kainos*) are sometimes used in the New Testament, as here, to contrast Judaism and Christianity; e.g. *we serve not under the old written code, but in the new life of the Spirit* (Rom. 7^6). The word *patch* (*plerōma*) is the noun from the verb 'to fulfil'; cf. Matthew's formula *All this took place to fulfil what the Lord had spoken by the prophet* (1^{22} etc.). The sense in which Christianity 'fulfilled' Judaism was one of the questions which troubled Matthew and his first readers; see 5^{17}ff., 23^2f..

The last words of the saying, *and so both are preserved*, are an addition by Matthew to the Marcan source. He seems to fight shy of the suggestion in Mark that Judaism is abolished by the kingdom. He sees Judaism and Christianity continuing side by side until the coming of Christ – cf. Rom. 11^{25}ff..

THE RAISING OF THE RULER'S   Mark 5^{21-43}
                  DAUGHTER AND THE CURE
                  OF A WOMAN WITH A
                  HAEMORRHAGE

18 *While he was thus speaking to them, behold, a ruler came in and knelt before him, saying, 'My daughter has just died; but come and lay your hand on her, and she will live.'* 19 *And Jesus rose and followed him, with his disciples.* 20 *And behold, a woman who had suffered from a haemorrhage for twelve years came up behind him and touched the fringe of his garment;* 21 *for she said to herself, 'If I only touch his garment, I shall be made well.'* 22 *Jesus turned, and seeing her he said, 'Take heart, daughter; your faith has made you well.' And instantly the woman was made well.* 23 *And when Jesus came to the ruler's house, and saw the flute players, and the crowd making a tumult,* 24 *he said, 'Depart; for the girl is not dead but sleeping.' And they laughed at him.* 25 *But when the crowd had been put outside, he went in and took her by the hand, and the girl arose.* 26 *And the report of this went through all that district.*

The last three paragraphs (9^{18-34}) in this section contain the third and last group of acts of power. These acts of power symbolize the coming of the kingdom. The daughter of the ruler has died, but Jesus makes her live; the woman had been sick, but Jesus makes her well. The word which is here translated 'make well' is *sōzein*, which is frequently used in the New Testament of 'to save' – e.g. *he will save his people from their sins* (1^{21}). Sickness and death are symbols of the condition of men apart from Christ; his coming brings them 'salvation' – that is, wholeness and life, which are here symbolized by restoration to health; cf. 10^{7f.}, where Jesus sends his apostles to preach the coming of the kingdom, and commands them to *Heal the sick, raise the dead*.

☙

Matthew has re-arranged Mark's order here; he has taken this paragraph from Mark 5^{21-43}, after the story of the healing of the man with the legion, which he had already used (8^{28-34}); and here, as there, he has considerably shortened Mark's account: in Mark, it consisted of twenty-three verses; here it is only nine.

18

Matthew says that the man was a *ruler*: Mark had, *a ruler of the synagogue*; Matthew abbreviates it because his readers would understand by *a ruler* a Jewish synagogue official. This representative of the old order comes to Jesus and kneels before him (the Greek can mean 'worshipped him', cf. 2^{11}) confessing his faith in Jesus' power to overcome death.

My daughter has just died: Contrast Mark $5^{23, 35}$; in Mark, the daughter dies between the setting out of the ruler and his meeting Jesus, and a message is brought to him to inform him of this. Matthew has omitted this, and therefore changed the words of the ruler.

20ff.

The woman's illness made her unclean according to the Law, and anything she touched would also be unclean (Lev. 15^{19}ff.). But Jesus is not defiled by her impurity: rather, he cures her of her illness.

20

Matthew, and Luke also, add the words *the fringe* (see also 14^{36} (= Mark 6^{56}), 23^{5}). Tassels or fringes were commanded, see Num. 15^{38}ff., Deut. 22^{12}, and they were intended to remind people of the commandments of God.

22

Take heart (added by Matthew, see 9^{2}) *daughter; your faith has made you well:* We can see how the story was adaptable for use by the Christians, who believed that they had been saved (= *made well*) by *faith* in Jesus.

23

the flute players are a Matthean addition; they were a regular feature of Jewish funeral customs, but they were also used on festive occasions, as in 11^{17}, *we piped to you, and you did not dance.*

24

the girl is not dead but sleeping: In the Old Testament, the word 'sleep' had been used figuratively of death, e.g. *many of those who sleep in the dust of the earth shall awake* (Dan. 12^{2}); and the Christians continued this usage, e.g. Paul said that Christ *died for us so that whether we wake or sleep* (i.e. live or die) *we might live with him* (1 Thess. 5^{10}). It is unlikely that Matthew, or those who told the story before him, meant that Jesus intended to say that the girl had not died; the Christians would not have told the story unless they believed that it was a miracle.

They understood Jesus to mean 'Death is not the end, because I have come to raise the dead, to awake those who are asleep'; cf. John 11^{11}: *our friend Lazarus has fallen asleep, but I go to awake him out of sleep.*

26

In Mark there is a command to silence at this point: *he strictly charged them that no one should know this* (Mark 5^{43}); Matthew, as usual, omits these commands to silence, and this verse replaces it as the conclusion to the story.

9^{27-31} THE BLIND RECEIVE   cf Mark 10^{46-52},
                      THEIR SIGHT 8^{22-26}

27And as Jesus passed on from there, two blind men followed him, crying aloud, 'Have mercy on us, Son of David.' 28When he entered the house, the blind men came to him; and Jesus said to them, 'Do you believe that I am able to do this?' They said to him, 'Yes, Lord.' 29Then he touched their eyes, saying, 'According to your faith be it done to you.' 30And their eyes were opened. And Jesus sternly charged them, 'See that no one knows it.' 31But they went away and spread his fame through all that district.

Matthew has two more acts of power to describe, before he writes the introduction to the second section of teaching; both of them describe the restoration of faculties – sight and speech; both of them are very largely Matthean constructions, not taken over from Mark in the way that the greater part of these two chapters has been. Behind Matthew's presentation of Jesus as the restorer of sight and speech may lie the following prophecy from Isaiah (35^{4-6}):

> *Say to those who are of a fearful heart*
>   *Be strong, fear not!*
> *Behold, your God*
>   *will come with vengeance,*
> *with the recompense of God.*
>   *He will come and save you* (Greek *sōsei hemas*: cf. 9^{21}f.).
> *Then the eyes of the blind shall be opened,*
>   *and the ears of the deaf* (Greek *kōphōn* – deaf or dumb) *unstopped;*

> *then shall the lame man leap like a hart,*
> *and the tongue of the dumb sing for joy.*

In this paragraph, *the eyes of the blind* (men – the word is plural in Greek) are *opened*; in the next paragraph, a man who is described as *kōphos*, deaf or dumb, is restored.

From other parts of this Gospel, we can see that Matthew thought of blindness as not only a physical incapacity, but also as a symbol for unbelief; e.g. Jesus says of the Pharisees, *They are blind guides. And if a blind man leads a blind man, both will fall into a pit* (15¹⁴), see also 23¹⁶, ¹⁷, ²⁴, ²⁶. Similarly, sight is a symbol of salvation; e.g. Jesus says of the disciples, *Blessed are your eyes, for they see* (13¹⁶). The two men in this story who have faith in Jesus, and are given sight by him because of their faith, symbolize the disciples whose unbelief will be taken away in order that they may know who Jesus is.

 KXX

There is no exact parallel to this paragraph in Mark (or in Luke), but there are some similarities in the Marcan account of the healing of blind Bartimaeus (Mark 10⁴⁶ff. = Matthew 20²⁹ff.). Bartimaeus, like the blind men here, addresses Jesus as *Son of David*; Jesus questions him, and here he questions the blind men; Jesus mentions his faith and theirs. Probably, therefore, Matthew has written this paragraph on the basis of Mark's story of Bartimaeus, and so created a doublet with Matthew 20²⁹ff., as he has also done when he has copied Marcan sayings twice over in his Gospel. There are also, however, certain points in Mark's story of the blind man at Bethsaida (Mark 8²²⁻²⁶) which are similar to this paragraph – a story which Matthew has not otherwise used. On the doubling of the number of people healed, see above, pp. 119ff.

27
Son of David is a favourite title for Jesus in this Gospel (1¹, 12²³, 15²², 21⁹, ¹⁵). For the Old Testament expectation of a Son of David see e.g. 2 Sam. 7¹²ff., Ps. 89.

29
he touched their eyes: This may have been taken from the other cure in Mark: *he laid his hands upon his eyes* (Mark 8²⁵).

30
Jesus sternly charged them: The word translated *sternly charged* (*enebrimēthē*)

can imply violent anger. Mark had used it in the account of the cleansing of the leper (Mark 1⁴³) and Matthew had omitted it when he was copying that paragraph (8⁴).

See that no one knows it is one of the few Matthean commands to silence (see also 8⁴, 12¹⁶, 16²⁰, 17⁹), and may possibly be based on Mark 8²⁶. No reason is given, either for the stern charge, or for the silence which is enjoined.

31
The story ends, like the previous paragraph, with the fame of Jesus spreading throughout all that district (cf. v. 26).

9³²⁻³⁴   THE DUMB MAN SPEAKS   cf. Mark 3²²

³²*As they were going away, behold, a dumb demoniac was brought to him.* ³³*And when the demon had been cast out, the dumb man spoke; and the crowds marvelled, saying, 'Never was anything like this seen in Israel.'* ³⁴*But the Pharisees said, 'He casts out demons by the prince of demons.'*

The last miracle in this section is the gift of speech to a dumb man (*kōphos*). Like the previous paragraph, it has no parallel in Mark or Luke, and is probably a creation of Matthew's. We can only guess at the reasons why he wanted to put in another act of healing, and why he wrote the particular verses which we have here.

First, as we saw at the beginning of Chapter 8, Matthew seems to have wanted to make up the number of Jewish people healed in this section to ten; he needed one more person to do this.

Secondly, as we saw on p. 143, he probably had the prophecy of Isa. 35⁵ᶠ· in mind:

> . . . *the ears of the deaf* (Greek *kōphōn*) shall be *unstopped*;
> . . . *the tongue of the dumb* shall *sing for joy.*

Thirdly, Matthew is about to give his second teaching section, in which Jesus will send the disciples out *to preach*, and in which he will tell them, *Do not be anxious how you are to speak or what you are to say; for what you are to say will be given to you in that hour* (10⁷, ¹⁹). The apostles are to be men with the gift of speaking: so Matthew may have thought it appropriate to conclude this section of Jesus' mighty works with the miracle of the gift of speech.

This particular story serves another purpose in Matthew; the latter half of it describes the reaction of the crowds on the one hand, and of the Pharisees on the other, to the exorcism of the dumb demoniac. The crowds marvel, but the Pharisees say that Jesus is in league with the demons. The disciples will find a similar division among those to whom they are sent (10$^{8-15}$), and they will be maligned just as their master has been (10$^{24f.}$).

❧

The miracle story has no parallel in Mark or Luke, but the words of the Pharisees in v. 34 are from Mark 3^{22} = Matthew 12^{24} – perhaps another case of Matthew duplicating a saying by copying it twice over from Mark.

32

dumb: The Greek word is *kōphos*: fundamentally it means 'dull' or 'blunt', and it was used both of speech and of hearing. In this story it is clear from the context that the word means *dumb*: the next verse says *the dumb man spoke*; and this is also the meaning of the word in 12^{22}, 15$^{30f.}$; but in 11^{5} it means *deaf*.

33f.

The contrasting reactions of the crowds and the Pharisees bring the whole series to a conclusion, in the division within Israel which Jesus has created by his teaching and preaching and healing; on the one side *the crowds*, who will eventually be the believers, the Church (cf. 7$^{28f.}$); on the other side *the Pharisees*, who stand for unbelief.

34

The whole of this verse is omitted by some of the authorities for the text, possibly because it is similar to 12^{24}; but the reference back in 10$^{25f.}$ guarantees the authenticity of this verse.

the prince of demons: The Jews of the time believed in the existence of thousands of evil spirits, or demons; they were believed to be the souls of the giants mentioned in Gen. 6$^{1-4}$. Satan (4^{10}, 12^{26}, 16^{23}) or *Beelzebul* (10^{25}, 12$^{24, 27}$) was their ruler. It was thought that they could enter into people and possess them, causing sickness or uncleanness; the cure must be by casting out the demon. One of the signs of the coming of God's kingdom would be the overthrow of these minions of Satan; see 12^{28}.

Matthew 9^{35}-10^{5a}

Introduction to the Second Discourse

The second section of collected sayings of Jesus is prefaced by a short introduction, which consists of two paragraphs and a sentence; cf. the introduction to the first section, 4¹⁸–5². The first paragraph describes in general terms the work of Jesus in Israel, and the need of the people; and this leads up to the command of Jesus to his disciples to pray for more labourers. As if in response to this prayer, Jesus then gives authority to the twelve to cast out unclean spirits and to heal; and the names of the twelve apostles are given. Then Jesus sends them out with instructions – and this introduces the next group of sayings.

9³⁵⁻³⁸   THE WORK OF JESUS, THE   Mark 6⁶, ³⁴
CROWDS, AND THE NEED FOR   Luke 10²
MORE LABOURERS

³⁵*And Jesus went about all the cities and villages, teaching in their synagogues and preaching the gospel of the kingdom, and healing every disease and every infirmity.* ³⁶*When he saw the crowds, he had compassion for them, because they were harassed and helpless, like sheep without a shepherd.* ³⁷*Then he said to his disciples, 'The harvest is plentiful, but the labourers are few;* ³⁸*pray therefore the Lord of the harvest to send out labourers into his harvest.'*

The threefold work of Jesus – *teaching, preaching,* and *healing* – continues, and reveals the state of Israel: they are *like sheep without a shepherd.* They need leaders who will guide them into the kingdom which is about to come, and these leaders can be provided only by God. Therefore, Jesus commands the disciples to pray God to send men who will do this work.

మ

This paragraph is a Matthean composition, made up mainly out of

149

Marcan material: v. 35a is from Mark 6^6, *And he went about among the villages teaching*; v. 35b is a repetition of Matt. 4^{23}; v. 36 is from Mark 6^{34}, *he saw a great throng, and he had compassion on them, because they were like sheep without a shepherd*. The other two verses 37f. are parallel to Luke 10^2, and may have been taken from another source. The paragraph illustrates well Matthew's knowledge of the text of Mark, probably by heart; and his fondness for formula-like phrases (9^{35}).

35
See note on 4^{23}.

36
like sheep without a shepherd is a description of Israel in the Old Testament, e.g. Num. 27^{17}, 1 Kings 22^{17}, Zech. 10^2. Israel is the flock of God, and God or his agent is the shepherd. For Jesus as the shepherd, see 25^{32}, 26^{31}.

37
the harvest is a term used in the Old Testament for the time when God will intervene in the world, and judge it (e.g. Hos. 6^{11}, Joel 3^{13}). For its use elsewhere in Matthew, see 13$^{30, 39}$, and compare 3^{12}, 24^{32}. For the Christian minister as a *labourer*, cf. 2 Tim. 2^{15} *a workman who has no need to be ashamed*, and 1 Cor. 3^9 etc., *fellow workmen*.

38
the lord of the harvest is God, and the disciples are to ask him to send labourers, that is, apostles and evangelists, into the world to prepare for the gathering of the harvest at the end of the world.

10$^{1-4}$ JESUS GIVES THE TWELVE Mark 6^7, 3$^{16-19}$
APOSTLES AUTHORITY
TO HEAL

10 *And he called to him his twelve disciples and gave them authority over unclean spirits, to cast them out, and to heal every disease and every infirmity.* ^{2}*The names of the twelve apostles are these: first, Simon, who is called Peter, and Andrew his brother; James the son of Zeb'edee, and John his brother;* ^{3}*Philip and Bartholomew; Thomas and Matthew the tax collector; James the son of Alphaeus, and Thaddaeus;^{a}* ^{4}*Simon the Cananean, and Judas Iscariot, who betrayed him.*

a Other ancient authorities read *Lebbaeus* or *Lebbaeus called Thaddaeus*

Matthew now introduces his readers to the twelve apostles. They are to become the labourers in the harvesting of the world of which Jesus has been speaking. No doubt Matthew thought of the twelve as the beginning of the ministry, as men who had authority which they could pass on to others. Here, however, he tells us only that Jesus gave them power to do a part of his work, namely, that of exorcizing unclean spirits and healing disease. This is the first mention of the *twelve disciples* in this Gospel; in Mark their appointment had been recorded at an earlier point in the narrative (Mark 3^{14}). Matthew's first readers would know that Jesus had appointed twelve, just as Paul could assume that the Corinthians knew about them (1 Cor. 15^{5}). The number twelve was probably chosen by Jesus to correspond to the number of tribes in Israel (cf. 19^{28} *you who have followed me will also sit on twelve thrones, judging the twelve tribes of Israel*). They are to be the leaders of the new Israel; and for this they are sent first to *the lost sheep of the house of Israel* (10^{6}) and after the resurrection to *all nations* (28^{19}).

తిజ

The calling and authorizing of the twelve is from Mark 6^{7}; their names are from Mark 3$^{16-19}$. Matthew has repeated his formula, *to heal every disease and every infirmity*, from 4^{23}, 9^{35}; and he has made two changes in the order of the names of the twelve in the list: he has brought *Andrew* from fourth place to second, to be a pair with his brother *Simon;* and he has changed Mark's *Matthew and Thomas* to *Thomas and Matthew the tax collector* (cf. 9^{9}).

1

Matthew has already drawn attention to the *authority* of Jesus: the authority of his *teaching* (7$^{28f.}$) and his authority *to forgive sins* (9^{6}). Jesus here begins to pass on this authority which he has received from God to others, cf. 9^{8}, 28$^{18ff.}$.

2

The word *apostles* is used only once in Matthew, just as it is used only once in Mark (6^{30}); in Luke, on the other hand, it is used more frequently. The literal meaning is 'one who is sent', and it became a technical term in the vocabulary of the Church, though it was not used only of the twelve.

first: Matthew adds this word; in his Gospel there is an underlining of the importance of Peter as the leader of the Church, though it should be noticed that his name always stands first in every list of the twelve. For *Peter* in this Gospel, see 4^{18}, 14^{28}ff., 16^{16}ff., 17^{24}ff.

For the meaning of the name *Peter*, see note on 16^{18}.

3
Thaddaeus is the name in Mark 3^{18}, but some of the manuscripts here have *Lebbaeus*, and this may be the correct reading.

4
Cananean means 'zealous', and it may refer to Simon's zeal for the Law, or that he was a Zealot (see Luke 6^{15}, Acts 1^{13}), i.e. one of those who favoured the use of force to expel the Romans from Palestine. There is, however, some doubt whether this party called themselves Zealots at this time.

Iscariot probably means 'from Kerioth' in southern Judea.

10^{5a}   THE MISSION AND CHARGE OF   Mark 6^{7f.}
THE TWELVE

5a *These twelve Jesus sent out, charging them,*

A final sentence introduces the sayings of Jesus about the work of the apostles. He *sent out* the twelve, Greek *apesteilen*, the verb from which the word *apostle* is formed: and he charged them where to go and what to do and to expect. Cf.5$^{1f.}$ for the similar introduction to the teaching on the mountain.

ဢဢ

These twelve Jesus sent out, charging them: Matthew has made use of Mark 6$^{7f.}$: *he began to send them out . . . He charged them.*

The sending of the twelve is a sign, that is, an action which shows who Jesus is. He has been sent by the Father, and given authority by God to proclaim the kingdom by his teaching, preaching, and healing. Now he sends others, to do what he does; and he will say to them, *He who receives you receives me, and he who receives me receives him who sent me* 10^{40}.

Matthew 10^{5b-42}

Instructions for the Apostles

Matthew's second collection of the words of Jesus is considerably shorter than the first, but about the same length as the fourth (18^{2-35}), with which it has some features in common: for example, in Chapter 10 Jesus instructs those whom he sends out on the mission how they are to do their work; in Chapter 18 he instructs the Church how it is to receive those whom he has sent to it.

Matthew has followed his usual practice of disturbing the Marcan framework as little as possible. Mark had recorded the sending out of the twelve, and the instructions which Jesus gave to them, in Mark 6^{7-11}; and Matthew has taken these few verses and expanded them with material which he found elsewhere in Mark and in other sources.

The identification of these other sources is a complicated question, and scholars have not been agreed on it. Some of the material comes in different contexts in Luke, and may therefore have been in Q. A few verses have no parallel in Mark or Luke. We can, however, say with some certainty that Matthew has collected together, in Chapter 10, sayings which he had from different traditions (Marcan and non-Marcan), and which had stood in different contexts in at least one of these traditions, i.e. Mark; and that he himself is responsible for weaving them into the pattern which they now have.

The section begins with instructions of Jesus to his apostles on the procedure they are to adopt: where they are to go, and what they are to do. He goes on to tell them that they are to expect persecution, hatred, and death; their lot will be no easier than his. But they are not to be afraid, because the Father has them in his keeping, and Jesus will speak for them to him. They share in Jesus' work of bringing division and judgement to the world, and so they must expect to be treated as he will be treated – with rejection and death. Finally, Jesus says that his apostles will be the means of bringing a reward to those who do receive them, the reward of receiving Christ who sent them, and the Father who sent him.

The whole section illustrates one of the tensions between the Evangelist's material, and his own purposes in the use of it. The traditional material recorded the belief of Jesus that his mission was to Israel and not to any other nations. Matthew, however, is writing at a time when the Church has come to believe that God is sending his evangelists to all the nations; and he writes his Gospel partly at least for use by evangelists outside Palestine, in his own time, and in the days ahead. He has resolved this practical problem in this chapter by beginning it with the clear and definite limitation imposed by Jesus who commands the apostles to go only to the Jews; and then gradually allowing the reader to see into the later times, when the limitation would be removed and the apostles would bear testimony to the Gentiles also. Why this will happen, and when and how it will happen, he does not tell us here; he reserves it until the end of the book (28$^{18-20}$).

| 10^{5b-15} | THE PROCEDURE WHICH IS TO BE FOLLOWED BY THE APOSTLES | Mark 6$^{8-11}$ Luke 9$^{2-5}$, 10$^{4-12}$ |

^{5b} 'Go nowhere among the Gentiles, and enter no town of the Samaritans, ^{6}but go rather to the lost sheep of the house of Israel. ^{7}And preach as you go, saying, "The kingdom of heaven is at hand." ^{8}Heal the sick, raise the dead, cleanse lepers, cast out demons. You received without pay, give without pay. ^{9}Take no gold, nor silver, nor copper in your belts, ^{10}no bag for your journey, nor two tunics, nor sandals, nor a staff; for the labourer deserves his food. ^{11}And whatever town or village you enter, find out who is worthy in it, and stay with him until you depart. ^{12}As you enter the house, salute it. ^{13}And if the house is worthy, let your peace come upon it; but if it is not worthy, let your peace return to you. ^{14}And if any one will not receive you or listen to your words, shake off the dust from your feet as you leave that house or town. ^{15}Truly, I say to you, it shall be more tolerable on the day of judgement for the land of Sodom and Gomor'rah than for that town.'

Jesus limits the present field of operations of the twelve to *the lost sheep of the house of Israel* whom he has seen in the course of his own work, and to whom he was sent by the Father (9^{35f}, 15^{24}). They are to go to them, and to do what he has done: preach that the kingdom is near, and perform the signs which are evidence that this is so. Moreover, like him they are to be poor, and to depend for their subsistence on the faith and generosity which their message will evoke. They are bearers of the peace of God, which some will accept and some will reject; those who reject imperil themselves at the day of judgement when the kingdom comes.

ಜಲ

The question of the sources which Matthew has used is, as we have said, extremely complicated at this point. Matthew has made use of the instructions to the twelve in Mark 6$^{8-11}$, and those verses are reproduced here in 10$^{9-11, 14}$. Verses 5–7 have no parallel in Mark or Luke: v. 6 picks up 9^{36} and is repeated in 15^{24}; v. 7 picks up the preaching of John and Jesus in 3^2, 4^{17}. The difficulty comes when we compare Luke 9$^{2-5}$, 10$^{4-12}$, the Lucan accounts of the mission of the twelve and the seventy; and we cannot be certain how these sayings lay in front of Matthew and Luke, before they incorporated them into their Gospels.

5b, 6
The twelve are not to go *among the Gentiles* (literally, 'on the road leading to the Gentiles') or to any Samaritan town; but to Israel alone. Jesus had been sent to Israel as King, to gather them and rule over them as a shepherd (an Old Testament title for the ruler). Now, Israel is *lost* (cf. *harassed and helpless* 9^{36}); the apostles are therefore given authority by Jesus, the shepherd of Israel, to be his assistants in the gathering together of his flock in his kingdom (cf. 18$^{10-14}$).

7, 8a
Two of the three parts of the work of Jesus, *teaching*, *preaching*, and *healing* (4^{23}, 9^{35}), are here extended to the apostles: *preaching* and *healing* (see also 10^1 and 28^{20}). *Preaching* is always used in Matthew of proclaiming the nearness of the kingdom, that God is soon to rule in the world in such a way that his will will be done on earth as it is in heaven. The acts of *healing* accompany or follow the *preaching*, as visible signs of the truth of the message. Did Matthew understand this command to do miracles literally or metaphorically? The question arises particularly in connexion with the second command, *raise the dead*. The letters of Paul show that he and his readers expected apostles to perform miraculous signs (e.g. 2 Cor. 12^{12}: *The signs of a true apostle were performed among you in all patience, with signs and wonders and mighty works*), and

157

the Acts of the Apostles shows that this could be believed to include raising the dead (Acts 9^{36}ff., 20^{7}ff.). On the other hand, sickness and death could be and were understood metaphorically – e.g. Eph. 2^{1f}., *And you he made alive, when you were dead through the trespasses and sins in which you once walked*; and see the note above on 8^{22}. These commands to heal may, therefore, have been taken to mean that by their preaching the apostles will bring life and salvation to the world.

8b

The twelve themselves had received their call and appointment and authority as a free gift from Christ; they are to treat others as they have been treated, dispensing God's gifts without charge.

9f.

They are to trust in the power of the message which they have been given, to call forth in their hearers generosity to them, and so they are forbidden to make any provision for themselves when they set out: that would be to go out in unbelief.

11

They are to find who is *worthy*, that is, willing to receive them, in every *town or village* which they enter, and *stay with him* as long as they remain there; that is, they are not to look out for better accommodation and move into it.

The word which is here translated *worthy* (*axios*) was translated *deserves* in the previous verse; and it is thus a 'stitch-word', linking these two sayings together, and linking them on to v. 13. *Worthy* suggests to us moral goodness; it would not have implied that for Matthew and his readers, but it could mean 'corresponding', 'comparable', 'congruous', i.e., in this case, willing to receive an apostle.

12f.

They are to *salute . . . the house* they enter, that is, bless the household with the *peace* of God; if however the household will not receive them, they are to withdraw the blessing.

14

Moreover, in these latter cases they are to *shake off the dust from* their *feet* as a sign that they will have nothing in common with those who have rejected them and their message, not even the dust of the place; so that they have no responsibility for them at the last judgement (cf. Pilate washing his hands, 27^{24}).

15

Sodom and Gomorrah were proverbial for their sinfulness and a standing warning of the judgement of God upon sinners (Gen. 19, Jude 7); yet even they will fare better in the last judgement than those who have refused to receive the messengers whom Jesus sends with the news of the coming kingdom.

10$^{16-23}$ THE PERSECUTION OF THE   Luke 10^3
APOSTLES   Mark 13$^{9-13}$

16*'Behold, I send you out as sheep in the midst of wolves; so be wise as serpents and innocent as doves.* 17*Beware of men; for they will deliver you up to councils, and flog you in their synagogues,* 18*and you will be dragged before governors and kings for my sake, to bear testimony before them and the Gentiles.* 19*When they deliver you up, do not be anxious how you are to speak or what you are to say; for what you are to say will be given to you in that hour;* 20*for it is not you who speak, but the Spirit of your Father speaking through you.* 21*Brother will deliver up brother to death, and the father his child, and children will rise against parents and have them put to death;* 22*and you will be hated by all for my name's sake. But he who endures to the end will be saved.* 23*When they persecute you in one town, flee to the next; for truly, I say to you, you will not have gone through all the towns of Israel, before the Son of man comes.'*

Just as the apostles share in the work of Jesus, so the treatment which the apostles will receive will be the same as that which Jesus will receive: as he is to be delivered up to the Jewish council, so will they; as he is to be hated, so will they; as he is to be put to death, so will they. But as he will come again in triumph from heaven at the end of the age, so will they have their vindication.

At this point in the chapter, when the horizon is extended to the end of the world, we begin to see that it is not just the original twelve who are being addressed here, but all the apostles and evangelists whom the Lord will send, not only to Israel (though Israel is still chiefly in mind, v. 23) but to the Gentiles also (v. 18).

Verse 16a is parallel to Luke 10³; vv. 17–22 are from Mark 13⁹⁻¹³; v. 23 has no parallel in Mark or Luke. Thus, for the greater part of his material here, Matthew has reached forward to the last teaching of Jesus in Mark 13, and reproduced it; when he comes to it again in the normal course of his rewriting of Mark, he omits most of the verses he has used already and substitutes other sayings, in order to avoid repetition and duplication (see 24⁹⁻¹³).

The last teaching in Mark 13 is given in answer to the disciples' question about the time of the destruction of the temple; Jesus foretells all that will happen before he comes again, and one item in the prophecy is the preaching of the gospel to all nations (Mark 13¹⁰). It may have been this saying which caused Matthew to incorporate these verses of Mark at this point in his own Gospel.

16

The disciples are compared to *sheep*, and those who will not receive them to *wolves* (cf. 7¹⁵). In one of the Jewish apocalyptic works, the righteous in Israel are spoken of as sheep and lambs, and their enemies as beasts which prey upon them. The apostles are the representatives of the new Israel, and those who will not hear them are the enemies who will persecute them. In this situation they will need the wisdom of *serpents* (cf. Gen. 3¹, *the serpent was more subtle than any other wild creature that the Lord God had made*) but the innocence of *doves*. This may have been a proverbial saying, 'The dove which, from the view-point of natural science in ancient times, has no bile, was for the early Christians the symbol of all kinds of virtues' (*Lexicon*, p. 657). The apostles will need both subtlety and innocence in order to use the time of persecution for bearing testimony.

17

They will be handed over to the local Jewish courts which were attached to the synagogues, and beaten – cf. 2 Cor. 11²⁴ where Paul says: *Five times I have received at the hands of the Jews the forty lashes less one.*

18

They will also suffer at the hands of the Roman *governors*, and of the emperor and his titular *kings* (e.g. the Herods), in their obedience to Christ and because of their testimony to him.

19

But on these occasions they are not to be anxious and worried what they are to say: God will give them words. *Will be given to you* is a passive for the action of God, and means 'God will give you'.

20

The Holy Spirit is referred to as *the Spirit of your Father*, and the expression is unique here in the New Testament. For the close connexion between the Spirit and preaching, see e.g. Luke 24⁴⁶⁻⁴⁹, Acts 1⁸, 2⁴, 1 Cor. 12⁸, 1 Peter. 1¹².

21

Jesus has come to bring division, to initiate the last judgement (see below, vv. 34–36); and this division will go through the middle of families, so that brothers will betray brothers, parents their children, and children their parents. This breaking up of families was a traditional piece of Jewish teaching about the woes that would come before the end; cf. Mic. 7⁶, quoted below on p. 165.

22

The apostles will be hated by everyone because they are the representatives of Jesus. They must endure this persecution and hatred, waiting in hope for *the end* when Christ will return and save them from their enemies.

23

The mission is not to be held up by persecution: those who can escape from one town are to go on to the next (cf. *wise as serpents*, v. 16). The time which is left before the end comes is short, so they must move on from place to place while they can; and even then the Son of man will return before they have completed the mission to Israel. This saying, which is almost certainly an authentic saying of Jesus, expresses his belief that the end will come soon.

There is another example of Matthew's use of 'stitch-words' here: in v. 22 *end* is *telos* and in v. 23 *gone through* is *telesēte*.

10²⁴, ²⁵   THE MASTER AND HIS SERVANTS   Luke 6⁴⁰

²⁴'*A disciple is not above his teacher, nor a servant[a] above his master; *²⁵*it is enough for the disciple to be like his teacher, and the servant[a] like his master. If they have called the master of the house Be-el'zebul, how much more will they malign those of his household.*'

a Or slave

It has been pointed out recently that the future which is foretold in Mark 13, follows in many respects the same pattern as the Passion and resurrection of Jesus in Mark 14–16, and it has been suggested that Mark intended his readers to see in the sufferings of the Church a 'repetition' of the sufferings of Christ. Matthew has been making use of part of Mark 13 in which the sufferings of the disciples are foretold: he underlines in this paragraph the necessary likeness between Christ's treatment at the hands of unbelievers and theirs.

✠

The only parallel to these verses is Luke 6⁴⁰, *A disciple is not above his teacher, but every one when he is fully taught will be like his teacher*; and John 13¹⁶, *A servant is not greater than his master; nor is he who is sent greater than he who sent him* (cf. John 15²⁰). There was a Jewish proverb: 'It is enough for the servant to be like his master.'

24

A disciple (which here has the meaning 'pupil') *is not* greater than *his teacher*, and so is not exempt from any persecution or ill-treatment which his teacher receives.

25

The aim of the pupil is to be *like his teacher*, and therefore, if his teacher has been ill-treated, he will expect to be ill-treated also. This has already happened in the case of Jesus; the Pharisees had said, *He casts out demons by the prince of the demons* (9³⁴). One of the names of this *prince of demons* is *Beelzebul*. It may mean 'Lord of the house', and if so then there is a play on the word here (see 12²⁴ff.).

10²⁶⁻³³   JESUS TELLS HIS APOSTLES NOT   Luke 12²⁻⁹
                    TO BE AFRAID   Mark 4²², 8³⁸

²⁶'*So have no fear of them; for nothing is covered that will not be revealed, or hidden that will not be known.* ²⁷*What I tell you in the dark, utter in the light; and what you hear whispered, proclaim upon the housetops.* ²⁸*And do not fear those who kill the body but cannot kill the soul; rather fear him who can destroy both soul and body in hell.*ᵃ ²⁹*Are not two sparrows sold*

*for a penny? And not one of them will fall to the ground without your Father's will.*³⁰*But even the hairs of your head are all numbered.* ³¹*Fear not, therefore; you are of more value than many sparrows.* ³²*So every one who acknowledges me before men, I also will acknowledge before my Father who is in heaven;* ³³*but whoever denies me before men, I also will deny before my Father who is in heaven.'*

a Greek *Gehenna*

Jesus has been warning the apostles that their lot will be like his, and the readers know that this will mean rejection and death. But they are not to be afraid, or to abandon their work; they are to remember that Jesus was vindicated by the Father in resurrection; and Jesus promises his apostles the safe-keeping of the Father and his own acknowledgement of them in heaven.

৩৩

Verse 26 is similar to a saying in Mark 4²², and v. 33 to Mark 8³⁸, but in neither case is the parallel close; apart from these verses this paragraph is completely non-Marcan. Luke, however, gives the whole of it with only slight variations (Luke 12²⁻⁹).

26f.
The command to *have no fear* is given three times in this paragraph (26, 28, 31). First, Jesus shows that the result of fear would be the abandoning of their work, which is to reveal and make known that thing which is at present a secret: the coming of the kingdom. God himself will reveal it to the world (*will not be revealed* means 'that God will not reveal'). The apostles are therefore not to fear persecution, because so long as they proclaim the kingdom they are doing God's will and are on his side.

28
Jesus goes on to give them reasons for not being afraid. Men can and will only kill *the body*; God can destroy *both soul and body in hell* (see 5²²). It is therefore more fearful to disobey God (who through Jesus is commanding them to preach the gospel) than to be put to death by persecutors.

29–31
Moreover, even *sparrows*, the cheapest living things that are sold for

food, are in the keeping of God, and cannot be destroyed against his will. Men are more valuable to God *than many sparrows*; therefore men are undoubtedly in God's keeping, and God records in his memory every detail of their lives.

32f.

Finally, Jesus, who is sending them out in their mission *to acknowledge* him as Messiah *before men*, will himself *acknowledge* them as his before the Father at the last judgement if they fulfil his command to preach the gospel; whereas if they disobey his command in fear of men, and deny him as Messiah, he will deny that they are his before the Father at the judgement; cf. *I never knew you; depart from me, you evil-doers* (7²³), and *Truly, I say to you, I do not know you* (25¹²).

before men may mean 'in earthly lawcourts'; *before my Father*, 'in the heavenly court where God is the judge'.

deny (*arneisthai*) is used again in this Gospel only of Peter's denial of Jesus, 26⁷⁰, ⁷², and see note on 26⁶⁹ff..

10³⁴⁻³⁹	JESUS	Luke 12⁵¹⁻⁵³,
	THE BRINGER OF DIVISION	14²⁶f., 17³³
	AND DEATH	Mark 8³⁴f.

³⁴'*Do not think that I have come to bring peace on earth; I have not come to bring peace, but a sword.* ³⁵*For I have come to set a man against his father, and a daughter against her mother, and a daughter-in-law against her mother-in-law;* ³⁶*and a man's foes will be those of his own household.* ³⁷*He who loves father or mother more than me is not worthy of me; and he who loves son or daughter more than me is not worthy of me;* ³⁸*and he who does not take his cross and follow me is not worthy of me.* ³⁹*He who finds his life will lose it, and he who loses his life for my sake will find it.*'

The instructions to the apostles now return to the subject which was mentioned in v. 21: the divisions which will appear within families. Although the apostles are the bringers of the gospel and the *peace* of God, this, as we have been told, will be rejected by those who are *not worthy*, and they will persecute those who have brought it and those who have received it. So, although in one sense Jesus brings *peace*, in another sense he brings division, war, and death. To be *worthy* of the peace, and to receive it, a man must be willing to be separated from those whom he loves most, and even from *life* itself.

ॐ

There is a partial parallel to vv. 38f. in Mark 8$^{34f.}$, but Matthew has reproduced it more exactly in 16$^{24f.}$. The parallels in Luke (12$^{51ff.}$, 14$^{26f.}$, 17^{33}) are closer. The question of the sources here is again uncertain.

34

The popular Jewish belief was that when the Messiah came, he would bring *peace* to the earth, though suffering would increase in the days immediately before his arrival. Jesus contradicts these ideas: he has indeed come, but the woes and tribulations will still increase.

a sword: The word had been used metaphorically in the Old Testament of war and death, e.g. Jer. 15^2.

35f.

These verses refer back to a passage in Micah which had been understood by the Jews as a prophecy of the messianic age:

> *for the son treats the father with contempt,*
>   *the daughter rises up against her mother,*
> *the daughter-in-law against her mother-in-law;*
>   *a man's enemies are the men in his own house.*
>
> Mic. 7^6

Jesus is saying, *I have come* to inaugurate the woes before the messianic age, of which Micah had spoken.

37

Jesus and his apostles will cause divisions in families, so the disciple must be prepared to have a greater loyalty to Jesus than to any member of his own household. Willingness to surrender a good thing for a better is one part of the meaning of being *worthy* (see also note on 10^{11}).

38

Worthiness involves even more than this: it requires a willingness to give up honour and life; *to take his cross and follow me.* Crucifixion was the Roman method of executing slaves for criminal and political offences. This is the first mention of the *cross* in this Gospel; for the idea of following Jesus, see above, 8$^{18ff.}$.

39

This leads on to the general statement that to *find* one's *life* is to *lose it*, and to *lose* one's *life* in obedience to Jesus is to *find it*. That is, those who establish themselves in the world in this age will be condemned at the judgement; those who have been killed in the course of the mission will be rewarded by God in the age to come.

IO^{40-42}	THE APOSTLES ARE	Mark $9^{37, 41}$
	REPRESENTATIVES OF JESUS	Luke 10^{16}
	AND OF THE FATHER	

⁴⁰*'He who receives you receives me, and he who receives me receives him who sent me.* ⁴¹*He who receives a prophet because he is a prophet shall receive a prophet's reward, and he who receives a righteous man because he is a righteous man shall receive a righteous man's reward.* ⁴²*And whoever gives to one of these little ones even a cup of cold water because he is a disciple, truly, I say to you, he shall not lose his reward.'*

The previous paragraph finished on the note of promise and reward: *he who loses his life for my sake will find it* (v. 39). The chapter as a whole ends with further promises of rewards. Whereas those who *will not receive* the apostles will be condemned *on the day of judgement* (vv. 14ff.), those who receive them will receive Christ and the Father who sent him, and will have their rewards from God in the age to come.

৵৩

For vv. 40 and 42, cf. Mark $9^{37, 41}$ and Luke 9^{48}; v. 41 has no parallel elsewhere.

The paragraph is made up of separate sayings, which have been placed side by side because of words or phrases which are common to them: i.e. *receive, reward, because he is, lose.*

40

To receive an apostle is to give him *food* (cf. v. 10) and to *listen to* his *words* (v. 14); and as the apostles are the representatives of Jesus, to receive them is to receive him; cf. the final parable in this Gospel, and the declaration of Jesus in it: *as you did it to one of the least of these my brethren, you did it to me* (25^{31}ff.).

41f.

Those who receive a *prophet* or a *righteous man*, and listen to him and obey his words, partake of his work, and so share the same reward as that which God will give to him (cf. 2 John^{10}ff. for the same idea, in a different context). *Prophets and righteous men* are mentioned together in 13^{17} – but there the reference is to those who lived before Jesus and *longed to see what you see* – and in 23^{29}; Christian *prophets* are foretold in 23^{34}, and it is these who are referred to here.

42

The *little ones* are here the *disciples*: Cf. *one of the least of these my brethren* (25^{40}), and 11^{25}, 18^{3}ff., and the notes thereon.

Matthew 11-12

The Unbelief of Israel

Matthew's procedure is to sort his material into two kinds, sayings and stories, and to arrange the sayings in speeches on a theme, the stories in groups which divide the speeches from one another; and he turns from speech to narrative with one of his formulas. We have had the second speech in 10^{5b-42}; we shall have the formula for the second time in 11^1; and after that we expect a narrative section, until the next speech begins.

The next speech, in fact, will be in Chapter 13 (the formula for its ending is at 13^{53}), so the section which we have to look at now is Chapters 11 and 12. There are some stories of the deeds of Jesus here: e.g. the restoring of the withered hand ($12^{9ff.}$) and the healing of a demoniac (12^{22}); but these are the only miracles in these chapters. The greater part of this section is taken up with what Jesus said, rather than with what he did. So what we have here is a departure from Matthew's normal procedure – alternate sections of words and deeds.

We shall see the reason for this, if we look first at the material which Matthew has grouped together in this section.

It begins with the question of John the Baptist, *Are you he who is to come, or shall we look for another?* and the answer of Jesus which directs John to his deeds, and ends *Blessed is he who takes no offence at me.* So the section begins with the problem of faith and unbelief. Then Jesus asks the crowd about John, and he says that John is Elijah who was expected to return from heaven, to make ready for the Messiah. But John and Jesus have both been rejected by this generation. So Jesus warns the cities where he has done most of his miracles of the judgement that is coming; he thanks the Father who has hidden the meaning of the miracles from some, but has revealed it to others; and he invites all those who are oppressed to come to him. Then come two stories of argument and conflict with the Pharisees on the sabbath, at the end of which they plan a way to destroy him. Jesus withdraws and is followed by many, and Matthew here quotes a prophecy of Isaiah which twice mentions the Gentiles as the recipients of God's mercy. But the Pharisees return, saying that

Jesus is in league with Beelzebul; and Jesus says that this is an unforgivable sin, and he denounces them as evil in the strongest terms. They ask for a miracle to authenticate the words of Jesus, but Jesus refuses: he calls them *an evil and adulterous generation*, who will be condemned at the last judgement by the people of Nineveh and by the Queen of Sheba, because of their impenitence. They will become worse than they were. They are no longer his brethren, because they do not do the will of his Father.

The theme which runs through this section is faith and unbelief; and Matthew has chosen his material so as to bring it out. This is why he begins with John's question, *Are you he who is to come?* and Jesus' answer . . . *Blessed is he who takes no offence at me.* As we shall see when we come to the text in detail, each paragraph is related to the theme, faith or unbelief, blessedness or offence.

The matters of faith which are mentioned here are that Jesus is the Christ (11^2) who has come after Elijah (11^{14}); he is the Son of man (11^{19}, $12^{8, 32, 40}$), the servant of the Lord (12^{18}), the Son of David (12^{23}), the one on whom the Spirit of God rests ($12^{18, 28, 32}$), whose miracles are signs of the coming kingdom ($11^{20ff.}$, 12^{28}). These things God has *hidden* from those who do not believe, who are spoken of as *this generation* (11^{16}, $12^{39, 41f., 45}$), *the wise and understanding* (11^{25}), the *scribes* and *Pharisees* ($12^{2, 14, 24, 38}$), Jesus' *mother and his brothers* (12^{46}). On the other hand, God has *revealed* these things to *the poor* (11^5), to those who take *no offence at him* (11^6), to those *who have ears to hear* (11^{15}), to *babes* (11^{25}), to those to whom he *chooses to reveal* them (11^{27}), who *labour and are heavy-laden* (11^{28}), the *Gentiles* ($12^{18, 21}$), *his disciples* (12^{49}), *whoever does the will of* the *Father* (12^{50}).

This section is therefore a turning-point in the Gospel. The kingdom has been announced to Israel by John the Baptist (Chapter 3), and by the words (Chapters 5–7) and deeds (Chapters 8–9) of Jesus and of his apostles (Chapter 10); but Israel rejects it, as we begin to see in this section, because of unbelief; Israel takes offence at Jesus. And because they reject the gospel, the way is now beginning to open up for salvation to be preached to the *Gentiles*; so that Isaiah's prophecy will be fulfilled in Jesus: *he shall proclaim justice to the Gentiles . . . in his name will the Gentiles hope* ($12^{18, 21}$). In this way the problem of witnessing to the Gentiles which was raised in Chapter 10 is beginning to be answered. (For a similar understanding of the relationship

between Israel and the Gentiles with regard to the gospel, see Rom·
9–11.)

If we are right in thinking that it was Matthew's intention in this
section to show how Israel rejected the gospel, and the consequences
of that rejection, then we may be able to see why he departed from
his usual procedure, and, instead of placing here a section of the
deeds of Jesus, why he has given us a section which is very largely
the words of Jesus. It may be that Matthew found that it was not
possible, by stories of the deeds of Jesus alone, to bring out the point
which he wanted to make here. The section had to contain material
which included discussion, argument, and denunciation, in order to
bring out the teaching about the unbelief of Israel.

Mark contained little of this kind of material, so Matthew had to
turn elsewhere for it. Chapter 11 is entirely non-Marcan; in 12¹⁻³²
Matthew was able to make use of stories of conflict and controversy
from Mark, and in 12⁴⁶ff. the Marcan story of the mother and brothers
of Jesus. Thus whereas Matthew's narrative sections are usually
largely Marcan, this one is not. Matthew has used what he thought
appropriate from Mark, but he has had to go to other sources for the
greater part of his material here.

11¹   THE TRANSITION FORMULA

11 *And when Jesus had finished instructing his twelve disciples, he went
on from there to teach and preach in their cities.*

This second use of the formula, which marks the end of a teaching
section and the beginning of a narrative section, looks back to
Chapter 10 as the instructing of the *twelve disciples*, and looks forward
to Jesus' continuation of his teaching and preaching in Galilee.

ॐ

Matthew records the sending out of the twelve in 10⁵, but he never
records their return to Jesus (contrast Mark 6³⁰, *the apostles returned to*

Jesus, and told him all that they had done and taught, and see note on 14¹²). *His disciples* are mentioned with Jesus again at 12¹.

went on from there (metebē ekeithen) is a phrase which Matthew uses again (12⁹, 15²⁹; cf. 8³⁴, 17²⁰ for Matthew's use of the verb), and is an example and mark of his editorial style. Matthew does not mean to say that Jesus transferred his work from Israel to the Gentiles yet (though he may be suggesting that he will), because he says that Jesus went *to teach and preach in their* (i.e. the Jews') *cities* (see 4²³ and the note on *their synagogues*). But notice that Matthew says *to teach and preach*, and not also *to heal* (contrast 4²³, 9³⁵): acts of healing, though they do still take place (12⁹ff., ²²ff. also 15²¹ff., ²⁹ff., 17¹⁴ff., 20²⁹ff., 21¹⁴), become less frequent from now on; cf. the comment after the visit of Jesus to his own country; *he did not do many mighty works there, because of their unbelief* (13⁵⁸). Jesus is beginning to withdraw his miraculous power from Israel, because their unbelief is becoming apparent.

11²⁻⁶   JOHN'S QUESTION AND   Luke 7¹⁸⁻²³
                         JESUS' ANSWER

²*Now when John heard in prison about the deeds of the Christ, he sent word by his disciples* ³*and said to him, 'Are you he who is to come, or shall we look for another?'* ⁴*And Jesus answered them, 'Go and tell John what you hear and see:* ⁵*the blind receive their sight and the lame walk, lepers are cleansed and the deaf hear, and the dead are raised up, and the poor have good news preached to them.* ⁶*And blessed is he who takes no offence at me.'*

John the Baptist's arrest had been mentioned in 4¹², and nothing further had been said about him since then, though his disciples approached Jesus on the question of fasting (9¹⁴). Now in *prison*, John hears about *the deeds of the Christ*, i.e. the miracles in Chapters 8 and 9, and he sends disciples to ask Jesus whether he is the one *who is to come*. Jesus' answer tells John to consider what Jesus is doing, and to see the fulfilment of prophecy in his miracles and his preaching.

Some commentators have built up out of this paragraph a fascinating picture of the state of John's mind as he lay in prison: how he began to doubt whether Jesus was the Messiah, and even perhaps to wonder whether he himself was the messenger sent to prepare his

way. Psychological reconstructions are uncertain at any time when we
have only Gospel material out of which to build them, because Gospel
material was not concerned with such matters (see Introduction, pp.
9f.); and in this particular instance, the whole case for the Baptist's
doubts depends on the historicity of Matthew 3$^{14ff.}$, because it is only
there in the Synoptic Gospels that John is said to have identified
Jesus as the one who was to be greater than himself. But Matthew
3$^{14ff.}$ is late material, possibly going no further back than the Evangelist himself. If the present passage comes from a source which did
not know 3$^{14ff.}$, then it could be that the meaning of John's question
here is that it was not until he was in prison, and had heard of the
miracles of Jesus, that he began to believe that Jesus was the Christ.
'The message may mark the beginning of faith, not of doubt'
(B. T. D. Smith).

We can be fairly certain that Matthew was not wanting to tell us
about John, but about Jesus, his works, and the possibility of faith or
offence. If Matthew had wanted to tell us about John, we should have
expected to hear from him what happened when the messengers
returned to the Baptist: did he believe, or did he go on doubting?
But there is not a word on this.

❧

The Lucan account (Luke 7$^{18ff.}$) is fuller at the beginning, but part of that
at least is Lucan editorial material; the rest of the account agrees almost
word for word with Matthew in the Greek.

2
Josephus says that John was imprisoned by Herod in the fortress of
Machaerus on the east side of the Dead Sea (*Antiquities*, XVIII, 5, 2).
See 14$^{3-12}$ for the reason for John's arrest.

the deeds of the Christ: Although *Christ* was eventually used as a proper
name, without the definite article, originally it was a title, and required the article, and this is how it is normally used in this Gospel. See
1^{17}, 2^4, 16$^{16,\ 20}$, 22^{42}, 23^{10}, 24$^{5,\ 23}$, 26^{63}; contrast 26^{68}.

3
he who is to come (*ho erchomenos*) may have been a Christian title for the
Messiah (3^{11}, 21^9, 23^{39}, etc.) though it may also go back to earlier times,
and derive from Ps. 118^{26}: *Blessed be he who enters* (Gk *ho erchomenos*) *in
the name of the Lord!*

or shall we look for another? (prosdokōmen): the word means 'wait for', *expect,* as in 24^{50}.

4

Jesus does not say directly and authoritatively 'I am the Christ', but invites John to consider what his messengers can *see and hear,* that is, the deeds and words of Jesus; these are the only way to come to faith. Those who do not believe are therefore *blind* and *deaf,* unable to interpret the signs which Jesus is giving; cf. 13^{16}, where Jesus says to his disciples *Blessed are your eyes, for they see, and your ears, for they hear.*

5

The words of Jesus recall three passages in Isaiah:

> In that day the deaf shall hear
>   the words of a book,
> and out of their gloom and darkness
>   the eyes of the blind shall see.
> The meek shall obtain fresh joy in the Lord
>   and the poor among men shall exult in the Holy One of Israel.
>
> (Isa. $29^{18f.}$)

> Then the eyes of the blind shall be opened,
>   and the ears of the deaf unstopped;
> then shall the lame man leap like a hart,
>   and the tongue of the dumb sing for joy.
>
> (Isa. $35^{5f.}$, see also on $9^{27ff.}$)

> The Spirit of the Lord God is upon me,
>   because the Lord has anointed me
> to bring good tidings to the poor (margin);
>   he has sent me to bind up the broken-hearted,
> to proclaim liberty to the captives (margin)
>   and the opening of the eyes, to those who are bound (Greek, *blind*);
>
> (Isa. $61^{1f.}$)

The miracles of healing in Chapters 8 and 9 are summarized in this list: *the blind,* $9^{27ff.}$; *the lame,* $8^{5ff.}$, $9^{1ff.}$; *the lepers,* $8^{1ff.}$; *the deaf,* $9^{32ff.}$ (*kōphos,* deaf or dumb, in both passages); *the dead,* $9^{18ff.}$. The climax of the list, however, is *the poor have good news preached to them,* an echo of Isa. 61^1. The miracles are signs of the preaching of the kingdom. For *the poor* see also 5^3.

6

blessed is he who takes no offence at me: To take offence means to sin (the word was translated *cause to sin* in $5^{29f.}$). Jesus does cause the Pharisees to sin (see below, 12²⁴, ³¹ff.); their sin is their unbelief in him, and they *will not be forgiven* in the judgement. Those who believe in him will be forgiven, and enter the kingdom: they are the *blessed* (cf. 5³ff·).

These vv. 2–6 are therefore a fitting introduction to this section (Chapters 11 and 12): they introduce the question, Faith or Offence? Blessedness or Condemnation? Jesus has come to bring division, and to set men against one another (10³⁴ff.). He himself, by his words and his deeds, is the cause of division. He divides men into believers and unbelievers, those who *have ears to hear* and those who are deaf, *the disciples* and *this generation*.

| 11⁷⁻¹⁵ | WHO IS | Luke 7²⁴⁻²⁸, 16¹⁶ |
| | JOHN THE BAPTIST? | |

⁷*As they went away, Jesus began to speak to the crowds concerning John: 'What did you go out into the wilderness to behold? A reed shaken by the wind?* ⁸*Why then did you go out? To see a man*ᵃ *clothed in soft raiment? Behold, those who wear soft raiment are in kings' houses.* ⁹*Why then did you go out? To see a prophet?*ᵇ *Yes, I tell you, and more than a prophet.* ¹⁰*This is he of whom it is written,*

> *"Behold, I send my messenger before thy face,*
> *who shall prepare thy way before thee."*

¹¹*Truly, I say to you, among those born of women there has risen no one greater than John the Baptist; yet he who is least in the kingdom of heaven is greater than he.* ¹²*From the days of John the Baptist until now the kingdom of heaven has suffered violence,*ᶜ *and men of violence take it by force.* ¹³*For all the prophets and the law prophesied until John;* ¹⁴*and if you are willing to accept it, he is Eli'jah who is to come.* ¹⁵*He who has ears to hear,*ᵈ *let him hear.'*

a Or *What then did you go out to see? A man . . .*
b Other ancient authorities read *What then did you go out to see? A prophet?*
c Or *has been coming violently*
d Other ancient authorities omit *to hear*

As John's disciples return with the answer of Jesus, he asks the crowds about John. *Jerusalem and all Judea and all the region about the Jordan* had gone out into the wilderness to him (3⁵); Jesus asks the crowds why they went. Who is this man who is now in Herod's prison? He is a prophet, and more than a prophet; he is the messenger of whom Malachi had spoken, sent to prepare the Messiah's way; he is the greatest man in this age. But he bears witness to one who is greater than anyone in this age, that is, to the Messiah. He marks the end of this age, and the beginning of the kingdom; in him, prophecy begins to be fulfilled.

ುಞ

Verses 7–11 are almost identical with Luke 7²⁴⁻²⁸; vv. 12, 13 are similar to Luke 16¹⁶; vv. 14, 15 have no parallel in Luke, but the identification of John as Elijah is made in Mark 9¹³ (which Matthew reproduces at 17¹²ff.).

7

John has preached in *the wilderness*, fulfilling the prophecy, *The voice of one crying in the wilderness* (Isa. 40³ in the Greek translation, quoted at 3³). People had gone out to him; why? Not only to see a reed shaken by the wind: that is, both the rushes in the Jordan valley which bend in the wind, and, figuratively, a weak and vacillating person, carried away by every wind of opinion; this could not be said of John, who was imprisoned for his denunciation of Herod's marriage (14³ᶠ.).

8

Neither would people have gone into the wilderness to see *a man clothed in soft raiment*, i.e. a courtier. Courtiers are found in palaces; John is now in prison. Moreover, we know that John's clothing was the *hair* and *leather* of the dress of a prophet (3⁴, 2 Kings 1⁸, Zech. 13⁴).

9

They went to see a *prophet*, that is, one who was able to speak the word of God. The Jews believed that the Holy Spirit ceased to be present in Israel when Haggai, Zechariah, and Malachi, the last of the prophets, died. Another prophet would therefore be a great occasion, marking a new epoch in Israel's history. Moreover, Jesus says that John is *more than a prophet* because he is the prophet in whom prophecy begins to be fulfilled, the messenger who comes before the Messiah and prepares his way.

10

The quotation is from Mal. 3^1, and it is quoted in Mark 1^2; Matthew had omitted it at the corresponding place in his Gospel, 3^3. The wording of the quotation in all the Synoptic Gospels differs from the Hebrew and the Greek of Malachi, which have *before my face, before me*: the Lord himself will come to his temple suddenly. There is, however, a saying in Exodus 23^{20}, *Behold, I send an angel* (the Greek can mean 'messenger') *before you* . . . , and there is some evidence that these two verses had been brought together in pre-Christian times.

11

John is therefore more than a prophet; he fulfils as well as prophesies. *among those born of women* is a Hebraic expression meaning 'among mortal men'; *there has arisen* is another Hebraic expression, meaning 'there has appeared in the world' (it is used again at 24$^{11,\ 24}$). No one has appeared in the world with a greater function than that of John, namely, to proclaim the coming of the Messiah.

yet he who is least in the kingdom of heaven is greater than he: This may mean that 'anyone, however humble and obscure, who shall be admitted into the kingdom, will be greater then than John is now' (McNeile); cf. the idea of entry into the kingdom as rebirth, Matthew 19^{28}, John 1^{13}, 3$^{3,\ 5}$, I Pet. 2^2. On the other hand, *he who is least in the kingdom of heaven* may refer to Jesus, who came as the servant (see 20^{28}). In this case, the saying means that Jesus is greater than John; and this would agree with the Baptist's witness: *he who is coming after me is mightier than I* (3^{11}).

12

This verse has been interpreted in a number of different ways. It is usually agreed that Luke's version is secondary: *The law and the prophets were until John; since then the good news of the kingdom of God is preached, and everyone enters into it violently* (Luke 16^{16}). Matthew's *has suffered violence* may mean *has suffered violence* through the opposition of evil spirits, or through the opposition of Herod, the Pharisees etc; or it may mean 'is sought with burning zeal'; and again, as in R.S.V. margin, it may be translated *has been coming violently* i.e. 'makes its way with triumphant force'.

men of violence take it by force may refer to the tax collectors, etc., who are entering the kingdom by repentance; or to the Zealots who are trying to bring in the kingdom by using force against the Romans; or to the Jews who are persecuting the Christians. The word here translated *take it by force* (*harpazousin*) is used again at 12^{29}, 13^{19} of seizing one's enemy's goods; if this gives us any guidance to the interpretation which Matthew gave to the saying here, then the reference will be to Herod who has imprisoned John, and to the Pharisees who are opposing Jesus.

13

The time before John was the time of prophecy and preparation: notice that Matthew writes *the prophets and the law*, and not, as usual, *the law and the prophets* (5[17], 7[12]), because he is thinking of the Old Testament as prophetic and pointing forward to Jesus.

14

Here, as in 17[13], Jesus identifies the Baptist with Elijah; see also 3[4] and Mal. 4[5].

15

The disciples, and the readers of the Gospel, have been given *ears to hear* by God (cf. 13[16]); they are commanded to use their gift of understanding.

11[16-19]   THIS GENERATION HAS NOT   Luke 7[31-35]
                              REPENTED

[16]'But to what shall I compare this generation? It is like children sitting in the market places and calling to their playmates,
          [17]"We piped to you, and you did not dance;
          we wailed, and you did not mourn."
[18]For John came neither eating nor drinking, and they say, "He has a demon"; [19]the Son of man came eating and drinking, and they say, "Behold, a glutton and a drunkard, a friend of tax collectors and sinners!" Yet wisdom is justified by her deeds.'[a]

a Other ancient authorities read *children* (Luke 7[35])

John the Baptist and Jesus have both called for repentance; but the Jews have not obeyed them. The Jews are like bad-tempered, quarrelsome children, satisfied with nothing: John lived among them as an ascetic and they called him a demoniac; Jesus was no ascetic, so they called him licentious and irreligious. Yet although this generation has found fault with John and with Jesus, God himself has not done so: the divine wisdom, who sent both John and Jesus is guiltless, and her deeds justify her – they will have their effect; there are those who do not disobey the call for repentance.

བོབ

These verses are almost exactly the same as Luke 7³¹⁻³⁵. It has been suggested that the difference between Matthew and Luke in the last line (Matthew, *deeds*; Luke, *children*) is due to independent translation of a common Aramaic source at this point. If that were the case, however, it would be difficult to account for the similarity of the Greek in the rest of the paragraph. It may be that Luke has changed the word, to bring out the meaning.

16

In the previous verse, Jesus invited those with *ears to hear*, to hear what he is saying, namely, that the age of fulfilment has begun, because Elijah has come in John the Baptist. But *this generation* has not heard Jesus or John, and has not responded to their preaching. *this generation* is a phrase which is used frequently in the Gospels – e.g. 12³⁹, ⁴¹f., ⁴⁵, 16⁴, 17¹⁷, 23³⁶, 24³⁴. It is usually found in contexts which show the failure of the Jews to believe and obey God. It can mean 'race, nation' or 'generation, contemporaries', and the latter is usually thought to be the sense in which it is used in the Gospels.

The formula *to what shall I compare* . . . ? *It is like* . . . is a translation of an Aramaic formula used in the introduction of rabbinic parables, and it means 'it is the case with . . . as with . . .'

17

Piping and dancing was a wedding-game; wailing and mourning was a funeral game. Probably the former was the boys' game, the latter the girls' game.

18f.

The two complaints in v. 17 are taken in the reverse order in vv. 18f.: the mourning is compared with John's fasting: the festivities with Jesus' eating and drinking.

18

John came neither eating nor drinking: Cf. 3⁴ *his food was locusts and wild honey,* i.e. the cheapest food possible. Jesus says of John to the Jewish leaders, later in this Gospel, *you did not believe him* (21³²). They said of John, as they also said of Jesus, *He has a demon.*

19

the Son of man is used here in the same way as in 8²⁰ and 9⁶, and may mean 'this man', 'I'.

a glutton and a drunkard: Cf. 9¹⁴ff. for Jesus' disciples not observing the Jewish fasts.

a friend of tax collectors and sinners: Cf. 9¹⁰ff. for Jesus' fellowship with those who are sick.

Yet wisdom is justified by her deeds: Wisdom is here the wisdom of God, in fact God himself, who has sent John and Jesus, and will prove himself righteous: there will be those who will accept the preaching of repentance – i.e. the Gentiles; see below, 12¹⁸, ²¹.

11²⁰⁻²⁴   JESUS WARNS THE CITIES   Luke 10¹³⁻¹⁵
                WHICH DID NOT REPENT

²⁰*Then he began to upbraid the cities where most of his mighty works had been done, because they did not repent.* ²¹*'Woe to you, Chora'zin! woe to you, Beth-sa'ida! for if the mighty works done in you had been done in Tyre and Sidon, they would have repented long ago in sackcloth and ashes.* ²²*But I tell you, it shall be more tolerable on the day of judgement for Tyre and Sidon than for you.* ²³*And you, Caper'na-um, will you be exalted to heaven? You shall be brought down to Hades. For if the mighty works done in you had been done in Sodom, it would have remained until this day.* ²⁴*But I tell you that it shall be more tolerable on the day of judgement for the land of Sodom than for you.'*

When Jesus sent the twelve to Israel, he told them to warn the towns which did not repent of the coming judgement, when *it shall be more tolerable . . . for the land of Sodom and Gomorrah* than for them (10¹⁴f.). What he had commanded the twelve to do, he now does himself: he reproaches the cities in which he had done most of his miracles, because they did not respond to the miracles with repentance, and he warns them of the severity of the judgement which is coming. The miracles were evidence that the kingdom was coming, and so the response to the miracles should have been the same as the response which is called for by the preaching of the kingdom, *Repent, for the kingdom of heaven is at hand* (3^2, 4^{17}). The judgement of Chorazin, Bethsaida, and Capernaum, the cities which are specified as the scene of Jesus' work, will be worse than the judgement of Tyre, of Sidon, even of Sodom, cities which had been denounced for their wickedness in the Old Testament, because these cities had not seen the miracles of Jesus; if they had, they would have repented.

❧

Verses 21, 22, 23 are almost exactly the same as Luke 10^{13-15}; in Luke they are part of the address to the seventy disciples and they follow the command to warn the impenitent cities of their judgement. The remaining verses of this paragraph have no parallel in the other Gospels.

20

In vv. 18f. Jesus said that *this generation* rejected John as a demoniac and himself as *a glutton and a drunkard*; this is what is meant by to take offence at him. The alternative is to see in the miracles of Jesus *the deeds of the Christ*, the signs that he is *he who is to come* (11^{2}ff.). To him who does so, Jesus says *Blessed is he*; but to the others he says *Woe to you*; contrast the Beatitudes, 5^{3}f. with the Woes, 23^{13}ff.. The cities in which Jesus has done his miracles have not repented, that is, accepted the miracles as signs of the coming kingdom, and turned away from pride to God. The word which is translated *mighty works* three times in this paragraph (*dynamis*) means literally 'powers' or 'acts of power'; cf. 7^{22}, $13^{54, 58}$, 14^2.

21

Woe to you is a formula which Matthew uses frequently (e.g. 23^{13}ff.), and it gives warning of the judgement of God which is coming at the end of this age; cf. Rev. 8^{13}, *Woe, woe, woe to those who dwell on the earth*; and, after the description of a plague of locusts, Rev. 9^{12}, *The first woe has passed; behold, two woes are still to come*.

Chorazin is only mentioned here (and in the Lucan parallel) in the Bible, and *Bethsaida* is not mentioned elsewhere in Matthew, but twice in Mark (Mark 6^{45}, 8^{22}), Luke, and John. For their possible sites see map, p. 8.

Tyre and Sidon were cities of the Philistines in Old Testament times, and the prophets had denounced their wickedness and foretold their doom; e.g. *What are you to me, O Tyre and Sidon, and all the regions of Philistia? ... I will requite your deed upon your own head swiftly and speedily* (Joel 3⁴).

sackcloth and ashes were signs of mourning and repentance; cf. Jonah 3⁶ *Then tidings reached the king of Nineveh, and he arose from his throne, removed his robe, and covered himself with sackcloth, and sat in ashes;* this incident is referred to in the next chapter, 12⁴¹.

22

For the formula *it shall be more tolerable on the day of judgement for ...* cf. 10¹⁵.

23

Capernaum was mentioned as the home of Jesus at 4¹³; see also 8⁵, 9¹, 17²⁴.

will you be exalted to Heaven? You shall be brought down to Hades is an echo of Isaiah's prophecy on Babylon:

> You said in your heart,
> I will ascend to heaven;
> above the stars of God
>   I will set my throne on high;
> I will sit on the mount of assembly in the far north;
> I will ascend above the heights of the clouds,
>   I will make myself like the Most High.
> But you are brought down to Sheol,
>   to the depths of the Pit.

(Isa. 14¹³ff.)

Capernaum's impenitence comes from pride, which tries to make itself like God, and is therefore unable to humble itself before God when he reveals himself as king. Jesus' miracles are signs of God's coming reign, but Capernaum, like Babylon, is too proud to repent; because it has not humbled itself in penitence, it will be humiliated by God in judgement. For this comparison between Capernaum and Babylon, compare Chapter 2, in which Herod is compared with Pharaoh, and Judea with Egypt. Those who should have been believers have in fact followed the ways of the proud and impenitent in the Old Testament. *Sodom* was another city which was proverbial for its wickedness in the Old Testament (see 10¹⁵); it was destroyed because God did not find *ten righteous* in it; but if the miracles of Jesus which have been done in Capernaum had been done in Sodom, the Sodomites would have repented, and God would not have destroyed their city.

24

This verse repeats the formula in v. 22 and 10²⁵.

       THE FATHER HIDES   Luke 10²¹, ²²
                    AND REVEALS

²⁵*At that time Jesus declared, 'I thank thee, Father, Lord of heaven and earth, that thou hast hidden these things from the wise and understanding and revealed them to babes;* ²⁶*yea, Father, for such was thy gracious will.*ᵃ ²⁷*All things have been delivered to me by my Father; and no one knows the Son except the Father, and no one knows the Father except the Son and any one to whom the Son chooses to reveal him.* ²⁸*Come to me, all who labour and are heavy-laden, and I will give you rest.* ²⁹*Take my yoke upon you, and learn from me; for I am gentle and lowly in heart, and you will find rest for your souls.* ³⁰*For my yoke is easy, and my burden is light.'*

    a *Or so it was well-pleasing before thee*

One of the themes in this section of the Gospel is the alternative, faith or unbelief. According to the biblical writers, this is the alternative before everyone, to believe in God or to disbelieve. But the biblical writers do not say that this choice is entirely in one's own hands; on the contrary, they say that to believe is a gift or blessing from God, and that to disbelieve is also the result of the action of God. For example, Paul says of God: *he has mercy upon whomever he wills, and he hardens the heart of whomever he wills* (Rom. 9¹⁸). In the same way, here in the Gospel the sayings of Jesus about the unbelief of *this generation* move back to the action of God, who hides the coming of the kingdom from some, and reveals it to others. Nevertheless, these actions of God are not capricious and unrelated to the lives of men: God hides the truth from *the wise and understanding*, that is, from those who in their arrogance and pride refuse to repent; and he reveals it to *babes*, that is, to the humble and lowly. This is the will of God, and Jesus gives thanks that it is so. He declares that he has been appointed by God as the revealer of God's law; and invites all those who are oppressed to believe in him, to learn his law, and to enter the kingdom;

he promises them that his law is not difficult, like the Law of the scribes and Pharisees, but easy to learn; it is the law of love.

෨෨

Verses 25–27 are parallel to Luke 10²¹f., with slight variations. Verses 28–30 have no parallel. The authenticity of the whole or part of this paragraph has been doubted; partly because of the use of the terms *the Father* and *the Son*, which is unusual in the words of Jesus; partly because the saying *I am gentle and lowly in heart* is unlikely in the mouth of Jesus himself. The passage reads more like a piece of Church writing based on a number of Old Testament quotations and put into the Lord's mouth (such as we have in the discourses in John's Gospel) than a tradition of Jesus' words spoken during the ministry.

25

At that time is a Matthean editorial link; he uses it again at 12¹, 14¹.

I thank thee, Father, Lord of heaven and earth recalls Ecclus 51¹, *I will thank thee Jehovah, O King*, the beginning of the prayer of Jesus ben Sirah, and Tobit 7¹⁸ the only other place in the Bible where *Lord of heaven and earth* is used.

thou hast hidden: See the quotation from Isa. 29¹⁴ below for this word; and see 13³⁵ for the idea of God 'hiding' his secrets from men. The meaning of *these things* is not clear, and suggests that Matthew himself did not compose this passage for this context; he probably intended it to refer to *the mighty works* in the previous paragraph.

the wise and understanding (*sophōn kai synetōn*): cf. *the wisdom of their wise men* (*sophōn*) *shall perish, and the discernment of their discerning men* (*synetōn*) *shall be hid* (Isa. 29¹⁴). The verse is quoted by Paul in 1 Cor. 1¹⁹.

and revealed them to babes: Later in this Gospel Jesus will say to Peter, *Flesh and blood has not revealed this* (that Jesus is the Christ) *to you, but my Father who is in heaven* (16¹⁷). *Babes* here means those who are not *wise and understanding*, like the Pharisees, but people like the tax collectors and sinners, who have received the preaching of Jesus, and become his disciples; in 10⁴² they were called *little ones;* see also 18¹ff., 19¹³ff..

26

such was thy gracious will is literally, as in the margin, *so it was well-pleasing before thee*, and it was a formula often used by the Jews in prayer, to avoid speaking directly of God's will.

27

The word which is here translated *have been delivered* (*paredothē*) is used of the handing over of tradition; and the meaning here may be that Jesus is the second Moses, to whom God has given the new Law; cf. Chapters 5–7.

The Father alone knows who Jesus is; to others, he is hidden and un-known, unless God reveals him; compare Jesus' words to Peter quoted in the note on v. 25 above. The Father is also unknown, and his will is not obeyed, except by the Son, and by those to whom the Son chooses to teach his law. The scribes and Pharisees, who think that they know God's law, are *blind guides* (23¹⁶).

28–30

The similarities between these sayings and the invitation of Jesus ben Sirah in Ecclus 51²³ff. are very close.

28

By those who *labour and are heavy-laden* is probably meant those who find the Law, as it was expounded by the scribes and Pharisees, too difficult to keep.

I will give you rest: The weekly sabbath rest was thought of as an anticipation of the final *rest* of the messianic age; see e.g. Hebrews 3⁷–4¹⁰, and compare the note on the genealogy, 1¹⁷. The same idea of rest from labour in the age to come is found in Rev. 14¹³ . . . *that they may rest from their labours*.

29

The idea of Jesus as the second Moses, the teacher of the new Law, is contained here in the expression *take my yoke upon you*. The rabbis spoke of *the yoke of the law*, and of the disciple as one who put his neck under this *yoke*.

I am gentle (*praüs*) *and lowly in heart:* The same word as that which is here translated *gentle* is translated *meek* in the Beatitudes (5⁵). Jesus himself is the pattern for his disciples; compare *he who is least in the king-dom of heaven* (11¹¹) which may refer to Jesus himself.

you will find rest for your souls is a quotation from Jer. 6¹⁶. The *yoke* or law of Jesus is not complicated, like the Law as it was expounded by the scribes and Pharisees, but is *summed up in this sentence, You shall love your neighbour as yourself* (Rom. 13⁹).

12 *At that time Jesus went through the grainfields on the sabbath; his disciples were hungry, and they began to pluck ears of grain and to eat.* [2]*But when Pharisees saw it, they said to him, 'Look, your disciples are doing what is not lawful to do on the sabbath.'* [3]*He said to them, 'Have you not read what David did, when he was hungry, and those who were with him:* [4]*how he entered the house of God and ate the bread of the Presence, which it was not lawful for him to eat nor for those who were with him, but only for the priests?* [5]*Or have you not read in the law how on the sabbath the priests in the temple profane the sabbath, and are guiltless?* [6]*I tell you, something greater than the temple is here.* [7]*And if you had known what this means, "I desire mercy, and not sacrifice," you would not have condemned the guiltless.* [8]*For the Son of man is lord of the sabbath.'*

The words of Jesus in 11^{25ff.} constitute a claim to authority as the teacher of God's law, and promise *rest* to those who come to him. These two themes, law and *rest* (or sabbath), carry on into this paragraph and into the paragraph which follows it. In both of them, the question is raised, What is lawful on the sabbath? The Pharisees taught that no work was to be done on the sabbath; but Jesus comes as the teacher of a law which *is easy*, and he therefore defends his disciples against the attacks of the Pharisees, and likewise his own practice of healing on the sabbath.

In the first paragraph, the disciples break the Law, according to the Pharisees, by plucking corn on the sabbath to satisfy their hunger. Jesus shows, first from the prophets, and then from the Law, that the Old Testament itself bears witness to his and the disciples' practice. We should recall here the principle which was laid down earlier in this Gospel, *Think not that I have come to abolish the law and the prophets; I have not come to abolish them but to fulfil them* (5¹⁷). Jesus shows how the new attitude to the sabbath fulfils both the story of David in the prophets, and the custom of the priests in the Law. Moreover, the word of God in Hosea, *I desire mercy and not sacrifice*, similarly points forward to a time when the Law will be fulfilled, and mercy will take the place of legalism; compare the words of Jesus to the scribes and

Pharisees: *you tithe mint and dill and cummin, and have neglected the weightier matters of the law, justice and mercy and faith* (23²³). The paragraph ends with the saying, *The Son of man is lord of the sabbath*, which Matthew may have understood to mean that Jesus is the true teacher of God's law on sabbath observance.

ഇ

Matthew has returned to Mark 2^{23ff.} for this paragraph and for the next – the last two of the five conflict-stories which form a group in Mark 2¹–3⁶. He has here reproduced almost the whole of Mark 2²³⁻²⁸, but he has omitted *when Abiathar was high priest*, which was inaccurate – it was *Ahimelech* not Abiathar (1 Sam. 21¹ff.) – and the saying *The sabbath was made for man, not man for the sabbath*, perhaps because he wanted to draw attention to the authority of Jesus as law-giver, rather than to the original purpose of the Law. Luke has also made both these omissions, and there are other minor agreements between Matthew and Luke against Mark in this paragraph. Matthew has also added in non-Marcan material, namely vv. 5–7; it is probably his own composition.

1

At that time is a Matthean editorial phrase, replacing Mark's 'And it came to pass'; cf. 11²⁵, 14¹. Matthew states explicitly, as Mark had not done, that *his disciples were hungry*, thus making more clear the parallel with David *when he was hungry, and those who were with him*, v. 3.

2

According to the scribes, all work was forbidden on the sabbath, including reaping.

3

The story of David and the *bread of the Presence* is in 1 Sam. 21¹⁻⁶. Matthew and his readers believed that Jesus was *the son of David* (1¹, etc.), and so the appeal to *what David did* would have deeper significance than the mere citing of texts.

4

the house of God was the sanctuary at Nob; but it is thought of here as an anticipation of the temple which Solomon built at Jerusalem, and which in turn foreshadowed and was replaced by the new temple which Jesus built (see 26⁶¹, 27⁴⁰).

the bread of the Presence: According to Lev. 24^{5ff.}, the high priest was to place twelve loaves on the golden altar each sabbath. Originally the idea may have been the offering of food to the god, which is found in other religions also; later it was thought of as an act of thanksgiving to God for his goodness to Israel. The regulation which forbade anyone except the priests to eat it is later than the time of David: in 1 Sam. 21 Ahimelech only requires that the men who eat it should be 'clean'.

he entered . . . and ate . . . : There is good evidence that the original text was 'he entered . . . and they ate . . .'

5
The story of David is in the prophets (i.e. the book of Samuel), but the same principle stands *in the law:* e.g. Lev. 24^8 commands the priests to change the bread on the sabbath. This is a breach of the sabbath law, and thus they *profane the sabbath*, but because they were commanded to do so, *they are guiltless. The temple* is more important than *the sabbath;* and laws concerning *the temple* take precedence over laws concerning *the sabbath.*

6
Jesus claims that *something greater than the temple is here:* God himself is beginning to rule in the world, and Jesus is his agent. Therefore laws concerning the sabbath are to give way in the face of the coming of *the Son of man*, v. 8. See also 12$^{41f.}$ for the formula *something greater than . . . is here.*

7
The disciples of Jesus are *guiltless* (the Greek word is plural), just as the priests are guiltless (v. 5); the disciples have followed the principle that the law of the kingdom takes precedence over the law of the sabbath. Matthew again quotes Hos. 6^6 (see above 9^{13}): the dispensation of *sacrifice* is to be replaced by the dispensation of *mercy* which is the fulfilment of *the law and the prophets* 7^{12}, 22$^{34ff.}$.

8
Another saying in which Jesus points to himself in the present as *the Son of man* (cf. 8^{20}, 9^6, 11^{19}). He has come and has brought release from the sabbath law. The disciples, plucking grain on the sabbath and eating it because they were hungry, have borne witness to this.

WHAT IS   Mark 3$^{1-6}$,
                  LAWFUL ON THE SABBATH?   Luke 14^{5}

⁹*And he went on from there, and entered their synagogue.* ¹⁰*And behold, there was a man with a withered hand. And they asked him, 'Is it lawful to heal on the sabbath?' so that they might accuse him.* ¹¹*He said to them, 'What man of you, if he has one sheep and it falls into a pit on the sabbath, will not lay hold of it and lift it out?* ¹²*Of how much more value is a man than a sheep! So it is lawful to do good on the sabbath.'* ¹³*Then he said to the man, 'Stretch out your hand.' And the man stretched it out, and it was restored, whole like the other.* ¹⁴*But the Pharisees went out and took counsel against him, how to destroy him.*

The controversy with the Pharisees on what is lawful on the sabbath continues in this paragraph. Jesus goes into a synagogue where there is a man with a withered hand, and the Pharisees ask Jesus whether it is lawful to heal on the sabbath, expecting him to say that it is, in order that they may have grounds for an accusation against him. Jesus answers with a counter-question: would they not rescue a sheep from a pit on the sabbath? A man is more valuable than a sheep; therefore it is lawful to do good on the sabbath. (We should recall here the saying from Hosea which was quoted in the previous paragraph, *I desire mercy. . . . To rescue a sheep, or to heal a man, is an act of mercy; and this is what God desires.) Jesus heals the man, and the Pharisees, having now a ground for accusing Jesus, go away from the synagogue to plan his destruction. This incident would probably have recalled in the minds of Matthew's readers a sign in the Old Testament: the prophet who came to Bethel, and foretold a son of David, Josiah, who would desecrate Bethel. The prophet gave as a sign of his prophecy the tearing down of the altar. The king stretched *out his hand* and said *Lay hold of him. And his hand, which he stretched out against him, dried up, so that he could not draw it back to himself.* Then the prophet prayed, *and the king's hand was restored to him, and became as it was before* (1 Kings 13$^{1ff.}$). The destruction of Bethel is used symbolically of the end of the synagogue and of the whole system which was represented by the synagogue; the final *son of David* has come and brought the old order to fulfilment.

ເວລ

Matthew is using the next paragraph in Mark (3^{1-6}); he has omitted the questions of Jesus in Mark $3^{4, 5a}$ and substituted the questions about the sheep, v. 11f., which are similar to Luke 14^5.

9

And he went on from there is another of Matthew's editorial phrases: cf. 11^1.

their synagogue: Matthew adds the word *their*; see note on 4^{23}.

10

In Mark, *they watched him, to see whether he would heal on the sabbath.* Matthew has changed this into a direct question, which uses again the word *lawful* from v. 4; and he will repeat *lawful* in v. 12. Thus the point of the paragraph for Matthew is what is lawful on the sabbath?

11

Question followed by counter-question was a usual method of disputation among the rabbis; cf. 21^{23}ff. for another example of it. But notice that it is the Evangelist who has introduced the first question (in v. 10) and the counter-question in this verse: he is conforming to rabbinic patterns.

For the use of a parable to elicit an answer which turns out to be a self-accusation, compare Nathan's parable of the lamb which he puts to David, 2 Sam. 12^1ff.

The word *one* should perhaps not be emphasized; it may have been used for the indefinite article 'a'. On the other hand, the argument may be that a man who possesses only *one* sheep will have greater concern for it – as in Nathan's parable, *The poor man had nothing but one little ewe lamb*.

12

For the formula, *of how much more value . . . ,* cf. 6^{26}, 10^{31}. *So it is lawful to do good on the sabbath* answers the question of the Pharisees in v. 10, and replaces Mark's question of Jesus to the Pharisees.

13

The words *stretch out* and the miracle of restoration echo 1 Kings 13^1ff.

14

Mark had a reference to *the Herodians*, but Matthew omits it here; he retains it at 22^{16} = Mark 12^{13}.

The Pharisees now begin to plot the destruction of Jesus, and this is an advance on their attitude to him in 9^{34} where they said that he was acting in the power of *the prince of demons*. Jesus had warned his disciples of persecution and death (10$^{26-39}$), and this now begins to close in upon him. Israel's rejection of Jesus is the theme of this section, and this verse marks an important stage in the process.

12$^{15-21}$ JESUS SEPARATES THE   Mark 3$^{7, 10, 12}$
                     CHURCH FROM ISRAEL

^{15}*Jesus, aware of this, withdrew from there. And many followed him, and he healed them all,* ^{16}*and ordered them not to make him known.* ^{17}*This was to fulfil what was spoken by the prophet Isaiah:*

> ^{18}'*Behold, my servant whom I have chosen,*
>   *my beloved with whom my soul is well pleased.*
> *I will put my Spirit upon him,*
>   *and he shall proclaim justice to the Gentiles.*
> ^{19}*He will not wrangle or cry aloud,*
>   *nor will any one hear his voice in the streets;*
> ^{20}*he will not break a bruised reed*
>   *or quench a smouldering wick,*
>   *till he brings justice to victory;*
> ^{21} *and in his name will the Gentiles hope.*'

Jesus leaves the synagogue because of the unbelief of the Pharisees and their decision to destroy him; and Matthew sees in this an anticipation or foreshadowing of the Church as the new Israel, which replaces the old. Many follow him, and he heals them – just as, in the Church, there will be many who follow his teaching, and are made new by his grace. But because this anticipates events which have not yet taken place, i.e. his death and resurrection, Jesus commands his followers not to make him known yet; and this fulfils the prophecy of Isaiah: Jesus is God's chosen servant, upon whom God's Spirit has come; he acts secretly and with mercy; and through him new life and hope will come to the Gentiles, because it is out of them that the new Israel will be formed.

ꭴꭴꭴ

In vv. 15, 16, Matthew has made a summary of Mark 3⁷⁻¹²: all the verbs in these two verses are from Mark 3⁷, ¹⁰, ¹²:

> *withdrew* is from Mark 3⁷: *Jesus withdrew with his disciples to the sea*
> *followed* is from Mark 3⁷: *and a great multitude from Galilee followed*
> *healed* is from Mark 3¹⁰: *for he had healed many*
> *ordered them not to make him known* is from Mark 3¹²: *he strictly ordered them not to make him known.*

Verse 17 is the formula for quoting an Old Testament prophecy; and vv. 18–21 are from Isa. 42¹⁻⁴.

15

Jesus . . . withdrew from there: Cf. the earlier 'withdrawals' of Jesus, 2¹³ff., ²²f., 4¹², each of which has been linked with an Old Testament quotation. The word is used again of Jesus leaving one district for another in 14¹³, 15²¹.

many followed him: For the use of *follow* in the sense 'be the disciple of', see 10³⁸ *he who does not take his cross and follow me is not worthy of me.*

and he healed them all: The Church is not simply those who 'follow' Jesus, and obey his teaching; it is also those who have received gifts from him. Healing may have been mentioned here with this figurative sense in mind; cf. note on 10⁸.

16

The third of the five commands to silence in Matthew (see above 8⁴, 9³⁰, and below 16²⁰, 17⁹). On this occasion, the silence which Jesus commands may have been thought of by Matthew as a fulfilment of the prophecy of the servant, which he is about to quote. The command may also point to the anticipatory nature of what is being said and done: the many who follow Jesus and are healed by him foreshadow the Church, but the Church has not yet been established by the new *covenant*; Jesus has not yet received *all authority*; and so his followers are not yet to *make disciples and teach* (26²⁸, 28¹⁸ff.).

17

See the note on 1²² where this quotation formula was used for the first time.

18–21

This is the longest Old Testament quotation in Matthew; and it has been shown that Matthew did not follow any one text of Isa. 42$^{1-4}$ (in Hebrew or in Greek) but drew upon several, according as they fitted into his purpose, which was to show the fulfilment of the prophecy in Jesus and his Church.

18

The first two lines of the quotation may have some connexion with the tradition of the *voice from heaven* at the baptism and transfiguration (3^{17}, 17^5). The third line, *I will put my Spirit upon him* (*ep' auton*) may have influenced Matthew to change Mark's account of the coming of the Spirit at the baptism, where he changes Mark's 'to him' to *on him* (*ep' auton* 3^{16}). For the Spirit at work in Jesus, see below vv. 28, 32. For proclamation *to the Gentiles* see 10^{18}, 24^{14}, 28^{19}.

19

The word which is translated *wrangle* (*erisei*) is not in the Greek version of Isa. 42^2, and Matthew may have chosen it because of its suitability for this context: the withdrawal of Jesus from controversy with the Pharisees, and the command to silence, vv. 15, 16.

21

Matthew has omitted two lines from Isa. 42^4, but retained the last line, because it fitted his purpose; and he uses the Greek translation, because it expressed best what Matthew believed the meaning of Isaiah to have been. The *Gentiles* will have *hope* through the preaching of the gospel by the disciples. For the same idea compare Eph. 2$^{11f.}$, *Remember that at one time you Gentiles ... were ... alienated from the commonwealth of Israel, and strangers to the covenants of promise, having no hope and without God in the world.*

12$^{22-32}$ THE PHARISEES BLASPHEME   Mark 3$^{22-30}$
              AGAINST THE SPIRIT   Luke 11$^{14-22}$, 12^{10}

22 *Then a blind and dumb demoniac was brought to him, and he healed him, so that the dumb man spoke and saw.* 23 *And all the people were amazed, and said, 'Can this be the Son of David?'* 24 *But when the Pharisees heard it they said, 'It is only by Be-el'zebul, the prince of demons, that this man casts out*

demons.' *25Knowing their thoughts, he said to them, 'Every kingdom divided against itself is laid waste, and no city or house divided against itself will stand; 26and if Satan casts out Satan, he is divided against himself; how then will his kingdom stand? 27And if I cast out demons by Be-el'zebul, by whom do your sons cast them out? Therefore they shall be your judges. 28But if it is by the Spirit of God that I cast out demons, then the kingdom of God has come upon you. 29Or how can one enter a strong man's house and plunder his goods, unless he first binds the strong man? Then indeed he may plunder his house. 30 He who is not with me is against me, and he who does not gather with me scatters. 31Therefore I tell you, every sin and blasphemy will be forgiven men, but the blasphemy against the Spirit will not be forgiven. 32And whoever says a word against the Son of man will be forgiven; but whoever speaks against the Holy Spirit will not be forgiven, either in this age or in the age to come.'*

The withdrawal of Jesus from the synagogue in the last paragraph was only an anticipation of the turning to the Gentiles which follows the crucifixion and resurrection; in this paragraph, the conflict between the old order and the new is renewed. The occasion is the exorcism of a blind and dumb man, which Matthew tells in the minimum number of words. The miracle causes a division: the crowds ask, Can this be the Son of David? But the Pharisees say that Jesus is only acting in the power of Beelzebul. The incident recalls the sayings of Jesus to the twelve in Chapter 10; he is being called Beelzebul, and he is bringing division into the house of Israel. Jesus' answer to the accusation of the Pharisees speaks of a divided kingdom, a divided city, and a divided house or household. Divisions are the signs of the end and destruction. If he is working in the power of Satan against Satan, by casting out demons, then Satan's rule is coming to an end, and the rule of God is beginning. And that is in fact the case: but Jesus is working in the power of God's Spirit, not of Satan; and his exorcisms are signs of the coming of the kingdom of God. The Pharisees should know that exorcism is done in the power of God, because their own pupils practise it: let them tell them that they work by Beelzebul.

There is another sense, however, in which these sayings about division may be understood. Jesus has brought division into Israel, so that some say 'Can this be the Son of David?' and others

'He is only doing it by Beelzebul'. The division in Israel is a sign that Israel's kingdom or city or house is coming to an end. Moreover the New Testament writers believed that the Israel of their day was possessed by Satan (see for example John 8⁴⁴, *You are of your father the devil, and your will is to do your father's desires*).

Judaism may, therefore, be called Satan's house; and Jesus has come to plunder it, having first bound Satan by his victory over him in the wilderness (4¹ff.). He has come to gather in the harvest or flock of God; but the Pharisees are on the side of Satan, not on the side of Jesus; scattering, not gathering. By saying that the Spirit which God has put upon Jesus, and by which he casts out demons, is Beelzebul, they are blaspheming against the Spirit; and God will not forgive them. God will forgive those who do not see that Jesus is the Son of man; but those who have seen the signs which Jesus has performed, and say that these signs are the work of Satan, will never be forgiven.

❧

There are parallels to these verses in both Mark and Luke, and Matthew's sources cannot be identified with any certainty. We can be sure that he has made use of Mark 3²²-³⁰; but a comparison of this paragraph of Matthew's with Luke 11¹⁴-²², 12¹⁰, shows a number of places in which Matthew and Luke agree against Mark, e.g. in vv. 25-28, 30, 32; this may indicate that they were using a non-Marcan written source, or that Luke used Matthew at this point.

Matthew has omitted Mark 3²⁰f. which describes the crowds that gathered at Jesus' house, *so that they could not even eat*; and how *his friends* (or possibly his family) went out to arrest him, saying, He is mad. Perhaps Matthew found this disrespectful to the family of Jesus.

22–24

Matthew provides a new introduction to the sayings about Beelzebul, an exorcism which is similar to that in 9³²ff.. There, the patient was *dumb*: here, he is *blind and dumb*. Matthew arranges the words as a chiasmus: *blind and dumb . . . spoke and saw*.

all the people would be better translated 'all the crowds', so as to avoid confusing two words which Matthew uses in different ways: Matthew uses *people* (*laos*) for Israel, the people of God; when he says *the crowds* (*hoi ochloi*) he means those who are usually bewildered and distressed, but often favourable to Jesus; they are the potential or future Church.

Son of David: See notes on 1^1, 9^{27}.

by Beelzebul: See note on 10^{25}.

25

kingdom, city, and *house* are used here as alternatives, and Matthew has added *city*, which was not in Mark. There may be a play on the name *Beelzebul,* which means 'Lord of the house'. For the identification of the *house* with Israel, or *this evil generation,* see below, vv. 43–45. Israel, which should be the *kingdom* of God, the *city* of God, the *house* of God, had become possessed by Satan. The verse can be taken in two ways: (*a*) as a *reductio ad absurdum*: Satan would not bring about his own destruction, therefore Jesus is not casting out demons in the power of Beelzebul; (*b*) as a warning of what is in fact happening: Jesus is bringing a division into Judaism which will cause its fall.

26

The former interpretation (*a*) is taken in this verse; in fact it is not Satan who is casting out Satan; he would not bring about his own destruction. Therefore Jesus must be the enemy of Satan.

27

your sons means 'your pupils', and refers to Jewish exorcists. The Jewish historian Josephus attributes knowledge of exorcism to Solomon: 'He left behind him the manner of using exorcisms, by which they drive away demons, so that they never return, and this method of cure is of great force unto this day'; and he goes on to describe an exorcism which he had seen performed by a Jew in the presence of the emperor Vespasian (*Antiquities,* VIII, 2, 5). Jewish exorcists would ascribe their power to God, and would, therefore, condemn the Pharisees when they attributed the power of Jesus to Satan.

28

The fact is, on the contrary, that Jesus' power to cast out demons has been given to him by God, and is *the Spirit of God* (see above 1^{20}, 3^{16}, 4^1, 10^{20}, 12^{18} for the Spirit of God as the active power of God, at work in Jesus and promised to his disciples). The exorcisms of Jesus are signs that God is active in the world, and that he is beginning to rule.

Notice that Matthew writes *kingdom of God* here, and not, as he usually does, *kingdom of heaven*: the less usual form in Matthew is used here to contrast with the other kingdom, the kingdom of Satan, v. 26. See also 19^{24}.

29

The *strong man* in this parable is Satan, and *his goods* are the people pos-

sessed by demons, like *the blind and dumb* man in v. 22; though in fact
that man is typical and symbolic of all Israel and of all men; cf.
the whole world is in the power of the evil one 1 John 5^{19}, and the implication of the devil's offer to give Jesus *all the kingdoms of the world* in 4$^{8f.}$.
The idea of binding Satan belongs to Jewish belief about the end of this
age, cf. Rev. 20$^{2f.}$. Jesus claims that his exorcisms show that he has
bound Satan and is therefore able to *plunder his house*, and hence that the
end of this age is here.

30

This saying, in this form, is not in Mark at this point, but there is a
similar saying in Mark 9^{40}. Matthew, or his source (cf. Luke 11^{23}), may
have placed it here because of the idea of 'gathering' in it, and because
of the division which it contains – see above, vv. 23f., 25f. Jesus, and
those who are *with* him, are gathering – either the harvest of the
kingdom of God (the Baptist had said of Jesus, He will *gather his wheat
into the granary*, 3^{12} and see 9$^{37f.}$), or the flock of God (9^{36}). The latter
is more likely, because the saying contrasts those who are *against* Jesus,
and scatter; compare *the wolf snatches them* [the sheep] *and scatters them*
(John 10^{12}). The Pharisees, the representatives of Judaism, are doing
the work of Satan.

31

the blasphemy against the Spirit refers back to the judgement of the
Pharisees in v. 24, *It is only by Beelzebul* . . . and the words of Jesus in
v. 28, *it is by the Spirit of God* . . . The Pharisees have called the work of
God the work of Satan. Jesus declares that God will not forgive this sin.

32

This verse has no parallel in Mark (but cf. Luke 12^{10}); the distinction
between saying a word against *the Son of man*, and speaking against the
Holy Spirit, is difficult; it may mean that to speak against Jesus is
forgivable, because he is hidden and unknown; but to speak against
his manifestation of God's coming kingdom is to speak against what is
revealed and can be known, and this is not forgivable.

Jesus uses the title *the Son of man* of himself here, as above in 8^{20}, 9^{6},
12^{8}; see notes on these verses.

³³'*Either make the tree good, and its fruit good; or make the tree bad, and its fruit bad; for the tree is known by its fruit.* ³⁴*You brood of vipers! how can you speak good, when you are evil? For out of the abundance of the heart the mouth speaks.* ³⁵*The good man out of his good treasure brings forth good, and the evil man out of his evil treasure brings forth evil.* ³⁶*I tell you, on the day of judgement men will render account for every careless word they utter;* ³⁷*for by your words you will be justified, and by your words you will be condemned.*'

The Pharisees have spoken against the Holy Spirit, they have said that Jesus' exorcisms are the work of Satan. Jesus says that their words are evidence of what they are. Just as fruit is evidence of the nature of the tree on which it grows, so words are evidence of the man who speaks them. Therefore, when God judges the world, he will judge men according to their words; what they have said will be a sure guide to what they are.

ಜಞ

This paragraph is similar to 7¹⁶⁻²⁰, and to Luke 6⁴³⁻⁴⁵. Matthew has probably adapted sayings of Jesus to fit this context.

33
make the tree good . . . should perhaps be translated 'suppose the tree is good, then its fruit is good; or suppose the tree is bad, then its fruit is bad' (*Lexicon*, p. 688). Later Jesus speaks of the Pharisees as a plant which God has not planted, and which he will root up, 15¹³.

bad (*sapros*) means 'unusable', 'unwholesome'; it is used in the next chapter of inedible fish, 13⁴⁸.

You brood of vipers! John the Baptist had also called the Pharisees (and Sadducees) *a brood of vipers*, and had commanded them to *bear fruit that befits repentance*, otherwise they would be cut down like trees which do not bear good fruit (3⁷ᶠᶠ·). The Pharisees have said that Jesus casts out demons *by the prince of demons*, and that John *has a demon*; they have judged Jesus and John in the same way. So John and Jesus condemn them with the same words.

the heart of a man is his mind or thoughts; and *his mouth* expresses his thoughts, that is, his real inner nature.

35

In this verse, *treasure* is substituted for *heart*; cf. *where your treasure is, there will your heart be also* (6^{21}). The *treasure* is the motives and purposes of a man, and his *heart* or thoughts follow his motives. His words then express what his thoughts are. There is thus a threefold division: treasure, heart, mouth; motives, thoughts, words.

36f.

Later in the Gospel, Jesus says that the Son of man will repay every man according to his deeds (16^{27}); here, he says that they will be judged according to their *words*. At first sight, this might seem to contradict what Jesus said in Chapter 7 about the importance of deeds and the unimportance of words (7^{21}ff.). But notice that *careless* (or useless, worthless) words are specified here, such as the Pharisees' blasphemy, whereas the point in Chapter 7 is the uselessness of words which do not correspond to deeds.

12$^{38-42}$ JESUS FORETELLS THE   Luke 11$^{29-32}$
CONDEMNATION OF THIS GENERATION

^{38} Then some of the scribes and Pharisees said to him, 'Teacher, we wish to see a sign from you.' ^{39} But he answered them, 'An evil and adulterous generation seeks for a sign; but no sign shall be given to it except the sign of the prophet Jonah. ^{40} For as Jonah was three days and three nights in the belly of the whale, so will the Son of man be three days and three nights in the heart of the earth. ^{41} The men of Nin'eveh will arise at the judgement with this generation and condemn it; for they repented at the preaching of Jonah, and behold, something greater than Jonah is here. ^{42} The queen of the South will arise at the judgement with this generation and condemn it; for she came from the ends of the earth to hear the wisdom of Solomon, and behold, something greater than Solomon is here.'

Jesus continues to denounce this generation and to warn them of their condemnation at the judgement. The occasion is the request of some of the scribes and Pharisees for a miracle from Jesus, to authenticate his teaching and prove his authority. The reader knows that the healing miracles have been signs: Jesus had pointed to them in answer to the question of the Baptist, and he had added, *blessed is he who takes no offence at me*. But the Pharisees have taken offence: they have attributed his miracles to the power of Satan, and being blind to the signs which Jesus has done, they ask for more. Jesus says that the only sign that God will give to this *evil and adulterous generation* will be *the sign of the prophet Jonah*, and this is then said to mean the burial of Jesus for three days and nights, like the three days and nights of Jonah in the whale. This sign will not be accepted by *this generation*; they will be condemned at the last judgement by the people of Nineveh, who repented at Jonah's preaching, and by the Queen of Sheba, who came to hear Solomon's wisdom. This generation has not repented or believed in Jesus, who is proclaiming something greater than Jonah or Solomon – the kingdom of God.

ಜಾ

Mark has a similar request for a sign from the Pharisees in Mark 8¹¹ff., which Matthew has used at the corresponding place, 16¹ff.. Luke has a section which is similar to the whole of this paragraph in Luke 11²⁹ff., though there are important differences (see e.g. note on v. 40). We cannot be certain that Luke gives an earlier form of the tradition here, though it has often been claimed that he does.

38
Teacher is a form of address which Matthew keeps for those who are outside the circle of Jesus' disciples or followers – see 8¹⁹ and note.

to see a sign, that is, a miracle; cf. Paul, *Jews demand signs and Greeks seek wisdom, but we preach Christ crucified, a stumbling-block to Jews and folly to Gentiles*, 1 Cor. 1²²f..

39
An evil and adulterous generation: The phrase occurs again in the other section in which Jesus refuses to give a sign, 16⁴, and Matthew may have taken it from Mark 8³⁸. The word *adulterous* is used in a metaphorical sense, of unfaithfulness to God, which goes back to the Old Testament prophets: 'God's relation to his people is depicted as a marriage, and

any beclouding of it becomes adultery' (*Lexicon*, p. 527); cf. God's command to Hosea, *Go again, love a woman who is beloved of a paramour and is an adulteress; even as the Lord loves the people of Israel, though they turn to other gods* (Hos. 3¹).

no sign shall be given means 'God will give no sign' (the passive tense avoids using the name of God).

the words *except the sign of the prophet Jonah* are not in Mark 8¹², and their meaning is not certain. Matthew takes *the sign* as Jonah's time in the whale (see next verse), though from the following verse it might be his *preaching* which is the sign, and this is how Luke understands it (Luke 11³⁰).

40
Jonah was three days and three nights in the belly of the whale is a quotation from the LXX translation of Jonah 1¹⁷. The whole verse is absent from Luke, and it may be a Matthean explanation of the sign of Jonah in the previous verse. Notice the use of the term *the Son of man* as a self-designation of Jesus, and cf. 8²⁰, etc.

41
There is a double contrast between the Ninevites and *this generation*; (*a*) the Ninevites *repented* (see Jonah 3⁶ff.), *this generation* has not repented (cf. *because they did not repent*, 11²⁰); (*b*) the Ninevites acted on *the preaching of Jonah*, *this generation* has not responded to *something greater than Jonah*, that is, the preaching and teaching and miracles of Jesus which proclaim the coming of the kingdom. For the formula, *something greater than . . . is here* see 12⁶ and next verse.

42
The queen of the South is the Queen of Sheba (see 1 Kings 10¹ff.); she also will condemn *this generation*, and here there are three contrasts: (*a*) she *came* to Solomon, but this generation has not come to Jesus (to *come* is used for to believe in 11²⁸, *Come to me*); (*b*) she came from outside Israel, *from the ends of the earth*, but this generation is near at hand, and still will not believe; (*c*) she came *to hear the wisdom of Solomon*, but *something greater than Solomon is here*; Jesus is proclaiming the kingdom, and he is the final *Son of David* and the wisdom of God (see e.g. 1 Cor. 1²⁴).

^{43}'*When the unclean spirit has gone out of a man, he passes through waterless places seeking rest, but he finds none.* ^{44}*Then he says, "I will return to my house from which I came." And when he comes he finds it empty, swept, and put in order.* ^{45}*Then he goes and brings with him seven other spirits more evil than himself, and they enter and dwell there; and the last state of that man becomes worse than the first. So shall it be also with this evil generation.*'

There is no real break between this and the preceding paragraphs: Jesus continues to warn the scribes and Pharisees of the condemnation which will come on *this generation* of the Jews at the last judgement. The paragraph is a parable, with an application added in the last line – the parable of a possessed man, who has been exorcized, but because he is *empty* the demon returns to him with reinforcements, so that the man is worse off in the end than he was before the exorcism took place. The application of the parable indicates how it is to be understood: the possessed man stands for *this generation* of the Jews; the exorcism is the ministry of Jesus; the emptiness of the man is the unbelief and unrepentance of the Jews; and their *last state* is their condemnation at the last judgement.

ॐ

These three verses are almost identical with Luke 11^{24}ff., except that Luke has not the application of the parable, *So shall it be also with this evil generation*. Matthew may have added this sentence – it is written in his characteristic style – or Luke may have omitted it, because in his Gospel the context in which he put the parable made it unnecessary to point out the interpretation of it.

43
An *unclean spirit* is a demon; cf. 8^{16} where the words are used interchangeably, and compare 10^1 with 10^8. Matthew may have preferred this term here, to contrast the *spirit* which goes out of a man with the Holy Spirit which should fill a man, so that he is not *empty*.

waterless places, that is, the wilderness, the home of demons; Jesus went there *to be tempted by the devil* (4^1).

seeking rest, but he finds none: The demon only finds satisfaction in destroying things, and in the desert there is nothing to destroy.

44

my house is the man who was possessed, and, in the application of the parable, *this generation*: see above (vv. 25, 29) for Israel as Satan's house, and below (23³⁸), *your house is forsaken and desolate.*

when he comes . . . should perhaps be taken as a conditional sentence: 'If he comes and finds it empty . . .' The return of the demon depends on the man: if he has repented, he will not be empty.

45

It will be worse for the man in the end than if he had never been exorcized; and it will be worse for Israel than it would have been if Jesus had never come; compare *it shall be more tolerable on the day of judgement for the land of Sodom and Gomorrah than for that town* (10¹⁵).

For the possible return of the demon after an exorcism, see the quotation from Josephus in the note on 12²⁷ (p. 198).

12⁴⁶⁻⁵⁰   JESUS DISOWNS HIS FAMILY;   Mark 3³¹⁻³⁵
ISRAEL

⁴⁶*While he was still speaking to the people, behold, his mother and his brothers stood outside, asking to speak to him.ᵃ* ⁴⁸*But he replied to the man who told him, 'Who is my mother, and who are my brothers?'* ⁴⁹*And stretching out his hand toward his disciples, he said, 'Here are my mother and my brothers!* ⁵⁰*For whoever does the will of my Father in heaven is my brother, and sister, and mother.'*

a Other ancient authorities insert verse 47; *Some one told him, 'Your mother and your brothers are standing outside, asking to speak to you'*

The last paragraph of this section on the rejection of Jesus by the Jews and the condemnation of the Jews by Jesus is one of those stories which were preserved because they contained a notable saying of Jesus. The saying in this case declares that the relatives of Jesus, *his mother and his brothers*, are no longer his true family: his disciples have taken their place. The only relationship which he recognizes is that of a common obedience to God. The relatives of Jesus, whom he disowns here, stand for the whole of Israel; the disciples, on the other hand, are the new Israel, the Church. We may recall here the warning of John the Baptist: *Do not presume to say to yourselves, We have Abraham as our father; for I tell you, God is able from these stones to raise up children to Abraham* (3⁹).

∝∝

Matthew has taken these verses from Mark 3³¹ff. where they followed immediately after the paragraph on blasphemy against the Spirit. He has made some slight alterations, one of which obscures a point which was much clearer in Mark: Mark says that *a crowd was sitting about him* in a house, so that his mother and his brothers could not approach him and had to remain outside. Matthew has omitted this, perhaps because he thought it unfitting that people should sit while Jesus was teaching. See notes on 13², 27³⁶.

46

Instead of *to the people* translate 'to the crowds' (*tois ochlois*) and see note on Matthew's use of *people* and *crowds* at 12²³.

his mother and his brothers: This is the only place in this Gospel, after Chapters 1 and 2, where the mother of Jesus appears. She is, however, mentioned again with his brothers and sisters in the next section of narrative, in the first paragraph (13⁵³ff.). Nothing is known about the relationship of these *brothers* to Jesus. Since the fourth and fifth centuries, it has been usually held that Mary had no children other than Jesus, and that the *brothers* were either children of Joseph by a previous marriage, or cousins. When Matthew says that Joseph *knew her* [Mary] *not until she had borne a son* (1²⁵) he could be taken to mean that the brothers and sisters of Jesus were the younger children of Joseph and Mary.

The positions of the two groups, his physical kindred *outside* and his disciples inside, are symbolic of the unbelievers and the faithful; Paul, for example, uses the terms *those outside* and *those inside* in this sense (1 Cor. 5¹²f.).

47

This verse should probably be omitted, as in R.S.V., since it is lacking in some of the Greek manuscripts and old versions.

49

Matthew has changed Mark's *looking around on those who sat about him* to *stretching out his hand towards his disciples*; in Matthew, 'the crowds' (see v. 46) are not yet the representatives of the Church, whereas the disciples are.

50

Mark had *whoever does the will of God*, but Matthew changed it to *whoever does the will of my Father in heaven*; *my Father in heaven* is a characteristic Matthean expression and in this context it expresses the one relationship which is constitutive of the real family of Jesus, namely, obedience to his Father. Jesus calls the disciples *my brethren* again at the end of the Gospel (28¹⁰).

13 *That same day Jesus went out of the house and sat beside the sea.* *²And great crowds gathered about him, so that he got into a boat and sat there; and the whole crowd stood on the beach. ³And he told them many things in parables, saying:*

Matthew's third section of teaching runs from 13³ᵇ to 13⁵², and in the next verse he gives us the formula for transition to narrative, *And when Jesus had finished these parables, he went away from there* . . . The third section of teaching is therefore a collection of *parables*, and of explanations of *parables*.

This section, like the other four, has an introduction, which sets the scene: Jesus is sitting in a boat on the lake of Galilee, the crowds are standing on the beach, and he speaks to them in parables.

There is one point about the section which we must notice now, in order to understand the role of the crowds at this point. The first two sections of teaching were unbroken: there were no interruptions, and no changes of scene. In this section, on the other hand, the disciples come and ask Jesus at one point why he is speaking to the crowds in parables, and later on he leaves the crowds and goes into the house where the disciples ask him to explain one of the parables; the section ends with Jesus asking them a question, *Have you understood all this?* and with their answer and his comment. (The fourth section of teaching also has a question from one of the disciples in the middle of it; and it is possible that the fifth contains a change of scene – see 18²¹, 24¹ff.)

These interruptions in Chapter 13 are important, because they are related to the subject-matter of the chapter: Jesus is speaking to *the crowds* and to *the disciples*, but because he is speaking in *parables* only *the disciples* can understand him, and even they need his help in order to do so. *The disciples* stand for all those to whom God has given the ability *to know the secrets of the kingdom of heaven*, and *the crowds* for those to whom *it has not been given* (v. 11).

ॐ

211

Matthew has taken the next two verses from Mark (Mark 4:1f.) but he has not left them as they were. Mark says that Jesus *taught* the crowd (he uses the word three times in these two verses), but Matthew will not say this, and writes instead *he told them many things in parables*: in Matthew the crowds do not understand, therefore it cannot be said that Jesus *taught* them. Matthew emphasizes that Jesus *sat* (cf. 5¹, 15²⁹, 24³, 26⁵⁵) and *the whole crowd stood* to listen (see note on 12⁴⁶ff.).

1

That same day is a Matthean editorial phrase, linking the teaching section to the previous narrative in which Jesus had condemned *this generation* of Jews. He teaches in parables here, because they have not repented in Chapters 11 and 12.

Jesus went out of the house: Mark had mentioned the house earlier on (3¹⁹), and Matthew omitted it at that point, and put it in here; see below, v. 36, where Jesus goes back *into the house*.

the sea is *the Sea of Galilee* (4¹⁸).

13³ᵇ⁻⁹   THE PARABLE OF THE SOWER,   Mark 4³⁻⁹
            THE SEED, AND THE SOIL

'*A sower went out to sow.* ⁴*And as he sowed, some seeds fell along the path, and the birds came and devoured them.* ⁵*Other seeds fell on rocky ground, where they had not much soil, and immediately they sprang up, since they had no depth of soil,* ⁶*but when the sun rose they were scorched; and since they had no root they withered away.* ⁷*Other seeds fell upon thorns, and the thorns grew up and choked them.* ⁸*Other seeds fell on good soil and brought forth grain, some a hundredfold, some sixty, some thirty.* ⁹*He who has ears,ᵃ let him hear.*'

a Other ancient authorities add here and in verse 43 *to hear*

There are seven parables in this chapter, and the first contrasts the seed which never grows and bears fruit with the seed which is fruitful. Four verses describe the seed which is wasted on bad ground, and one verse the seed which is fruitful because it falls into good soil; nevertheless the fruitful seed makes up for the waste which has been involved. The idea of fruitfulness sends us back to what was said earlier in this Gospel about the Pharisees: John had commanded them to *bear fruit* (3^8), and Jesus had said that *the fruit* was the test of the tree (12$^{33\text{ff.}}$). The fruitless ground here in the parable stands for *the Pharisees*, who have not believed in Jesus. Whereas the *good soil* is *the disciples*: Jesus has just said of them that they do the will of his Father (12^{50}).

This is the immediate interpretation of the parable, and the meaning which it has at this point in the Gospel. But because both *the Pharisees* and *the disciples* are representative figures, standing for unbelievers and believers generally, a wider interpretation of the parable can and will be given later (see vv. 18$^{\text{ff.}}$).

❧

Matthew has taken the parable from Mark 4$^{3\text{ff.}}$, and has made only very slight and unimportant changes in it.

In the study of the parables of Jesus, it is usual to distinguish three questions: (*a*) What does the parable mean at this point in the Gospel? that is, how does it fit into the development of the story or plot of the Gospel? and why did the Evangelist put it in here? (*b*) What did the parable mean to the Church which preserved it, before it was used by the Evangelist? For what purposes was it used in the Christian communities which handed it on in their preaching and teaching? (*c*) What did the parable mean when it was first spoken by Jesus? Why did he use it?

(*a*) We have already seen that this parable of the seed and the different kinds of ground follows on from the contrasts in Chapters 11 and 12 between *the Pharisees* and *the disciples*; see for example 11^{25}, *thou hast hidden these things from the wise and understanding and revealed them to babes*. Jesus' preaching has borne no fruit in the leaders and official representatives of Judaism, but his *disciples* have paid attention to it and acted on it.

(*b*) Matthew will give us the Church's understanding of the parable in vv. 18$^{\text{ff.}}$, and there the emphasis will be on the quality of faith in the disciples themselves. The parable will be understood, not so much as a parable of faith and unbelief, but as a parable of different degrees of faith.

(*c*) When Jesus used the parable, the point of it may have been different again: he may have used it to contrast the wasted seeds with the final harvest which justifies the waste, and his meaning will then have been that although God does not seem to be at work in the world, and does not seem to be King, nevertheless his kingdom is coming, and will make up for all the apparent failures and disappointments that have gone before. (See further D. E. Nineham, *The Gospel of St Mark*, pp. 125ff.)

4–7
In Palestine, sowing preceded ploughing; the sower could not tell what the ground was like at the time when he sowed – e.g. whether there was any depth of earth.

8
grain is in Greek the word *karpos*, which has previously been translated *fruit* ($3^{8\text{ff.}}$, $7^{16\text{ff.}}$, 12^{33}). The quantities, *a hundredfold, sixty, thirty*, are apparently far higher than was usual even in a good year; seven and a half was average, ten was good. The improbably large numbers draw attention to the point of the parable, which was originally the immense value and richness of the kingdom when it does come (*c*), and later, the fruitfulness of the disciples (*a* and *b*).

9
For this formula, see note on 11^{15}.

13^{10-17}	JESUS EXPLAINS TO THE	Mark $4^{10-12, 25}$
	DISCIPLES WHY HE TEACHES	Luke 10^{23}f.
	IN PARABLES	

^{10}*Then the disciples came and said to him, 'Why do you speak to them in parables?' ^{11}And he answered them, 'To you it has been given to know the secrets of the kingdom of heaven, but to them it has not been given. ^{12}For to him who has will more be given, and he will have abundance; but from him who has not, even what he has will be taken away. ^{13}This is why I speak to them in parables, because seeing they do not see, and hearing they do not hear, nor do they understand. ^{14}With them indeed is fulfilled the prophecy of Isaiah which says:*

> *"You shall indeed hear but never understand,*
> *and you shall indeed see but never perceive.*
> ^{15}*For this people's heart has grown dull,*
> *and their ears are heavy of hearing,*

and their eyes they have closed,
lest they should perceive with their eyes,
and hear with their ears,
and understand with their heart,
and turn for me to heal them."

[16]*But blessed are your eyes, for they see, and your ears, for they hear.* [17]*Truly, I say to you, many prophets and righteous men longed to see what you see, and did not see it, and to hear what you hear, and did not hear it.'*

Matthew probably considered the previous paragraph the first parable in his Gospel; he had used parables of Jesus before this point (e.g. $7^{24ff.}$, $9^{15ff.}$, $11^{16ff.}$, etc.), but he did not call any of them parables, and none of them were as developed as the parable of the seed and the soil. So this is the point at which it seems right to Matthew (as it had to Mark also) to give an explanation of the reason why Jesus used this way of speaking. The reason which Matthew gives is that the parables hide the message from the unbelievers, but convey it to those who believe. The disciples have been given power by God to know about the kingdom, and they learn more about it through the parables; the crowds have not been given power to know, and so they receive nothing from the parables. The crowds' blindness and deafness and incomprehension fulfil the prophecy of Isaiah. The disciples, on the other hand, have received sight and hearing from God, so that they can understand the ministry of Jesus as the fulfilment of the hopes of prophets and righteous men in the Old Testament.

Although much of this paragraph may go back to authentic sayings of Jesus, it is doubtful whether those sayings originally referred to the reason why he spoke in parables. For example, the words *This is why I speak to them in parables* are a Matthean adaptation of a different saying in Mark, and the Marcan form may originally have meant something quite different, and quite unrelated to the teaching in parables (see note on 13^{11}). When Jesus used a parable, its meaning was probably clear to his audience from the context in which he used it – though his audience may not always have wanted to understand his meaning. What seems to have happened is: the parables were remembered without their context, new meanings were read into them, they were put to new uses in the life of the Church, and the original intention of the parables was forgotten. It was then thought that Jesus had used parables in order to hide his message, and sayings of Jesus from another context were used to express this attitude.

ജ

These verses have a basis and framework in Mark, but Matthew has added to them, from elsewhere in Mark, from the Old Testament, and from Christian sources. Verses 10, 11, 13 correspond to Mark 4$^{10–12}$; v. 12 is from Mark 4^{25} (and it will be used again at 25^{29}); in vv. 14ff. Matthew has written out in full the quotation from Isa. 6$^{9f.}$ of which the Marcan passage reminded him. The last two verses 16, 17 are non-Marcan, and they are found in a shorter form in Luke 10$^{23f.}$.

10

Matthew has rewritten Mark's verse, in order to avoid some of the difficulties in it; notice in particular that he has changed Mark's . . . *asked him concerning the parables* to *Why do you speak to them in parables?* and so made it clear that this is to be an explanation of parabolic speaking in general and not an explanation of a specific parable.

11

To you it has been given to know: it has been given is a passive for the action of God; God has given the disciples understanding of Jesus' teaching. Matthew has added *to know the secrets of the kingdom of heaven*: in Mark (and in some ancient versions of Matthew) *the secret*. Notice the agreement here between Matthew and Luke against Mark. *The secrets (ta mystēria)* are the ways of God which only he knows, and only he can reveal to men so that they may know them. In this context the meaning is that God has revealed Jesus to the disciples as the Messiah, who proclaims the coming kingdom.

but to them it has not been given replaces Mark's *but for those outside everything is in parables*; and the original meaning of this saying in Mark may have been, 'everything is obscure', and it may not have referred to the parables at all. Matthew, like the other New Testament writers, is prepared to say that as faith is the gift of God, unbelief is the withholding of a gift by God; *it has not been given* means 'God has not given it'.

12

From Mark 4^{25}, but Matthew has added *and he will have abundance*. The passive verbs stand for God's action: God will give more understanding to the man to whom he has given faith, and he will abound in knowledge; God will take away in hell from him who does not believe, even his life.

13

This is why I speak to them in parables is added by Matthew, and answers the disciples' question in v. 10.

see, hear, and *understand* anticipate the quotation in the next two verses.

Matthew has changed Mark's *so that* to *because*; the speaking in parables is according to Matthew a punishment of Israel *because* of their blindness, whereas in Mark it is a means of hiding the gospel *so that* they may not see.

14

The quotation is from Isa. 6^{9}f.; it was clearly in the mind of Mark when he wrote Mark 4^{12} and it was a favourite Old Testament text among the first Christians, because it 'explained' the rejection of the Messiah by the Jews. Matthew's text here agrees exactly with LXX.

16f.

The disciples' eyes and ears have been opened by God to see and hear and understand the words and signs of Jesus, which are the beginning of the kingdom, that for which the Old Testament writers longed. The disciples are *blessed* because they live now, in this time of fulfilment, and because God has given them the faith which enables them to *see* and *hear* and *understand*. Matthew uses the expression *prophets and righteous men* again in 10^{41}, 23^{29}.

13$^{18-23}$ JESUS EXPLAINS THE PARABLE   Mark 4$^{13-20}$
OF THE SOWER

^{18}'*Hear then the parable of the sower.* ^{19}*When any one hears the word of the kingdom and does not understand it, the evil one comes and snatches away what is sown in his heart; this is what was sown along the path.* ^{20}*As for what was sown on rocky ground, this is he who hears the word and immediately receives it with joy;* ^{21}*yet he has no root in himself, but endures for a while, and when tribulation or persecution arises on account of the word, immediately he falls away.*^{a} ^{22}*As for what was sown among thorns, this is he who hears*

*the word, but the cares of the world and the delight in riches choke the word,
and it proves unfruitful.* [23] *As for what was sown on good soil, this is he who
hears the word and understands it, he indeed bears fruit, and yields, in one
case a hundredfold, in another sixty, and in another thirty.'*

  a Or *stumbles*

Jesus continues to address the disciples, not the crowds, and explains
the parable of the sower. The four kinds of ground stand for four kinds
of people: the man who *does not understand*, the man who does not
persevere in persecution, the man who is worldly, and the man who
is fruitful in good works.

This interpretation of the parable is almost certainly the work of the
early Church, and not an explanation of the parable given by Jesus
himself. The evidence for this is partly that it is unlikely that Jesus
needed to explain his parables; partly that the language in this
paragraph is nearer to the language of the early Church than to Jesus'
words; partly that the allegorical, detailed interpretation of the
parable is unlike Jesus' usual method; partly that the harvest in the
parable is not interpreted in terms of the coming of the kingdom, as
it is in other parables of Jesus.

∽∾

18
In Mark, a rebuke is here addressed to the disciples: *Do you not understand this parable? How then will you understand all the parables?* Matthew
has omitted it, because in his Gospel the disciples are presented as people
who do understand (vv. 16f.); and in its place he writes, 'You, therefore,
hear the parable of the sower'; the 'You' is emphatic in the Greek –
you who are blessed, who see and hear and understand; you who are
not like *this people* of Israel who do not understand. *The parable of the
sower* is Matthew's title for the parable, and it is not altogether appropriate: the parable is really about different kinds of ground. This title,
and the title in v. 36, are the only examples of titles of parables in the
New Testament.

19
hears ... and does not understand: Matthew has rewritten Mark at this
point, to bring the explanation into line with the beginning of the
quotation in v. 14, *You shall indeed hear but never understand.* In the
context of the Gospel, this refers first to the scribes and Pharisees, and

then to *this people* Israel as a whole; but Matthew means it to apply also to all who will not understand the preaching of the kingdom in the future.

20f.
The interpretation of the parable anticipates a time when the disciples will be persecuted and some will stumble and renounce their faith, because they have no stability and endurance.

22
The third kind of ground stands for those who have not *left everything* and are not *poor in spirit*. Love for God and men is choked by self-love, and so *the word* does not bear fruit in good works.

23
The fourth kind of ground stands for the man who *hears* and *understands* the gospel, as the disciples do; and he will bear fruit in good works.

in one case a hundredfold, in another sixty, and in another thirty means that there will be different 'grades' of disciples; cf. *shall be called least in the kingdom of heaven . . . shall be called great in the kingdom of heaven* (5¹⁹).

13²⁴⁻³⁰   THE PARABLE OF THE WEEDS   Mark 4²⁶⁻²⁹
                        OF THE FIELD

²⁴*Another parable he put before them, saying, 'The kingdom of heaven may be compared to a man who sowed good seed in his field;* ²⁵*but while men were sleeping, his enemy came and sowed weeds among the wheat, and went away.* ²⁶*So when the plants came up and bore grain, then the weeds appeared also.* ²⁷*And the servantsᵃ of the householder came and said to him, "Sir, did you not sow good seed in your field? How then has it weeds?"* ²⁸*He said to them, "An enemy has done this." The servantsᵃ said to him, "Then do you want us to go and gather them?"* ²⁹*But he said, "No; lest in gathering the weeds you root up the wheat along with them.* ³⁰*Let both grow together until the harvest; and at harvest time I will tell the reapers, Gather the weeds first and bind them in bundles to be burned, but gather the wheat into my barn."'*

   a Or *slaves*

The explanation of the reason for speaking in parables, and of the first parable, is followed by three more parables: the explanation had been given to *the disciples alone*, but these other three parables, like the first, are to be understood as spoken to *the disciples* and *the crowds*.

The first of these three parables contrasts two kinds of *seed*, in much the same way as the parable of the sower had contrasted *good soil* with unfruitful ground. The disciples are the good seed; the crowds, the scribes and Pharisees, and all unbelievers are the weeds, sown not by God, but by the evil one. As the farmer leaves wheat and weeds in his field side by side until the harvest, so God will leave the Church and the synagogue side by side in the world until the end of this age.

৩৩

There is no parallel to these verses in Mark or Luke, but Mark has at this point the parable of the seed growing secretly (Mark $4^{26ff.}$) and there are a number of words which are common to both: *sleep, come up, wheat, harvest, grain*. This may be due to the fact that both are parables of growth and harvest; but the possibility remains that Matthew has either combined Mark's parable with another, or rewritten Mark's parable.

If we ask again the three questions, (*a*) What does the parable mean at this point in the Gospel? (*b*) What did it mean in the life of the Church? (*c*) What did it mean when Jesus used it? the answers may be as follows:

(*a*) It follows on from the saying in $12^{33ff.}$ about the *good tree* and its *good fruit*, the *bad* tree and its *bad* fruit; and it is referred to again at $15^{13f.}$ *Every plant which my heavenly Father has not planted will be rooted up. Let them alone.*

(*b*) Matthew gives the Church's explanation of the parable in $13^{36ff.}$: the judgement which is coming at the end of this age, when the wicked and the righteous will be separated, and each will receive his deserts.

(*c*) If the parable comes from Jesus originally, the emphasis may have been on the words of the farmer in vv. 29f.; the disciples must wait until God brings this age to an end, and leave the separating of men to him and his angels; compare Paul's command to the Corinthians, *do not pronounce judgement before the time, before the Lord comes, who will bring to light the things now hidden in darkness and will disclose the purposes of the heart. Then every man will receive his commendation from God* (1 Cor. 4^5).

24

Another parable he put before them, saying: A Matthean formula, cf.
vv. 31, 33, and 21^{33}. *Them* does not refer to *the disciples* as one might
have expected from v. 10, but picks up v. 3; this is clear when we get
to v. 34, *All this Jesus said to the crowds in parables.*

The kingdom of Heaven may be compared to a man who . . .: This method
of introducing a parable is a translation of an Aramaic expression, and
it means 'It is the case with . . . as with . . .'; the *kingdom* is not like
a *man*, but like *the harvest*.

25f.

weeds (Greek *zizania*): 'Darnel, cheat, a troublesome weed in the grainfields, resembling wheat' (*Lexicon*, p.340). Another authority says that
its botanical name is 'lolium temulentum' (Jeremias, *The Parables of
Jesus*, p. 224).

27

the servants of the householder: Jesus has been called *the householder* (= *the
master of the house*) and his disciples his *servants*, in 10^{24}f..

28f.

The experts say that it was usual to root out darnel before the harvest,
and that this was sometimes done more than once.

30

Darnel was dried and used for fuel. *Gather the wheat into my barn:*
cf. John the Baptist, *he will . . . gather his wheat into the granary* (in Greek
the words are identical), 3^{12}.

13^{13-32} THE PARABLE OF THE   Mark 4^{30-32}
                                 MUSTARD SEED

^{31}*Another parable he put before them, saying, ' The kingdom of heaven is like
a grain of mustard seed which a man took and sowed in his field; ^{32}it is the
smallest of all seeds, but when it has grown it is the greatest of shrubs and
becomes a tree, so that the birds of the air come and make nests in its branches.'*

The parables of the sower and the weeds have contrasted fruitfulness
and unfruitfulness, the disciples and the unbelievers. Two more

parables follow, which have another contrast – the beginning of the kingdom and the completion of it.

In the first of these two parables the emphasis is on the great end which will follow from a small beginning; the mustard seed is *the smallest of all seeds*, but it grows into *the greatest of shrubs*. The kingdom will also grow from small beginnings in the preaching of the Baptist and the ministry of Jesus and his disciples to a great end when the Gentiles are brought into it.

৩৩

This parable is in each of the Synoptic Gospels, and it raises the problem of Matthew's sources in an acute form, because there are agreements in Matthew and Luke against Mark. It is usually held that Matthew has combined two versions of the parable, Mark's and Q's; but a good case has been made out for thinking that Luke used Matthew's and Mark's.

It may well be that the Evangelist, the Church, and Jesus, all used this parable for the same purpose.

31

For the editorial formula, *Another parable . . .* and for the introductory formula to the parable, *The kingdom of heaven is like . . .*, see v. 24; the meaning of the latter is 'it is with the kingdom as with the mustard seed': it begins as something insignificant, it becomes something great. Matthew has added the words *which a man took and sowed in his field*: they are a link phrase, joining the last parable to this one, and this one to the next (see vv. 24 and 33); the similar words in Luke suggest that he used Matthew here.

32

when it is grown it is the greatest of shrubs and becomes a tree is an exaggeration, and exaggeration or hyperbole is a characteristic of Jesus' parables (cf. note on v. 8); the mustard plant will, however, grow to a height of from eight to ten feet by the Lake of Gennesaret.

the birds of the air come and make nests in its branches is a quotation from Dan. 4^{21}; in Daniel, the tree is the kingdom of Nebuchadnezzar, and *the birds* stand for the nations which have come under his dominion; here *the birds* are the Gentiles, who will be brought into God's kingdom.

³³*He told them another parable. 'The kingdom of heaven is like leaven which a woman took and hid in three measures of meal, till it was all leavened.'*

The last parable to *the crowds* forms a pair with the mustard seed, and like it contrasts the beginning with the completion of the kingdom: the woman takes a small piece of leaven and mixes it in a large quantity of meal, and the effect is out of all proportion to the cause. Notice in the parable the word 'hide': the kingdom has started to come, God is already at work in the world in the exorcisms, but this is at present hidden from the majority.

ಐಐ

The parable is not in Mark, but is in Luke in almost identical wording, apart from the introductory formulas.

33
For the formulas, see note on v. 24.

Compare *Do you not know that a little leaven ferments the whole lump of dough?* (1 Cor. 5⁶.)

three measures of meal is a large quantity, enough to feed some 160 people. The exaggeration is intentional, and stands for the universal transformation which the kingdom will effect.

13³⁴, ³⁵   THE PARABLES AND THE   Mark 4³³f.
FULFILMENT OF PROPHECY

³⁴*All this Jesus said to the crowds in parables; indeed he said nothing to them without a parable.* ³⁵*This was to fulfil what was spoken by the prophet:ᵃ*

'*I will open my mouth in parables,*
I will utter what has been hidden since the foundation of the world.'

a Other ancient authorities read *the prophet Isaiah*

The section on parables is divided into two parts, in the first part Jesus is addressing *the crowds* and his *disciples*, in the second his disciples only. So Matthew rounds off the first part with an editorial passage, which shows that the use of parables fulfils prophecy. Jesus spoke to the crowds in parables, and only in parables; he did not explain what he was saying to them, because they had refused to hear him. This fulfilled Ps. 78² in which God had prophesied that he would speak in parables the hidden things, his secrets, which he had concealed from men since the beginning of the world, but is now declaring through Jesus to those who have ears to hear.

ൟ

Matthew has adapted Mark's ending to his section on parables, to suit this position in Matthew in the middle of the section, concluding the parables to *the crowds*. He has added his formula for introducing an Old Testament quotation, and the quotation from Ps. 78², partly in LXX and partly in a different version.

34
Jesus speaks to the crowd *in parables*, because they do not believe, see above, vv. 10ff.

35
For the quotation formula, see note on 1²².

The quotation is from a Psalm, and so we should expect Matthew to have said 'spoken by David' (cf. 22⁴³); the text is uncertain: either *the prophet*, or *the prophet Isaiah* which is the reading of some of the important manuscripts. Later on in the Gospel, a quotation from Zechariah is attributed to Jeremiah (27⁹), and a similar mistake may have been made here; i.e. *the prophet Isaiah* may well be the original reading.

What has been hidden since the foundation of the world is the time of the coming of the kingdom which Jesus is proclaiming in the parables.

13^{36-43} JESUS EXPLAINS THE PARABLE
OF THE WEEDS

³⁶*Then he left the crowds and went into the house. And his disciples came to him, saying, 'Explain to us the parable of the weeds of the field.'* ³⁷*He*

*answered, 'He who sows the good seed is the Son of man; ³⁸the field is the
world, and the good seed means the sons of the kingdom; the weeds are the
sons of the evil one, ³⁹and the enemy who sowed them is the devil; the harvest
is the close of the age, and the reapers are angels. ⁴⁰Just as the weeds are
gathered and burned with fire, so will it be at the close of the age. ⁴¹The Son
of man will send his angels, and they will gather out of his kingdom all
causes of sin and all evildoers, ⁴²and throw them into the furnace of fire; there
men will weep and gnash their teeth. ⁴³Then the righteous will shine like
the sun in the kingdom of their Father. He who has ears, let him hear.'*

The scene for the second half of this section of parables is in the house;
Jesus leaves the crowds, and explains the second parable – the parable
of the weeds – to the disciples in private; then he adds three more
parables, and explains one of them.

The parable of the weeds is explained in terms of the last judgement: the separation of the evildoers from the righteous, their
destruction or salvation.

⚬⚬⚬

The parable of the weeds (vv. 24ff.) was not in Mark or Luke, so the
explanation of it here is also unparalleled in the other Gospels; but the
introductory sentences in v. 36 may be based on a later verse in Mark
(7¹⁷). *And when he had entered the house, and left the people* (Greek
'crowd'), *his disciples asked him about the parable.*

This explanation, like that of *the parable of the sower* in vv. 18ff., is
not an original part of the words of Jesus; and it is doubtful whether it
goes back any further than Matthew himself, because it is full of his
own idioms, and some of the ideas in it are peculiar to this Gospel.

36

We suggested in the Introduction that this Gospel is arranged symmetrically round a 'middle point': this verse, where Jesus leaves *the crowds*
and goes *into the house* to teach his disciples is the turning-point; it is the
middle of the central section of teaching, and it anticipates his turning
from the Jews to the Gentiles. (In pages of text, this verse is slightly less
than half-way through the Gospel.)

the parable of the weeds of the field: See note on v. 18.

37

The title *Son of man* is put into Jesus' mouth as his self-designation;
cf. 16¹³.

38

the field is the world: The scope of Jesus' work is universal; everything will be put in subjection to him.

The phrase *the sons of the kingdom* here means the disciples of Jesus; in the only other place where it is used in Matthew it means the unbelieving Jews (8¹²). 'The son of' means 'obedient to'; *the sons of the kingdom* are those who obey God; *the sons of the evil one* are those who obey the devil.

39f.

the close of the age is a purely Matthean idiom, and a sign of the editor's own composition; see 13⁴⁹, 24³, 28²⁰.

41

his kingdom means the world over which Jesus will be given authority, after his resurrection (28¹⁸); good and evil will remain side by side in the world until the end of this age.

all causes of sin and evildoers is a quotation from Zeph. 1³, and means here false teachers; see 7²³, 18⁶⁻⁹, 24¹⁰⁻¹².

42

For *the furnace of fire* see note on 3¹⁰.

there men will weep and gnash their teeth: See note on 8¹².

43

Cf. Dan. 12³ *And those who are wise shall shine like the brightness of the firmament.*

in the kingdom of their Father: Matthew distinguishes between 'the kingdom of the Son of man' (v. 41) and the kingdom of the Father: the former begins with the coming of Jesus and ends at the judgement, when the latter begins; Paul expresses the same ideas to the Corinthians: *Then comes the end, when he delivers the kingdom to God the Father after destroying every rule and every authority and power. For he must reign until he has put all his enemies under his feet* (1 Cor. 15²⁴ᶠ·).

13⁴⁴   THE PARABLE OF THE TREASURE

⁴⁴'*The kingdom of heaven is like treasure hidden in a field, which a man found and covered up; then in his joy he goes and sells all that he has and buys that field.*'

This parable and the next form a pair, and it is possible that they were originally spoken by Jesus one after the other, and were always preserved side by side in the tradition. Both parables point to the joy of the disciples.

The first parable is about a poor man who finds treasure which is hidden in a field, and sells everything to buy the field: he must be poor, if he has to sell everything he has to buy a field. The disciples also have found treasure, because they know the King who is soon to reign, and they have been adopted as his brothers. The King is hidden at present, and their secret is at present covered up – no one else knows that they know. They are leaving everything to follow him, but without any complaint.

ഇരൂ

There is no parallel in Mark or Luke.

For the formula, see v. 24.

Hiding valuables in the ground was normal in Palestine especially in times of invasion. If the owner were killed or died before he recovered his property, it would remain until someone found it. The man in the parable seems to us to act dishonestly, deceiving the owner of the field: but apparently the strict letter of the law permitted him to do this; and in any case the characters in the parables of Jesus are not always moral; see for example the Unjust Steward, Luke 16^{1}ff..

The disciples were told in 6^{19}ff. to lay up treasure for themselves in heaven – that is, to look to God for their reward, and not to men. Their treasure is to inherit the earth, and to share in God's rule over it; but this is given only to those who are poor and meek (5$^{3, 5}$). Later on in the Gospel, Jesus will say to a young man, *Sell what you possess and give to the poor, and you will have treasure in heaven; and come, follow me* (19^{21}). Jesus, the coming King of the world, the Son of man, is the treasure, and his disciples have found him, although he is hidden. In order to reign with him they must *sell all*, share his poverty and meekness, and *follow him*. Moreover, they will do this *in joy*, because just as the man in the parable obtains the field and the treasure at the cost of *all that he has*, so they obtain the world and a share in God's dominion over it at the cost of their possessions.

13^{43, 46}   THE PARABLE OF THE PEARL

⁴⁵'*Again, the kingdom of heaven is like a merchant in search of fine pearls,*
⁴⁶*who, on finding one pearl of great value, went and sold all that he had and*
bought it.'

The second parable in the pair makes the same point as the first.
As in other pairs of parables, the main characters are contrasted; here,
the first was a poor man, the second is a pearl merchant; but rich as
he is, he must still sell all his stock to have enough ready money to
buy the exceptionally valuable pearl. The first man found the
treasure by chance: the second is looking for pearls in the course of
his work. The disciples are to see that the claims of the kingdom are
total, and leave no room for self-interest: or rather, wise self-interest
dictates a total response.

❧❧

There is no parallel in Mark or Luke.

45f.
For the formula for introducing the parable, *the kingdom of heaven is*
like, see note on v. 24.

pearls were, with gold, the most valuable things in the ancient world,
and even sometimes 'more in demand than gold' (*Lexicon*, p. 492);
cf. *do not throw your pearls before swine* (7⁶) where *pearls* are again used
of valuables, and may stand for *the kingdom of heaven* as here.

13⁴⁷⁻⁵⁰   THE PARABLE OF THE NET

⁴⁷'*Again, the kingdom of heaven is like a net which was thrown into the sea*
and gathered fish of every kind; ⁴⁸*when it was full, men drew it ashore and*
sat down and sorted the good into vessels but threw away the bad. ⁴⁹*So it*
will be at the close of the age. The angels will come out and separate the evil
from the righteous, ⁵⁰*and throw them into the furnace of fire; there men will*
weep and gnash their teeth.'

The fourth paragraph in this second part of the section returns to the ideas in the first paragraph, the explanation of the parable of the weeds of the field. We have here a parable with an explanation attached to it, teaching the separation at the end of the age by the angels. Matthew is not adding anything that was not in the first paragraph, and even his wording contains repetitions: apparently he wanted another item to balance up this part of the section, in his favourite arrangement, *a, b, b, a*.

༄

There is no parallel in Mark or Luke, but cf. the miracles in Luke 5⁴ff., John 21⁴ff..

47
The introductory formula means that it will be with the kingdom as it is with catching fish in a net: fish must be sorted; and so there will be a separation at the end.

fish of every kind may mean clean and unclean fish – Lev. 11⁹ff. laid down which fish might be eaten and which not; or it may mean all the possible kinds of fish – the commentators on John 21¹¹ say that it was sometimes reckoned by ancient writers that there were 153 different kinds of fish. If the first is chiefly in mind, then *the evil* and *the righteous* of v. 49 are meant; if the latter, then *all the nations* (25³²).

48
when it was full suggests not only the filling of the net with fish, but also the fulfilling of the time until the last judgement; compare *Let both grow together until the harvest* in v. 30. There is to be no separation before the end. The *vessels* here, like the *barn* in v. 30, stand for eternal life in the age to come. *The bad* are the inedible fish; see note on 12³³.

49f.
These verses are full of Matthean formulas and idioms, most of them also used in vv. 40–43.

^{51}*'Have you understood all this?' They said to him, 'Yes.'* ^{52}*And he said to them, 'Therefore every scribe who has been trained for the kingdom of heaven is like a householder who brings out of his treasure what is new and what is old.'*

The whole section of parables which began at 13^1 is concluded by these two verses, and after them will come the regular formula for transition from teaching to narrative. Jesus asks his disciples – he has been addressing them, and not the crowds, in the second part of this section – whether they have understood *all this*, that is, no doubt, both the first (public) part of the section, and the second (private) part of it. We know that *it has been given* to the disciples *to know the secrets of the kingdom of heaven*; so we are not surprised when they answer *Yes*. Jesus says to them that they are *like a householder who brings out of his treasure what is new and what is old*; but the meaning of this is not at all clear; it may refer to the quotation from the Psalm in v. 35. Jesus has taught them in his parables the things that have been hidden since the foundation of the world; so what they know is both *new* and *old* – *old*, because it was determined by God at the beginning; and *new*, because it has only now been revealed by Jesus.

❧

These two verses have no parallel in Mark and Luke. The presentation of the disciples as those who understand is typically Matthean (see vv. 11ff.).

52

every scribe: In 23^{34} Jesus foretells that he will send *scribes* to the Jews. In Matthew's Church there may have been a class of Christian scribes, and he may have thought of himself as one of them.

who has been trained (mathēteutheis): The word is used again at 27^{57}, 28^{19}, but not elsewhere in the Gospels; did Matthew (Greek *Matthaios*) pun on his own name? The householder has among his treasures *new* things and *old* things; in what sense can this be said of the disciples? The words *new* and *old* are often used in the New Testament to mean the Law and the Gospel (see note on 9^{17}), and so the meaning here may be that the disciple 'teaches men both the Gospel and the Law' (B. T. D. Smith) – see 5^{17}ff., 23^{23}. On the other hand, if the chiasmus which we have already noticed in vv. 36–50 extends on either side, then these two verses will correspond to vv. 34f. (... *what has been hidden since the foundation of the world*). The things that are *new* and *old* are the secrets of the kingdom and its coming, beginning now and coming finally at the end of the age. The disciples will be able to teach these things.

Unbelief and Little Faith

The section of the Gospel which we are to consider now runs from the end of the parables to the beginning of the fourth collection of sayings in Chapter 18. As R.S.V. sets it out, there are twenty-one paragraphs, and all except two of them have fairly close parallels in Mark. The two exceptions are the account of Peter walking on the water, and the conversation between Jesus and Peter about the half-shekel tax, 14²⁸ff. and 17²⁴ff.. In the other nineteen paragraphs Matthew has sometimes edited Mark, and sometimes added fresh material to the Marcan tradition, but on the whole he has made very few changes. And whereas up to the end of Chapter 13 Matthew had considerably rearranged the order of the Marcan paragraphs, from Chapter 14 to the end of the Gospel he hardly ever varies the sequence in which they had stood in his source. He must, therefore, have been satisfied with Mark's arrangement in this part of his Gospel and decided not to improve on it.

We shall try to see what was the purpose of the two Evangelists in this section of their Gospels.

In Mark, this section (Mark 6¹–9³²) leads up to the confession of Peter *You are the Christ* and the revelation of Jesus at the transfiguration. In the earlier part of it the disciples are again and again shown as blind and ignorant; Peter only 'sees' after Jesus has opened the eyes of a blind man; and the miracle of the blind man's seeing is told in such a way that the reader is made to think that Jesus is opening Peter's eyes.

Matthew, as we have seen, takes this section over ready-made from Mark: he underlines the story of Peter's confession by his additions to it, and adds another confession of all the disciples, *Truly you are the Son of God* (14³³). We might say that Matthew is giving here the disciples' answer to two questions which had been asked earlier on in the Gospel: *What sort of man is this, that even winds and sea obey him?* and *Can this be the Son of David?* (8²⁷, 12²³).

The disciples' faith is a gift from the Father: he has revealed to them who Jesus is, and he has revealed it by means of the miracles of Jesus. So Matthew (like Mark) continues to give us Jesus' miracles in this section: two feeding-miracles; the healing of many sick people, a Gentile girl, and an epileptic boy; and the transfiguration.

The reader of this Gospel cannot help sensing a certain incongruity in the Evangelist's work at this point. Either he has not revised Mark, in this section, as much as he should have done, or he should not have allowed his treatment of the disciples in Chapter 13 to reach the stage that it did. In Chapter 13, the disciples were presented as those who, through the grace of God, saw and heard and understood the meaning of the ministry of Jesus. But in Mark this was not the case; and Matthew finds it difficult to take up Mark again, and use it as it stands.

Matthew therefore has to introduce the conception of *little faith* (14^{31}, 16^8, 17^{20}). The disciples, he has to say, were not yet perfect believers: they did not yet understand all the implications of who Jesus was, and what his work would involve for him and for them.

If Matthew had some difficulty in his presentation of the disciples it was otherwise with his presentation of the Jews in general. They continue to stand for *unbelief*. We shall hear of Herod the tetrarch's execution of John; the Pharisees' and the scribes' transgression of the commandment of God; and the denunciation of the Jews as an evil and adulterous generation.

But in contrast with the Jews, the Gentiles will be mentioned again: a Canaanite woman will be commended for her great *faith*; numbers of Gentiles will be healed; and it is possible that one of the feedings is intended to be read as the feeding of a Gentile crowd.

So in this section Matthew puts himself into the hands of Mark much more than he had done earlier in his Gospel, and this creates some difficulties for him. He continues to show the Jews and in particular their leaders in the role of unbelievers; and the Gentiles as those who will take their place in the new Israel. Meanwhile, the picture of the disciples is Matthew's main difficulty; and his solution is to say that they are imperfect believers, men of *little faith* which must grow and develop.

JESUS IS REJECTED IN HIS Mark 6^{1-6a}
OWN COUNTRY

⁵³*And when Jesus had finished these parables, he went away from there,* ⁵⁴*and coming to his own country he taught them in their synagogue, so that they were astonished, and said, 'Where did this man get this wisdom and these mighty works?* ⁵⁵*Is not this the carpenter's son? Is not his mother called Mary? And are not his brothers James and Joseph and Simon and Judas?* ⁵⁶*And are not all his sisters with us? Where then did this man get all this?'* ⁵⁷*And they took offence at him. But Jesus said to them, 'A prophet is not without honour except in his own country and in his own house.'* ⁵⁸*And he did not do many mighty works there, because of their unbelief.*

The incident which Matthew has chosen from Mark to follow the parables is the rejection of Jesus in a synagogue in his own country. The congregation think that they know him and his family, and they take offence at his words and deeds. The story appealed to Matthew for inclusion at this point, because he had been comparing Israel to fruitless ground, and weeds, and the fish that men throw away: now he shows again that the words of Jesus were justified; the people in his own country did not believe in him. They did not recognize his *wisdom* and his *mighty works* as the Spirit of God; they did not know that he was *the Son of God*, and that his true brethren were his disciples, not his physical family. They stumbled in unbelief, and so Jesus refused to do many miracles, just as he had refused to teach them earlier in this chapter, but had spoken to them in parables which they could not understand.

ॐ

Matthew has abbreviated Mark 6^{1-6a}, and made some additions to it. Verse 53 is an addition: it is the third appearance of the formula for transition from teaching to narrative. Matthew repeats the question *Where then did this man get all this?* at the end of the words of the congregation – an example of his fondness for *inclusio* (see p. 51). He has changed Mark's *Is not this the carpenter?* to *Is not this the carpenter's son?* possibly in order to contrast the unbelief of the people with the Christian faith that Jesus is the Son of God, not the son of Joseph; and he has omitted Mark's *. . . and among his own kin* in the words of Jesus, perhaps because he believed that the true kindred of Jesus were the disciples, not the people of his own country (cf. 12⁴⁹ᶠ.). Finally he has changed Mark's last sentence, *And he could do no mighty work there, except that he laid his hands upon a few sick people and healed them. And he marvelled because of their unbelief*, to *And he did not do many mighty works there, because of their unbelief*: and so removed any suggestion of the inability of Jesus to do miracles, and stressed his refusal to do them.

53

For the other examples of this formula, see 7²⁸, 11¹, 19¹, 26¹.

these parables summarizes the contents of the teaching section which preceded this use of the formula, 13³ᶠᶠ.

54

Matthew and Mark call the place *his own country*; Luke says *Nazareth* (Luke 4¹⁶): see note on *his own city* in 9¹ which seemed to mean *Capernaum*. We cannot be sure whether Matthew meant *his own country* to be Nazareth, or Capernaum, or Galilee as a whole. He may have left it vague, in order to let it stand for *this generation* of the Jews in general, which has rejected Jesus and his message.

he taught them in their synagogue: This is the last reference to teaching in a synagogue in this Gospel; for earlier references see 4²³, 9³⁵, 12⁹. For teaching here, contrast Matthew's avoidance of the word in 13¹ᶠᶠ. and the note there. Matthew has added *their* (synagogue): see note on 4²³. The astonishment of the congregation is the result of *their unbelief* (v. 58). To the believing the *wisdom* and *the mighty works* (i.e. the miracles) of Jesus are from God: cf. 12²⁸ᶠ., *it is by the Spirit of God that I cast out demons . . .*

55f.

Contrast the sayings about Jesus' family in 12⁴⁶ᶠᶠ., the story which came immediately before the teaching section.

57

The congregation takes offence, because their eyes have not been opened; compare *blessed is he who takes no offence at me*, and *blessed are your eyes, for they see* (11⁶, 13¹⁶): and Rom. 9³²ᶠ., *They have stumbled over the stumbling stone, as it is written, Behold I am laying in Zion a stone that will make men stumble, a rock that will make them fall; and he who believes in him will not be put to shame.*

A prophet is not without honour . . . was a well-known proverb.

58

'Our Lord is depicted in St Matthew as deliberately restricting his acts of power among his own people in consequence of and almost as a punishment for unbelief' (R. H. Lightfoot).

14$^{1-12}$ THE DEATH OF JOHN THE   Mark 6$^{14-30}$
BAPTIST

14 *At that time Herod the tetrarch heard about the fame of Jesus;* ^{2}*and he said to his servants, 'This is John the Baptist, he has been raised from the dead; that is why these powers are at work in him.'* ^{3}*For Herod had seized John and bound him and put him in prison, for the sake of Hero'di-as, his brother Philip's wife;^{a}* ^{4}*because John said to him, 'It is not lawful for you to have her.'* ^{5}*And though he wanted to put him to death, he feared the people, because they held him to be a prophet.* ^{6}*But when Herod's birthday came, the daughter of Hero'di-as danced before the company, and pleased Herod,* ^{7}*so that he promised with an oath to give her whatever she might ask.* ^{8}*Prompted by her mother, she said, 'Give me the head of John the Baptist here on a platter.'* ^{9}*And the king was sorry; but because of his oaths and his guests he commanded it to be given;* ^{10}*he sent and had John beheaded in the prison,* ^{11}*and his head was brought on a platter and given to the girl, and she brought it to her mother.* ^{12}*And his disciples came and took the body and buried it; and they went and told Jesus.*

a Other ancient authorities read his brother's wife

This paragraph begins with the report of Jesus' miracles which had reached Herod Antipas, one of the sons of Herod the Great. Herod believed that Jesus was John the Baptist risen from the dead, and that this was the reason for his doing miracles. The paragraph then goes on to explain how John had met his death: John had rebuked Herod for marrying Herodias, his sister-in-law; Herod had imprisoned him, but had not dared to kill him, until he was caught up in the intrigues of Herodias and her daughter. Matthew makes it clear in his Gospel that Jesus and John suffer the same fate: both of them are prophets (13^{57}, 14^5); both of them are rejected by *this generation* (11$^{16ff.}$); both of them are put to death – *I tell you that Elijah has already come, and they did not know him, but did to him whatever they pleased. So also the Son of man will suffer at their hands* (17¹²). Matthew, like Mark, believed that John was Elijah returned from heaven; and just as Jezebel, king Ahab's wife, had tried to kill Elijah (1 Kings 19²), so now Herodias, king Herod's wife, succeeds in bringing about John's death.

৯৯

Matthew tells in twelve verses the story which Mark had told in twenty-seven verses. In order to shorten Mark's version, Matthew has omitted the other opinions about Jesus which were current, and abbreviated the account of Herod's birthday celebrations. He has also made certain alterations in the story, among which notice first that whereas in Mark it is said that Herodias wanted to kill John but could not because Herod knew that he was a righteous and holy man and protected him, in Matthew it is Herod who wants to kill John, and does not do so because he is afraid of the people who believe John to be a prophet; and secondly that Mark's statement at the beginning of the next paragraph that *The apostles returned to Jesus, and told him all that they had done and taught* in their mission (Mark 6³⁰) is misunderstood by Matthew as a reference to the disciples of the Baptist, and is made the conclusion of this paragraph: *and they went and told Jesus*. The first alteration may have been made because Matthew was thinking of Herod as a second Ahab, who had wanted to remove Naboth (1 Kings 21). The second alteration makes it possible for Matthew to continue in the next verse (14¹³) with a sentence which is very similar to 4¹² (see note on 14¹³).

1

At that time is a Matthean editorial phrase (cf. 11²⁵).
Matthew and Luke both change Mark's *King Herod* to *Herod the tetrarch*; a *tetrarch* was the ruler of the fourth part of a district, and it was the correct title for Herod Antipas; but Matthew, following Mark, calls him *the king* in v. 9.

2

these powers (*hai dynameis*) means 'these miracles': see 7²², 11²⁰, 13⁵⁴, ⁵⁸. Herod is giving his answer to the people's question *Where did this man get this wisdom and these mighty works?* (13⁵⁴).

3f.

Mark was almost certainly wrong in saying that Herodias was the wife of *Philip*: she was the wife of another Herod who was half-brother to

Herod Antipas. The omission of *Philip* in a few of the authorities from the text here may be a later attempt to correct this mistake, in which Matthew followed Mark. The complications of the Herod family relationships are so great that mistakes could very easily arise.

5

See the notes after the text above for the change which Matthew has made in Mark; and notice how he has taken the explanation *because they held him to be a prophet* from Mark 11^{32} = Matthew 21^{26}.

6–11

Josephus also records the execution of 'John who was called the Baptist' at the command of Herod 'who feared lest the great influence John had over the people might put it into his power and inclination to raise a rebellion (for they seemed ready to do anything he should advise)' (*Antiquities* XVIII, 5, 2).

12

and they went and told Jesus: This is Matthew's adaptation of Mark 6^{30} *The apostles returned to Jesus, and told him all that they had done and taught,* which in Mark is the beginning of the next paragraph, and refers to the twelve who had been sent out in Mark 6$^{7\text{ff}}$.

14$^{13-21}$ JESUS FEEDS THE Mark 6$^{32-44}$
FIVE THOUSAND

^{13}Now when Jesus heard this, he withdrew from there in a boat to a lonely place apart. But when the crowds heard it, they followed him on foot from the towns. ^{14}As he went ashore he saw a great throng; and he had compassion on them, and healed their sick. ^{15}When it was evening, the disciples came to him and said, 'This is a lonely place, and the day is now over; send the crowds away to go into the villages and buy food for themselves.' ^{16}Jesus said, 'They need not go away; you give them something to eat.' ^{17}They said to him, 'We have only five loaves here and two fish.' ^{18}And he said, 'Bring them here to me.' ^{19}Then he ordered the crowds to sit down on the grass; and taking the five loaves and the two fish he looked up to heaven, and blessed, and broke and gave the loaves to the disciples, and the disciples gave them to the crowds. ^{20}And they all ate and were satisfied. And they took up twelve *baskets full of the broken pieces left over. ²¹And those who ate were about five thousand men, besides women and children.*

The news of the death of John is followed by another 'withdrawal' of Jesus, but as the reader of this Gospel has learnt to expect, the 'withdrawal' is followed by a new further revelation of the power and authority of Jesus. The scene of this revelation is the desert, and Jesus not only heals the sick, but also feeds the hungry. The miracle recalls the Old Testament story of the manna in the wilderness (Exod. 16), and Elisha feeding a hundred men (2 Kings 4⁴²ff.), and no doubt the Christians, as they used the story, saw in this feeding an anticipation of the eucharist (26²⁶ff.): these interpretations are brought out more clearly in the treatment of the feeding in John 6. The basic idea, however, is probably simpler than this; in the next chapter, Jesus will speak of the salvation which he is bringing as *bread*: *It is not fair to take the children's bread and throw it to the dogs* (15²⁶). *Bread* had also been used as a symbol of life and truth in the Old Testament; e.g.

> *Why do you spend your money for that which is not bread,*
> *and your labour for that which does not satisfy?*
> *Hearken diligently to me, and eat what is good,*
> *and delight yourselves in fatness.*
> *Incline your ear, and come to me;*
> *hear, that your soul may live;*

(Isa. 55²f.)

There is evidence also that some of the Jews expected that when the Messiah came there would be a repetition of the miraculous feeding at the time of the Exodus; for example a first-century Jewish writer says: 'And it shall come to pass at that self-same time that the treasury of manna shall again descend from on high, and they will eat of it in those years, because these are they who have come to the consummation of time' (i.e. the messianic age), 2 *Baruch* 29⁸; and compare Rev. 2¹⁷, *To him who conquers I will give some of the hidden manna.*

We cannot get back now, behind all the Christian interpretations of this story, to what actually happened; but we can see what it meant to Matthew and his readers: Jesus as the prophet like Moses; the Messiah who brings new food and gives eternal life; the sign of the age to come.

Matthew has used Mark 6³²⁻⁴⁴, omitting the description of the crowd as *like sheep without a shepherd* which he had already used in 9³⁶; changing Mark's *and he began to teach them many things* to *and healed their sick* (Luke makes the same alteration, Luke 9¹¹); and abbreviating the conversation between Jesus and the disciples.

13

Now when Jesus heard this, he withdrew from there: Cf. the similar expression in 4¹² *Now when he heard that John had been arrested, he withdrew into Galilee*. For other 'withdrawals' of Jesus in this Gospel, see 2¹⁴, ²², 12¹⁵, 15²¹.

to a lonely place (eis erēmon topon): Literally 'to a desert place': the same word is used for 'desert' or *wilderness*, in Exod. 16.

14

The *compassion* of Jesus is mentioned four times in this Gospel; 9³⁶, here, 15³² (the other feeding miracle), and 20³⁴.

healed their sick replaces Mark's reference to teaching, possibly because Matthew intended to avoid saying that Jesus taught the crowd (see note on 13¹ff.): and because Matthew had omitted two references to the sick (*arrōstoi*) in Mark 6⁵, ¹³.

15ff.

The disciples cannot see any other possible course to take except that of sending the crowds away to *buy food for themselves*; Jesus says that there is no need to do this. The disciples *doubt* the power of Jesus, because they have *little faith*: cf. the words of Jesus to Peter, *O man of little faith, why did you doubt?* (v. 31).

19

he looked up to heaven, and blessed, and broke and gave the loaves to the disciples: In Jewish households, the father of the family said grace before meals by taking a loaf, thanking God for the gift of food, breaking the loaf, and giving each person present a piece of it to eat. *Blessed* here means therefore *blessed* God, i.e. praised him and thanked him for food; not *blessed* the bread. Cf. Acts 27³⁵f., Paul *took bread, and giving thanks to God in the presence of all he broke it and began to eat. Then they all were encouraged and ate some food themselves*.

20

were satisfied (echortasthēsan): The same word is used in the Beatitudes of the messianic feast in the kingdom; *Blessed are those who hunger and thirst for righteousness, for they shall be satisfied*, 5⁶; this feeding in the desert is the sign of the kingdom. For the mention of food *left over*, cf. the account of Elisha's miracle, *they ate, and had some left, according to the word of the Lord* (2 Kings 4⁴⁴).

21

Matthew adds the words *besides women and children* here and at the end of the other feeding in 15³⁸.

14^{22-27} JESUS WALKS ON THE SEA   Mark 6⁴⁵⁻⁵⁰

²² Then he made the disciples get into the boat and go before him to the other side, while he dismissed the crowds. ²³ And after he had dismissed the crowds, he went up into the hills by himself to pray. When evening came, he was there alone, ²⁴ but the boat by this time was many furlongs distant from the land,ᵃ beaten by the waves; for the wind was against them. ²⁵ And in the fourth watch of the night he came to them, walking on the sea. ²⁶ But when the disciples saw him walking on the sea, they were terrified, saying, 'It is a ghost!' And they cried out for fear. ²⁷ But immediately he spoke to them, saying, 'Take heart, it is I; have no fear.'

a Other ancient authorities read *was out on the sea*

After the feeding, Jesus first sends the disciples in the boat to the other side, then dismisses the crowds, and goes up 'the mountain' alone to pray. He is thus separated from the disciples when, in the fourth and last watch of the night, they are caught by a storm out on the lake, facing a head-wind. He walks to them on the sea, but they do not recognize him: they cry out for fear. He says to them, It is I. Jesus had already revealed himself as Lord over the winds and sea by commanding them to obey him (8²³ff.), but although the calming of the wind is mentioned in the next paragraph (14³²) this is not the main point here. The emphasis here is on the separation of the disciples from Jesus, and their terror and fear, which are not removed until the fourth watch of the night when Jesus miraculously comes to them. The significance of the story for the Church may have been that although Jesus is apparently separated from them, since the crucifixion, yet he is praying for them, and will come to them again as the Son of man;

they are to *take heart* and *have no fear*, although they are *beaten by the waves* of persecution, and *the wind* is *against them*.

ನಐ

Matthew uses the next six verses of Mark (Mark 6$^{45-50}$): he has omitted the name of the place on *the other side* to which he sent the disciples (*Bethsaida*), and the statement that Jesus *meant to pass by them*.

22

the boat: They had come *in a boat* to the desert place where Jesus fed the crowds (14^{13}).

23

the hills (to oros): Literally, 'the mountain'; the other references to the mountain in Matthew are 4^8, 5^1, 8^1, 15^{29}, 17$^{1, 9, 20}$, 28^{16}.

to pray: Here and in Gethsemane (26^{36}ff.) are the only places where Matthew says that Jesus prayed.

25

the fourth watch of the night: The Romans divided the time between 6 p.m. and 6 a.m. into four equal periods called watches.

14$^{28-33}$	PETER'S DOUBT AND HIS RESTORATION	Mark 6$^{51, 52}$, 15^{39}

^{28}*And Peter answered him, 'Lord, if it is you, bid me come to you on the water.' ^{29}He said, 'Come.' So Peter got out of the boat and walked on the water and came to Jesus; ^{30}but when he saw the wind,^{a} he was afraid, and beginning to sink he cried out, 'Lord, save me.' ^{31}Jesus immediately reached out his hand and caught him, saying to him, 'O man of little faith, why did you doubt?' ^{32}And when they got into the boat, the wind ceased. ^{33}And those in the boat worshipped him, saying, 'Truly you are the Son of God.'*

  a Other ancient authorities read *strong wind*

Peter asks to be allowed to come to Jesus on the water, and Jesus tells him to come to him; he walks on the water until, afraid of the wind, he begins to sink, and cries out to Jesus to save him. Jesus takes hold of him, and rebukes him for his doubt. They both get into the boat, the wind ceases, and the disciples worship Jesus as the Son of God.

This is one of the two paragraphs which Matthew has added to Mark in this section: the greater part of it has no parallel outside this Gospel, and the style in which it is written is typically Matthean. We have seen already that the Church for which Matthew wrote his Gospel had a particular reverence for Peter as the *first* of the apostles, and the *rock* on which the Church is built (10^2, 16^{18}). Nevertheless, this reverence for Peter did not cause Matthew to omit Peter's denial of Jesus during the Passion ($26^{69\text{ff.}}$); and here also Matthew presents Peter as a man of *little faith*, a doubter. The failure of Peter here, and his restoration by Jesus, may be an anticipation of Peter's failure during the Passion, and his restoration after the resurrection.

What we have in this paragraph is therefore best regarded as a preacher's elaboration on a theme by means of a story; another example of this kind of writing in this Gospel is the account of the resurrection of dead saints after the death of Jesus, $27^{52\text{f.}}$.

ΙΧΘΥΣ

Verses 28–31 have no parallel in Mark, but v. 32 is adapted from Mark 6^{51}, and v. 33 is Matthew's rewriting of Mark 6^{52}, making use of Mark 15^{39}.

28

Peter asks Jesus' permission to do what Jesus is doing; in the Passion also he will attempt to follow Jesus (26^{58}).

Notice how Matthew uses the word *water* (here and in the next verse) when he is composing 'out of nothing', but copies *sea* from Mark when he is following a written source closely (vv. 25f.); perhaps *sea* would suggest the Mediterranean to Matthew's readers.

30

With Peter's fear, fall, and cry, cf. his denials of Jesus and weeping, $26^{69\text{ff.}}$.

31

Jesus restores Peter, reproving him for *little faith* (a characteristic Matthean expression, see 6^{30}, 8^{26}, 16^8, 17^{20}) and for *doubt* (another Matthean word, see 28^{17}). The restoration of Peter after the resurrection is not recorded in Matthew; perhaps this story was created in order to fill that gap. For other evidence of the restoration of Peter, see 1 Cor. 15⁵ (*he appeared to Cephas, then to the twelve*), Mark 16⁷ (*tell his disciples and Peter that he is going before you to Galilee*), John 21¹⁵ᶠᶠ. (the conversation between Jesus and Peter).

33

Mark had at this point, *And they were utterly astounded, for they did not understand about the loaves, but their hearts were hardened* (Mark 6⁵¹ᶠ.). Matthew omits this, because in his Gospel the disciples are presented as men who have been given insight. He therefore puts in its place a confession of faith, *Truly you are the Son of God*, which he has adapted from the centurion's confession after the death of Jesus, Mark 15³⁹. And notice also the word *worshipped*, another favourite word of Matthew's, on which see note on 8²; Matthew will use it twice in his last chapter, of the worship of Jesus by the women and his disciples after the resurrection, 28⁹, ¹⁷.

14³⁴⁻³⁶   JESUS HEALS THE SICK   Mark 6⁵³⁻⁵⁶
                    AT GENNESARET

³⁴*And when they had crossed over, they came to land at Gennes'aret.* ⁴⁵*And when the men of that place recognized him, they sent round to all that region and brought to him all that were sick,* ³⁶*and besought him that they might only touch the fringe of his garment; and as many as touched it were made well.*

These three verses describe the welcome which Jesus receives at Gennesaret: Jesus is recognized as the healer, the sick of the district are brought to him, and all who touch the fringe of his garment are made well.

The purpose of these verses may be to contrast the welcome from the people with the criticism which the Pharisees and scribes from Jerusalem will make in the paragraph which follows (15¹ᶠᶠ.). Matthew has twice given us a miracle of Jesus, followed first by a favourable reception, then by a hostile criticism; in 9³²ᶠᶠ. the exorcism of a dumb demoniac – *the crowds marvelled, saying, Never was anything like this seen in Israel. But the Pharisees said, He casts out demons by the prince of demons.* And in 12²³ᶠ·, after another exorcism, the crowds said *Can this be the Son of David?* But the Pharisees said, *It is only by Beelzebul, the prince of demons, that this man casts out demons.* In much the same way here, we have first the manifestation of Jesus (14²²⁻³³), then the favourable reaction of the men of Gennesaret (14³⁴ᶠᶠ·), then the criticism of the Pharisees and scribes (15¹ᶠᶠ·).

ஐ

Matthew is using Mark 6⁵³⁻⁵⁶, but abbreviating the source, which implied a considerable tour in the district – e.g. *Wherever he came, in villages, cities, or country, they laid their sick in the market places . . .*

34
Gennesaret is located on the western side of the lake, south of Capernaum, but it is not certain whether it was a town (or village), or a district, namely, the whole fertile plain.

35
For *the fringe of his garment* see notes on 9²⁰ and 23⁵.

15¹⁻⁶   JESUS ACCUSES THE PHARISEES   Mark 7¹⁻¹³
AND SCRIBES OF TRANSGRESSING
THE COMMANDMENT OF GOD

15 *Then Pharisees and scribes came to Jesus from Jerusalem and said,* ²'*Why do your disciples transgress the tradition of the elders? For they do not wash their hands when they eat.*' ³*He answered them,* '*And why do you transgress the commandment of God for the sake of your tradition?* ⁴*For God commanded,* "*Honour your father and your mother,*" *and,* "*He who speaks evil of father or mother, let him surely die.*" ⁵*But you say,* "*If any one tells his father or his mother, What you would have gained from me is given to God,ᵃ he need not honour his father.*" ⁶*So, for the sake of your tradition, you have made void the wordᵇ of God.* ⁷*You hypocrites! Well did Isaiah prophesy of you, when he said:*
> ⁸"*This people honours me with their lips,*
> *but their heart is far from me;*

> ⁹in vain do they worship me,
>   teaching as doctrines the precepts of men." '

a Or *an offering*
b Other ancient authorities read *law*

The Pharisees and scribes return on to the scene, with a question about the behaviour of Jesus' disciples. The disciples, they say, do not keep the oral Law, or *tradition of the elders*; for example, they do not practise ritual washing before meals. Jesus answers the Pharisees and scribes with a counter-question which accuses them of using the tradition of the elders as a way of breaking *the commandment of God*, that is, the written Law. He then illustrates this: the Fifth Commandment laid down a duty to parents; but the oral tradition permitted a man to devote his possessions to God, in such a way that his parents would derive no benefit from them. They are *hypocrites*, and they fulfil Isaiah's prophecy of people who honour God with words but not with the will, who worship God in vain and teach human commands and not those of God.

∞

Matthew has taken Mark 7¹⁻¹³, and abbreviated it by omitting two verses which explained the customs of the Jews, an explanation which Mark thought necessary for his readers who were apparently not in close contact with Jews, but which Matthew's readers could dispense with. Matthew has also re-arranged the material in the paragraph: in Mark, the prophecy from Isaiah comes before the sayings about the commandment and the tradition: Matthew takes the Law first, and then the prophet.

1f.
The *Pharisees and scribes*, unlike the Sadducees, observed a large body of unwritten laws, called *the tradition of the elders*; these regulations were later written down by Rabbi Judah ha-Nasi (A.D. 135–c. 220) and formed the Mishnah. Washing the hands was for the removal of ceremonial defilement caused by contact with people or things that were unclean.

3
Jesus answers their question with a counter-question in the rabbinic manner; the pattern 'question, counter-question' is the work of the

Evangelist, who has contrived it by the manipulation of his source
(cf. 12^{9ff} and notes).

Jesus contrasts *the commandment of GOD* with YOUR *tradition*; i.e.
God's will with man's will.

4

This verse and the next illustrate the charge in the previous verse: the
example of *the commandment of God* is the fifth of the Ten Commandments (Exod. 20^{12}); and *He who speaks evil of father or mother, let him
surely die* is quoted from Exod. 21^{17}.

5

The example from *your tradition* (v. 3) is a regulation for vows: a man
could set apart his property for God, while retaining the right to use it
himself, and thus prevent its use by anyone else – e.g. in this case, by his
father.

6

This verse repeats the general charge in v.3 , and is thus an example of
Matthew's use of *inclusio*; moreover, the items in the two verses are
repeated in the opposite order (*commandment, tradition . . . tradition, word*
= commandment), so as to make a chiasmus (on these stylistic
idioms of Matthew, see Introduction, pp. 15f. and 51).

7

Matthew has added *You hypocrites!* See note on 6^2.

8f.

The quotation is from Isa. 29^{13} in the LXX. *This people* (*ho laos houtos*),
is taken to mean Israel, of whom the *Pharisees and scribes* are the leaders.
By making it possible for a man not to contribute from his possessions
to his parents, and thus dishonour his parents, they are teaching men to
dishonour God, who commands them to honour their parents. They
still pay respect to the commandments of God *with their lips*, but *their
heart* (= thoughts, motives) is directed to themselves, and not to him;
their *worship* is to no purpose, because they teach, not God's commandments, but merely human instruction. Cf. the sayings about words
and deeds in 7^{21ff}.

^{10}And he called the people to him and said to them, 'Hear and understand: ^{11}not what goes into the mouth defiles a man, but what comes out of the mouth, this defiles a man.' ^{12}Then the disciples came and said to him, 'Do you know that the Pharisees were offended when they heard this saying?' ^{13}He answered, 'Every plant which my heavenly Father has not planted will be rooted up. ^{14}Let them alone; they are blind guides. And if a blind man leads a blind man, both will fall into a pit.' ^{15}But Peter said to him, 'Explain the parable to us.' ^{16}And he said, 'Are you also still without understanding? ^{17}Do you not see that whatever goes into the mouth passes into the stomach, and so passes on?^{a} ^{18}But what comes out of the mouth proceeds from the heart, and this defiles a man. ^{19}For out of the heart come evil thoughts, murder, adultery, fornication, theft, false witness, slander. ^{20}These are what defile a man; but to eat with unwashed hands does not defile a man.'

    a Or is evacuated

Jesus now returns to the subject which the Pharisees and scribes had raised at the beginning of the previous paragraph. They had asked why the disciples did not observe the tradition about washing before eating. Jesus calls together the crowd, and speaks to them in a parable: it is not what enters through the mouth that defiles, but what goes out from the mouth. This saying is not explained to the crowd, but first the disciples tell Jesus that the Pharisees were offended by it, and Jesus says that the Pharisees are not 'of God', and so they will be destroyed; and then Peter asks Jesus to explain the parable, and Jesus says that what enters through the mouth is food, what goes out of the mouth is evil words and evil actions, which defile a man.

This paragraph raises a number of problems, as Matthew was no doubt aware; it seems, for example, to involve a complete rejection of the Old Testament laws about clean and unclean meats, and Mark certainly drew this conclusion, because he adds in parentheses, *Thus he declared all foods clean* Mark 7^{19}. Matthew has omitted this comment, probably because he and his readers did not believe that Jesus had abolished the Old Testament law about food (see e.g. 23^3). Matthew has added the concluding line, *to eat with unwashed hands does not defile a man,* perhaps in order to limit the scope of the teaching of Jesus here to the original question, which was whether the disciples should keep the tradition of the elders or not. Matthew is saying: Jesus taught us that it is not necessary to keep this tradition; but we should keep the written commandments of God.

Another problem is whether Mark was right in thinking that Jesus did teach the abolition of the laws about clean and unclean food. From what we can discover about the Church in the years after the resurrection by means of Paul's letters and the Acts of the Apostles, it seems highly unlikely that Jesus did give such explicit instructions as Mark implies in Mark $7^{14ff.}$: otherwise the Church would not have had so much difficulty in admitting the Gentiles to its fellow-ship, and eating with them. See, for example, Acts 10^1-11^{18}, 15, Gal. $2^{11ff.}$. Mark has probably read the attitude of the Church of his time and place into the original sayings of Jesus.

ಐಐ

Verses 10, 11, 15–20 are from Mark 7^{14-23}, with some alterations for which see the notes below. Verses 12–14 have no parallel in Mark, and of these three verses only 14b, *if a blind man . . . ,* has a parallel in Luke 6^{39}; the remainder are probably of Matthean composition, because they are in his style.

10

In v. 2, the Pharisees and scribes raised two questions: (i) the tradition of the elders, (ii) defilement. Verses 3–9 answered (i); vv. 10–20 answer (ii).

he called the people unto him: The words translated *the people* here are *ton ochlon,* and they would be better translated 'the crowd'; Matthew distinguishes between Israel (the people of God) and the crowd – see on 4^{23}.

Hear and understand is taken from Mark; Matthew, one suspects, would not have expected the crowd to understand; cf. 13^{14} *You shall indeed hear but never understand.*

11

Matthew changes Mark's *into him . . . out of man* to *into the mouth . . . out of the mouth*; the amendment is not altogether happy, because though the first refers to food and is satisfactory, the second refers not only to words, but also to deeds, and this is not so satisfactory. See vv. 18ff.

12–14

These verses are an editorial addition, and they interrupt the subject. The question of the disciples implies that the Pharisees have understood the parable, whereas the disciples themselves have not understood it; see vv. 15ff. For the word *offended* (*eskandalisthēsan*) see note on 11⁶.

Every plant ... cf. the parable of the weeds of the field and its explanation, 13²⁴ᶠᶠ·, ³⁶ᶠᶠ·.

blind guides: This charge is repeated against the Pharisees in Chapter 23 – e.g. 23¹⁶. Paul uses a similar idea: *if you are sure that you are a guide to the blind* (Rom. 2¹⁹).

15

In Mark, *his disciples asked him about the parable*; but Matthew changes this, to make *Peter* speak on behalf of the disciples.

16

Matthew slightly softens down the rebuke of Jesus in Mark.

17

What goes into the mouth in v. 11 is now explained as food, but Matthew omits the words in Mark which said explicitly that no food can defile a man.

18

Cf. 12³⁴, *Out of the abundance of the heart the mouth speaks.* A man is defiled by his words, which express his thoughts.

19

Matthew has abbreviated Mark's list of thirteen evil things, to seven, and has re-arranged them so that after the first (*evil thoughts*) the other six follow the order of the Sixth, Seventh, Eighth, and Ninth Commandments: *murder* (the Sixth); *adultery* and *fornication* (Seventh); *theft* (Eighth); *false witness* and *slander* (Ninth).

20

These are what defile a man; but to eat with unwashed hands does not defile a man: This verse repeats v. 11, and reverses the order of terms in it: *not what goes into the mouth defiles a man, but what comes out of the mouth, this defiles a man.* It thus rounds off this paragraph (*inclusio*) and is an example of a chiasmus; cf. v. 6 above. Matthew has added *but to eat with unwashed hands* . . . perhaps limiting the application of the parable to *the tradition of the elders* (v. 2), and not (like Mark) taking it as a declaration that Jesus abolished the Old Testament food laws.

15²¹⁻²⁸   THE FAITH OF A GENTILE   Mark 7²⁴⁻³⁰

²¹*And Jesus went away from there and withdrew to the district of Tyre and Sidon.* ²²*And behold, a Canaanite woman from that region came out and cried, 'Have mercy on me, O Lord, Son of David; my daughter is severely possessed by a demon.'* ²³*But he did not answer her a word. And his disciples came and begged him, saying, 'Send her away, for she is crying after us.'* ²⁴*He answered, 'I was sent only to the lost sheep of the house of Israel.'* ²⁵*But she came and knelt before him, saying, 'Lord, help me.'* ²⁶*And he answered, 'It is not fair to take the children's bread and throw it to the dogs.'* ²⁷*She said, 'Yes, Lord, yet even the dogs eat the crumbs that fall from their masters' table.'* ²⁸*Then Jesus answered her, 'O woman, great is your faith! Be it done for you as you desire.' And her daughter was healed instantly.*

In the two paragraphs before this, the question What is it that defiles? had been raised. In this paragraph, the subject is the relation between Jews and Gentiles. The two subjects are connected, because the Jews' belief concerning defilement made them keep themselves separate from the Gentiles; and the eventual Christian faith that *the dividing wall of hostility* between Jews and Gentiles had been broken down by Christ enabled them to accept Gentiles into the Church on equal terms with the Jews (see e.g. Eph. 2¹¹⁻²²).

This paragraph looks forward to the time when this will happen, and the story of the Gentile woman whose daughter Jesus healed was no doubt told among the Christians at the time when the debate about the admission of Gentiles was proceeding. Matthew has made various additions to Mark, which may reflect his attitude to this debate. He inserts the request of the disciples that Jesus should *send her away*, much as some of the Jewish Christians had opposed preaching to Gentiles and contact with them (e.g. Acts 11¹ff.). And he repeats here a saying of Jesus which he has recorded earlier in a slightly different form and context, *I was sent only to the lost sheep of the house of Israel*: thus agreeing with those who said that Jesus himself had not gone outside Israel during his ministry. Matthew has also retold the story in such a way as to create a delay between the coming of the woman and Jesus' answer to her request – a delay which corresponds to the interval between the ministry of Jesus and the time when Gentiles were admitted to the Church.

ΙΟΟΙ

Matthew has kept this paragraph almost exactly the same length as Mark 7^{24-30}, and so in order to add new material of his own he has omitted some of Mark's details.

21

Jesus went away from there: The last place-name was Gennesaret (14^{34}).

and withdrew: Matthew has added this word here: see note on 2^{14}, etc.

to the district of Tyre and Sidon: Matthew has added *and Sidon* (though the text of Mark is uncertain and Mark has it in 7^{31}); these towns are about thirty to fifty miles north-west of Gennesaret on the Mediterranean coast (see map on p. 8) and are the farthest north that Jesus is said to have gone. Matthew's interest may have been due to his writing in and for a Church in this same district. The two towns were mentioned before in $11^{21f.}$.

22

Matthew changes Mark's description *a Greek, a Syrophoenician by birth* to *a Canaanite*: there is some evidence to show that the words Canaan and Canaanite were used of Phoenicia, and possibly of the countryside as opposed to the Greek towns, at this time.

Matthew has put her request into direct speech; for *Have mercy on me,* cf. 9^{27}, 17^{15}, $20^{30f.}$. *O Lord:* Jesus is frequently addressed as *Lord* in Matthew but seldom in Mark; *Son of David* is also a characteristic title of Jesus in this Gospel (see 1^1).

23

The silence of Jesus, and the request of the disciples, have both been added by Matthew. *Send her away* may mean either 'Dismiss her', or 'Do what she asks and so let her go away'. The latter is more likely, in view of the next verse.

24

Another Matthean addition, a repetition of the command of Jesus to

the twelve, . . . *Go rather to the lost sheep of the house of Israel* (10⁶).
Matthew sees the time before the crucifixion as the time when the
Gospel is offered to the Jews, and the time after the resurrection as the
time for preaching to the Gentiles (28¹⁹).

25

Matthew has added this second request by the woman.

26

the children are the Jews, God's people; *the dogs* are the Gentiles. The
Jews used to call the Gentiles *dogs*, and the Christians, claiming to be the
true Jews, in turn called the unbelieving Jews *dogs*, e.g. *Look out for the
dogs, look out for the evil-workers, look out for those who mutilate the flesh.
For we are the true circumcision . . .* (Phil. 3²f·). *Bread* is used in this saying as
a symbol of salvation, as in the feeding miracles (14¹³ff., 15³²ff.).
Cf. also 7⁶, *Do not give dogs what is holy.*

27

Matthew has changed Mark's *the children's* to *their masters'*; the faith of
the woman is heightened by this admission that the Jews are the
masters over the Gentiles.

28

Matthew has rewritten this verse to make it agree more closely with
the saying of Jesus to the Gentile centurion in 8¹³.

15²⁹⁻³¹   JESUS HEALS MANY   cf. Mark 7³¹⁻³⁷
                    SICK PEOPLE

²⁹*And Jesus went on from there and passed along the Sea of Galilee. And he
went up into the hills, and sat down there.* ³⁰*And great crowds came to him,
bringing with them the lame, the maimed, the blind, the dumb, and many
others, and they put them at his feet, and he healed them,* ³¹*so that the throng
wondered, when they saw the dumb speaking, the maimed whole, the lame
walking, and the blind seeing; and they glorified the God of Israel.*

Jesus returns from Tyre and Sidon in the north, to the Sea of Galilee,
and goes up the mountain; great crowds bring sick people to him, and
he heals them, so that the crowd is amazed, and glorifies *the God of
Israel.*

In order to understand these verses, it is necessary to compare the parallel passage in Mark 7³¹ff. There, a man was healed by Jesus who is described as one who *was deaf and had an impediment in his speech* (*kōphon kai mogilalon*). The second word, which means literally 'a stammerer', was rare, but it had been used in the LXX translation of Isa. 35⁵ᶠ·:

> Then the eyes of the blind shall be opened,
>   and the ears of the deaf unstopped;
> then shall the lame man leap like a hart
>   and the tongue of the dumb sing for joy.

Matthew has picked up Mark's reference back to Isaiah, and re-written the paragraph in terms of the fulfilment of it, bringing in just those kinds of sickness which Isaiah had mentioned, *the lame, the maimed, the blind, the dumb* (or 'deaf', *kōphous*).

Two points in this paragraph suggest that we are to think here of a Gentile crowd rather than a Jewish crowd: (i) *The Sea of Galilee* is only so called in this Gospel here and at 4¹⁸, where it follows the pro-phecy of Isaiah which promised *light* to *Galilee of the Gentiles*; (ii) the crowd here glorifies *the God of Israel*, implying that they themselves are not of Israel.

༺༻

29
And Jesus went on from there (*metabas ekeithen*) is a characteristic Matthean introduction to a paragraph; see e.g. 12⁹.

And he went up into the hills (literally, the mountain) *and sat there:* Cf. 5¹ for almost exactly the same words.

30
The four kinds of sick people in Isaiah's prophecy were *the blind* (*typhlōn*), *the deaf* (*kōphōn*), *the lame* (*ho chōlos*), *the dumb* (*mogilalōn*). Matthew uses three of these words, but he uses *kōphōn* in the sense of *dumb* (as he had done at 9³²ᶠ·, 12²²ᶠ·, contrast 11⁵), and he employs another word which is translated *maimed* (*kyllos*) to make up the four.

31
the throng (*ton ochlon*): The same word as *the crowds* in the previous verse.

[32] *Then Jesus called his disciples to him and said, 'I have compassion on the crowd, because they have been with me now three days, and have nothing to eat; and I am unwilling to send them away hungry, lest they faint on the way.'* [33] *And the disciples said to him, 'Where are we to get bread enough in the desert to feed so great a crowd?'* [34] *And Jesus said to them, 'How many loaves have you?' They said, 'Seven, and a few small fish.'* [35] *And commanding the crowd to sit down on the ground,* [36] *he took the seven loaves and the fish, and having given thanks he broke them and gave them to the disciples, and the disciples gave them to the crowds.* [37] *And they all ate and were satisfied; and they took up seven baskets full of the broken pieces left over.* [38] *Those who ate were four thousand men, besides women and children.* [39] *And sending away the crowds, he got into the boat and went to the region of Mag'adan.*

The next incident in Matthew is another miracle of feeding, very similar to the one already described in $14^{13\text{ff.}}$. Again it begins with a conversation between Jesus and his disciples, and mentions the *compassion* of Jesus; only a small number of loaves and fish are available, but Jesus commands the crowds to sit down, and he gives thanks and distributes the food; and after everyone has eaten, a large quantity of fragments is collected. One of the main differences between the two stories is the numbers: seven loaves here, five in Chapter 14; seven baskets of fragments here, twelve in Chapter 14; four thousand men here, five thousand in Chapter 14.

Why has Matthew given his readers two miracle stories which are so similar? It has been suggested that the two stories are separate accounts of a single incident, but, while this is possible, it does not account for Matthew's (and Mark's) inclusion of both of them in their Gospels. Nor is it altogether satisfactory to say that Matthew is following Mark, his source, and that because Mark had two accounts of Jesus feeding crowds, Matthew reproduced both of them: Matthew was capable of omitting Marcan material when he chose to do so (and Luke has in fact omitted the second feeding miracle), and here he has not chosen to omit. We must therefore look for another explanation of this apparent repetition.

In $15^{1\text{ff}}$ the Pharisees and scribes complained that the disciples of Jesus were eating without first washing their hands, as the tradition of the elders ordered. In answer to this complaint, Jesus said that a man is not defiled by what he eats: and this statement would, as we saw, have the effect of abolishing the rule that Jews should not eat with Gentiles. In the next paragraph a Gentile woman asked for *the crumbs that fall from their masters' table*, and her request was granted, her daughter was healed. After that, *great crowds* brought sick people to Jesus who healed them, and we saw that these crowds may have stood for the Gentiles in Matthew's mind, who would eventually come into the Church. There is no real break between vv. 29^{ff} and vv. 32^{ff} – the crowd which Jesus feeds in 32^{ff} are those who brought the sick in 29^{ff}. It may be, therefore, that these *four thousand men, besides women and children* stand for the Gentiles who will be fed (or, saved) by Christ through his coming Passion and resurrection and the ministry of his disciples.

ဢ

Matthew has only made slight changes in Mark $8^{1\text{ff}}$, and the tendency has been to make this account closer to the previous feeding. See the notes on 14^{13-21} for many of the points in this paragraph.

34

Because the numbers in the two stories are the main difference between the narratives, it has been suggested that the Evangelists intended the readers to understand them symbolically; e.g. the number of loaves here is *seven*, and this has been understood as a reference to the seventy nations, or to the seven 'deacons' who were appointed to minister to the *Hellenists* in Jerusalem, Acts $6^{1\text{ff}}$. The *five* loaves in the previous feeding have similarly been taken as a reference to the five books of the Law.

37

The number of baskets here is *seven* (in the previous feeding it was *twelve*); and the word for *baskets* here is different from the word which was used in the earlier story; there is some evidence that the word used in the first feeding described the kind of basket which was 'typical of the Jews' (*Lexicon*, p. 448).

38

The number *four thousand* has been said to be connected with the four corners of the earth, or the *four winds* (24^{31}) – i.e. the whole world.

39

Matthew has changed Mark's *Dalmanutha* to *Magadan*. The location of both places is uncertain; and so is the reason for Matthew's alteration.

16^{1-4} JESUS REFUSES TO GIVE   Mark 8^{11-13}
A SIGN TO THE PHARISEES AND
SADDUCEES

16 *And the Pharisees and Sad'ducees came, and to test him they asked him to show them a sign from heaven.* [2]*He answered them,[a] 'When it is evening, you say, "It will be fair weather; for the sky is red."* [3]*And in the morning, "It will be stormy today, for the sky is red and threatening." You know how to interpret the appearance of the sky, but you cannot interpret the signs of the times.* [4]*An evil and adulterous generation seeks for a sign, but no sign shall be given to it except the sign of Jonah.' So he left them and departed.*

   a Other ancient authorities omit the following words to the end of verse 3

The Pharisees and Sadducees, who are always in this Gospel the representatives of unbelief, come to Jesus and ask him to perform a miracle which will prove his claims. Jesus refuses to give them any sign except *the sign of Jonah*. A similar incident was recorded earlier in the Gospel, and *the sign of Jonah* was explained there as the resurrection of the Son of man (12^{38}ff.).

This paragraph raises a number of difficulties:

(i) As the R.S.V. margin indicates, most of vv. 2, 3 is omitted by some of the authorities from the text. The majority of writers take the view that they are a later addition to the text, and not part of Matthew's original Gospel.

(ii) The Pharisees and Sadducees ask for a sign from heaven, and Jesus refuses to give them one, *except the sign of Jonah*, which means as we saw above, the resurrection. The words *except the sign of Jonah* have been added here by Matthew; they are not in the corresponding place in Mark. In the original saying, therefore, Jesus refused to give them any sign at all. But according to the answer which Jesus gave to the Baptist, his miracles and his preaching were signs (11²ff.). (And note that according to vv. 2, 3 the Jewish leaders are rebuked for not knowing how to interpret *the signs of the times,* i.e. the miracles of Jesus.) Are we therefore to conclude that Jesus himself did not understand his miracles as signs?

(iii) Even if this were the case, it would still not explain why Matthew says that the only sign which will be given to this generation is the sign of Jonah, because he clearly believed that the miracles were signs, and that Jesus had performed many of them for this generation.

Perhaps the second and third difficulties are lessened if we recall that Jonah came to Nineveh preaching repentance (cf. 12⁴¹), and that the purpose of Jesus' miracles was that men should repent (11²⁰ff.). The miracles of Jesus are only effective as signs when they produce repentance.

৵৵

If vv. 2, 3 are part of Matthew's original text then Matthew has added them at this point himself, since they are not in Mark 8¹¹f.. Apart from this, he has added *and Sadducees* in v. 1; omitted Mark's *he sighed deeply in his spirit*; and added *evil and adulterous* and *except the sign of Jonah,* as in 12³ff..

1

Sadducees have been mentioned once before this in Matthew, when they came to John for baptism (3⁷). One would not expect to find them in Galilee, or anywhere far from Jerusalem, because they were closely associated with the temple. Nowhere else in the New Testament are they encountered outside Judea. As they disappeared from history after the fall of Jerusalem in A.D. 70, Matthew may have had little knowledge of them.

2, 3

The words which are not certainly authentic fit awkwardly into the context: v. 4 follows smoothly after *He answered them,* but not so smoothly after v. 3. There is a similar saying in Luke 12⁵⁴ff.. There is, moreover, some doubt whether the rule 'Red sky at night . . . Red sky in the morning . . .' applies to conditions in Palestine. Even if these verses are not part of Matthew's text, and are not true of Palestinian weather conditions, their meaning is in accordance with the mind of the Evangelist. The unbelievers have not understood the miracles of Jesus as signs of the coming of the kingdom. They *cannot interpret* the signs; for the 'impossibility', compare Jesus' question, *How can you speak good, when you are evil?* (12^{34}).

4

evil and adulterous: See note on 12^{39}.

the sign of Jonah: See note on 12^{39}.

Matthew adds the words, *So he left them and departed*; Jesus will not compel them to believe in him.

16$^{5-12}$ JESUS WARNS HIS DISCIPLES   Mark 8$^{13-21}$
AGAINST THE TEACHING OF THE
PHARISEES AND SADDUCEES

^{5}*When the disciples reached the other side, they had forgotten to bring any bread.* ^{6}*Jesus said to them, 'Take heed and beware of the leaven of the Pharisees and Sad'ducees.'* ^{7}*And they discussed it among themselves, saying, 'We brought no bread.'* ^{8}*But Jesus, aware of this, said, 'O men of little faith, why do you discuss among yourselves the fact that you have no bread?* ^{9}*Do you not yet perceive? Do you not remember the five loaves of the five thousand, and how many baskets you gathered?* ^{10}*Or the seven loaves of the four thousand, and how many baskets you gathered?* ^{11}*How is it that you fail to perceive that I did not speak about bread? Beware of the leaven of the Pharisees and Sad'ducees.'* ^{12}*Then they understood that he did not tell them to beware of the leaven of bread, but of the teaching of the Pharisees and Sad'ducees.*

In this paragraph, a saying of Jesus is at first misunderstood by the disciples. When the misunderstanding has been cleared up, they understand the meaning of the original saying. The disciples had forgotten to bring any bread with them, and Jesus tells them to beware of the leaven of the Pharisees and Sadducees. At first they think that he is referring to their having no bread; but Jesus rebukes them for their little faith, recalling the two feeding miracles and the quantity of food left over. He has not been speaking about bread, and they should have known it. He was referring to the teaching of the Pharisees and Sadducees. Matthew has made a number of alterations in Mark here, in order to simplify and explain the incident.

☙

Matthew has omitted Mark's statement that the disciples had only one loaf with them in the boat (Mark 8¹⁴), and he has added v. 12 to explain the meaning of the saying of Jesus about leaven. (Cf. 17¹³ for a similar explanatory addition to Mark.) Moreover, he has changed Mark's *beware of the leaven of the Pharisees and the leaven of Herod* to *beware of the leaven of the Pharisees and Sadducees*: he had added *Sadducees* in the previous paragraph (16¹), but that may not be his only reason for bringing them in here also: since he understands *leaven* as *teaching* (v. 12), he could hardly speak of the teaching of Herod. (In Mark, leaven may have meant something less precise than teaching – e.g. influence.) Matthew has also omitted Jesus' rebukes of the disciples for not understanding, and the answers of the disciples to his questions.

6
leaven, in the rabbinic writers, and elsewhere in the New Testament except for 13³³, is always used of something evil. There is an apparent contradiction between the warning against the teaching of the Pharisees here, and the command in 23²f. *. . . practise and observe whatever they tell you.*

7
they discussed it among themselves (dielogizonto): The word is always used, in Matthew as in Mark, of faithless or evil thoughts. The noun is in fact translated *evil thoughts* in 15¹⁹. So here they doubt Jesus' power to provide them with bread.

8
O men of little faith: See note on this characteristically Matthean word at 6³⁰.

why do you discuss . . . ? See note on previous verse.

9f.
The two feeding miracles should have shown the disciples that **he is** able to supply them with food.

II, 12

Matthew now returns to the original saying of Jesus in v. 6, and explains what Jesus had meant. (In Mark, the reader was left to understand this for himself.) Verse 11 first declares that the saying about leaven did not refer to bread, and then repeats the saying. Verse 12 interprets it as a warning against the teaching of the Pharisees and Sadducees, and says that the disciples *understood*. In Mark, the paragraph ends quite differently, with the unanswered question of Jesus, *Do you not yet understand?*

16¹³⁻²⁰   JESUS IS REVEALED TO THE   Mark 8²⁷⁻³⁰
                    DISCIPLES AS THE CHRIST

¹³*Now when Jesus came into the district of Caesare'a Philippi, he asked his disciples, 'Who do men say that the Son of man is?'* ¹⁴*And they said, 'Some say John the Baptist, others say Eli'jah, and others Jeremiah or one of the prophets.'* ¹⁵*He said to them, 'But who do you say that I am?'* ¹⁶*Simon Peter replied, 'You are the Christ, the Son of the living God.'* ¹⁷*And Jesus answered him, 'Blessed are you, Simon Bar-Jona! For flesh and blood has not revealed this to you, but my Father who is in heaven.* ¹⁸*And I tell you, you are Peter,ᵃ and on this rockᵇ I will build my church, and the powers of deathᶜ shall not prevail against it.* ¹⁹*I will give you the keys of the kingdom of heaven, and whatever you bind on earth shall be bound in heaven, and whatever you loose on earth shall be loosed in heaven.'* ²⁰*Then he strictly charged the disciples to tell no one that he was the Christ.*

    a Greek *Petros*
    b Greek *Petra*
    c Greek *the gates of Hades*

Not many verses in the New Testament can have been more discussed than those which make up this paragraph, and particularly the words of Jesus to Peter in vv. 17–19. We shall first give a summary of the whole paragraph, anticipating the discussion of the meaning of the words, and then go on to consider some of the problems which it raises.

The scene of the incident is the district of Caesarea Philippi, about twenty miles north of the Sea of Galilee. Jesus asks his disciples who men say that he is, and they say John, Elijah, Jeremiah, or one of the prophets. Then he asks them who they themselves say that he is, and Simon Peter replies, You are the Christ, the Son of the living God. Jesus says to Simon that he is *blessed*, that is, that God has given him the ability to know who Jesus is, and that he is the *rock* on which he will build the new Israel, over which death will have no power. Moreover he will give him power to admit people into the kingdom which is coming, because his teaching and his disciplinary actions in the community will be ratified and endorsed by God. Finally, he commands all the disciples to tell no one that he is the Christ.

The framework and part of the contents of this paragraph are from Mark: Mark records the place, the two questions of Jesus, and the command to silence (Mark 8²⁷ff.); and there are some problems even about these verses in the earlier Gospel: for example, it is not agreed among all scholars that Jesus thought of himself as the Messiah, and therefore that he would have welcomed the statement of Peter, *You are the Christ*, though in Mark this is so placed, after the miracle of the opening of the eyes of a blind man at Bethsaida, as to imply that Peter is responding to divine revelation. It may be, then, that even in Mark the story has been adapted for its context in the Gospel, and that Peter's statement has been made into Peter's confession of faith.

This process of heightening the importance of Peter's statement has proceeded further in Matthew. To the Marcan words, *You are the Christ*, Matthew adds *the Son of the living God:* and Matthew also adds the words of Jesus which follow in vv. 17–19 which declare Peter *Blessed*, give him the new name, *rock*, and the promise of being the foundation of the Church and of having the power of the keys of the kingdom. From this it can be seen that the present context of these sayings is probably not original; Matthew has followed his usual practice of inserting into Mark's narrative, at points which seemed to him appropriate, sayings which he had from other sources. Mark had suggested, by placing the story of Peter's answer to Jesus after the opening of the eyes of a blind man, that Peter's eyes had been opened to see who Jesus was. Matthew's saying of Jesus in v. 17 makes the same point in a different way. And having begun to speak about Peter, Matthew continues with other sayings of Jesus.

We should notice next that this emphasis on the position of Peter as the leader of the twelve is in line with certain other details which are characteristic of this Gospel: e.g. in the list of the twelve Matthew added the word *first* before *Simon, who is called Peter* (10²); he added the story of Peter walking on the water (14²⁸ᶠᶠ·), and changed the text in 15¹⁵ so that it was Peter who asked the question about the meaning of the parable of defilement. Later on, he will add other references to Peter which were not in Mark (17²⁴ᶠᶠ·, 18²¹). On the other hand, it must be remembered that Matthew has not created 'the primacy of Peter' out of nothing: there is a saying in Luke which can also be understood as conferring upon Peter a position of leadership (Luke 22³¹ᶠᶠ·) and another in John (John 21¹⁵ᶠᶠ·) and cf. Mark 16⁷; and in all the Gospels Peter is represented as the spokesman of the twelve, and is placed first in all the lists of the twelve. We must not therefore exaggerate the difference between Matthew and the other New Testament writers in their attitude to Peter.

This raises the questions of the authenticity and meaning of 16¹⁷⁻¹⁹, and authenticity and meaning cannot be separated here. Verse 17 contains a number of characteristic Matthean expressions, and in its present form it may not be authentic. For *blessed are you*, cf. *blessed are your eyes, for they see, and your ears for they hear* (13¹⁶, another non-Marcan saying) and *Blessed is he who takes no offence at me* (11⁶); for *has not revealed this to you*, cf. 11²⁵⁻²⁷ (*revealed them to babes . . . to whom the Son chooses to reveal him*); and the expression *my Father who is in Heaven* is only found in Matthew. Verse 17 may therefore be Matthean, and may compensate for his omission of the Marcan story of the opening of the eyes of the blind man (Mark 8²²ᶠ·).

Verse 18 may be a separate saying; the introductory *And I tell you* is evidence that it is (see 19⁹). Although its authenticity has been doubted, there are now a number of scholars who think that it may be original. Part of the difficulty is that the word *church* is only used in the mouth of Jesus here and in 18¹⁷. The real problem, however, is what Aramaic word is here translated by the Greek word *ekklēsia*, *church*. It may be a word meaning 'assembly' or 'synagogue'; and it may mean the new Israel, the flock, of which the twelve are the nucleus. If this is so, then the reasons for doubting the authenticity of the saying are removed.

Similarly, v. 19 has been regarded as unauthentic on the ground that it seemed to identify the church with the kingdom. But this need not be so: the exact meaning of the power to bind and loose is uncertain, but it may mean that Peter (and all the twelve of which he is leader) have power to remit sins: that just as Jesus has given them power to heal, so also he gives them a share in his power to forgive.

Thus, while the present context of these sayings in vv. 17–19 may not be the original occasion on which Jesus spoke them (some have suggested that they were originally spoken during the Last Supper; cf. Luke $22^{31f.}$), and while the present form of v. 17 may owe something at least to the style of the Evangelist, it may be that the sayings themselves are authentic; more will be said about their meaning in the notes which follow the text.

❧

On Matthew's use of Mark $8^{27ff.}$, see the introduction to this paragraph, and the notes on the individual verses below.

13
Caesarea Philippi: Philip, the son of Herod the Great (2^1) and the half-brother of Archelaus (2^{22}) and Antipas (14^1), ruled over the district north and east of Galilee from the death of his father (2^{19}) in 4 B.C. until his own death in A.D. 34. He is mentioned in this Gospel at 14^3 (but see note). He rebuilt Paneas and called it *Caesarea* in honour of the emperor; and *Philippi* to distinguish it from the sea-port also called Caesarea (see map, p. 8).

Matthew has inserted *the Son of Man* here; Mark had *Who do men say that I am?* Some commentators take Matthew to mean that Jesus inquired first who men say that *the Son of Man*, who is still to come, is to be. But this is unlikely: (i) because of the parallelism of v. 15, *But who do you say that I am?*, where *you* is emphatic; (ii) because in other places Matthew has used *the Son of man* not as the title of a person other than Jesus, but as Jesus' description of himself (8^{20} etc.); in this Gospel, it had almost ceased to be a title, and become a name, in the same way that *Christ* became another name for Jesus, and ceased to be used as a title of his office.

14
Some say John the Baptist: Herod Antipas had said this, see 14^2.

others say Elijah: If the Baptist was believed to be Elijah returned from heaven (11^{14}, $17^{10ff.}$), and if Jesus was believed to be John resurrected, then he would in fact be Elijah. *Jeremiah* has been added by Matthew: there is some evidence that some Jews expected Jeremiah (and other *prophets*) to return at the end of the world.

15

In Greek, the word *you* is emphatic (*hymeis de*), and contrasts the opinions of *men* (vv. 13f.) with the faith of the disciples which is based on divine revelation (v. 17).

16

the Christ is a title, the Greek translation of the Hebrew word Messiah (meaning 'anointed' and thus 'king'). Matthew has already used it in the genealogy (1^1, $^{16f.}$), and in editorial passages (1^{18}, 11^2), and as the equivalent of *King of the Jews* in the mouth of Herod (2^4). Its use by Peter marks a new step in the revelation of Jesus, but it is not to be made known until after his resurrection (see v. 20). Matthew has added *the Son of the living God*, a title which he had put into the mouth of the disciples at 14^{33}; see also 2^{15}, 3^{17}, 4$^{3, 6}$, 8^{29}, 27$^{40, 43, 54.}$.

17

Peter's answer shows that he is in receipt of divine revelation; cf. 11$^{25f.}$ where Jesus says that the Father reveals the coming of the kingdom *to babes*. Peter is therefore the object of the Father's *gracious will*, and is therefore *Blessed* (cf. 5$^{3ff.}$, 11^6, 13^{16}, 24^{46}).

Simon is a Greek name; the disciple's Jewish name was Simeon, but Matthew does not use this form (contrast Acts 15^{14}).

Bar-Jona means son of Jonah; Simon's father is mentioned by name again in the New Testament only in the fourth Gospel (John 1^{42}, 21$^{15ff.}$).

flesh and blood means man over against God, man in his weakness, and without the help and inspiration of the Spirit, e.g. Paul says that after his conversion *he did not confer with flesh and blood* – i.e. with 'mere men' (Gal. 1^{16}).

18

you are Peter (*Petros*): There is no evidence that anyone had the name Peter before Christian times, either in its Greek form or in Aramaic, Cephas. In fact it is not a name at all, but a nickname, and it should really be translated 'Rock'. There are a number of examples in the Old Testament of people receiving a new name which will describe their future life; e.g. *No longer shall your name be Abram* [that is *exalted father*], *but your name shall be Abraham* [here taken to mean *father of a multitude*]; *for I have made you the father of a multitude of nations* (Gen. 17^5).

and on this rock I will build my church: The pun on the words Peter and rock goes back into Aramaic, Kepha, and Kephas. For the idea of building upon a rock, see $7^{24f.}$. Simon, to whom God has revealed who Jesus is, will be the foundation of the *church* which Jesus is to build. The future tense, *I will build*, looks forward to the time after the crucifixion, when the disciples will be sent out to baptize and to teach ($28^{19f.}$). For the idea of the new Israel as made from a rock, compare Isa. $51^{1f.}$,

> Look to the rock from which you were hewn,
>   and to the quarry from which you were digged.
> Look to Abraham your father.
>   and to Sarah who bore you;

and compare the rabbinic comment on this: 'When God looked upon Abraham who was to arise, he said, Behold, I have found a rock on which I can build and found the world' (quoted in J. Lowe, *St Peter*, p. 56f.).

my church (*mou tēn ekklēsian*): The Greek word used here had been used in the Greek translation of the Old Testament for 'the people', 'the assembly', 'the congregation'. The community of the disciples of Jesus is therefore to be the true Israel, the *children of Abraham* (3^9). Aramaic scholars do not agree what Aramaic word lies behind the Greek translation in Matthew, but one of the suggestions is the word *kenishta*', which could, apparently, be used both for the Church as a whole (*ekklēsia*) and for the local congregation (*synagōgē*, synagogue).

and the powers of death shall not prevail against it: The purpose of building upon a rock in the parable at the end of Chapter 7 was to ensure the permanence of the house ($7^{24f.}$); in much the same way here, the Church which is to be built upon the rock will withstand *the powers of death*, a phrase which is literally *the gates of Hades* (R.S.V. margin), and means that Hades, the place of the dead, cannot close its gates to imprison the members of Jesus' congregation, the new Israel. In Chapter 10 Jesus promised that they will share in his sufferings (10^{38}), now he promises that they will share in his resurrection.

19

I will give you the keys of the kingdom of heaven: The kingdom is here pictured as a place to be entered, as in 7^{21} *Not everyone who says to me, Lord, Lord, shall enter the kingdom of heaven,* and cf. $7^{13f.}$ *the narrow gate* through which men enter *life* (that is, the kingdom). Peter is therefore given authority to admit, or refuse admittance, to the kingdom. *The kingdom of heaven* is not used here as an equivalent for the Church, but the Church is the community of those who wait and pray for the coming of the kingdom (6^{10}). The way in which Peter opens and closes the door into the kingdom is explained in the next sentence.

and whatever you bind on earth shall be bound in heaven, and whatever you loose on earth shall be loosed in heaven: There are two equally possible meanings of binding and loosing: (i) laying down rules and granting exemption from rules; (ii) condemning and acquitting, i.e. the power to forgive sins which Jesus claimed in 9⁶, and now grants to Peter also. Both interpretations mean much the same in the end: Peter has authority in the Church to make pronouncements (whe her legislative or disciplinary) which will be ratified at the last judgement. Much the same authority had been given to all the twelve in 10¹³⁻¹⁵, and see also 18¹⁸, John 20²³.

in heaven here is a periphrasis for 'in the sight of God'; and the future tenses, *shall be bound, shall be loosed,* refer to the last judgement.

20
The command to keep silent is from Mark, and was the conclusion of Mark's paragraph; because Matthew inserted the sayings in vv. 17ff., he adds here the words *that he was the Christ,* to make it clear what they were to tell no one. For the other commands to keep silence in Matthew, see note on 8⁴.

16²¹⁻²³   JESUS FORETELLS HIS DEATH   Mark 8³¹⁻³³
                 AND RESURRECTION

²¹*From that time Jesus began to show his disciples that he must go to Jerusalem and suffer many things from the elders and chief priests and scribes, and be killed, and on the third day be raised.* ²²*And Peter took him and began to rebuke him, saying, 'God forbid, Lord! This shall never happen to you.'* ²³*But he turned and said to Peter, 'Get behind me, Satan! You are a hindranceᵃ to me; for you are not on the side of God, but of men.'*

    a Greek *stumbling-block*

The title *Christ* would not suggest suffering or death to the majority of the Jews, perhaps even to any of them; they would associate it with victory and glory. The Christians, on the other hand, living after the crucifixion, preached *Christ crucified*, and believed that his death had happened according to the will and foreknowledge of God, and in fulfilment of the scriptures. Peter's confession is therefore followed immediately by Jesus' predictions of his coming suffering at Jerusalem, and his resurrection; and this is declared to be necessary – i.e. the will of God. Peter speaks for the disciples when he rebukes Jesus for this saying, but Jesus denounces him in very strong terms.

This is the first explicit prediction of the Passion, and Matthew takes it from Mark, where it comes in the same relative position in the Gospel. Matthew has slightly increased the number of details in the predictions, and the number of predictions themselves. We may wonder whether Mark also had not developed this material out of less precise sayings of Jesus; but it is usually thought that some such predictive sayings go back to Jesus.

ಜಿ

Matthew's source is Mark 8^{31}ff. and he has added the detail *go to Jerusalem*; changed Mark's *after three days* to *on the third day*; put Peter's rebuke into direct speech; and added *You are a hindrance to me*.

21
From that time Jesus began . . . marks a new phase in the Gospel; from now until the end of the book there will be a new emphasis on the death and resurrection of Jesus, and on his teaching on this subject (see 17$^{9, 12, 22}$f., 20^{18}f., ^{28}, 21^{38}f., 26^2).

Jesus: Some of the manuscripts have here 'Jesus Christ', as in 1$^{1, 18}$. The manuscripts have been modified considerably in places where the titles of the Lord were mentioned, and it is therefore not always possible to be certain what the original reading was. But the full title, 'Jesus Christ' would be appropriate here (as it was in the title of the book and the beginning of the birth-story, 1$^{1, 18}$), at the beginning of a new phase in the Gospel, and after Peter's confession in 16^{16}.

he must go to Jerusalem: The sense in which Matthew understood the word *must* is shown by two of his additions to Mark: 3^{15} *thus it is fitting for us to fulfil all righteousness*; and 26^{54} *how then should the scriptures be fulfilled, that it must be so?* The necessity is the will of God, expressed in the scriptures. We shall see which scriptures Matthew had particularly in his mind, when we come on to his account of the Passion in Chapters 26, 27.

the elders and chief priests and scribes constituted the Sanhedrin, the supreme court of the Jews in Jerusalem. Matthew has made explicit what Mark only implied at this point, and has added the reference *to Jerusalem* as the scene of Jesus' sufferings.

on the third day: Matthew always substitutes this for Mark's *after three days*, as a more precise description of the event.

22

Peter, who had been the spokesman of the disciples in the previous paragraph in which he had declared Jesus' Messiahship, now acts as their spokesman in declaring he does not believe in the necessity for the Messiah's death and resurrection.

23

Matthew has softened Mark's *he rebuked Peter* to *said to Peter*.

Get behind me, Satan! (The same expression was used at the end of the temptations, 4^{10}.) To oppose the divine will is to be the agent of Satan; a *hindrance* or stumbling-block (*skandalon*) – i.e. a teacher of wickedness, see 13^{41}.

for you are not on the side of God, but of men is a paraphrase; the Greek is literally, 'You are not intent upon God's affairs, but upon men's.' Notice that to be on the side of man, as opposed to that of God, is to be on the side of Satan. For the alternatives, cf. *He who is not with me is against me*, etc. (12^{30}); and for the possession of the world by Satan, see $4^{8f.}$

16^{24-28} JESUS TEACHES HIS DISCIPLES Mark $8^{34}-9^{1}$
                 THE WAY OF DISCIPLESHIP

24 *Then Jesus told his disciples, 'If any man would come after me, let him deny himself and take up his cross and follow me.* 25 *For whoever would save his life will lose it, and whoever loses his life for my sake will find it.* 26 *For what will it profit a man, if he gains the whole world and forfeits his life? Or what shall a man give in return for his life?* 27 *For the Son of man is to come with his angels in the glory of his Father, and then he will repay every man for what he has done.* 28 *Truly, I say to you, there are some standing here who will not taste death before they see the Son of man coming in his kingdom.'*

Peter has been addressed as Satan, because he opposes Jesus' obedience to the will of God which will involve him in suffering and death as the way to his glory. The ignorance of Peter is not just ignorance about the future of Jesus: it reveals that he is ignorant about the future of the disciples, and so about his own future also. Jesus therefore begins to teach his disciples that if they wish to come after him as his pupils, and enter with him into the glory of the age to come, they must follow him in his obedience to the will of God, and this will mean following him in his Passion. They must make no efforts to secure themselves in this age, because that would involve them in losing their lives in the age to come. Jesus is soon to come from heaven and reward everybody according to his deeds: so soon that some of his contemporaries will still be alive when it happens; and the reward will be either eternal life or eternal punishment.

໑໑

Matthew has made only slight alterations in Mark 8³⁴–9¹: e.g. he has omitted the reference to *the multitude* (or crowd) whom Jesus addresses with the disciples in Mark, probably because Matthew considers them incapable of receiving this teaching; he has omitted the saying in Mark 8³⁸, perhaps because he has used it, or a similar saying, in 10³³; he has added a quotation from Ps. 62 in v. 27, and changed the last line of the paragraph.

24
If any man would come after me: The word translated *would* here means 'wants to', 'desires to'.

let him deny himself: The same word is used of Peter denying Jesus in 26³⁴ᶠ·, ⁷⁵, and a similar word is used in 10³³, 26⁷⁰ᶠᶠ·. From these passages, it is clear that the word means 'to disown somebody', 'to disclaim any connexion with somebody'. The condition of discipleship is therefore the breaking of every link which ties a man to himself; cf. *You are not your own,* 1 Cor. 6¹⁹.

take up his cross and follow me: See note on 10³⁸, where taking up the cross was first mentioned. The Romans crucified rebels and the world will execute those who go over to the other side (see v. 23 for the opposition between God and men).

25

whoever would save his life will lose it: i.e. whoever wants to save his life ... Jesus has said that discipleship involves crucifixion, that is, death. There is therefore no possibility of both being a disciple and saving, or preserving, one's life. Those who want to save their lives will not enter the kingdom, but will be condemned at the judgement.

whoever loses his life for my sake will find it: The disciple who follows Jesus will lose his life for his sake (or because of his command), and he will find it – i.e. have it restored to him at the resurrection and judgement. (For many of the disciples this meant martyrdom, but not for all.)

26

For the idea of gaining *the whole world*, see the last temptation of Jesus ($4^{8f.}$): and for the blessedness of poverty, the first Beatitude (5^3). The alternatives are: gain in this age, loss in the age to come; or poverty in this age, and riches in the age to come.

what shall a man give in return for his life? is a proverb, and it means that a man's life is more valuable to him than anything else. It is therefore worth his while losing anything, if by this means he gains his life; and the paradox here is that he must lose his life, in order to gain it.

27

The reason why the disciples must act in this way is because Jesus, who speaks of himself here as *the Son of man*, is coming in glory, with his angels, to *repay every man for what he has done* (an allusion to Ps. 62^{12}); see $13^{41ff.}$, *The Son of man will send his angels, and they will gather out of his kingdom all causes of sin and all evildoers*, etc.

28

Matthew has rewritten the last few words; Mark had *before they see the kingdom of God come with power*, and Matthew changes this to *before they see the Son of man coming in his kingdom*; cf. 13^{41} (quoted in note on previous verse) for *his kingdom*, and see note on 13^{41}.

17^{1-8} THE TRANSFIGURATION   Mark 9^{2-8}

17 *And after six days Jesus took with him Peter and James and John his brother, and led them up a high mountain apart.* [2]*And he was transfigured before them, and his face shone like the sun, and his garments became white*

as light. ³*And behold, there appeared to them Moses and Eli'jah, talking with him.* ⁴*And Peter said to Jesus, 'Lord, it is well that we are here; if you wish, I will make three booths here, one for you and one for Moses and one for Eli'jah.'* ⁵*He was still speaking, when lo, a bright cloud overshadowed them, and a voice from the cloud said, 'This is my beloved Son,ᵃ with whom I am well pleased; listen to him.'* ⁶*When the disciples heard this, they fell on their faces, and were filled with awe.* ⁷*But Jesus came and touched them, saying, 'Rise, and have no fear.'* ⁸*And when they lifted up their eyes, they saw no one but Jesus only.*

a Or *my Son, my* (or *the*) *Beloved*

Matthew has just given us two sayings which direct the reader's attention forward to the coming of the Son of man in glory, to reign on the earth. *Six days* later – the precise note of time links this para-graph to the previous sayings – Jesus is revealed to three of the disciples in the glory in which he will come at the end of this age. The revela-tion is given on a *mountain*, where Jesus is seen transformed, his face shining like the sun, and his clothes white as light. Moreover, two of the greatest characters in the Old Testament, *Moses and Elijah*, appear with Jesus, and the sign of the divine presence, the *cloud*, over-shadows them; and God speaks from the cloud, declaring Jesus to be his Son.

This passage recalls the story of Jesus' baptism at the beginning of the Gospel: in both, there is a *voice*; in both the voice says the same words, *This is my beloved Son, with whom I am well pleased* (3¹⁷). Both stories are 'epiphanies', or manifestations of Jesus as he is, or as he will be; and they are therefore in the same category as the first manifesta-tion of Jesus in Chapter 2, to the Magi from the East. Epiphany stories of this kind are common in ancient writing about holy men: in these stories, the veil which separates the invisible from the visible world, and the future from the present, is removed for a moment, and the truth is revealed.

The story of the transfiguration of Jesus may be the earliest of the epiphany stories about Jesus – older than the account of the voice at the baptism (though the baptism of Jesus by John is certainly historical), and older than the manifestation of Jesus to the Magi (or, in Luke, to the shepherds). What kind of basis has it in history? What really happened? We shall see, when we come on to the detailed study of

Matthew's account of it, and compare that with Mark's, that Matthew has added certain features which were not in his source: he has 'embroidered' Mark. If this could happen to a written account, how much more will it not have happened before anything was put in writing – i.e. before Mark wrote his Gospel in the sixties of the first century? And how shall we know what features in the Marcan account are additions, and what are historical? Some have suggested that the historical part is an account of a resurrection appearance of Jesus which Mark, or the tradition before Mark, had misplaced. Others think that the historical basis is a mystical experience, like those sometimes recorded in the lives of the saints. In this realm there is very little to go on, and therefore very little to be said.

But if we ask what the story meant to Matthew (or to Mark before him) there is more to be said. Jesus takes a small group of the disciples apart, in order to reveal something to them. Matthew will describe another occasion when he does the same, and it is the same three disciples who are taken; and there what is revealed is the obedience of Jesus to the will of his Father ($26^{37\text{ff.}}$), that is, the inner meaning of the crucifixion. Here, however, as the context suggests, what is revealed is the glory in which the Son of man will come to rule at the end of the age ($16^{27\text{f.}}$). Jesus' face shines *like the sun*, just as, when the kingdom comes, *the righteous will shine like the sun* (13^{43}); and his garments become *white as light* (cf. the description of the angel armies who come with Jesus at the end of the world in the Revelation, *And the armies of heaven, arrayed in fine linen, white and pure, followed him on white horses*, Rev. 19^{14}). *Moses and Elijah* appear, who were believed by the Jews to have been taken up to heaven alive, and not to have descended into Sheol; and who were expected to return to earth before the Messiah (they are the *two witnesses* in Rev. $11^{3\text{ff.}}$, the embodiment of the Law and the prophets). The voice of God from the *bright cloud* tells the disciples that Jesus is the Son, the fulfilment of Old Testament expectations, the one who is to be heard by men because he is the judge of God at the last day. When the disciples hear these words, they fall on their faces as Daniel had done before the vision of the heavenly man, and (like him) they are touched by Jesus, who tells them to rise and fear not (Dan. 10^{5-12}).

മ

Matthew has made a large number of small changes in Mark 9^{2-8}, and re-arranged the paragraph so that the fear of the disciples follows the voice from heaven, instead of following the vision of Jesus transfigured, as in Mark. Matthew's alterations are editorial and explanatory: it is unlikely that he had any other source than Mark for this paragraph.

1

And after six days: Precise notes of time like this are unusual in the Synoptic Gospels outside the account of the last days in Jerusalem and the Passion narrative itself. Here, it may be historical reminiscence, or it may be due to reminiscence of Exod. $24^{16\text{ff.}}$, *The glory of the Lord settled on Mount Sinai, and the cloud covered it six days; and on the seventh day he called to Moses out of the midst of the cloud . . . And Moses entered the cloud, and went up on the mountain.*

For *Peter and James and John* here, cf. Jesus *taking with him Peter and the two sons of Zebedee* in Gethsemane, 26^{37}.

and led them up a high mountain apart: See 14^{23} for the other references to mountains in Matthew; Moses and Elijah had both received revelations from God on mountains (Exod. 24, 1 Kings 19).

2

he was transfigured before them: The Greek word (*metemorphōthē*, literally 'metamorphosed') means 'changed, transfigured'. This is explained in the description which follows:

and his face shone like the sun is a Matthean addition. Cf. the description of *the righteous* in the kingdom, 13^{43}, and of *one like a son of man* in Rev. $1^{13\text{ff.}}$ . . . *his face was like the sun shining in full strength.* Cf. also Exod. $34^{29\text{ff.}}$, *the skin of* Moses' *face shone because he had been talking with God.* This passage is referred to by Paul in 2 Cor. 3, and there the same word, *transfigured*, is used of the changing of Christians which is going on now and will be completed at the end of this age (2 Cor. 3^{18}).

and his garments became white as light: white is the colour of heavenly things; see the Revelation, where the word is used sixteen times.

3

For other references to Elijah in this Gospel, see 11^{14}.

4

Matthew changes Mark's *Master* (= Rabbi) to *Lord*; in Matthew, only Judas Iscariot addresses Jesus as 'Rabbi' ($26^{25,\ 49}$).

What does Peter's question mean? It may mean that he wanted to make permanent a vision which could only be temporary: I can build

shelters for all three of you. (Matthew has changed Mark's *let us make
... to I will make*; cf. note on 15¹⁵.)

5
a bright cloud: Matthew has added the word *bright*. The cloud is the sign
of God's presence in the Exodus, and from it he speaks here.

overshadowed (epeskiasen): The word is used of the cloud covering the
tent of meeting in Exod. 40³⁵.

For *This is my beloved Son, with whom I am well pleased* see 3¹⁷, the voice
at the baptism of Jesus. Matthew has added here, from there, *with
whom I am well pleased*, to make the two occasions similar to one
another: this is one of his characteristic editorial methods.

listen to him may be a quotation from Deut. 18¹⁵, ¹⁹, the prediction of
a prophet like Moses, which is quoted in Acts 3²²f., 7³⁷. Matthew has
already shown how the early life of Jesus was like that of Moses (Chapter 2), and how Jesus is greater than Moses because he teaches the new
Law which fulfils the old (Chapters 5–7).

6f.
These verses are a Matthean addition to the story, and, as we saw above,
they may be modelled on Daniel's description of the effect of his vision
upon himself, Dan. 10⁷ff..

17⁹⁻¹³   ELIJAH AND THE SON OF MAN   Mark 9⁹⁻¹³

⁹*And as they were coming down the mountain, Jesus commanded them, 'Tell
no one the vision, until the Son of man is raised from the dead.' ¹⁰And the
disciples asked him, 'Then why do the scribes say that first Eli'jah must
come?' ¹¹He replied, 'Eli'jah does come, and he is to restore all things; ¹²but
I tell you that Eli'jah has already come, and they did not know him, but
did to him whatever they pleased. So also the Son of man will suffer at their
hands.' ¹³Then the disciples understood that he was speaking to them of
John the Baptist.*

While Jesus and the three disciples descend the mountain to rejoin
the rest of the disciples, a conversation takes place between them
which arises out of what they have seen. Jesus tells them to remain

silent about the vision of his glory, which has been revealed to them, until after his resurrection – *until the Son of man is raised from the dead*. The disciples remember that Jesus has said that the Son of man will come soon (16^{28}), and that it was said in the Old Testament that Elijah would come before the day of the Lord to make men repent; moreover, they have just seen Elijah on the mountain with Moses. If Jesus is to die, and if he (the Son of man) is to come soon, then why is it said that Elijah will come? There will not be time, and he will not have brought men to repentance if the Son of man is killed. Jesus replies that Elijah does come and restore all things: but this has already happened; and he was put to death, just as Jesus himself will be put to death. The disciples understand that Jesus is speaking of the Baptist. The lives of Elijah, John, and Jesus are thus similar: they are all three persecuted by the leaders of the nation, because they are not known for what they are.

ಜಿ

The meaning of Mark's paragraph (Mark 9^{9}ff.) was obscure: Matthew has re-arranged it; Luke has omitted it altogether. Matthew has left out the sentence which said that the disciples *kept the matter to themselves, questioning what the rising from the dead meant*, and has added v. 13 for the sake of his readers, to clarify the meaning of what Jesus said about Elijah; cf. 16^{12}.

9
Matthew substitutes direct speech for indirect, and changes Mark's *what they had seen* to *the vision*. The disciples are not to speak of the glory of the Son of man which they have seen, until after the resurrection, when they will preach it to the Church, to warn and to encourage. This is the fifth and last command to keep silent in Matthew – see 8^{4}.

10f.
Mal. 4$^{5f.}$ is the basis of the scribal teaching here referred to. *To restore all things* is in the Greek version of Malachi, but not in the Hebrew. Verse 11 may be a question: 'Does Elijah come first, and will he restore all things?' or it may be a statement of the tradition, which Jesus proceeds to correct with his own *but I tell you* – cf. 5$^{21f.}$, etc.

12
Elijah has already come: See 3^{4}, 11^{7}ff., 14^{1}ff.

and they did not know him is a Matthean addition, and an example of

Matthew's interest in faith and knowledge. *They* here probably refers to the Jewish leaders, not the crowd who held that John was a prophet, 21^{26}.

but did to him whatever they pleased: See 14^{1-12} for the account of the death of John, and 1 Kings $19^{2, 10}$ for Jezebel's desire to kill Elijah, which has now been repeated in Herodias.

So also the Son of man will suffer at their hands is a Matthean addition: the fate of both the forerunner and the Messiah will be the same; cf. 11^{16}ff.

13
An explanatory note for the readers, inserted as a statement of the disciples' understanding. To *understand* (*synienai*) is a favourite word of this Evangelist.

| 17^{14-20} | JESUS HEALS AN EPILEPTIC BOY | Mark 9^{14-29} |

^{14}*And when they came to the crowd, a man came up to him and kneeling before him said,* ^{15}*'Lord, have mercy on my son, for he is an epileptic and he suffers terribly; for often he falls into the fire, and often into the water.* ^{16}*And I brought him to your disciples, and they could not heal him.'* ^{17}*And Jesus answered, 'O faithless and perverse generation, how long am I to be with you? How long am I to bear with you? Bring him here to me.'* ^{18}*And Jesus rebuked him, and the demon came out of him, and the boy was cured instantly.* ^{19}*Then the disciples came to Jesus privately and said, 'Why could we not cast it out?'* ^{20}*He said to them, 'Because of your little faith. For truly, I say to you, if you have faith as a grain of mustard seed, you will say to this mountain, "Move hence to yonder place," and it will move; and nothing will be impossible to you.'*^{a}

a Other ancient authorities insert verse 21, *But this kind never comes out except by prayer and fasting*

During the absence of Jesus and the three disciples, the rest of the disciples have been unable to help a man who brought his epileptic son to them to be healed. The man now appeals to Jesus, telling him about both the condition of the boy and the failure of the disciples.

Jesus rebukes the demon so that it comes out of the boy, and rebukes the disciples for the weakness of their faith: if they believed, they could do anything.

In Mark, the story illustrated the destructiveness of evil – the symptoms of the boy's illness were described in greater detail – and the apparent death and resurrection of the boy, as well as the failure of the disciples in the absence of Christ. Matthew has concentrated on this failure and its cause – unbelief. The reader is reminded of Peter's failure to walk on the water, when Jesus rebuked him for *little faith*, and the discussion about the lack of bread (14$^{28ff.}$, 16$^{5ff.}$). The disciples will only be able to *follow* Jesus (that is the main subject now; see 16^{24}) if they have faith in the power of God to work in them and through them.

☙❧

The miracle and the conversation which follows it are recorded in sixteen verses in Mark (9$^{14ff.}$), but Matthew has reduced them to seven by making extensive omissions. (Luke has also abbreviated Mark, and often at the same points and in the same way as Matthew.)

14
Matthew has added *kneeling before him*; see note on 8^2.

15
Matthew has changed Mark's *Teacher* to *Lord*: See note on 8^{19}.

he is an epileptic: Literally 'he is a lunatic'; Matthew has introduced the word here, as also at 4^{24} (the only places where it is used in the New Testament); Mark had described the symptoms, Matthew gives the name of the complaint.

16
For the failure of the disciples in this part of the Gospel, see also 14$^{16ff.}$, $^{26ff.}$, $^{28ff.}$, 15$^{16,\ 23,\ 33}$, 16$^{5ff.,22}$, 17$^{4,\ 10f.}$.

17
O faithless and perverse generation is an echo from Deut. 32^5, *They are a perverse and crooked generation* (other allusions to this Old Testament passage in the New Testament are in Acts 2^{40}, Phil. 2^{15}). Although the words seem to be addressed by Jesus to the disciples in Matthew, it is usually Jesus' practice to speak of the crowd or the leaders of the Jews in this way.

18
Jesus rebuked him: i.e. the demon in the boy.

20

Matthew has added this verse.

Because of your little faith: See 6³⁰, 8²⁶, 14³¹, 16⁸, for this characteristically Matthean expression.

The rest of the saying in this verse is similar to Luke 17⁶ and Mark 11²²ᶠ·. The smallness of *a grain of mustard seed* has been mentioned, 13³¹ᶠ·. To move mountains was a proverbial Jewish expression, which Paul uses in 1 Cor. 13²; Matthew may have put the saying here partly because of the recent references to the *mountain* in 17¹, ⁹.

The saying is hyperbolic, like the saying about the beam in the eye, 7³ᶠᶠ·.

21

This verse (see R.S.V. margin) is found only in one group of authorities for the text: it is almost certainly an addition, put in from Mark 9²⁹ by a scribe who was using a manuscript of Mark in which the words *and fasting* had been added.

17²², ²³   JESUS AGAIN FORETELLS HIS   Mark 9³⁰⁻³²
                        DEATH AND RESURRECTION

²²*As they were gathering*ᵃ *in Galilee, Jesus said to them, 'The Son of man is to be delivered into the hands of men,* ²³*and they will kill him, and he will be raised on the third day.' And they were greatly distressed.*

a Other ancient authorities read *abode*

In this, the second of the main predictions of the Passion, Jesus speaks of the coming handing-over of the Son of man into the hands of men, his death, and his resurrection on the third day. The word which is used here for handing-over or delivering is a word which acquired almost a technical meaning through its use in connexion with the Passion: it is used in the Gospels of Judas' betrayal of Jesus to the chief priests; of the Sanhedrin, sending Jesus to Pilate; and of Pilate committing Jesus to the executioners. It is used also in the Epistles; and one of the senses in which it is used by Paul is of God handing Jesus over to death: *He who did not spare his own Son but gave him up for us all, will he not also give us all things with him?* (Rom. 8³²). The use of the verb in the passive here, *The Son of man is to be delivered*, may also refer to the action of God, just as the other passive tense, *he will be raised on the third day* refers to God's action: God will hand the Son of man over to men; they will kill him; God will raise him (or waken him) on the third day.

ᔕᙢ

Matthew has abbreviated Mark 9³⁰ff. and rewritten the introduction to the saying of Jesus, and the conclusion. Mark's introduction was one of his 'secrecy' passages: *They went on from there and passed through Galilee. And he would not have anyone know it*, but Matthew will not keep any more of Mark's commands to silence. Mark's conclusion was a more definite statement of the failure of the disciples than Matthew would allow: *But they did not understand the saying, and they were afraid to ask him.*

22

As they were gathering (*systrephomenōn*): The variant reading, *as they abode* (*anastrephomenōn*), is almost certainly an alteration of the more difficult *as they were gathering*: it may mean gathering round Jesus, crowding round him; or it could mean gathering together to go up to Jerusalem for the Passover (see note on next paragraph).

into the hands of men: Note the contrast between *the Son of man*, one sent by God from heaven, and his suffering at *the hands of men*.

23

on the third day: See note on 16²¹.

And they were greatly distressed: In Mark they did not understand and were afraid to ask; in Matthew they do understand, but fail to rejoice – if St Matthew means their sorrow to be a failure: he may, however, mean that they were *distressed* at the sin of men, which would bring about this rejection of the Son of man; cf. 26³⁷ where Matthew uses the word again, of Jesus.

17²⁴⁻²⁷   THE QUESTION OF THE TEMPLE TAX   Mark 9³³

²⁴*When they came to Caper'na-um, the collectors of the half-shekel tax went up to Peter and said, 'Does not your teacher pay the tax?'* ²⁵*He said,*

'Yes.' And when he came home, Jesus spoke to him first, saying, 'What do you think, Simon? From whom do kings of the earth take toll or tribute? From their sons or from others?' ²⁶And when he said, 'From others,' Jesus said to him, 'Then the sons are free. ²⁷However, not to give offence to them, go to the sea and cast a hook, and take the first fish that comes up, and when you open its mouth you will find a shekel; take that and give it to them for me and for yourself.'

The last paragraph in this long narrative section (which began at 13⁵³) illustrates the teaching which is to be given in the discourse which follows it: the disciples are not to *cause offence* to others. The story is one of the two non-Marcan incidents in the whole of this section, and, as in the other, Peter figures prominently (14²⁸ff.). A law in the book Exodus (30¹¹ff.) commanded that every Jew over nineteen years of age should pay half a shekel a year to the temple; the collectors of this tax ask Peter if Jesus pays it, and he says that he does. Later, there is a conversation between Jesus and Peter, in which Jesus claims that because he and his disciples are the *sons* of God the King, they should not pay any tax. But because this would cause offence, Peter is to find a shekel in the mouth of a fish, which will pay for Jesus and for Peter.

Although the contents of this paragraph are not in Mark or Luke, their setting is Marcan – the reference to *Capernaum* at the beginning of the paragraph, and to the house in the second verse, have both been taken from the next verse in Mark (Mark 9³³). The wording of the paragraph, on the other hand, is Matthean. So it is very unlikely that Matthew had these verses in written form: he himself first put them in writing, 'embroidering' on Mark.

It has been suggested that the story has been enlarged 'to suit the times': that the original form of it ended at v. 26, and that v. 27 was added after A.D. 70 when the temple tax was directed by the Romans to the temple of Jupiter Capitolinus.

෴

24
your teacher: See 8¹⁹ for *teacher* in the mouth of the opponents of Jesus.

25f.

Jesus spoke to him first: If this is intended to imply supernatural knowledge, then cf. $12^{15, 25}$.

What do you think? is a Matthean phrase: cf. 18^{12}, 21^{28}, $22^{17, 42}$, 26^{66}.

kings of the earth is a phrase from Ps. 2^2; see the note on 22^{34} where the same Psalm is used again. The point of the question is that, just as princes are exempt from paying taxes by virtue of their relation to the king, so are the disciples because of their relation to God (see $12^{49f.}$ for Jesus and his disciples as *brothers*).

27

The same argument from fear of offence is used by Paul: though he is free to claim money from his converts, he has not done so, in order not to *put an obstacle in the way of the gospel of Christ* (1 Cor. 9^{12}); and similarly, he refuses to eat meat, if doing so will cause offence to his Christian brother who has a weak conscience (ibid., 8^{13}). Jesus will not allow his freedom, which is also the right of his disciples, to give offence to the authorities. The saying about the coin in the fish's mouth has the ring of legend about it; cf. $27^{52ff.}$ for another legend.

Matthew 18

Life in the Church

In Chapter 18, Matthew gives the fourth of the sections of teaching, and then returns to narrative in 19¹ with the usual formula. This collection of Jesus' sayings is about the same length as the second, in Chapter 10, and like the second it is about Church affairs: there the subject was the evangelistic work of the Church, here it is the relations between Christians.

Having reached the point in Mark where the disciples were arguing amongst themselves *who was the greatest*, and where Jesus said to them that if anyone would be first, he must be the last of all and servant of all (Mark 9³³ff.), Matthew uses that, and some of the sayings which follow it in Mark, as the basis for this section.

The chapter begins with the disciples' question, *Who is the greatest in the kingdom of heaven?* Jesus says that they must humble themselves, and become like children, in order to be great in the kingdom. They must welcome and care for the little ones in the Church, and not cause them to sin; everything that causes sin must be thrown away; they must care for one another as God cares for them. This leads on to instructions on what they are to do when they see another member of the Church sinning. Then Peter asks Jesus the question how often he should forgive his fellow-Christian, and the answer of Jesus introduces a parable on forgiveness.

Matthew's subject here was suggested by the sayings which he found in Mark at this juncture: but that does not completely account for his stopping at this particular point, and making this subject the theme of his fourth section of teaching. He had mentioned *the church* in Chapter 16, and so now he tells his readers more about the relations which must obtain between the members of it: the care which they must show for one another; the mutual and unlimited forgiveness with which they must treat one another.

Matthew's Gospel shows signs of such careful arrangement that we can say with some certainty that he had planned out at least the main structure of it before he began to write. If that was so, then he would have known that his fifth and last section of teaching was to be about the coming of the kingdom. The kingdom is to the Church as the main building is to the porch or entrance hall.

The way that the disciples live now, in the Church, determines whether they will enter the kingdom when Jesus comes again as the judge at the end of the world. So Matthew prepares the way for the teaching about the coming of the kingdom in the fifth discourse, by the teaching about the Church in the fourth.

Moreover, there are a number of verbal links which bind Chapter 18, to the chapters which came immediately before it: *Church, to bind and loose, to cause to sin, maimed and lame, to repay, to gain*. (We saw the same relationship between the narrative of Chapters 8 and 9, and the teaching in Chapter 10.)

18¹⁻⁴　　　HUMILITY IN THE CHURCH:　Mark 9³³⁻³⁶,
　　　　　GREATNESS IN THE KINGDOM　　　　　10¹⁵

18 *At that time the disciples came to Jesus, saying, 'Who is the greatest in the kingdom of heaven?' ²And calling to him a child, he put him in the midst of them, ³and said, 'Truly, I say to you, unless you turn and become like children, you will never enter the kingdom of heaven. ⁴Whoever humbles himself like this child, he is the greatest in the kingdom of heaven.'*

The first paragraph shows how we are to think of the relationship between the present and the future, the Church and the kingdom, the fourth section of teaching and the fifth. The disciples ask, Who is the greatest in the kingdom of heaven? and Jesus tells them that they will never even enter the kingdom unless they give up all desire for being great, and become like children, without any status or privileges. Those who do that will be great in the kingdom.

ॐ

Matthew has considerably recast Mark 9³³ff., making the disciples ask Jesus the question, instead of Jesus asking the disciples what they had been arguing about; and he reaches over to the next chapter in Mark (Mark 10¹⁵) for 18³, which he has adapted for its new context.

1

Matthew had used part of Mark 9^{33} already (see on 17^{24}ff.). For the use of the disciples' questions in the sections of teaching, see 13$^{10,\,36}$, 18^{21}, 24^{3}.

Who is the greatest in the kingdom of heaven? Matthew did not think that there would be no distinctions in the kingdom; he had already said that some *shall be called least in the kingdom of heaven*, and others *shall be called great in the kingdom of heaven* (5^{19}).

2

Jesus' taking of a child is an acted parable: cf. his blessing the children (19^{13}ff.), his riding into Jerusalem on an ass and a colt (21^{1}ff.), and the Last Supper (26^{26}ff.).

3

unless you turn and become like children ... is Matthew's rephrasing of Mark's *whoever does not receive the kingdom of God like a child*. The *child* is for Matthew the symbol of humility (see next verse), not because a child is humble (most of them are not), but because a child has no status in society: *the heir, as long as he is a child, is no better than a slave, though he is the owner of all the estate* (Gal. 4^{1}). See also the first Beatitude, *Blessed are the poor in spirit, for theirs is the kingdom of heaven* (5^{3}): the child is unable to own property. See also the sayings about following Jesus and losing everything, in 16^{24}ff.

4

This saying has no parallel in Mark, and is probably a Matthean creation. It repeats what was said negatively in the previous verse, in a positive form: i.e. If you do not ... you will not ... if you do ... you will. ... And it rounds off the paragraph by repeating the words in the question at the beginning ... *is the greatest in the kingdom of heaven* (another example of Matthew's use of *inclusio*).

18$^{5,\,6}$ RECEIVING OR OFFENDING   Mark 9$^{37,\,42}$

^{5}*'Whoever receives one such child in my name receives me; ^{6}but whoever causes one of these little ones who believe in me to sin,^{a} it would be better for him to have a great millstone fastened round his neck and to be drowned in the depth of the sea.'*

    a Greek *causes ... to stumble*

The *child* is the link between this paragraph and the one before. The *child* is the symbol of the Christian: and because Christianity is a social religion involving a community of disciples, and not an individualistic religion, 'alone with the Alone', Jesus teaches what must be the relation between one Christian and another. This subject is the theme of the rest of the section.

The paragraph presents us with an either/or: either we *receive* (that is, welcome, and so care for) one another, or we *cause* one another to *sin*. To each of these alternatives there corresponds a reward: those who receive one another receive Christ; those who cause one another to sin will incur judgement.

At this point it is very clear that this section is the pair of the second section of teaching in Chapter 10, which had ended with a similar saying, *He who receives you receives me, and he who receives me receives him who sent me*, 10⁴⁰.

∽∾

Matthew's careful use of Mark is well illustrated at this point. Verse 5 is Mark 9³⁷ᵃ; he had used the rest of that verse in 10⁴⁰ (see above). Verse 6 is from Mark 9⁴². Four verses come between these in Mark – i.e. Mark 9³⁸⁻⁴¹: Matthew had used Mark 9⁴⁰ in 12³⁰ and Mark 9⁴¹ in 10⁴²; but he has omitted Mark 9³⁸ᶠ, the saying about the exorcist who did not follow the disciples. (Possibly Matthew wanted to leave out another of the occasions when Jesus rebuked his disciples; possibly the saying of Jesus did not appeal to Matthew's love of discipline and organization.) Matthew has thus split up the sayings in Mark 9³⁷ᶠᶠ, and put some in Chapter 10, some in 12, some in 18.

5
On the meaning of receiving one another, see 10¹⁴, ⁴⁰ᶠ. It involves welcoming, listening to, and acting upon what is heard.

one such child: Jesus has taken the child as the symbol and standard of what every Christian ought to be; cf. *thou hast hidden these things from the wise and understanding and revealed them to babes*, 11²⁵; and in this chapter, the *little ones* vv. 6, 10, 14.

in my name: The *name* of a person is a way of saying 'the person himself'; *in my name* may therefore mean 'because of me'.

6

'To cause to sin' (*skandalizein*) is here contrasted with *to receive*; and it means to put something in the way of somebody else's obedience to God, so that he stumbles. Death is better than the punishment that God will give to those who cause Christians to sin, because this punishment will mean not the death of the body alone, but the destruction of *both soul and body in hell* (10²⁸). There is evidence that the Romans used death by drowning as a method of execution, and Josephus describes how Galileans drowned Herod's supporters in the lake (*Antiquities*, XIV, 15, 10).

187-9   ON STUMBLING-BLOCKS   Mark 9⁴³⁻⁴⁷
                                                Luke 17¹

⁷'*Woe to the world for temptations to sin!ᵃ For it is necessary that temptations come, but woe to the man by whom the temptation comes!* ⁸*And if your hand or your foot causes you to sin, cut it off and throw it from you; it is better for you to enter life maimed or lame than with two hands or two feet to be thrown into the eternal fire.* ⁹*And if your eye causes you to sin, pluck it out and throw it from you; it is better for you to enter life with one eye than with two eyes to be thrown into the hellᵇ of fire.*'

  a Greek *stumbling-blocks*
  b Greek *Gehenna*

The words *stumbling-block* and *cause to stumble* link this paragraph to the one before it. Those who make others sin bring judgement, or woe, upon the world. They are necessary, being part of the nature of things, the result of the devil's supremacy in this age. But this does not remove man's responsibility for becoming the devil's agent and allowing himself to be used by him. The man who becomes a stumbling-block to others will be judged by God; compare the explanation of the parable of the weeds of the field: *The Son of man will send his angels, and they will gather out of his kingdom all causes of sin* (*skandala*, stumbling-blocks) *and all evildoers*, 13⁴¹. The paragraph continues with the sayings about the *hand*, the *foot*, and the *eye* which cause men to stumble: it is better to enter life without them than to be thrown into hell by God with them. These sayings may be understood of the causes which make the individual to sin; or they may be understood of the individuals in the community who cause offence – they must be excluded. In this context, the latter is perhaps more likely – cf. v. 17.

రచ్చ

Verse 7 has no parallel here in Mark, but is similar to Luke 17¹; on the other hand, cf. Mark 14²¹ where Jesus says of Judas: *The Son of man goes as it is written of him, but woe to that man by whom the Son of man is betrayed! It would have been better for that man if he had not been born.* Matthew may have constructed this verse (18⁷) out of it. Verses 8, 9 are Matthew's abbreviated version of Mark 9⁴³ff. (cf. Matthew 5²⁹f. where he has also used these Marcan sayings, and both there and here he has added *and throw it from you*).

7
For the expression *Woe to* see 11²¹.

it is necessary that temptations come: Stumbling-blocks are part of the sufferings which will come before the end of the world (see 24⁹ff., and notice *this must take place* (24⁶); and compare Paul's statement, *There must be factions among you in order that those who are genuine among you may be recognized* 1 Cor. 11¹⁹).

but woe to the man, etc.: For the responsibility of man, which is not abrogated by the divine necessity, cf. the saying about Judas in 26²⁴ (= Mark 14²¹ quoted above).

8f.
'It is possible that in this context the words are intended to suggest that members who lead others into sin should be cut off from the body of the Church' (B. T. D. Smith). If that is the way in which Matthew understood and used these sayings here, then they show that he thought of the Church as a body, in the same way that Paul also thought of the Church – e.g. 1 Cor. 12¹²ff..

THE CARE WHICH MEMBERS SHOULD   Luke 15^{3-7}
          HAVE FOR ONE ANOTHER

10'See that you do not despise one of these little ones; for I tell you that in
heaven their angels always behold the face of my Father who is in heaven.^a
12What do you think? If a man has a hundred sheep, and one of them has
gone astray, does he not leave the ninety-nine on the hills and go in search of
the one that went astray? 13And if he finds it, truly, I say to you, he rejoices
over it more than over the ninety-nine that never went astray. 14So it is not
the will of my^b Father who is in heaven that one of these little ones should
perish.'

> a Other ancient authorities add verse 11, For the Son of man came to
>   save the lost
> b Other ancient authorities read your

In vv. 5f. Matthew stated the alternatives: (i) receiving one another;
(ii) causing one another to stumble. He then took up (ii), the case of
those who cause others to stumble (vv. 7^{ff.}); now he returns to (i), not
despising the *little ones* (vv. 10ff.). Each member of the Church is to
care for the others, and bring back any that stray, just as the shepherd
cares for his sheep. The Father does not want any to perish; and the
Christians must share his mind. Everyone has his heavenly representative, an angel who guards him and prays to God for him.

శ⊂శ

Verse 10 is peculiar to this Gospel, and v. 11 (see R.S.V. margin) is
probably a later scribe's addition to Matthew from Luke 19^{10}. The
parable of the lost sheep (vv. 12^{ff.}) is found also in Luke 15^{3ff.} and
Luke's form and use of it are usually thought to be nearer to Jesus' than
Matthew's.

10
See that you do not (horate mē) is a Matthean introductory phrase (see
8^4, 9^{30}, 24^6), and the sentence as a whole, with its reference to the
little ones, is an editorial link to vv. 5f. where the *little ones* were last
mentioned. Notice how Matthew rounds off the paragraph by another
reference to them in v. 14.

in heaven their angels always behold the face of my Father who is in heaven:
The Jews believed that the nations had angelic representatives in heaven
(see e.g. Dan. 10¹³, ²⁰), and that individuals also had their guardian-
angels (see e.g. Gen. 48¹⁶, and Acts 12¹⁵ where the Christians say of
Peter, *It is his angel!*). The angels have access to God (that is the meaning
of *always behold the face of my Father*), and can intercede with him on behalf of those over whom they watch, and protect them. God will therefore care for his little ones: his other children should do so too.

12f.
What do you think? A Matthean expression; see note on 17²⁵. The parable
of the lost sheep is here used to teach care for one another, and
particularly for those who have *gone astray* in sin, in the Christian
community. In Luke, the parable is part of Jesus' defence of his attitude
to tax collectors and sinners.

14
The application of the parable – probably another Matthean addition:
God, like a shepherd, cares for and values each of his sheep; the disciples
must do the same, and restore those who sin to the fold. This will be
explained further in the next paragraph, vv. 15ff.

18¹⁵⁻²⁰   TREATMENT OF THE BROTHER   Luke 17³
                      WHO SINS

¹⁵'*If your brother sins against you, go and tell him his fault, between you and
him alone. If he listens to you, you have gained your brother.* ¹⁶*But if he
does not listen, take one or two others along with you, that every word may
be confirmed by the evidence of two or three witnesses.* ¹⁷*If he refuses to
listen to them, tell it to the church; and if he refuses to listen even to the
church, let him be to you as a Gentile and a tax collector.* ¹⁸*Truly, I say to
you, whatever you bind on earth shall be bound in heaven, and whatever you
loose on earth shall be loosed in heaven.* ¹⁹*Again I say to you, if two of you
agree on earth about anything they ask, it will be done for them by my Father
in heaven.* ²⁰*For where two or three are gathered in my name, there am I in
the midst of them.*'

This paragraph explains how they are to fulfil the teaching in vv. 10ff.
The parable had mentioned the sheep that goes astray, and this is

now expounded in the words, *If your brother sins* . . . (The words which follow in R.S.V., *against you*, should probably be omitted; this subject will be dealt with later (v. 21): the question now is not forgiveness, but the sin of one member of the community.) Every effort is to be made to bring the erring brother to repentance: first in private, then before a few, finally before the whole assembly of disciples. If he is still impenitent, he must be excluded from the congregation of the new Israel. The decision of the Church will be the decision of God: as he inspires them in making the decision, so he will also honour it; and Christ himself will be with them, guiding them and directing them.

৵৽

Verse 15 has a slight parallel in Luke 17^3 *If your brother sins, rebuke him, if he repents, forgive him*; otherwise none of this material appears in the other Gospels. There is, however, a passage in I Cor. 5^{1-8} which should be compared with these instructions; Paul is telling the disciples to exclude one of their members; and he uses the expression *in the name of the Lord Jesus* and the presence of *the power of our Lord Jesus* in the community (cf. v. 20).

15
your brother: i.e. another member of the Christian community.

against you should probably be omitted, as in some of the most important manuscripts.

If he listens to you: i.e. pays attention and acts upon what is said by repenting.

you have gained your brother: i.e. you have saved him from perishing, and thus restored him to the flock or family of the Church (cf. v. 14).
  Behind this verse there lies a passage in the Old Testament which was frequently quoted by the first Christians: *You shall not hate your brother in your heart, but you shall reason with* [= same word in Greek as *tell him his fault* in this verse] *your neighbour, lest you bear sin because of him. You shall not take vengeance or bear any grudge against the sons of your own people, but you shall love your neighbour as yourself: I am the Lord* (Lev. $19^{17f.}$). Matthew refers to this passage again at 5^{43}, 19^{19}, 22^{39}.

16
If a private rebuke fails, then, before the matter is brought before the Church, it must be heard before one or two others, in fulfilment of

another passage in the Old Testament: *A single witness shall not prevail against a man for any crime or for any wrong in connexion with any offence that he has committed; only on the evidence of two witnesses, or of three witnesses, shall a charge be sustained* (Deut. 19¹⁵).

17

the church (see also 16¹⁸): Here presumably the local congregation, or Christian synagogue. If the sinner refuses to listen (i.e. to repent), he is to be treated *as a Gentile and a tax collector*, that is, he is to be excommunicated from the congregation. A *Gentile*, because the Church is the new Israel, and so those who are not members of it are now Gentiles; a *tax collector*, because *tax collectors* were excluded from the old Israel by their trade and their uncleanness. See also 5⁴⁶ᶠ· for the two words in the same context.

18

Bind and *loose* may mean here banish from the community and recall to it: Josephus uses the words in this way (*Jewish Wars*, 1, v. 2); cf. 16¹⁹ for the same words. *In heaven* means 'with God': he will stand by the decision of the Church.

19

The idea of the relationship between *earth* and *heaven*, the Church and God, continues in this verse. The prayer of two who are in agreement will be heard and answered by God, just as the decisions of the Church are his decisions.

20

two or three (cf. v. 16): Even where there are only two or three gathered together as Christians (*in my name*, cf. v. 5), Jesus is present with them.

The Jews had a similar saying: 'Rabbi Hanina ben Teradion said: When two sit and there are not between them words of Torah, lo, this is "the seat of the scornful", as it is said: "Nor sitteth in the seat of the scornful". But when two sit, and there are between them words of Torah, the Shechinah [i.e. the presence of God] rests between them . . .' (Pirqe Aboth 3³). Rabbi Hanina ben Teradion was executed in A.D. 135.

Notice here that the first verse of the next paragraph repeats the first words of this paragraph: v. 15 was *if your brother sins*, v. 21 is *How often shall my brother sin against me . . . ?* It may be that Matthew has again arranged his sayings as a chiasmus: (*a*) *If your brother sins* (v. 15), (*b*) *two or three witnesses* (v. 16), (*c*) the *church* is to exclude him (v. 17): (*c*) the *church* is to *bind* and *loose*, to exclude and to recall (v. 18), (*b*) *two or three* (vv. 19f.), (*a*) *how often shall my brother sin against me . . . ?* (vv. 21f.)

²¹ *Then Peter came up and said to him, 'Lord, how often shall my brother sin against me, and I forgive him? As many as seven times?'* ²² *Jesus said to him, 'I do not say to you seven times, but seventy times seven.*ᵃ

    a Or *seventy-seven times*

Peter now raises a new question, that of sin between brothers, i.e. fellow-Christians. If the Church is to banish its unrepentant members, are the individual Christians also to cut themselves off by refusing to forgive those who persistently sin against them? Jesus says that they are to make no limitation. The individual Christian has no position of authority on the basis of which he can make a rule or draw a line: because he is completely at the disposal of God, and nothing in himself, he cannot claim to himself as an individual God's prerogative of condemning.

ಬಂ

The Lucan parallel is: *and if he* [your brother] *sins against you seven times in the day, and turns to you seven times, and says, I repent, you must forgive him* (Luke 17⁴).

21
For a question in the middle of a teaching section, see note on v. 1.
    For Peter as the leader and spokesman of the disciples, cf. 10², 14²⁸, 15¹⁵, 16¹⁶, 17²⁴.

22
The numbers *seven* and *seventy-seven* are used in Gen. 4²⁴ of vengeance, the opposite of the forgiveness which is taught here. *Seventy times seven* (or *seventy-seven times* margin, the Greek can be taken either way) means that forgiveness must be unlimited; and this is further explained in the next paragraph, where it is shown that what the disciple has to forgive is minute compared with what God has already forgiven him.

THE PARABLE OF THE UNMERCIFUL
OFFICIAL

²³'*Therefore the kingdom of heaven may be compared to a king who wished to settle accounts with his servants.* ²⁴*When he began the reckoning, one was brought to him who owed him ten thousand talents;ª* ²⁵*and as he could not pay, his lord ordered him to be sold, with his wife and children and all that he had, and payment to be made.* ²⁶*So the servant fell on his knees, imploring him, "Lord, have patience with me, and I will pay you everything."* ²⁷*And out of pity for him the lord of that servant released him and forgave him the debt.* ²⁸*But the same servant, as he went out, came upon one of his fellow servants who owed him a hundred denarii;ᵇ and seizing him by the throat he said, "Pay what you owe."* ²⁹*So his fellow servant fell down and besought him, "Have patience with me, and I will pay you."* ³⁰*He refused and went and put him in prison till he should pay the debt.* ³¹*When his fellow servants saw what had taken place, they were greatly distressed, and they went and reported to their lord all that had taken place.* ³²*Then his lord summoned him and said to him, "You wicked servant! I forgave you all that debt because you besought me;* ³³*and should not you have had mercy on your fellow servant, as I had mercy on you?"* ³⁴*And in anger his lord delivered him to the jailers,ᶜ till he should pay all his debt.* ³⁵*So also my heavenly Father will do to every one of you, if you do not forgive your brother from your heart.'*

a This talent was probably worth about £300
b The denarius was worth about a shilling
c Greek *torturers*

This section of teaching on the relations between Christians ends with the parable of a court official who had been shown great mercy by the king, but failed to show mercy to one of his equals over a much smaller matter. Jesus says that this is the situation in which the disciples find themselves: God has forgiven them their sins which are innumerable; but at the last judgement this remission will be revoked, if they have not shown mercy to one another in the Church – not mercy in word, but *from* the *heart*, that is, in reality.

This parable is only found in Matthew.

23

Therefore is a Matthean link, attaching the parable to the answer to Peter to which it probably did not originally belong: it does not in fact illustrate repeated and unlimited forgiveness, which is the point of the previous saying. The original setting of the parable may have been Jesus' teaching about the last judgement, cf. the last parable in the Gospel (25³¹ff.).

the kingdom of heaven may be compared to a king who ... means that the judgement which comes before the kingdom begins is like the settling of accounts. Cf. in the Lord's Prayer, after the petition for the coming of the kingdom, *And forgive us our debts, As we also have forgiven our debtors* (6¹²); and also 25¹⁹.

24

one was brought: i.e. from prison.

ten thousand talents: The sum is intended to be exaggeratedly large; *ten thousand* is the largest unit of number, and *talents* are the largest unit in currency; as we might say, 'a billion pounds'. The *servant* (v. 23) is therefore thought of as a governor of a province, responsible for the payment of the taxes of his country.

25

The sale of the official, *his wife, and children* would not realize more than a fraction of the debt: it is therefore a punishment.

26

Although the official asks for *patience* and promises to *pay everything*, it is clear that he cannot possibly do so (see note on v. 34). The sin of man against God is a debt which cannot be wiped out by man; and if it is not wiped out, it involves the debtor in eternal bondage.

27

The king does not take up this 'promise' of repayment: he forgives *the debt* completely. For the *pity* (or compassion) of the king, cf. 9³⁶, 14¹⁴, 15³², 20³⁴: the works of Jesus have been signs of this divine forgiveness.

28

a hundred denarii: A very small sum, out of all proportion to the original debt.

29

The *fellow servant* repeats the request made in v. 26, but omits the words *Lord* and *everything*, because he is addressing an equal, and because the sum involved is so small.

30

There is no question here of selling the debtor, because the sum is too small (contrast v. 25 and cf. 5²⁵ᶠ. . . . *you* will *be put in prison; truly, I say to you, you will never get out till you have paid the last penny*).

31

greatly distressed: Perhaps 'shocked'; cf. 17²³.

32f.

The parable asks a question of one of the characters in it, which the hearers of the parable are to answer for themselves.

34

jailers: R.S.V. margin rightly translates *torturers:* the man might have hidden part of the money (cf. 13⁴⁴).

till he should pay all his debt: He will never be able to raise so large a sum; therefore his imprisonment will be unending.

35

The application of the parable is probably Matthean: God will revoke the remission of sins at the last judgement in the case of those who have not forgiven one another. *my heavenly father* is a Matthean term, cf. v. 14. *from your heart* means not merely in words, but sincerely, really; cf. *This people honours me with their lips, but their heart is far from me* (15⁸).

Matthew 19-22

The Way to Jerusalem

The beginning of the next section of the Gospel is clearly marked by the formula in 19¹, but it is not as clear where it ends; we shall take the last verse of Chapter 22 as the conclusion; *... nor from that day did anyone dare to ask him any more questions* has a ring of finality about it. (On this way of dividing the Gospel, see p. 363.)

The section begins with the statement that after Jesus had taught the disciples about the Church he left Galilee *and entered the region of Judea beyond the Jordan.* The reader recalls Jesus' prediction that he must go to Jerusalem and die there (16²¹), and it becomes clear as this section proceeds that he is on his way to that city: in Chapter 20 Matthew says that he *was going up to Jerusalem* (20¹⁷); later in that chapter they pass through *Jericho* (20²⁹), in 21 they reach Jerusalem; and from there on, everything takes place in or near Jerusalem, until, in the last chapter of the Gospel, the scene changes back again to Galilee.

The subject of this section of Matthew is therefore the coming of Jesus to Jerusalem. But Jesus does not come merely as a pilgrim for the Passover feast. He is the *king* of Zion, foretold by the prophets, and he comes to claim from his people the obedience that is due to him. Moreover the reader knows already that Israel will not listen to him, but that their leaders will kill him.

In the New Testament, Jerusalem is not only the capital and headquarters of the Jews, but also a parable or 'symbol' of eternal life. In one sense, we may say, Jerusalem is the kingdom of God. It is therefore appropriate that as Jesus goes to Jerusalem, he should teach his disciples who are following him about the kingdom, and tell them what their following of him into the kingdom will involve.

Matthew has taken over this section from Mark ready-made (Mark 10¹–12³⁷), but he has added a few sayings which concern the kingdom and the way to it (19¹⁰ff., 20¹ff., 21¹⁴ff., ²⁸ff., 22¹ff.).

19 *Now when Jesus had finished these sayings, he went away from Galilee and entered the region of Judea beyond the Jordan;* [2]*and large crowds followed him, and he healed them there.*

When Jesus came into Galilee at the beginning of the Gospel, Matthew quoted a prophecy from Isaiah: *The people who sat in darkness have seen a great light.* This *light* of the gospel has now been revealed: Jesus has taught and healed and preached in Galilee, and all that can be given, including and culminating in the teaching about the Church in the previous chapter, has been reported by Matthew. Therefore Jesus leaves Galilee, the place of revelation, and enters Judea, the place of rejection and death. Matthew suggests that Jesus' work in Galilee has not been in vain; he says that large crowds follow Jesus.

≈≈≈

Matthew has attached his transition formula to Mark 10^1, the statement that Jesus *went to the region of Judea*; but he has made some changes in Mark, on which see the notes that follow.

1

Now when Jesus had finished these sayings . . . See 7^{28}, 11^1, 13^{53} for previous uses of this formula; and 26^1 for the fifth and last appearance of it.

he went away from Galilee: The verb here (*metairein*) is used only by Matthew in the New Testament, and the only other place in which he uses it is after the teaching in parables, 13^{53}. There it introduced the account of Jesus' rejection in *his own country*; here it leads up to his rejection in Jerusalem. For *Galilee* as the place of revelation, see in particular 4^{12}ff.

and entered the region of Judea beyond the Jordan: The district was usually called Perea (see map); and this was the usual route for pilgrims going from Galilee to Jerusalem, because it avoided Samaria.

2

and large crowds followed him: Contrast Mark's *and crowds gathered to him again:* the crowds following Jesus may be a prefiguring of the Church.

306

and he healed them there: Contrast Mark's *and again, as his custom was, he taught them.* Matthew has avoided saying that Jesus taught the crowds: see notes on 13¹, 14¹⁴.

19³⁻⁹   THE QUESTION ABOUT   Mark 10²⁻¹²
                    DIVORCE

³*And Pharisees came up to him and tested him by asking, 'Is it lawful to divorce one's wife for any cause?'* ⁴*He answered, 'Have you not read that he who made them from the beginning made them male and female,* ⁵*and said, "For this reason a man shall leave his father and mother and be joined to his wife, and the two shall become one"?ᵃ* ⁶*So they are no longer two but one.ᵃ What therefore God has joined together, let no man put asunder.'* ⁷*They said to him, 'Why then did Moses command one to give a certificate of divorce, and to put her away?'* ⁸*He said to them, 'For your hardness of heart Moses allowed you to divorce your wives, but from the beginning it was not so.* ⁹*And I say to you: whoever divorces his wife, except for unchastity,ᵇ and marries another, commits adultery.'ᶜ*

  a Greek *one flesh*
  b Other ancient authorities, after *unchastity*, read *makes her commit adultery*
  c Other ancient authorities insert *and he who marries a divorced woman commits adultery*

The first incident which Matthew records in this section is the Pharisees' question about divorce. The rabbis held different opinions on the question, What constitutes adequate grounds for divorce? Divorce itself was practised because it was allowed in Deuteronomy. Jesus replies that God never intended that there should be divorce, and he quotes Genesis to prove this. The permission granted by Moses in Deuteronomy was a concession to the hardness of heart of Israel. To divorce one's wife (*except for unchastity* – on the meaning of this see below) and marry another is to commit adultery.

At first sight, this paragraph seems out of place in Matthew's arrangement of his material: partly because this subject has already been raised and dealt with in the teaching on the mountain (5³¹ᶠ·);

and partly because we do not expect to find this kind of material in this section of the Gospel, where the subject is the journey of Jesus to his death and resurrection in Jerusalem, and the way of the disciples who follow Jesus to the kingdom of heaven. Matthew, however, has not re-arranged Mark at this point; and the reasons may be, (i) because the question is asked by Pharisees who are 'testing' Jesus; i.e. they are looking for grounds on which to accuse him and condemn him; there will be other stories of this kind, in which Jesus comes into conflict with the Jewish leaders, in Chapters 21, 22. (ii) In his answer to the Pharisees Jesus draws a distinction between two levels in the Law: the permission given by Moses *for your hardness of heart*, and the purpose of God *from the beginning*; Jesus has come to call men into the kingdom of God, and this kingdom will restore the world to its condition at the beginning. Jesus' teaching about divorce is teaching about the kingdom; and in giving it Jesus is revealed as the one who is greater than Moses.

∞

Matthew has re-arranged Mark 10²ᶠᶠ.. In Mark, Jesus asked the Pharisees what Moses commanded, they answered, and then Jesus said that this was commanded because of their hardness of heart, but was not so from the beginning. Matthew re-arranges this so that the reference to Genesis comes before the reference to Deuteronomy, and so that Jesus does not ask the Pharisees what Moses commanded. Matthew has also added *for any cause* (v. 3) and *except for unchastity* (v. 9); and omitted Mark's note that the last sayings were given privately to the disciples *in the house*, and the saying which contemplated the possibility of a woman divorcing her husband.

3
tested him: In this Gospel, Jesus is *tested* or tempted (*peirazein*) first by Satan, and then by the various Jewish sects: *Pharisees, Sadducees,* and *Herodians* (4¹, ³, 16¹, 22¹⁸, ³⁵).

for any cause: Matthew has added these words either because he knew that the question of permissible causes for divorce was disputed by the rabbis, and he meant that the Pharisees wanted to see with which group Jesus would identify himself; or because Matthew was preparing for the exception which is allowed in v. 9.

4

The words *made them male and female* are a quotation from Gen. 1^{27}. *From the beginning* of the world God made the two sexes, and made them for marriage – see next verse.

5

and said: This can be taken of Jesus: i.e. 'And he said . . .'; but it is more likely that R.S.V. is right, and that the subject of *said* is God (= *he who made them from the beginning*), who spoke through Moses, the author (as was supposed) of Genesis; the words which follow, *For this reason . . .* are a quotation from Gen. 2^{24}.

the two shall become one: Literally, *one flesh*: that is, as closely related as the members of one family, or as the limbs of one body: see Gen. 2^{21}ff. and notice in particular Adam's words about Eve, *This at last is bone of my bones and flesh of my flesh.*

6

This verse repeats and underlines the point of the quotation from Gen. 2^{24}.

7

The Pharisees refer to Deut. 24^{1}, *When a man takes a wife and marries her, if then she finds no favour in his eyes because he has found some indecency in her, and he writes her a bill of divorce and puts it in her hand and sends her out of his house . . .*

8

Notice the contrast between *command* in v. 7 and *allowed* in this verse. In Mark, Jesus uses *command*, and the Pharisees use *allowed*; so Matthew's re-arrangement has made a new point here: it was not a commandment, of Moses, but his permission.

9

And I say to you: According to Mark this was a separate saying, spoken to the disciples privately *in the house*; cf. 16^{18}.

except for unchastity: The same exception is found at 5^{32}, but nowhere else in the New Testament. Most commentators agree that these words were not spoken by Jesus, but were added by the Church which had his authority to make regulations (16^{19}, 18^{18}). It is not certain what *unchastity* (*porneia*) means in this context – it may mean pre-marital fornication or post-marital adultery; but probably the latter (see also note on 5^{32}).

The additional clauses (see margin) are not well attested in the authorities for the text, and are probably due to assimilation to the parallel passage in Mark.

[10] *The disciples said to him, 'If such is the case of a man with his wife, it is not expedient to marry.'* [11]*But he said to them, 'Not all men can receive this precept, but only those to whom it is given.* [12]*For there are eunuchs who have been so from birth, and there are eunuchs who have been made eunuchs by men, and there are eunuchs who have made themselves eunuchs for the sake of the kingdom of heaven. He who is able to receive this, let him receive it.'*

These three verses introduce a comment by the disciples on the previous words of Jesus, and his reply to their comment. The disciples say that, in view of Jesus' teaching on marriage, it is better not to marry at all; as it stands, this seems to mean that in view of Jesus' prohibition of divorce, it is better not to marry; but it may be that there was originally a different connexion between these sayings and the previous paragraph. Jesus says that only some people will be able to give up marriage, and not everyone is able to do so, because not everyone has been made by God for the celibate life. Some can, because they have been born impotent; others, because they have been made impotent by men; others, because they have accepted celibacy for the sake of the kingdom. Those who can accept this saying are to accept it.

৩৫

The occasion, but not the material, is Marcan. Mark had a question from the disciples, and an answer from Jesus at this point (Mark 10^{10}ff.); Matthew has used that material in his previous paragraph (19^9), and he brings in new material here which may originally have stood in quite a different context.

10

Although some scholars think that this comment of the disciples refers to a saying of Jesus which is now lost, the verse has at least one mark of Matthean style: *it is (not) expedient* is a phrase which is used only by Matthew in the Synoptic Gospels (5^{29}ff., 18^6, and here). The disciples are therefore portrayed here as expressing amazement at the teaching of Jesus on divorce and drawing the conclusion that it is better not to marry. Cf. their astonishment in v. 25.

11

this precept (ton logon touton): Literally, 'this saying'; it probably refers to the saying of the disciples in the previous verse, that *it is not expedient to marry*.

those to whom it is given – i.e. by God; cf. 13¹¹ *To you it has been given to know the secrets of the kingdom of heaven*. There are only some who have been called to celibacy by God, and given the gift of continence; cf. 1 Cor. 7⁷ *Each has his own special gift from God, one of one kind and one of another*.

12

Three classes of celibate are distinguished: those born impotent, those made impotent, those who have renounced marriage for the sake of the kingdom. In fact, there are really only two categories here, the unwilling and the willing celibates; and the distinction is between force of circumstances and freedom of the will. The latter group are those who are called by God; of them Jesus says, repeating the word *receive* from v. 11 (an example of *inclusio*), *He who is able to receive this, let him receive it*; cf. *He who has ears let him hear*, 11¹⁵, 13^{9, 43}.

19¹³⁻¹⁵   CHILDREN AND THE KINGDOM Mark 10¹³ff.

¹³ *Then children were brought to him that he might lay his hands on them and pray. The disciples rebuked the people;* ¹⁴*but Jesus said, 'Let the children come to me, and do not hinder them; for to such belongs the kingdom of heaven.'* ¹⁵*And he laid his hands on them and went away.*

The subject of Jesus' teaching on the way to Jerusalem is the way of the follower of Jesus to the kingdom of heaven. In the previous verses, for example, Jesus said that there were those who had renounced marriage for the sake of the kingdom. And in this paragraph also one of the essentials of the way to the kingdom is taught. The story is a typical example of the way in which a saying of Jesus has been remembered within a setting of narrative. People bring children to Jesus for blessing; the disciples rebuke them; Jesus tells the disciples to let the children come, because the kingdom belongs to those who are like them; and he blesses the children.

The story recalls the sayings at the beginning of Chapter 18 about becoming like children in order to enter the kingdom of heaven, and the meaning of it is the same: the child is the symbol of the disciple who will enter the kingdom, because the child has no status in the world. By blessing the children Jesus is blessing the disciple who is poor and unencumbered by the things of this age: a 'nobody'.

∞

Matthew has made some changes in Mark 10¹³ff.: for example, he had already used Mark 10¹⁵ in 18³, so he omits it here; and he omits Mark's statement that Jesus *was indignant* with the disciples when they rebuked those who brought the children.

13
Those who brought the children to Jesus may have believed that 'the rabbi' had some magic power which would benefit the children. Possibly this is why the disciples *rebuked them*: but their motive is not in fact stated in the text. The story was preserved for the sake of the saying of Jesus which it contained, and unessential details were omitted.

14
Jesus used the occasion to teach by action (cf. 18²). *Let the children come to me:* Jesus is the herald and agent of the coming of the kingdom, so to *come* to him is to enter it: cf. his words, *come to me . . . and I will give you rest* (11²⁸); in order to come to him, or enter the kingdom, the disciples must *become like children* (18³) – i.e. *be poor in spirit, meek,* etc. (5⁵ff.).

15
he laid his hands on them: See v. 13 and note the *inclusio*.

| 19^{16-22} | POSSESSIONS AND THE KINGDOM (A) | Mark 10¹⁷ff. |

¹⁶*And behold, one came up to him, saying, 'Teacher, what good deed must I do, to have eternal life?' *¹⁷*And he said to him, 'Why do you ask me about*

what is good? One there is who is good. If you would enter life, keep the commandments.' [18]*He said to him, 'Which?' And Jesus said, 'You shall not kill, You shall not commit adultery, You shall not steal, You shall not bear false witness,* [19]*Honour your father and mother, and, You shall love your neighbour as yourself.'* [20]*The young man said to him, 'All these I have observed; what do I still lack?'* [21]*Jesus said to him, 'If you would be perfect, go, sell what you possess and give to the poor, and you will have treasure in heaven; and come, follow me.'* [22]*When the young man heard this he went away sorrowful; for he had great possessions.*

The theme of entering the kingdom is carried on in this paragraph. A young man asks Jesus what he must do to have *eternal life*, that is, to enter the kingdom. Jesus tells him to keep the Commandments, and then tells him which ones. The young man claims that he has observed them, and Jesus tells him to sell his possessions, give to the poor, and follow him. The young man goes away sad.

The story recalls the teaching in Chapters 5–7 about poverty and treasure in heaven and being perfect, and about the impossibility of serving two masters, God and mammon. Similarly, the sayings here about the Commandments recall Jesus' commentary on the Commandments in Chapter 5; the obedience which he demands from those who want to enter the kingdom is so much greater than that which the young man had expected that he goes away sad.

Matthew has made a number of changes in the first question of the young man and Jesus' answer (Mark 10[17f.]); he has omitted *Do not defraud*, but added *You shall love your neighbour as yourself*; and whereas in Mark the man said *all these I have observed from my youth*, suggesting that he is no longer a youth, Matthew rewrites this as *The young man said to him, All these I have observed*.

16

Teacher: The title is never used in Matthew by disciples of Jesus; see 8[19].

what good deed must I do . . . Matthew has changed Mark's *Good teacher what must I do*, and has also changed the answer of Jesus in the next verse, in order to remove the suggestion that Jesus disclaimed the use of *good* of himself.

to have eternal life: *life* and *eternal life* are equivalents for *the kingdom of heaven*; see vv. 23, 29; and the alternatives, *destruction* or *life*, in 7[13f.], etc.

17

Why do you ask me about what is good? One there is who is good: Contrast Mark: *Why do you call me good? No one is good but God alone.* See note on previous verse.

18f.

The first five of these commandments are from the Ten Commandments in Exod. 20¹²ff., Deut. 5¹⁶ff.; the sixth is a quotation from Lev. 19¹⁸, and Matthew has added it here (see also 22³⁹). This passage from Leviticus is quoted with four of the Ten Commandments by Paul in Rom. 13⁹, and there is evidence to show that the rabbis taught that this command sums up the Law.

20

Matthew has rewritten Mark, making the man ask Jesus what he still lacks, and omitting *Jesus looking upon him loved him.*

21

If you would be perfect is a Matthean addition: by perfection is not meant a stage higher than entering *life* (v. 17), as though one could choose either of two levels, salvation (= the kingdom), or perfection. To be *perfect* means the same as *to enter life*; this is seen (i) from the similarity of the phrases in v. 17 and in this verse: *If you would enter life . . . If you would be perfect*; and (ii) because Jesus had said before *You, therefore, must be perfect, as your heavenly Father is perfect* (5⁴³).

you will have treasure in heaven: i.e. God's approval and reward at the judgement; see 6¹⁹f..

and come, follow me: See 8²², etc.

22

The young man rejects the call of Jesus, and is *sorrowful*: contrast the parable of the man who sold everything *in his joy*, 13⁴⁴.

19²³⁻³⁰	POSSESSIONS AND THE KINGDOM (B)	Mark 10²³⁻³¹ Luke 22²⁸⁻³⁰

²³*And Jesus said to his disciples, 'Truly, I say to you, it will be hard for a rich man to enter the kingdom of heaven.* ²⁴*Again I tell you, it is easier for a camel to go through the eye of a needle than for a rich man to enter the*

kingdom of God.' ²⁵*When the disciples heard this they were greatly astonished, saying, 'Who then can be saved?'* ²⁶*But Jesus looked at them and said to them, 'With men this is impossible, but with God all things are possible.'* ²⁷*Then Peter said in reply, 'Lo, we have left everything and followed you. What then shall we have?'* ²⁸*Jesus said to them,'Truly, I say to you, in the new world, when the Son of man shall sit on his glorious throne, you who have followed me will also sit on twelve thrones, judging the twelve tribes of Israel.* ²⁹*And every one who has left houses or brothers or sisters or father or mother or children or lands, for my name's sake, will receive a hundredfold,ᵃ and inherit eternal life.* ³⁰*But many that are first will be last, and the last first.*

a Other ancient authorities read *manifold*

The subject of riches and the kingdom is continued in a discussion between Jesus and the disciples. He says that it will be difficult for a rich man to enter the kingdom; in fact, he adds, it will be impossible for a rich man to enter it, as impossible as it is for a camel to go through the eye of a needle. The disciples ask whether anyone can be saved, and Jesus says God is able to do everything: entry into the kingdom, or salvation (they are the same thing), is his work, and not man's. Peter asks what he and the other disciples who have left everything and followed Jesus will have as their reward when they enter the kingdom, and Jesus says that they will have a share in his dominion and glory in the age to come, and so likewise will all who have left possessions of any kind in obedience to him. Wealth in this age will be rewarded with poverty in the age to come, but poverty in this age with wealth in the age to come.

ಜಜ

Verses 23–27 and 29f. are from Mark 10²³ff.. with some alterations, and Matthew has omitted Mark 10²⁴; v. 28 has been inserted by Matthew – it is similar to Luke 22²⁸ff..

23

For the difficulty of entering the kingdom, cf. *the gate is narrow and the way is hard, that leads to life* (7¹⁴). For the rich man, this difficulty lies in the temptation to divide his loyalty between God and his possessions, treasure in heaven and treasure on earth.

24

Matthew has omitted Mark 10²⁴, *And the disciples were amazed at his words. But Jesus said to them again, Children, how hard it is to enter the kingdom of God!* That is to say, in Mark the subject is changed from the case of the rich man, to the general situation of all men: and it may be that the question of the disciples *Then who can be saved?* originally followed the statement of the universal difficulty of entering the kingdom. (The order of verses in Mark is uncertain at this point.) Matthew omits the general statement, and keeps the discussion on the subject of riches and the kingdom.

It is easier for a camel . . . is a proverb, and an example of Jesus' use of hyperbole: it will be as impossible for a rich man to enter as for a camel to go through the eye of a needle; cf. 23²⁴. The various attempts which have been made to find a 'possibility' in this parable are to be discounted: e.g. the suggestion that the needle's eye was a small gate; or that *camel* means 'piece of camel-hair'.

kingdom of God – not the usual Matthean expression, kingdom of heaven: perhaps because of the emphasis on God's power in v. 26; cf. 12²⁸.

25

Who then can be saved? The disciples, arguing from the Old Testament teaching that wealth is a mark of divine favour, ask, If a rich man cannot be saved, then surely no one can be saved? To be *saved* means to *enter the kingdom*; see also 10²², 24¹³, ²².

26

God alone is able to bring men into the kingdom; cf. the saying about faith in 17²⁰ *if you have faith . . . nothing will be impossible to you.* Faith is man's response to the omnipotence of God.

with God all things are possible is an Old Testament saying (Gen. 18¹⁴, Job 42², Zech. 8⁶).

27

Matthew has added the words, *What then shall we have?* – i.e. what will be our reward in the kingdom. Notice how Matthew has taken the two expressions, *left everything, followed you,* and reversed their order in vv. 28f.: *you who have followed me . . . everyone who has left houses,* etc.

28

This verse has been added by Matthew, and it may owe a great deal to his phrasing.

in the new world: Literally, 'in the regeneration', or 'in the rebirth' *(en tē palingenesia)*; this was a technical term with the Stoics and in the mystery religions, but it was also used by the Hellenistic Jewish writer, Philo. The experts say that it cannot be the translation of a Hebrew or Aramaic word, and that it must therefore be attributed to the Evangelist, or to one of his predecessors. It refers to the kingdom as the time when everything will be new, born again, because God's will will be done on earth (6¹⁰).

when the Son of man shall sit on his glorious throne: Cf. the Matthean introduction to his last parable, *When the Son of man comes in his glory . . . then he will sit on his glorious throne* (25³¹). He sits as judge to reward, and as king to rule. *His glorious throne* is the throne of God: the Jewish book called *The Similitudes of Enoch* has various parallels to this idea of a representative of God sitting on God's throne.

you who have followed me: See v. 27 for these words, in Peter's question; in the answer of Jesus they are limited to the twelve, see next words.

will also sit on twelve thrones: i.e. will share in my dominion over the new age. Luke's version omits the number *twelve* here, possibly because Luke was thinking of Judas Iscariot.

judging the twelve tribes of Israel: judging may mean either (i) rewarding, or (ii) ruling (cf. the title *judges* for rulers in the Old Testament); and *the twelve tribes of Israel* may mean either (*a*) the Jewish people, or (*b*) the new Israel, the Church (it is so used in James 1¹). Of the possible combinations of these, the choice is between (1) judging the Jews, and (2) ruling the Church. The latter (2) is perhaps more likely because of Matthew's interest in the Church, and because, in this context, it is more appropriate: to be a ruler is more of a reward than to be a judge.

29
Matthew returns to Mark; the promise here is to all Christ's disciples, *everyone who has left* . . . and not only to the twelve: contrast v. 28.

for my name's sake: i.e. 'for my sake', 'to be my disciple'; cf. 10²².
will receive, from God, as his reward, in the kingdom. Matthew has abbreviated Mark here: in Mark there was a distinction between rewards with persecution *now in this time*, and eternal life *in the age to come*: Matthew puts all the rewards into the age to come.

a hundredfold: Probably *manifold* (margin) was the original reading in Matthew, as in Luke; they agree against Mark who has *a hundredfold*.

and inherit eternal life (Mark: *receive . . . eternal life*): Matthew always uses the verb to inherit, and the noun, *inheritance*, of entering into the life of the age to come: 5⁵, 21³⁸, 25³⁴. For *eternal life* see note on 19¹⁶.

30

many that are first (i.e. the rich, powerful, and 'religious' in this age)
will be last (in the kingdom, where they will have *no reward* 6^1 and be
least 5^{19}), *and the last* (i.e. the poor, the meek, the sinners) will be *first*
(in the kingdom, where they will be *great*, and have a great reward
and treasure). This saying is repeated in the reverse order of phrases
after the parable which follows (21^{16}) to form both an *inclusio* and a
chiasmus.

20$^{1-16}$ A PARABLE OF GOD'S REWARDS

20 *'For the kingdom of heaven is like a householder who went out early
in the morning to hire labourers for his vineyard. ²After agreeing with the
labourers for a denarius^a a day, he sent them into his vineyard. ³And going
out about the third hour he saw others standing idle in the market place; ⁴and
to them he said, "You go into the vineyard too, and whatever is right I will
give you." So they went. ⁵Going out again about the sixth hour and the
ninth hour, he did the same. ⁶And about the eleventh hour he went out and
found others standing; and he said to them, "Why do you stand here idle all
day?" ⁷They said to him, "Because no one has hired us." He said to them,
"You go into the vineyard too." ⁸And when evening came, the owner of the
vineyard said to his steward, "Call the labourers and pay them their wages,
beginning with the last, up to the first." ⁹And when those hired about the
eleventh hour came, each of them received a denarius. ¹⁰Now when the
first came, they thought they would receive more; but each of them also
received a denarius. ¹¹And on receiving it they grumbled at the householder,
¹²saying, "These last worked only one hour, and you have made them equal
to us who have borne the burden of the day and the scorching heat." ¹³But
he replied to one of them, "Friend, I am doing you no wrong; did you not
agree with me for a denarius? ¹⁴Take what belongs to you, and go; I choose
to give to this last as I give to you. ¹⁵Am I not allowed to do what I choose
with what belongs to me? Or do you begrudge my generosity?"^b ¹⁶So the
last will be first, and the first last.'*

a The denarius was worth about a shilling
b Or is your eye evil because I am good?

Matthew inserts a parable at this point in Mark to illustrate the teaching about rewards in the kingdom, which has been the subject of the previous paragraphs. The parable is the story of an owner of a vineyard who employed men at different times in the day, and at the end of the day paid them all the same wage. Matthew understands the owner as being God, and the payments as his reward, i.e. *eternal life*. He also relates the parable to the saying about the *last* and the *first* which precedes and follows the parable: the men who are employed first are paid last, and those who are employed last are paid first.

The parable came to Matthew from a non-Marcan source, and so it probably came to him without any context in the teaching and ministry of Jesus. Matthew has chosen this context for it, and his choice is not altogether suitable. First, the order of paying the workmen is of no real significance in the story: it merely permits those who were employed first to see how much those who were employed last received, and gives them time to suppose that they would receive more. Secondly, as all the workmen receive the same payment, the parable does not illustrate the meaning of the saying about *first* and the *last*, which was, according to Matthew, the different rewards which would be given by God to different people.

The original emphasis of the parable probably lay in the saying of the owner, *I choose to give to this last as I give to you* (v. 14). God is not answerable to man for what he does with his rewards. He can do as he pleases with his gifts, and his generosity is not to be complained of by men. And the setting in the ministry of Jesus is probably his controversy with the Pharisees over his treatment of the tax collectors and sinners: he admits them to his fellowship, he eats and drinks with them, he invites them into the kingdom, because God who has sent him is generous with his forgiveness and mercy; those who complain in the parable are the Pharisees, who, like the older brother in the Lucan parable of the prodigal son, claim more from the Father because of their good works (Luke 15^{11ff.}).

Matthew, or the Church before him, has taken a parable which originally applied to the ministry of Jesus, and used it of the judgement at the end of this age.

ॐ

There is no parallel in Mark or Luke; but the awkwardness with which the parable fits into this context indicates that it was not composed by Matthew, but came to him from some non-Marcan source.

1

the kingdom of heaven is like: The formula does not mean that the king-dom is like a householder, but that it is like the reckoning which the householder makes at the end of the day. For the formula see note on 13²⁴; for the idea of the judgement as a reckoning of accounts, cf. 18²³, 25¹⁴ff.

early: i.e. about 6 a.m.

2

a denarius a day: A denarius was 'a workman's average daily wage' (*Lexicon*, p. 178).

3

the third hour: i.e. between 8 and 9 a.m.
standing: Perhaps 'sit about idly gossiping' (Jeremias, ibid. p. 136).

4

It is important to notice that the sum of money to be paid for the work done is only fixed beforehand with the first group of men, v. 2; this accounts for the situation at the end of the parable, vv. 10ff.

5

the sixth and the ninth hour: i.e. between 11 a.m. and noon, and between 2 and 3 p.m.

6

the eleventh hour: i.e. between 4 and 5 p.m. The work was urgent, if the owner took on more labourers so late in the day; it was the vintage, and the work must be done before the rains came (Jeremias, ibid p. 136).

Why do you stand here idle all day? (see v. 3 for *stand*): Perhaps a reproach; there would be plenty of work at that time of the year.

7

Because no one has hired us may be an excuse to cover up laziness, rather than the truth.

8

the owner of the vineyard: The word translated *owner* is the Greek word often used for God (*kyrios*, Lord).

their wages (ton misthon): Perhaps 'the wage', i.e. the denarius mentioned in vv. 2 and 9f. The same word is translated *reward* in 5¹², etc.

beginning with the last, up to the first: This may mean no more than, 'Pay them all, including the last' (Jeremias); but in any case, the order of payment had no special importance, except that it allowed the situation which follows to develop. Matthew has related it to the sayings in 19^{30}, 20^{16}.

11f.

If the parable originally referred to the Pharisees and their grumbling at Jesus' treatment of the sinners, then this will mean that Jesus is treating sinners with the same mercy as that which he has for those who have *borne the burden* of the Law. For the idea of the Law as a burden, cf. the letter to the Gentile Churches, *For it seemed good to the Holy Spirit and to us to lay upon you no greater burden than these necessary things* (Acts 15^{28}); and, *Come to me, all who labour and are heavy laden* (11^{28}).

13

Friend (hetaire): The word as used in Matthew implies reproach – see 22^{12} (the man without a wedding garment), 26^{50} (Judas Iscariot).

14

There may be a contrast here between *what belongs to you* (i.e. what you have earned and is therefore now yours) and the gift of the vineyard owner (*to give to this last*). The denarius is paid as a wage to the first group, but given as a gift to the last group. *As I give to you* is literally, in the Greek, 'as also to you'. Thus the emphasis is on the choice of the owner: '*I choose*, and there is no appeal against my choice, because I am master of my own property.'

15

God's mercy, revealed in Jesus' fellowship with the sinners, is inexplicable to the Pharisees, but it is undeniable that God is free to do as he wishes – cf. Paul on God's mercy to Jews and Gentiles: *What shall we say then? Is there injustice on God's part? By no means! For he says to Moses, I will have mercy on whom I have mercy, and I will have compassion on whom I have compassion. So it depends not upon man's will or exertion, but upon God's mercy* (Rom. 9$^{14ff.}$).

do you begrudge my generosity: Literally, as in R.S.V. margin, *is your eye evil because I am good? An evil eye* is 'one that looks with envy or jealousy upon other people' (*Lexicon*); Mark had used it for *envy* in Mark 7^{22}.

16

This verse repeats, in the reverse order of members, the saying in 19^{30}.

[17]*And as Jesus was going up to Jerusalem, he took the twelve disciples aside, and on the way he said to them,* [18]*'Behold, we are going up to Jerusalem; and the Son of man will be delivered to the chief priests and scribes, and they will condemn him to death,* [19]*and deliver him to the Gentiles to be mocked and scourged and crucified, and he will be raised on the third day.'*

The teaching of Jesus about the rewards of the kingdom is interrupted here to tell the readers about the journey to Jerusalem on which the teaching was given, and the outcome of the journey: the handing over of the Son of man to the Jewish leaders, his condemnation by them, their surrender of him to the Gentiles for suffering and death, and his resurrection by God on the third day. The paragraph interrupts the teaching of Jesus on rewards in the kingdom, but it does not break the line of thought in this part of the Gospel: Jesus has just said, *The last will be first.* He is *the last*, in his condemnation, mockery, and death; and he *will be first* when God raises him from the dead and exalts him to the position of authority over the world. The teaching about rewards is exemplified in Jesus; and his disciples must *follow* him.

৩৯

Matthew has taken these verses from Mark 10^{32}ff., but he has omitted the references to the amazement and fear of the disciples as they followed Jesus, and made a few detailed alterations in the prediction.

17

And as Jesus was going up to Jerusalem: A different text is found in some of the authorities here, and it may be original. It is: 'When he was about to go up to Jerusalem, Jesus . . .' If this is what Matthew wrote, then this prediction of the Passion and resurrection will be the final warning of what is to happen, before Jesus and his disciples set out for the city.

18

the Son of man will be delivered to the chief priests and scribes refers to the actions of Judas Iscariot (26^{14}ff., 47ff.), but the passive tense, *will be delivered,* may also mean that God's hand and purpose are in these actions, cf. 26²⁴ *the Son of man goes as it is written of him* (i.e. in scripture, and therefore as God intends).

19
to the Gentiles here must mean 'to the Romans', who exercised authority to execute criminals.

to be mocked and scourged: See 27²⁶ff.

and crucified (Mark: *they will . . . kill him*): The previous references to the cross in this Gospel are 10³⁸, 16²⁴; and it is only in Matthew that Jesus explicitly predicts his death by crucifixion.

20²⁰⁻²⁸   SUFFERING AND THE KINGDOM
Mark 10³⁵⁻⁴⁵

²⁰*Then the mother of the sons of Zeb'edee came up to him, with her sons, and kneeling before him she asked him for something.* ²¹*And he said to her, 'What do you want?' She said to him, 'Command that these two sons of mine may sit, one at your right hand and one at your left, in your kingdom.'* ²²*But Jesus answered, 'You do not know what you are asking. Are you able to drink the cup that I am to drink?' They said to him, 'We are able.'* ²³*He said to them, 'You will drink my cup, but to sit at my right hand and at my left hand is not mine to grant, but it is for those for whom it has been prepared by my Father.'* ²⁴*And when the ten heard it, they were indignant at the two brothers.* ²⁵*But Jesus called them to him and said, 'You know that the rulers of the Gentiles lord it over them, and their great men exercise authority over them.* ²⁶*It shall not be so among you; but whoever would be great among you must be your servant,* ²⁷*and whoever would be first among you must be your slave;* ²⁸*even as the Son of man came not to be served but to serve, and to give his life as a ransom for many.'*

In this paragraph the theme is again the relation between the kingdom and suffering. Those who hope to be first in the kingdom, must be last in the world, and this will involve sharing the same treatment from the world as Jesus received.

The mother of James and John asks Jesus that they may have the chief places on either side of him when he rules as King. Jesus asks them whether they are able to share in his sufferings, and they say that they are. Then Jesus says that it is the Father, and not he, who rewards men in the kingdom. This leads on to further teaching to the ten other disciples, who are angry with James and John, on greatness and humiliation: anyone who wants greatness in the kingdom must accept the lowest place among the disciples here and now, just as Jesus, the Son of man and judge of the world, gives his life as the servant of the world.

ᛜᚱᛜ

Matthew has made some changes and omissions in Mark 10³⁵ff., the most important is that whereas in Mark, the two disciples themselves made the request, in Matthew it is their mother who comes to Jesus and (a characteristic of this Gospel) kneels before him.

20
Why has Matthew taken the request from James and John and put it into the mouth of their mother? It is unlikely that he had access to the historical facts at this point: few of his changes elsewhere suggest that he had such access. Possibly he did it in order to present the disciples themselves in a more favourable light, though the words of Jesus in vv. 22ff. are all addressed to the two disciples, in the plural, and not to their mother. It is just possible that Matthew had in mind Bathsheba's request to David for Solomon to succeed him as King and sit upon his throne (I Kings 1¹⁵f.).

the mother of the sons of Zebedee: See 4²¹, 10².

21
in your kingdom: i.e. when you rule as King. Mark had *in your glory*; Matthew has made the same change from *glory* to *kingdom* in 16²⁸.

22
You do not know what you are asking: Plural in Greek, addressed to James and John; the disciples do not yet understand the relationship between suffering and the kingdom.

Are you able to drink the cup I am to drink? For suffering as a cup, see also later in the Gospel the words of Jesus to the Father, *If it be possible, let this cup pass from me* (26³⁹). The expression is used in the Old Testament, e.g. Isa. 51¹⁷ where the prophet says of Jerusalem after its destruction:

> *Rouse yourself, rouse yourself,*
>   *stand up, O Jerusalem,*
> *You who have drunk at the hand of the Lord*
>   *the cup of his wrath,*
> *who have drunk to the dregs*
>   *the bowl of staggering.*

(Mark has a parallel reference to the *baptism* of Jesus, which also refers to his death: but Matthew has omitted it.)

We are able: At the time of the Passion of Jesus, the disciples did not follow him and share his cup; *all the disciples forsook him and fled* (26⁵⁶). But through the power which his Passion and resurrection brought to them, they were enabled to follow him. Cf. *Where I am going you cannot follow me now; but you shall follow afterward* (John 13³⁶).

23

You will drink my cup: The martyrdom of James is recorded in Acts 12²; nothing is known for certain about the death of John.

it has been prepared by my Father: Cf. 25³⁴, ⁴¹. The belief that everything is known by God from the beginning of the world and pre-ordained is common in the Bible. For the limited knowledge of the Son, cf. 24³⁶. Matthew has added the words *by my Father*, to explain the passive periphrasis in Mark (*it has been prepared*).

24

the two brothers: Mark had *James and John*, and Matthew has avoided their names, as also in v. 20.

25ff.

Among *the Gentiles*, greatness is demonstrated by power and authority. In the Church it will not be so: those who hope for places of authority in the kingdom must be servants and slaves of the community.

28

The pattern of slavery and glory is set by *the Son of man*, who is the *first* among the disciples, the ruler, and great one (v. 25). He *came* into the world *not to be served* as a King is served by his attendants, *but* as a servant, *to serve* others; and the supreme moment of his service will be his death, in which he will *give his life* in humiliation *for many* – that is, his death will have the effect of releasing all men (*many* is a Hebraism for 'all') from their captivity and slavery; cf. *He will save his people from their sins* (1²¹); *This is my blood of the covenant, which is poured out for many for the forgiveness of sins* (26²⁸).

²⁹*And as they went out of Jericho, a great crowd followed him.* ³⁰*And behold,
two blind men sitting by the roadside, when they heard that Jesus was passing
by, cried out,ᵃ 'Have mercy on us, Son of David!'* ³¹*The crowd rebuked
them, telling them to be silent; but they cried out the more, 'Lord, have mercy
on us, Son of David!'* ³²*And Jesus stopped and called them, saying, 'What
do you want me to do for you?'* ³³*They said to him, 'Lord, let our eyes be
opened.'* ³⁴*And Jesus in pity touched their eyes, and immediately they
received their sight and followed him.*

a Other ancient authorities insert *Lord*

The request of the two disciples has revealed their blindness: they
do not understand yet the teaching of Jesus about his Passion, or
about their discipleship. Matthew follows it with the request of two
blind men for their sight; this is granted, and they follow Jesus
(as disciples). The juxtaposition of these two paragraphs is Marcan;
and in Mark it is a repetition of a device which he had used earlier
in the Gospel – when the opening of the eyes of a blind man at
Bethsaida came immediately before the confession of Peter (Mark
8²²ff.). The miracle, in both cases, is related to the narrative about the
disciples. In Mark 8, Peter 'sees' who Jesus is, through the grace of
Christ. Here and in the parallel in Mark 10, the two disciples are and
will remain blind, until Jesus opens their eyes; then they will follow
him. Matthew has made this more clear than Mark, by changing the
one blind man in Mark into *two blind men*, who thus correspond
to *the two brothers* in v. 24. We can now see how it will happen that
Jesus' prediction to the two brothers, that they will drink his cup,
can be fulfilled. The *pity* or compassion of Jesus in his Passion and
resurrection will touch them; they will receive their sight and
follow him.

ΙΩΣ

Matthew has omitted from Mark 10⁴⁶ff. the account of the crowds talking to the blind man and other details, but added some words from the Marcan account of the healing of a different blind man (Mark 8²²ff.) – a story which he had omitted at the corresponding point in his Gospel.

29

And as they went out of Jericho: This is the first point in the journey south which Matthew has specified since 19¹ (*he ... entered the region of Judea beyond the Jordon*). From now on, the topography becomes more exact; see, e.g., 21¹, ¹², etc.

30

two blind men: Contrast Mark: *Bartimaeus, a blind beggar, the son of Timaeus.* Notice that Matthew has omitted the name, as above in v. 24, possibly because he wanted to apply the teaching here to all Christians. For the doubling of the number of people healed, cf. 8²⁸ff. (two demoniacs), 9²⁷ff. (two blind men).

Jesus: Mark had *Jesus of Nazareth,* but Matthew omits *of Nazareth* as in the other places where it stood in Mark (Mark 1²⁴, 14⁶⁷, 16⁶).

Probably the word *Lord* should be added before *Have mercy on us* (as in R.S.V. margin); it is certainly part of the text in v. 31, and Matthew tends to make similar passages exactly the same as each other.

32

What do you want me to do for you? is parallel to Jesus' words to the mother of the disciples in v. 21, *What do you want?*

33

Lord: Matthew has translated Mark's Aramaic word *rabbouni, master.*

34

in pity: Literally, 'being moved with compassion'.

touched their eyes: The particular word for *eyes* (*ommata*) is only used in the New Testament here and in the Marcan account of the blind man at Bethsaida (Mark 8²³).

and followed him: Sight is a symbol of faith, and following Jesus on his journey to Jerusalem is similarly a symbol of discipleship (see, e.g., 10³⁸).

21 *And when they drew near to Jerusalem and came to Beth'phage, to the Mount of Olives, then Jesus sent two disciples, ²saying to them, 'Go into the village opposite you, and immediately you will find an ass tied, and a colt with her; untie them and bring them to me. ³If any one says anything to you, you shall say, "The Lord has need of them," and he will send them immediately.' ⁴This took place to fulfil what was spoken by the prophet, saying,*

> ⁵*'Tell the daughter of Zion,*
> *Behold, your king is coming to you,*
> *humble, and mounted on an ass,*
> *and on a colt, the foal of an ass.'*

⁶*The disciples went and did as Jesus had directed them; ⁷they brought the ass and the colt, and put their garments on them, and he sat thereon. ⁸Most of the crowd spread their garments on the road, and others cut branches from the trees and spread them on the road. ⁹And the crowds that went before him and that followed him shouted, 'Hosanna to the Son of David! Blessed be he who comes in the name of the Lord! Hosanna in the highest!' ¹⁰And when he entered Jerusalem, all the city was stirred, saying, 'Who is this?' ¹¹And the crowds said, 'This is the prophet Jesus from Nazareth of Galilee.'*

Matthew describes the arrival of Jesus at Jerusalem with the greatest solemnity. He sees it as a moment of great significance in the ministry of Jesus, being the entry of the King into his capital and the coming of God's Son to his disobedient people and, like the transfiguration, a preview of his coming in glory at the end of the world.

Jesus himself chooses the manner in which he will enter Jerusalem: riding on an ass and a colt. The evangelist points to the Old Testament passages which had foretold this, and which have now been fulfilled. There is a sense of mystery about the arrangements: two of the disciples are told where they will find the animals, and what to say to anyone who speaks to them.

When Jesus first foretold his Passion to his disciples, he said that he *must go to Jerusalem* (16²¹); and the word *must* meant, as we saw, the divine command, the will of the Father. Jesus has obeyed the Father's command, and come near to Jerusalem; and now he fulfils it by the manner in which he enters the city.

The actions and words of the crowd bear witness to the kingship of Jesus: they spread their clothes on the road along which he is to pass, which is a sign that he who will come is King; and they cut down branches and spread them also on the road – another sign of a festival. Moreover they shout his royal title, *Son of David*; and proclaim him to the city as *the prophet*.

Although there may be a historical element in the tradition of Jesus' 'Triumphal Entry', the description which Matthew gives is at least to some extent idealized, as we can see by comparing it with the Marcan parallel. The purpose of the story was to sound the note of majesty and kingship before the Passion narrative began, at the moment of Jesus' arrival in the city, and to adumbrate the second coming of Jesus in glory.

సౌ

Matthew has both abbreviated Mark 11^{1ff.} and added material of his own, so that in the end his paragraph is about the same length as Mark's. He has abbreviated the instructions given to the two disciples, and the account of finding the animal(s); but added the Old Testament prophecies and the descriptions, in the last two verses, of the effect of the events on the city. Some of his other detailed alterations will be noted below.

1
Bethphage: Mark had *Bethphage and Bethany*; both villages were on the east side of Jerusalem.

the Mount of Olives is mentioned in the Old Testament in Zech. 14⁴: *On that day his* [i.e. the Lord's] *feet shall stand on the Mount of Olives which lies before Jerusalem on the east.* . . . The place was thus associated in the minds of the Jews with Messianic hopes, and it is no accident therefore that it is the scene later in the Gospel for the foretelling of the coming of Christ at the end of the world (24³).

2
an ass tied, and a colt with her: Contrast Mark, *a colt tied, on which no one has ever sat;* Mark almost certainly had the prophecy in Zech. 9⁹ in mind when he wrote this, and in the Greek translation it described the animal on which the King would ride into Jerusalem as 'a beast

and a young colt' (*hypozygion kai pōlon neon*). Matthew has picked up the reference to Zechariah (which he quotes in v. 5), and has changed the words of Jesus to the disciples to make them a more exact fulfilment of the prophecy. For this relationship between Mark, the Old Testament, and Matthew, cf. 15^{29}ff..

3

. . . '*The Lord has need of them*,' *and he will send them immediately*: Matthew has changed the singular (*it . . . it*) in Mark into the plural; and altered the second part of the sentence: in Mark it ran: '*The Lord has need of it and will send it back immediately.*'

4

Matthew inserts here his formula for the fulfilment of a prophecy; see 1^{22}.

5

Matthew has combined two Old Testament prophecies. The first, *Tell the daughter of Zion* (i.e. God's people, Israel, the Bride of God), is from Isaiah 62^{11}, and the prophecy continues with these words of encouragement:

> Behold, your salvation comes;
>> behold, his reward is with him,
>>> and his recompense before him.
>> And they shall be called The holy people,
>>> The redeemed of the Lord;
>> and you shall be called Sought out,
>>> a city not forsaken.

The other part of the prophecy is from Zech. 9^9:

> Rejoice greatly, O daughter of Zion!
>> Shout aloud, O daughter of Jerusalem!
> Lo, your king comes to you;
>> triumphant and victorious is he,
> humble and riding on an ass,
>> on a colt the foal of an ass.

The last two lines are an example of Hebrew poetic parallelism – i.e. repetition of the same idea in different words. Matthew seems to have taken this literally, and thus introduced two animals into the story.

6

Matthew has considerably abbreviated Mark's detailed account of the finding of the colt and of the conversation which Jesus had foretold (Mark 11^{4}ff.).

7

Matthew has altered the wording here also, to bring in the second animal; *he sat thereon* is a translation that obscures what Matthew in fact wrote, viz. 'he sat on them' (*epekathisen epanō autōn*).

8

Most of the crowd spread their garments on the road: For this act of homage, compare 2 Kings 9¹³, *Then in haste every man of them took his garment, and put it under him on the bare steps, and they blew the trumpet, and proclaimed, Jehu is king.*

and others cut branches from the trees and spread them on the road: Branches are mentioned in the accounts of the rededication of the temple in the year 165 B.C., at the Feast of Tabernacles, 1 Macc. 13⁵¹, 2 Macc. 10⁷.

9

Hosanna: From Ps. 118²⁵; the word is Hebrew, and it means, Save, or Help; but it became a liturgical formula, and a greeting, as here.

to the Son of David has been added by Matthew, to emphasize the kingship of Jesus at this moment when he is entering the royal city. Cf. also v. 15 where Matthew repeats the cry; and for the title, see note on 1¹.

Blessed be he who comes in the name of the Lord is also from Ps. 118 (v. 26). *He who comes* may have been used as a title for the Messianic king; see note on 11³.

Hosanna in the highest: the highest means 'heaven', and heaven is a periphrasis for God; therefore these words may mean 'God bless him'.

10

all the city was stirred is another Matthean addition; cf. the description of the coming of the Magi with their question about the *king of the Jews* – *When Herod the king heard this, he was troubled, and all Jerusalem with him* (2³); and for the 'idealizing' use of *all* see also 3⁵, 4²³ᶠ.

11

the crowds explain who Jesus is, and announce him to Jerusalem. We might have expected Matthew to have used a greater title of Jesus than *the prophet*; e.g. 'King', 'Son of David', etc. He may have had 16¹⁴ in mind, where the disciples said that some were saying that Jesus was *one of the prophets*; and later in this chapter he says that the crowd *all held him to be a prophet* (v. 46). Perhaps Matthew intends to portray the understanding of *the crowds* as something less than the faith of the disciples.

^{12}*And Jesus entered the temple of God^a and drove out all who sold and bought in the temple, and he overturned the tables of the money-changers and the seats of those who sold pigeons.* ^{13}*He said to them, 'It is written, "My house shall be called a house of prayer"; but you make it a den of robbers.'*

a Other ancient authorities omit *of God*

The prophecy of the messenger who would prepare the way of the Lord, which Matthew had quoted in connexion with John the Baptist (11^{10}), continues: *and the Lord whom you seek will suddenly come to his temple . . . But who can endure the day of his coming, and who can stand when he appears?* (Mal. 3$^{1f.}$). Matthew's next paragraph shows the fulfilment of this part of the prophecy: Jesus enters the temple, and his actions and his words rebuke the Jews for their misuse of God's house: it should have been a place of prayer, but they have made it a robber's den.

∞

This is one of the few places in this Gospel after Chapter 13 where Matthew re-arranges the order of the Marcan paragraphs; in Mark, the cleansing of the temple takes place on the day after Jesus' arrival in Jerusalem, and thus after the cursing of the fig tree: Matthew brings the cleansing forward to the first day in Jerusalem, and keeps the material about the fig tree for the second day (vv. 18ff.). His reason for bringing forward the cleansing to this point may have been to fulfil the Malachi prophecy, or to bring the cleansing closer to the entry into Jerusalem because the account of the entry may have reminded him of the feast of dedication, which celebrated the Maccabean cleansing of the temple.

12

The words *of God* are only found in some of the manuscripts. If they are part of Matthew's original text, then he added them to Mark.

the tables of the money changers: All financial transactions in the temple had to be made in the coinage of Tyre; therefore other coins had to be changed into Tyrian coins, and large profits were made for the temple in these exchanges.

the seats of those who sold pigeons: Pigeons were required as sacrifice, e.g. by those who could not afford a lamb (Lev. 5^7, 12^8, etc.).

13

My house shall be called a house of prayer is a quotation from Isa. 56^7; *shall be called* means 'shall be', as in 5^9. Mark continued the quotation . . . *a house of prayer for all the nations,* but Matthew has omitted this, perhaps because he believed that the time of the *nations* (or Gentiles) did not begin until after the resurrection.

a den of robbers is a phrase from Jer. 7^{11} where Jeremiah is predicting the destruction of the temple as a punishment for its misuse; for Jesus' prediction of its destruction, see $23^{37ff.}$, 24^2.

21^{14-17} THE SON OF DAVID IN   Mark 11^{11b}
THE TEMPLE

¹⁴*And the blind and the lame came to him in the temple, and he healed them.* ¹⁵*But when the chief priests and the scribes saw the wonderful things that he did, and the children crying out in the temple, 'Hosanna to the Son of David!' they were indignant;* ¹⁶*and they said to him, 'Do you hear what these are saying?' And Jesus said to them, 'Yes; have you never read,*

    "Out of the mouth of babes and sucklings thou hast brought perfect praise"?'
¹⁷*And leaving them, he went out of the city to Bethany and lodged there.*

These four verses are a Matthean addition to Mark, built out of Old Testament passages, and underlining the kingship of Jesus – he is the Son of David, the Messiah. First there is the healing of *the blind and the lame . . . in the temple.* This short reference to healing by Jesus in Jerusalem, which has no parallel in Mark, may have been added by Matthew (or by a commentator on Mark, before Matthew) as a 'fulfilment' of an incident recorded in 2 Sam. $5^{6ff.}$: *David and his men went to Jerusalem,* which was at that time a stronghold of the Jebusites, and the Jebusites thought that their citadel could not be taken; they said, *the blind and the lame will ward you off,* meaning *David cannot come in here.* David said, *Whoever would smite the Jebusites, let him get* up the water shaft to attack *the lame and the blind, who are hated by David's soul*; and he took the stronghold. The author of 2 Samuel then adds, *Therefore it is said, The blind and the lame shall not come into the house* (of the Lord, LXX). Matthew is thus contrasting the first David, who killed the blind and the lame, and forbade them to enter the temple, with the second David, to whom the blind and the lame come in the temple, and by whom they are healed.

Another Old Testament passage is also recalled here: *Children* repeat the shouts of the crowd at the entry into Jerusalem, *Hosanna to the Son of David!* and the chief priests and scribes are angry; but Jesus says that this is in fulfilment of Ps. 8².

This is the first appearance of *the chief priests and the scribes* since 2⁴, when Herod assembled them to find the answer to the question of the Magi. From now on they will play an important part in the narrative.

ॐ

The only words which Matthew has taken from Mark are in the last verse, *he went out* and *to Bethany* (Mark 11¹¹). The rest of the paragraph is probably a Matthean construction, based on the two Old Testament passages, 2 Sam. 5^{6ff.} and Ps. 8². The vocabulary is characteristically Matthean.

14

the blind and the lame: The Greek words used are the same as those in 2 Sam. 5^{6ff.}. This is the last account of healing in this Gospel. Jesus has driven out those who bought and sold the material for sacrifice, and in its place he has healed the sick: that is to say, he has replaced the Law with the gospel.

15

the chief priests and the scribes have been mentioned in the predictions of the Passion (16²¹, 20¹⁸): their appearance, now, warns the reader that these predictions will shortly be fulfilled.

the wonderful things that he did refers, presumably, to the healings in the previous verse.

the children crying out in the temple anticipates the quotation from Ps. 8 in the next verse.

Hosanna to the Son of David! See v. 9.

16

Out of the mouth of babes and sucklings ... Matthew quotes the LXX of
Ps. 8^2, which differs from the Hebrew text; the latter would not have
been appropriate. This indicates that the passage was composed among
people who used the Old Testament in Greek, rather than in
the Hebrew or Aramaic; or who could choose which version to use.
The contrast between *the chief priests and the scribes* and the *babes and
sucklings* recalls the words of Jesus earlier: *I thank thee, Father, Lord of
heaven and earth, that thou hast hidden these things from the wise and
understanding and revealed them to babes* (11^{25}).

17

leaving them: The implication is that Jesus turns away from those who
have rejected the possibility of faith: see 4^{13}, where he left Nazareth
after the arrest of John the Baptist; and 16^4, where he left the Pharisees
and Sadducees when they had asked him for a sign from heaven.

the city is Matthew's term for Jerusalem.

21$^{18-22}$ THE FIG TREE   Mark 11$^{12-14, 20-25}$

^{18}*In the morning, as he was returning to the city, he was hungry.* ^{19}*And seeing a fig tree by the wayside he went to it, and found nothing on it but
leaves only. And he said to it, 'May no fruit ever come from you again!' And
the fig tree withered at once.* ^{20}*When the disciples saw it they marvelled,
saying, 'How did the fig tree wither at once?'* ^{21}*And Jesus answered them,
'Truly, I say to you, if you have faith and never doubt, you will not only
do what has been done to the fig tree, but even if you say to this mountain,
"Be taken up and cast into sea," it will be done.* ^{22}*And whatever you ask
in prayer, you will receive, if you have faith.'*

This story is unique in the Gospels, in that it describes the only
miracle of Jesus which is purely destructive. Jesus looks for fruit on
a fig tree because he is hungry, but finding only leaves he utters a
powerful word which makes the tree immediately wither. The
disciples ask how this has happened, and Jesus says that those who
have faith will not only be able to make trees wither, but will also
be able to move *this mountain* into the sea.

We shall see, from a comparison with Mark, that the incident has suffered some change since it was written down in the earlier Gospel; and it may well be that it was also changed before it came to Mark. Possibly the origin of the story was not an incident, but a saying of Jesus about the fate of fruitless trees – compare the words of John the Baptist, *Every tree therefore that does not bear good fruit is cut down and thrown into the fire* (3[10]); and the parable in Luke 13[6ff.].

Although Matthew uses the miracle to teach the necessity of faith, he probably understood it also as a sign of the coming judgement of God upon faithless Israel. It leads up to the parables which come in vv. 28ff., and notice in particular the words which Matthew has added in v. 43: *Therefore I tell you, the kingdom of God will be taken away from you and given to a nation producing the fruits of it*; that is to say, the Jews are like the fruitless fig tree, and they will be condemned by God for their fruitlessness.

∞

In Mark, Jesus looks for fruit on the tree, and 'curses' it, on one day; then on the next day Peter draws Jesus' attention to it (Mark 11[12ff.], 20ff.). The result of Matthew's re-arrangement here is that the whole incident takes place on the same day; he has therefore added the sentence, *And the fig tree withered at once*, and changed the words of the disciples in v. 20, to the question why the fig tree withered at once. This has had the effect of making the miracle into an example of faith's powerfulness; whereas in Mark it was a sign of God's judgement, with little emphasis on the miraculous element.

19

Matthew has omitted Mark's note, *it was not the season for figs* (Mark 11[13]), possibly because his readers would know this, or because its inclusion made the story more confusing.

For *fruit* as a symbol of good works, see 3[8], etc.

21

For *faith* and moving *mountains*, see 17[20].

22

The saying about *faith* and *prayer* links this paragraph back to the cleansing of the temple: the temple should have been a *house of prayer*, but it was condemned, because the Jews had no *faith* in God; their worship was not the giving of *fruit* which God commands, but they were *robbers*, making themselves rich instead of rendering it to God.

²³*And when he entered the temple, the chief priests and the elders of the people came up to him as he was teaching, and said, 'By what authority are you doing these things, and who gave you this authority?'* ²⁴*Jesus answered them, 'I also will ask you a question; and if you tell me the answer, then I also will tell you by what authority I do these things.* ²⁵*The baptism of John, whence was it? From heaven or from men?' And they argued with one another, 'If we say, "From heaven," he will say to us, "Why then did you not believe him?"* ²⁶*But if we say, "From men," we are afraid of the multitude; for all hold that John was a prophet.'* ²⁷*So they answered Jesus, 'We do not know.' And he said to them, 'Neither will I tell you by what authority I do these things.*

The official leaders of the Jews return with the fundamental question: Jesus has provoked people to address him as *Son of David*, and *the prophet*; he has ridden into Jerusalem on an ass and a colt, turned people out of the temple, and healed others in the temple. Is his authority to do these things an authority which God has given to him, or has he assumed it for himself? In a typically rabbinic way, Jesus replies with a counter-question, concerning the authority of John the Baptist. The chief priests and elders are unable to answer, because if they confess John's divine authority, Jesus will ask them why they did not believe him, and if they deny it, the crowd will revolt against them, since they believed that John was sent by God.

The counter-question of Jesus is not a mere evasion of the original question of the official leaders of the Jews. We have already seen that Jesus did not make explicit and open claims for himself, but spoke in riddles (see e.g. 11^2ff.). Therefore he does not answer their question with a simple answer; but nevertheless his counter-question does imply the answer which he believes to be true: John the Baptist and he himself are both sent by God to Israel, and *this generation* has rejected both of them (see 11^{16}ff., 17^{11}ff.).

Matthew has made very few alterations in Mark 11²⁷ᶠᶠ. and those are only minor verbal changes which scarcely affect the sense.

23

as he was teaching, if original, has been added by Matthew (and by Luke 20¹); but it is omitted in some of the ancient witnesses to the text, and may not be part of what Matthew wrote. (See note on 13¹ᶠᶠ. On the other hand, notice the reference to *teaching* in the temple at 26⁵⁵.)

By what authority are you doing these things? these things may refer to *teaching* (if that is original); or to the entry into Jerusalem, the cleansing of the temple, and the healings; or to the ministry in general.

24

Another possible line of interpretation here is that only those who have attended to John's preaching of repentance and accepted his baptism will be able to understand who Jesus is, and whence he receives his authority.

For question followed by counter-question, see also 12¹¹, 15³.

25

from heaven means 'from God'; *from men* as the opposite of *from heaven* means 'merely human', and thus 'self-assumed', 'wicked'.

Why then did you not believe him? believe here implies 'obey'; i.e. they did not repent, and were not baptized, and did not follow John when he bore witness to Jesus.

27

We do not know: Their pretended ignorance is in fact a cover for their unwillingness to decide and to act upon John's preaching.

. . . by what authority I do these things repeats the words of the question in v. 23, and thus rounds off the paragraph.

21²⁸⁻³²   THE PARABLE OF THE TWO SONS   Luke 7²⁹f.

²⁸'*What do you think? A man had two sons; and he went to the first and said, "Son, go and work in the vineyard today." ²⁹And he answered, "I will not"; but afterward he repented and went. ³⁰And he went to the second and said the same; and he answered, "I go, sir," but did not go. ³¹Which of the*

two did the will of his father?' They said, 'The first.' Jesus said to them,
'Truly, I say to you, the tax collectors and the harlots go into the kingdom of
God before you. [32]*For John came to you in the way of righteousness, and you*
did not believe him, but the tax collectors and the harlots believed him; and
even when you saw it, you did not afterward repent and believe him.'

The question of Jesus in the previous paragraph revealed the unbelief
of the Jewish leaders in John the Baptist, and this is pressed home now
in the parable of the two sons: one of them obeys, and one of them
does not obey his father. This is applied to the tax collectors and
harlots who obeyed John, and the Jewish leaders who did not.

As in other places in the Gospels, a parable of Jesus seems to have
been used here for a different purpose from that for which Jesus
himself had used it. The original parable, in vv. 28–30, was probably
used to illustrate the difference between saying and doing: compare
Not every one who says to me, Lord, Lord, shall enter the kingdom of
heaven, but he who does the will of my Father who is in Heaven, 7^{21}
(notice the parallel expressions, *say, Lord* [= *Sir*], *do the will of the*
Father, enter [or *go into*] *the kingdom*); and compare also the saying
about the true family of Jesus, *Whoever does the will of my Father in*
heaven, is my brother, and sister, and mother (12^{50}). This kind of teaching
may have been the original setting of this parable; and Matthew, or
the Church before him, has applied it to the contrast between the
response of the sinners to John, and the disobedience of the Jewish
leaders to him.

❧

Verses 28–31 have no parallel in Mark or Luke, but v. 32 has a partial
parallel in Luke $7^{29f.}$. Matthew has added the whole paragraph at this
point, possibly because at Mark 12^1 he read *And he began to speak to*
them in parables (plural) though only one parable followed in Mark; but
even more, because the disobedience of the son to the father in the
parable fitted the context, namely the disobedience of the Jewish leaders
to John. At the end of the next parable Matthew can therefore say,
When the chief priests and Pharisees heard his parables, they perceived that
he was speaking about them (21^{45}).

28
What do you think? is a Matthean introduction: see 17^{25}.

the vineyard: See below, v. 33, where *a vineyard* stands for Israel; and above, 20¹, where working in a vineyard means serving God in this age, for a reward in the age to come.

29

he repented (*metameletheis*): This word is used by Matthew alone of the four Evangelists, and here it can have the weaker sense, 'he changed his mind'; see also 27³.

30

I go, sir: sir here is the word which is also translated *Lord* (*kyrie*). It is the son who does not go, who says *Lord*; cf. 7²¹ (quoted above) that it is not everyone who says *Lord, Lord* who does the will of the Father.

31

the tax collectors and the harlots have believed and obeyed John, therefore they precede *the chief priests and the elders* (v. 23) into the kingdom.

the kingdom of God, not, as usually in Matthew, the kingdom of heaven – see 12²⁸, 19²⁴, 21⁴³.

32

This verse explains the statement in the previous verse in terms of the parable; notice how vv. 31 and 32 are related to each other chiasmically: (*a*) *tax collectors and harlots*, (*b*) *you*; (*b*) *you*, (*a*) *tax collectors and harlots*.

you did not afterward repent: The same word is used as in v. 29.

The text of Matthew is uncertain in vv. 29–31: in some manuscripts the disobedient son who did not go comes first, and the one who changed his mind is second; and this may be the original order. In that case, the chiasmus begins in v. 29; 29(*b*) disobedient son, 30(*a*) obedient son, 31(*a*) *tax collectors and sinners*, (*b*) *you*, 32(*b*) *you*, (*a*) *tax collectors and sinners*.

21³³⁻⁴¹   THE PARABLE OF THE VINEYARD   Mark 12¹⁻⁹

³³'*Hear another parable. There was a householder who planted a vineyard, and set a hedge around it, and dug a wine press in it, and built a tower, and let it out to tenants, and went into another country.* ³⁴*When the season of*

fruit drew near, he sent his servants to the tenants, to get his fruit; ³⁵*and the tenants took his servants and beat one, killed another, and stoned another.* ³⁶*Again he sent other servants, more than the first; and they did the same to them.* ³⁷*Afterward he sent his son to them, saying, "They will respect my son."* ³⁸*But when the tenants saw the son, they said to themselves, "This is the heir; come, let us kill him and have his inheritance."* ³⁹*And they took him and cast him out of the vineyard, and killed him.* ⁴⁰*When therefore the owner of the vineyard comes, what will he do to those tenants?'* ⁴¹*They said to him, 'He will put those wretches to a miserable death, and let out the vineyard to other tenants who will give him the fruits in their seasons.'*

Jesus tells the Jewish leaders another parable, and asks for an answer to it: tenants of a vineyard have refused to pay the landlord, and have ill-treated his servants and killed his son and heir; what will the landlord do to the tenants when he comes? They answer that he will kill them and let the vineyard out to other tenants who will pay.

The parable is an allegory of God's dealings with his people; the description of the vineyard at the beginning quotes a passage from the book of Isaiah, in which the prophet spoke of Israel in terms of a vineyard, and her disobedience in terms of wild grapes. The servants stand for the prophets, and the son and heir for Jesus himself. The tenants are the chief priests and other leaders of the Jews, as they themselves recognize (v. 45). The son is killed, the tenants will be put to death, and the vineyard will be let out to other tenants, just as Jesus will be crucified, Jerusalem destroyed, and the Gentiles will replace the Jews as God's people.

Matthew has made the details in the story match the events to which they refer more exactly than they did in Mark; and no doubt the same process went on before the story was written down. It is therefore difficult to know how much of the allegory goes back to Jesus himself: some have suggested that the sending and death of the son of the owner of the vineyard have been added by the Church (see D. E. Nineham, *The Gospel of St Mark*, pp. 308ff.).

ॐ

Matthew takes up Mark from the point at which he had left him (Mark 12¹) and will not leave the earlier Gospel again until he inserts another parable (Matthew 22¹ff.). Matthew has made small changes in Mark, usually to bring the allegory into line with the history of God and Israel.

33
Hear another parable: Matthew's introduction; cf. 13¹⁸.

There was a householder: Mark had simply *A man.* Matthew uses the word *householder* for God in other parables, e.g. 20¹.

planted a vineyard, and set a hedge around it, and dug a wine press in it, and built a tower, is a quotation from Isa. 5², which Matthew has slightly altered from its Marcan form, to conform with the LXX.

let it out to tenants: i.e. the covenant which God made with Israel at the time of the patriarchs and again after the Exodus.

and went into another country: Many estates in Galilee in the first century were owned by absentee foreign landlords.

34
When the season of fruit drew near: The Greek here is similar to Mark's words at the beginning of his Gospel, *The time* (or season) *is fulfilled, and the kingdom of God is at hand* (or, has drawn near), Mark 1¹⁵.

his servants: Mark, *a servant*; Matthew is thinking of the prophets.

his fruit: Mark, *some of the fruit*; Matthew is thinking of all that is due to God from man.

35
killed another, and stoned another: Matthew has added *stoned another,* to recall the persecution of the prophets in Israel; cf., *O Jerusalem, Jerusalem, killing the prophets and stoning those who are sent to you!* (23³⁷). The only prophet whose stoning is recorded in the Old Testament is *Zechariah the son of Jehoiada* (2 Chron. 24²⁰f.); it is possible, however, that there were apocryphal lives of the prophets (e.g. The Martyrdom of Isaiah) which recorded the killing of the prophets; cf. Heb. 11³⁷, *They were stoned, they were sawn in two, they were killed with the sword.*

36
other servants, more than the first: Contrast Mark, *another servant.* Matthew's second and larger group may correspond to 'the latter prophets'. Mark has a third servant, but Matthew omits him, probably to fit the Jewish distinction between 'the former' and 'the latter prophets'. In later Jewish literature 'the former prophets' means the books of the Old Testament from Joshua to 2 Kings inclusive (which were

thought to be the works of Joshua, Samuel, and Jeremiah) and 'the latter prophets' means the books from Isaiah to Malachi inclusive, omitting Daniel.

37

Afterward he sent his son to them: Contrast Mark, *He had still one other, a beloved son; finally he sent him to them.* It is not at all clear why Matthew has omitted the word *beloved*, which he has used at the baptism and transfiguration (3^{17}, 17^5) and in the quotation from Isaiah, in 12^{18}.

38

If the landlord was supposed to be a foreigner living abroad, the tenants would have hoped that, if he had only one son (so Mark), then, on the death of the son (and of the owner), they would be able to take possession of the vineyard.

39

they took him and cast him out of the vineyard, and killed him: Matthew has re-arranged Mark in the light of the death of Jesus outside Jerusalem; Mark's order was more natural, *they took him and killed him, and cast him out of the vineyard.*

40

As in vv. 25 and 31 Jesus forces the Jewish leaders to answer the question for themselves, and thus condemn themselves. In Mark at this point the question is rhetorical, and Jesus answers it himself; Matthew on the other hand puts the answer into the mouth of the Jewish leaders.

41

put those wretches to a miserable death: Mark had simply, *destroy the tenants.* Matthew is more conscious of the wrath of God against the Jews, and may have in mind the destruction of Jerusalem in A.D. 70. *and let out the vineyard to other tenants who will give him the fruits in their seasons* is an expansion of Mark's *and give the vineyard to others:* if the first covenant was suggested by the first 'letting out' of the vineyard, v. 33, then this letting will suggest the new *covenant* (26^{28}), and the *other tenants* are the Church, the faithful, from both the Jews and the Gentiles, who give the *fruit* of their good works to God.

^{42}*Jesus said to them, 'Have you never read in the scriptures:*

> "*The very stone which the builders rejected*
> *has become the head of the corner;*
> *this was the Lord's doing,*
> *and it is marvellous in our eyes*"?

^{43}*Therefore I tell you, the kingdom of God will be taken away from you and given to a nation producing the fruits of it.*'^{a}

> *a* Other ancient authorities add verse 44, '*And he who falls on this stone will be broken to pieces; but when it falls on any one, it will crush him*'

The parable of the vineyard tells in allegorical form the main events in the dealings of God with his people: covenant, prophecy, the coming of Christ, the crucifixion, the Church. One notable event is absent – the resurrection. This is now made good by the addition of an Old Testament quotation, which foretells the reversal of men's judgement by God. And just as men's rejection of Jesus will be reversed by God, so also the plan of the tenants to acquire the vineyard will be forestalled by him, and he will give it to others.

༄

Verse 42 is from Mark 12^{10}f. with the addition of the introductory words, *Jesus said to them*. Verse 43 has no parallel in Mark, and is presumably Matthew's own composition, since it could hardly have stood on its own as an independent saying of Jesus. On v. 44 see note below.

42

The quotation is from Ps. 118^{22}f. – and the same verses are quoted in Acts 4^{11}, 1 Pet. 2^7 (see also 21^9 above and 23^{39} below). The *stone* is identified with Jesus, and *the builders* with the Jewish leaders.

the head of the corner means either 'cornerstone' or 'keystone' – a position of importance. Jesus' resurrection will be *marvellous* in the eyes of both the Jews and the Christians (see Chapter 28).

43

Matthew underlines the significance of the answer which the Jewish leaders have themselves given in v. 41. Matthew again uses the expression *the kingdom of God* (see v. 31); this may indicate that the saying is older than Matthew; or Matthew may have used it intentionally, as in the other places where it appears in his Gospel, to emphasize that the vineyard is God's and not man's; cf. *the Most High rules the kingdom of men, and gives it to whom he will*, Dan. 4²⁵.

... *given to a nation producing the fruits of it* - i.e. to the Gentiles (24¹⁴, 28¹⁹); *producing* is the word which is also translated *bear* (e.g. 3⁸, ¹⁰). The Christians are here thought of as fruitful trees; cf. Ps. 1³: *He is like a tree planted by streams of water, that yields its fruit in its season*.

44

This verse is omitted by Codex Bezae and other authorities, but is found in nearly all the other manuscripts etc. Most of the commentators and editors of the text of Matthew omit it, perhaps because it is almost exactly parallel to Luke 20¹⁸, and if it is genuine it is a remarkable example of an agreement between Matthew and Luke against Mark. It may allude to Isa. 8¹⁴f., *He* [the Lord] *will become a sanctuary, and a stone of offence, and a rock of stumbling to both the houses of Israel, a trap and a snare to the inhabitants of Jerusalem. And many shall stumble thereon; they shall fall and be broken; they shall be snared and taken*; cf. also Dan. 2³⁴f., ⁴⁴f.. To stumble on this stone (or *take offence at Jesus*, 11⁶) will involve loss here and now; *when it falls on anyone* (perhaps at the last judgement), *it will crush him* (in the destruction of *soul and body in hell*, 10²⁸).

21⁴⁵, ⁴⁶   THE REACTION OF THE CHIEF   Mark 12¹²
PRIESTS AND PHARISEES

⁴⁵*When the chief priests and the Pharisees heard his parables, they perceived that he was speaking about them.* ⁴⁶*But when they tried to arrest him, they feared the multitudes, because they held him to be a prophet.*

The Jewish leaders understand the meaning of the two parables (21²⁸ff.): they are the disobedient son of the Father, and they are the tenants who have killed the servants of the owner of the vineyard.

They want to arrest Jesus, but they are afraid of the crowds, because the crowds believe that Jesus is a prophet.

৩৫৪

Matthew has rewritten Mark 12¹², and thus removed a possible mis-understanding in Mark; and adapted the Marcan comment for his own Gospel. Mark had: *And they tried to arrest him, but feared the multitude, for they* [i.e. the Jewish leaders, not the multitude] *perceived that he had told the parable against them; so they left him and went away.* Matthew adds (to explain why *they feared the multitude*), *because they held him to be a prophet.*

45
the chief priests and the Pharisees: The chief priests were mentioned above at vv. 15 and 23; the Pharisees had not been mentioned before since the arrival in Jerusalem.

his parables: Mark, *the parable*; Matthew has added another parable vv. 28ff.

46
the multitudes: Matthew, as usual, uses the word in the plural; in Mark it is singular.

because they held him to be a prophet: Cf. 21¹¹, ²⁶.

22¹⁻¹⁰   THE PARABLE OF THE   Luke 14¹⁶⁻²⁴
INVITATIONS TO THE WEDDING

22 *And again Jesus spoke to them in parables, saying,* ²'*The kingdom of heaven may be compared to a king who gave a marriage feast for his son,* ³*and sent his servants to all those who were invited to the marriage feast; but they would not come.* ⁴*Again he sent other servants, saying,* "*Tell those who are invited, Behold, I have made ready my dinner, my oxen and my fat calves are killed, and everything is ready; come to the marriage feast.*" ⁵*But they made light of it and went off, one to his farm, another to his business,* ⁶*while the rest seized his servants, treated them shamefully, and killed them.* ⁷*The king was angry, and he sent his troops and destroyed those murderers and*

burned their city. [8] *Then he said to his servants, "The wedding is ready, but those invited were not worthy.* [9] *Go therefore to the thoroughfares, and invite to the marriage feast as many as you find."* [10] *And those servants went out into the streets and gathered all whom they found, both bad and good; so the wedding hall was filled with guests.'*

Matthew inserts two more parables into Mark – the marriage feast and the wedding garment. The first, in this paragraph, has been highly allegorized, and as in most allegories, the story as a story hardly stands by itself: it only makes sense when the reader sees what the story stands for. A king invites guests to his son's wedding feast, but they refuse to come; so he sends other servants, and they still refuse to come, and ill-treat and kill the servants. So the king sends his army and burns their city. Then the king sends the servants to find other guests – as many as they can find, both bad and good.

We should notice first the similarities between this parable and the parable of the vineyard which it follows in Matthew: in both, two groups of servants are sent; those to whom the servants are sent refuse to do what the servants say, and kill some of them; those who have refused to obey are themselves destroyed; and they are replaced by others, who make up for what the first have failed to do.

Matthew clearly means his readers to understand the two parables in the same way: he is describing God's dealings with the Jews, their disobedience to him, and the new covenant which will include the Gentiles.

The allegorical elements in the story, which strike the reader as strange and unnatural, e.g. the killing of those who bring an invitation to a wedding, the destruction of guests, and burning of a city while a meal is waiting to be served, are no doubt additions, made by the Church or the Evangelist to an earlier and more straightforward parable; and to some extent these additions show the influence of the parable of the vineyard in its Matthean form (e.g. 22^4 repeats words in 21^{36}).

Moreover, there is a similar parable in Luke 14$^{16ff.}$, which is in some ways less allegorized, in other ways more developed – e.g. the reasons why the guests do not come are given more fully.

It is difficult to reconstruct the original parable of Jesus out of Matthew's allegory, but the purpose of it may have been to defend his fellowship with the tax collectors and sinners on the grounds that the Pharisees had refused his invitation to repent and to join him at his table, which was the anticipation of the messianic feast.

ಐಐ

Matthew inserts this parable, and the parable which follows, between Mark 12¹² and Mark 12¹³ (= Matthew 22¹⁵). It is usually thought that this parable, and the parable in Luke 14¹⁶ff., are independent expansions of an original shorter parable; but it may be that here too Luke has used Matthew.

1

This verse is Matthew's composition, to introduce the two parables which he is inserting here.

2

The kingdom of heaven may be compared to: See 13²⁴ for this formula.

a king: The *king* here is God, as in 5³⁵ (Jerusalem *is the city of the great King*), 18²³ (*a king who wished to settle accounts with his servants*). In other places in this Gospel, Jesus himself is the King, e.g. 25³⁴.

a marriage feast: The kingdom is compared to a *marriage feast* again at 25¹⁰, and in Rev. 19⁷ff..

3

Cf. the first group of servants sent for the fruit of the vineyard in 21³⁴f.; perhaps Matthew means the former prophets in both places.

4

Cf. the second group of servants in 21³⁶; one would expect these to be the latter prophets, though it has been suggested that the apostles are meant, and their mission to Israel, 10⁵ff..

5f.

The story is inexplicable unless we recall the interpretation – the refusal of Israel to repent, and the persecution of the prophets (or of the apostles).

7

Cf. 21⁴¹, ⁴³. The city stands for Jerusalem, destroyed by the Romans in A.D. 70.

8

those invited were not worthy: Cf. the instructions to the apostles in 10¹³ff..

9

Go therefore (poreuesthe oun): Cf. the words with which Jesus sends the apostles to the Gentiles. *Go therefore and make disciples of all nations (poreuthentes oun)* 28¹⁹. The new mission of the servants corresponds to the mission to the Gentiles which begins after the resurrection.

10

both bad and good anticipates the next parable, in which a 'bad' guest is cast out of *the wedding hall*.

22¹¹⁻¹⁴ THE PARABLE OF THE WEDDING GARMENT

¹¹'*But when the king came in to look at the guests, he saw there a man who had no wedding garment;* ¹²*and he said to him, "Friend, how did you get in here without a wedding garment?" And he was speechless.* ¹³*Then the king said to the attendants, "Bind him hand and foot, and cast him into the outer darkness; there men will weep and gnash their teeth."* ¹⁴*For many are called, but few are chosen.*'

The second parable continues the story of the first: the king who has invited the guests comes into the hall to inspect them, and finds one who has no wedding garment: the king commands him to be thrown out. Again the parable has been allegorized – the outside of the hall is described as *the outer darkness*, where *men will weep and gnash their teeth*; that is, the hall is the life of the age to come, and outside it is hell. Also, it is clear that originally this was a separate parable; how could a guest be blamed for not being correctly dressed for a wedding, when he had been brought in in the manner described at the end of the previous parable?

There is a similar parable attributed to a rabbi who lived about the year A.D. 80, which describes a king sending invitations to a banquet, but giving no time. 'The wise attired themselves, while the foolish went on with their work. Suddenly the summons came, and those who were not dressed in clean clothes were not admitted to the banquet' (Jeremias, *The Parables of Jesus*, p. 131). If Jesus' parable was originally used for the same purpose, then it taught readiness, that is, repentance; cf. 25¹ff.

Matthew uses it to show that it is not enough to hear the preaching: there must be a response to it, in good works: *Bear fruit that befits repentance* (3⁸); compare the seed sown on the good soil, *he who hears the word and understands it; he indeed bears fruit* . . . (13²³). Matthew says that *many are called* – that is, invited into the kingdom by the preaching of the gospel; *but few are chosen* – that is, few will respond, and are *worthy*. The Jews themselves have demonstrated this principle: it will operate among the Gentiles also; they will be judged at the end of the world (see 25³¹ff.). Cf. also the parable of the *net* (13⁴⁷ff.) for the idea of *good* and *bad* together in the Church.

ಜಃ

These verses have no parallel in the other Gospels; and the latter part is full of Matthean expressions.

11
when the king came in to look at the guests: This is the last judgement; compare the parables in Chapter 13 (e.g. weeds of the field, the net), and in Chapter 25 (the ten bridesmaids, the talents, the sheep and the goats): in all of these there is a division or sorting out of the bad and the good.

a man who had no wedding garment: The wedding garment was not, apparently, a special garment, but ordinary clean clothes. It stands for the new life of good works which is to follow the preaching of the gospel; cf. *The fine linen is the righteous deeds of the saints* (Rev. 19⁸).

12
Friend (hetaire): A word used only by Matthew in the New Testament, and always of people who are in the wrong; see 20¹³.

how did you get in here without a wedding garment? The only demand which John and Jesus make is that men should *repent* in order to enter the kingdom (3², 4¹⁷): this repentance expresses itself in a life of good works, or charity. The man has tried to enter without this new life, and therefore he is condemned.

he was speechless: The Jews thought of good works as 'intercessors' before God; e.g. 'He who fulfils a command gains for himself an intercessor', Pirqe Aboth 4¹³; cf. Acts 10⁴. The man has done no good works, therefore he is silent, and there is no one to speak for him.

13

the attendants: A different word in the Greek from the *servants* in the previous parable. They stand for *the angels*; see 13$^{39ff.}$, 39f.

Bind him hand and foot: Cf. the command to the servants in the parable of the weeds of the field, *Gather the weeds first, and bind them in bundles to be burned* (13^{30}).

cast him into the outer darkness; there men will weep and gnash their teeth: For the same expression; see 8^{12} and cf. 13$^{42, 50}$, 24^{51}, 25^{30}.

14

For many are called, but few are chosen: The word *called* (*klētoi*) is from the same root as the word translated *invited* in vv. 3ff.

chosen (*eklektoi*) means chosen by God for the life of the kingdom; the *chosen* or *elect* will be gathered into the kingdom by the angels (24^{31}). The saying may be a Jewish proverb; and it means that though many are offered the gospel by the preaching of the prophets and apostles, few will respond to it by repentance and good works, and those who do respond do so because God has *chosen* them, and not because of their own goodness.

22$^{15-22}$ THE QUESTION OF THE   Mark 12$^{13-17}$
PHARISEES AND HERODIANS:
TAXES

15 Then the Pharisees went and took counsel how to entangle him in his talk. 16 And they sent their disciples to him, along with the Hero′di-ans, saying, 'Teacher, we know that you are true, and teach the way of God truthfully, and care for no man; for you do not regard the position of men. 17 Tell us, then, what you think. Is it lawful to pay taxes to Caesar, or not?' 18 But Jesus, aware of their malice, said, 'Why put me to the test, you hypocrites? 19 Show me the money for the tax.' And they brought him a coin.^{a} 20 And Jesus said to them, 'Whose likeness and inscription is this?' 21 They said, 'Caesar's.' Then he said to them, 'Render therefore to Caesar the things that are Caesar's, and to God the things that are God's.' 22 When they heard it, they marvelled; and they left him and went away.

a Greek *a denarius*

The rest of this chapter describes the questions which the Jewish leaders ask Jesus, and the question which he puts to them. Their aim is to trap him, so that they may have a charge to bring against him before the council of the Jews, and before the Roman governor.

First come the Pharisees with the Herodians: they begin with a flattering introduction, and then ask whether it is lawful for the Jews to pay the Roman taxes. Jesus perceives the reason why they ask this question: it is a test question, to see whether Jesus will declare himself on the side of the zealots who refuse to pay, or on the side of those who collaborate with the Romans. Jesus says that the money for the tax bears the emperor's portrait and name, and is therefore his; so it should be paid to him. But then he goes beyond the terms of the question, and demands that the Jews should also return to God what belongs to him; and we recall here that in the parable of the vineyard the Jews were accused of not rendering to God the fruit which was his (21^{33ff}.).

※

Matthew has taken up Mark at the point he had reached, and he continues to copy him with few changes for the rest of this chapter. This paragraph reproduces Mark 12^{13ff}. with only slight modifications, mainly at the beginning and end.

15f.
Matthew rewrites Mark 12^{13}; the reference to *the Herodians* in Mark here seems to have reminded him of the only other place where they are mentioned in Mark (Mark 3^6), and Matthew's rewritten introduction in these verses makes use of expressions which he and Mark had used (see 12^{14}).

to entangle (*pagideuein*): The word is rare in Greek, and is only used here in the New Testament. It is a hunting term, meaning to 'snare' or 'trap'.

16
their disciples: Disciples of the Pharisees are only mentioned here and in Mark 2^{18}; the word 'disciples' implies a teacher, and the Pharisees were not teachers, except for those of them who were also scribes.

the Herodians were the supporters of Herod the Great and of his family; they favoured collaboration with the Romans, who were ruling Palestine with the Herods as their puppet-kings. The Herodians would have been in favour of paying taxes to Caesar; the Pharisees would not.

17

Tell us, then, what you think is a Matthean addition; for *what you think* cf. 17²⁵, etc.

18

aware of their malice ... you hypocrites: Matthew has expanded and rewritten Mark's *their hypocrisy;* possibly he has in mind the attack on the hypocrisy of the scribes and Pharisees in Chapter 23.

19

As in 17²⁴ff., it seems as though Jesus and his disciples have no money.

20

Whose likeness and inscription is this? The denarius would bear a portrait of the emperor Tiberius (A.D. 14–37) and this inscription: Ti[berius] Caesar Divi Aug[usti] F[ilius] Augustus.

21

Render (apodote) is a different word from *pay* (literally, 'give', *didonai*) which was used in v. 17; the change in words may mean, The taxes are not a gift, but a debt. The same word, *render (apodidonai)* was used in 21⁴¹ of the tenants who would render to God his fruit.

22

and they left him and went away: Matthew has taken these words from Mark 12¹², the end of the parable of the vineyard; he had omitted them there, because he wanted to keep the *Pharisees* on the scene until this point.

22²³⁻²⁸   THE QUESTION OF THE   Mark 12¹⁸⁻³³
SADDUCEES: RESURRECTION

²³ *The same day Sad'ducees came to him, who say that there is no resurrection; and they asked him a question,* ²⁴*saying, 'Teacher, Moses said, "If a man dies, having no children, his brother must marry the widow, and raise up children for his brother."* ²⁵*Now there were seven brothers among us; the first married, and died, and having no children left his wife to his brother.* ²⁶*So too the second and third, down to the seventh.* ²⁷*After them all, the woman died.* ²⁸*In the resurrection, therefore, to which of the seven will she be wife? For they all had her.'*

The second question is put by a different group, the Sadducees.

Matthew tells his readers all that it is necessary for them to know about the Sadducees in order to understand the present story: they did not believe in the resurrection of the dead.

The Sadducees observed the written Law, but did not acknowledge any oral traditions or any beliefs which could not be clearly proved from the scriptures. The Law had commanded that a man should marry his brother's widow, if the brother had died without children. The Sadducees produce a test case: a family of seven brothers, each dying in turn, and the widow marrying the next; and no children by the marriages; whose wife will she be in the resurrection? The story is intended as a *reductio ad absurdum* of the belief in resurrection, which the Sadducees do not mention until the end of their question; and it is held by them to show the impossibility of believing in the resurrection, according to the Law: the Law would not have commanded such marriages, if it had looked forward to a life after death. (It should be remembered that the belief in life after death was not held by the Jews until after most of the Old Testament books had been written.)

৩৫৩

Matthew has abbreviated Mark 12¹⁸ff. and made a few unimportant stylistic alterations.

23
The same day is a Matthean addition, to improve the connexion with the previous paragraph.

The *Sadducees* have been mentioned before in this Gospel at 3⁷, 16¹⁻¹².

who say there is no resurrection: Josephus says of the Sadducees, 'But the doctrine of the Sadducees is this: That souls die with the bodies; nor do they regard the observation of anything besides what the law enjoins them. . . .' (*Antiquities*, XVIII, 1, 4.)

24
The quotation is from Deut. 25⁵, but the unusual word used for *marry* (*epigambreuein*) is not in Deuteronomy; it was used in a manuscript of the LXX translation of Gen. 38⁸, where *Onan* was commanded to marry his deceased brother *Er's* widow, whose name was *Tamar*; she was mentioned in the genealogy (1³).

28
In the resurrection: The Sadducees mean, If there be a resurrection; whereas this, they suppose, proves that there cannot be a resurrection.

²⁹But Jesus answered them, 'You are wrong, because you know neither the scriptures nor the power of God. ³⁰For in the resurrection they neither marry nor are given in marriage, but are like angelsᵃ in heaven. ³¹And as for the resurrection of the dead, have you not read what was said to you by God, ³²"I am the God of Abraham, and the God of Isaac, and the God of Jacob"? He is not God of the dead, but of the living.' ³³And when the crowd heard it, they were astonished at his teaching.

a Other ancient authorities add of God

Jesus says that the error of the Sadducees springs from two causes, their ignorance of the scriptures, and of the power of God. The power of God will transform men in such a way that they do not marry in the age to come. And the scriptures do in fact presuppose belief in the resurrection: God said that he was the God of the patriarchs, in the book Exodus, after the patriarchs had died; this implies that they were or would be alive. The method of arguing here is typically rabbinic.

☙❧

Matthew makes few changes in Mark 12²⁴ff., though as usual he abbreviates his source. In v. 33 he has used an editorial comment of Mark's from another context to round off the incident.

29
you know neither the scriptures nor the power of God: These two causes of error are taken in the reverse order in the exposition of them which follows.

30
the power of God will introduce a new kind of life, in which there will be no marriage or birth, because there will be no death. Cf., e.g., 1 Cor. 15⁵¹, *We shall all be changed.*

31f.
the scriptures contain the saying (in Exod. 3⁶), *I am the God of Abraham.* . . . The argument appears thin to us, but it would not have seemed so to

first-century Jews who used the scriptures in this way. The text meant
that the God who was speaking to Moses was the God who had called
the patriarchs and made promises to them. The conclusion which is
drawn from the text in this argument is that the patriarchs are still
alive, or will be raised up in the resurrection because the living God
would not define himself in terms of the dead.

33
This verse is adapted from Mark 11^{18b}, the conclusion of the account of
the cleansing of the temple; Matthew had omitted it at that point in
his Gospel (21¹³).

22³⁴⁻⁴⁰   THE QUESTION OF THE   Mark 12²⁸⁻³¹
PHARISEE: THE GREAT
COMMANDMENT

³⁴*But when the Pharisees heard that he had silenced the Sadducees, they came
together.* ³⁵*And one of them, a lawyer, asked him a question, to test him.*
³⁶*'Teacher, which is the great commandment in the law?'* ³⁷*And he said to
him, 'You shall love the Lord your God with all your heart, and with all
your soul, and with all your mind.* ³⁸*This is the great and first commandment.* ³⁹*And a second is like it, You shall love your neighbour as yourself.*
⁴⁰*On these two commandments depend all the law and the prophets.'*

The Pharisees plan another attack on Jesus, when they hear that their
rivals, the Sadducees, have been silenced. One of them asks Jesus the
question which was frequently discussed among the rabbis, Which is
the great commandment in the Law? Jesus replies that the first and
great commandment is the commandment to love God; and that there
is another like it, to love your neighbour as yourself. Both of these
commandments are quotations from the Old Testament: the first is
part of the words which every Jew was expected to recite every day.
The second is like an answer which a rabbi had given to a similar
question, 'What thou hatest for thyself, do not to thy neighbours.'
It is possible, though not certain, that the commandments to love
God and to love your neighbour had been brought together by the
Jews in pre-Christian times.

Matthew here considerably shortens Mark 12^{28}ff., omitting Mark 12$^{32-34}$. There are agreements here with Luke 10^{25}ff., and it has sometimes been thought that Matthew and Luke had in addition a source other than Mark for this section.

34

In Mark, the question is asked by a scribe: Matthew brings back the Pharisees.

they came together (synēchthēsan epi to auto) is a quotation from Ps. 2^2, (the rulers) take counsel together, which Matthew uses again at 26^3.

35

a lawyer (nomikos): This is the only place where Matthew uses this word; Luke uses it six times, Mark never. Even here in Matthew it is omitted by a small group of authorities, and may be a later addition, from Luke 10^{25}.

to test him: Matthew adds these words; cf. 22^{18}.

36

Teacher is another Matthean addition, to make the introduction to this question conform to the introductions to the two previous questions, vv. 16 and 24.

37

The quotation is from Deut. 6^5.

39

The quotation is from Lev. 19^{18}; it has been quoted before in this Gospel at 5^{43}, 19^{19}.

40

Mark had *There is no commandment greater than these*; Matthew changes it, to say that *all the law and the prophets* can be deduced from these two commandments; cf. 7^{12}. This was the teaching of the Jewish rabbis, and Matthew is here bringing Jesus into line with them.

22$^{41-46}$ JESUS' QUESTION TO   Mark 12$^{34b, 35-37}$
THE PHARISEES: WHOSE SON IS
THE CHRIST?

^{41}*Now while the Pharisees were gathered together, Jesus asked them a question,* ^{42}*saying, 'What do you think of the Christ? Whose son is he?'*

They said to him, 'The son of David.' 43*He said to them, 'How is it then that David, inspired by the Spirit,ᵃ calls him Lord, saying,*

44*"The Lord said to my Lord,*
    Sit at my right hand,
      till I put thy enemies under thy feet"?

45*If David thus calls him Lord, how is he his son?'* 46*And no one was able to answer him a word, nor from that day did any one dare to ask him any more questions.*

    a Or *David in the Spirit*

Jesus has answered the three test questions put to him by the leaders of the Jews. Before this section of the Gospel ends, Matthew records one question which Jesus put to the Pharisees: Whose son do they think the Messiah will be? The Pharisees reply that he will be the son of David – an opinion which was widely held by Jews of the first century and could claim much Old Testament support. Jesus tells them that this answer raises a difficulty: David was inspired by the Spirit as a prophet, and in one of his Psalms he spoke of the Messiah as *my Lord*, and said that the Messiah would sit at the right hand of God. This implies that the Messiah is greater than David; he cannot, therefore, be his son.

The Psalm which is here used by Jesus (Ps. 110) was one of the most-quoted passages of the Old Testament in early Christian writings. Opinion is divided on whether its use goes back to Jesus himself (as these verses claim) or whether it was first used by the Church after the resurrection, as an explanation of the delay between the exaltation of Jesus and the end of the world – *Sit at my right hand, till I put thy enemies under thy feet*; it is so used in 1 Cor. 15²⁵, for example. If Jesus did use the Psalm, it is still not certain that he applied it to himself: in this paragraph he does not at any point identify himself with David's Lord.

Matthew clearly believed that Jesus was both the *son of David* and *the Christ* (see 1¹). Matthew therefore cannot have meant that Jesus was denying that the Christ was the son of David. He may have understood this saying to mean that Jesus was more than *son of David*, just as he had said earlier in the Gospel that Jesus brought into the world *something greater than Jonah,* and *something greater than Solomon,* and *something greater than the temple* ($12^{6f.}$, $^{41f.}$).

The public disputations in the temple end with this question: in the next chapter Jesus addresses *the crowds and his disciples,* but not the Pharisees or the other Jewish leaders; and the Jewish leaders do not ask him any more questions. The meeting of Jesus with those who fill the place of unbelievers in this Gospel therefore ends with a question, to which the unbelievers cannot give an answer. This is how it must be, because the knowledge of who Jesus is is only given by the Father (16^{17}), and he hides it from *the wise and understanding* (11^{25}).

৩০

Matthew has provided a new introduction and conclusion to Mark 12^{35}ff..

41
In Mark, there was a reference to Jesus teaching in the temple, which Matthew has omitted; and Matthew has made Jesus ask *the Pharisees* the question, whereas in Mark it was not said whom he asked.

42
What do you think of the Christ? is another Matthean addition: for *what do you think* see 22^{17}, and for *the Christ* see 11^2.

The son of David: The Old Testament passages on which this answer was based are, e.g., Isa. 9^{2}ff., 11^{1}ff..

43
David was believed to be the author of the Psalms, and many passages in the Psalms were taken by Christians as references to Christ (cf. Acts 2^{25}ff. where Pss. 16, 132, and 110 are quoted); it was also believed that David was inspired by the Spirit of God to foretell the messianic days; cf. the words of David, *The Spirit of the Lord speaks by me, his word is upon my tongue,* 2 Sam. 23^2. It is now known that many of the Psalms were not written by David, but belong to a later date; and that passages in them which Christians read as prophecies of the Messiah originally had a different meaning.

45
The question is intended to leave the Pharisees in the confusion of unbelief and ignorance.

46

The last part of this verse is from Mark 12^{34b}, the conclusion of the previous paragraph, which Matthew had omitted there and put here instead to round off the section. Jesus is supreme in the debates with the Jewish leaders, and their opposition to him now goes underground, to reappear in Chapters 26f. and achieve its purpose.

Matthew 23-25

The Last Section of Teaching

There is no doubt where the last section of teaching finishes; the formula in 26[1] marks the end of it. As there is no break between Chapters 24 and 25, it is usually said that the last section of teaching in Matthew begins at 24[3], when the disciples come to Jesus as he is sitting on the Mount of Olives, and ask him about his coming and the end of the age.

On the other hand, it is possible that Matthew intended Chapter 23 to be taken with Chapters 24 and 25 as the last teaching section. He has rounded off the narrative at the end of Chapter 22, so that the reader expects a new beginning in Chapter 23. There is certainly a break between 23 and 24, a change of scene, and a question asked by the disciples; but we have already had a change of scene in the third teaching section (Chapter 13); and there were questions asked by disciples in the third and the fourth (Chapters 13 and 18). If we take 23 with 24 and 25, then the last teaching section is about the same length as the first, and this seems to have been planned by Matthew (see pp. 14ff.); and like the first, it is addressed (at first) to *the crowds* and *his disciples* (23[1], cf. 5[1], 7[28f.]). Moreover, the seven Woes in 23 balance the eight Beatitudes in Chapter 5, so that the first teaching begins with the promise of blessing, and the last with the warning of woe. (In Luke 6[20ff.] Beatitudes and Woes are brought close together, and clearly contrasted.)

For these reasons we shall take it that Matthew intended to include Chapter 23 as part of the last section of teaching.

As in the other sections of this kind in Matthew, he has found a passage in Mark which he could adapt for his purpose. He had, in Mark 13, one of the two long collections of continuous teaching in his source, and he has expanded it by the addition of other material to make Chapters 24, 25. In Mark 12[38-40] he had a short warning against the scribes, and he has expanded this to form Chapter 23.

So the sources which he has used in 23–25 are: First, Mark for the greater part of this section. Secondly, material which he shares with Luke – e.g. some of the Woes and the lament over Jerusalem in Chapter 23; the sayings about the flood, the thief, and the faithful servant in 24; and the second parable in Chapter 25. And thirdly, material which only comes in Matthew's Gospel – e.g. part of the warning against the Jewish leaders in 23, and the first and last parables in 25.

The section as a whole forms a most impressive conclusion to the teaching of Jesus in this Gospel. It begins with warnings against the practices of the scribes and Pharisees, and calls woes upon them and upon Jerusalem. This takes place in the temple, and as they are going out of it Jesus tells the disciples that it will be destroyed. Then, on the Mount of Olives, in answer to their question when this will be, Jesus foretells the stages which will lead up to the coming of the Son of man and the end of this age, and warns the disciples to be ready, like a steward set over a household, like bridesmaids waiting for the bridegroom, and like servants entrusted with money; because the Son of man will come to judge and divide men, and the alternatives are *eternal punishment* or *eternal life*.

23: *The Woes on the Scribes and Pharisees*

This chapter has a very simple and clear arrangement; it begins with an introduction, in which Jesus warns the crowds and his disciples against the practices of the scribes and Pharisees (23^{1-12}); then comes the main subject, the seven Woes on the scribes and Pharisees (23^{13-36}); and finally there is a short conclusion, a lamentation over Jerusalem which has always been the centre of disobedience to God (23^{37-39}).

There are two points which the reader should bear in mind in this chapter. First, the experts on the Judaism of the first century tell us that the scribes and Pharisees have been considerably caricatured here; they were not all like this picture of them, indeed many were extremely loving and holy men. Second, the warnings against the scribes and Pharisees are not meant to be taken as just warnings against those particular men of the first and second century, but as a portrait of unbelief at any time, anywhere. The scope of this chapter is much wider than it might at first seem: it is addressed to the Church, and it is part of a Church book: its purpose is to warn Christians against an attitude to God which is not impossible within the Church, and among disciples. The scribes and Pharisees are used as lay-figures, or representatives of practical atheism which masquerades as piety. The reader may feel that Matthew has been severe and cold in his condemnation of the Jewish leaders; and we are told that in fact he has misrepresented them. Matthew's defence of what he has done might well be to repeat Nathan's words, *You are the man.*

23 1-12   WARNING AGAINST THE   Mark 12 37b-40
               PRACTICE OF THE SCRIBES   Luke 11 46
                     AND PHARISEES

23 *Then said Jesus to the crowds and to his disciples, 2'The scribes and the Pharisees sit on Moses' seat; 3so practise and observe whatever they tell you, but not what they do; for they preach, but do not practise. 4They bind heavy burdens, hard to bear,ᵃ and lay them on men's shoulders; but they themselves will not move them with their finger. 5They do all their deeds to be seen by men; for they make their phylacteries broad and their fringes long, 6and they love the place of honour at feasts and the best seats in the synagogues, 7and salutations in the market places, and being called rabbi by men. 8But you are not to be called rabbi, for you have one teacher, and you are all brethren. 9And call no man your father on earth, for you have one Father, who is in heaven. 10Neither be called masters, for you have one master, the Christ. 11He who is greatest among you shall be your servant; 12whoever exalts himself will be humbled, and whoever humbles himself will be exalted.'*

   a Other ancient authorities omit *hard to bear*

Jesus warns the crowds and his disciples not to follow the example of the scribes and Pharisees. They increase the duties of religion for others, but do not practise any charity; they are ostentatious in the performance of religious practices, and look for honour and reward from men in the present, rather than from God in the future. The true way is the opposite of this: to be a servant and humble in the present, and so to be exalted by God in the age to come.

᙭᙭᙭

Matthew has used Mark 12 37bff. as the occasion for this much longer denunciation of the scribes and Pharisees; but he has also made use of some of the Marcan wording in vv. 1f., 6f. Verse 4 is similar to Luke 11^{46}; vv. 11f. may be alternative versions of sayings in Mark 9^{35}, Luke 18^{14}, etc. Verses 3, 5, 8ff. have no parallel in the other Gospels.

1

Then said Jesus to the crowds and to his disciples: Cf. the first section of teaching, which is given to *the disciples* in the presence of *the crowds* (5$^{1f.}$, 7^{28}).

2

The scribes and the Pharisees sit on Moses' seat: sit on Moses' seat is not just a figurative expression, meaning 'have the teaching authority of Moses'; Moses' seat is the name of a piece of furniture in the synagogue, the seat from which the teacher delivered the sermon; cf. Luke 4$^{20ff.}$.

3

Their teaching is to be followed, but not their example; cf. 7$^{21ff.}$ for the antithesis between saying and doing. In *they preach but do not practise, preach* is an unfortunate translation of the Greek word (*legein*): in Matthew, *preach* is a different word, *kērussein*, and it means to proclaim the coming of the kingdom; the word used here means 'speak', 'talk'.

It is difficult to believe that Jesus really commanded obedience to the teaching of the scribes and Pharisees; this seems to have been the attitude of Matthew or of one of his sources; see 5^{19}.

4

They bind heavy burdens: See 16^{19}, 18^{18} for binding and loosing, i.e. making regulations and exceptions. The charge against the scribes and Pharisees here is that they increase the regulations; contrast what Jesus says of his own teaching, *My yoke is easy, and my burden is light* (11^{30}); and the *two commandments* on which *all the law and the prophets* depend (22^{40}).

they themselves will not move them with their finger: The meaning of this may be that they have nothing positive and constructive to say to those who have broken the laws.

5

A different charge begins in this verse – the charge of religious ostentation; a repetition of 6$^{1ff.}$, *Beware of practising your piety before men in order to be seen by them*. Examples of this follow.

for they make their phylacteries broad: This is the only place in the New Testament where phylacteries are mentioned. Apparently they were texts written on parchment and worn on the forehead and forearm at times of prayer, perhaps to ward off demons.

and their fringes long: The fringes may be in fact 'tassels' 'which the Israelite was obliged to wear on the four corners of his outer garment, according to Num. 15^{38}f., Deut. 22^{12} (*Lexicon*, p. 449); see also 9^{20}, 14^{36}. The Marcan parallel is: *Beware of the scribes, who like to go about in long robes* (Mark 12^{38}): Matthew may be explaining what *long robes* means.

6

they love the place of honour at feasts and the best seats in the synagogues (from Mark 12^{39}): The best seats in the synagogues were those on the bench in front of the ark where the scrolls were kept, facing the congregation.

7

salutations in the market places (from Mark 12^{38}): The rule was that 'a man must salute his superior in the knowledge of the Law'; therefore to love salutations is to love to be, or to be recognized as, superior to others.

and being called rabbi by men: The word *rabbi* originally meant 'great' and so, 'lord, master, teacher'. In this Gospel, Jesus is addressed as rabbi only by Judas Iscariot (26$^{25, 49}$).

8

But you is emphatic in the Greek; the disciples are to be different from the scribes and Pharisees; cf. 20^{26}.

you have one teacher: i.e. Jesus.

and you are all brethren: The word 'brother' was used of members of the Church; cf. 1 Cor. 8^{11}. The idea of brothers leads on to the idea of father in the next verse.

9

call no man your father on earth: The title 'abba', *father*, was used of the patriarchs and great Jewish teachers of the past.

for you have one Father, who is in heaven: The fatherhood of God is more frequently mentioned in this Gospel than in the others; and Matthew is particularly fond of the antithesis *on earth . . . in heaven.*

10

This verse repeats v. 8; the word *master* (*kathēgētēs*) means 'teacher', possibly 'interpreter'.

11

He who is greatest among you shall be your servant: Notice the play on *rabbi* (great) in v. 8. The saying appears in different forms elsewhere in the Gospels. In this context, *shall be* seems to be a warning of what will be the punishment for pride, rather than the way of humility as the means to greatness.

12

This verse has a number of parallels in Jewish literature. The passive tense, *will be humbled, will be exalted*, refers to the punishment and reward of God at the judgement.

21^{13-36} *The Seven Woes*

Seven sections, each of them beginning *Woe to you*, now follow. *Woe to you* expresses a double idea: first, grief or indignation at the sin which is defined in the following clause; secondly, a warning of punishment from God for those who have committed this sin.

The word *hypocrites* may mean, not so much consciously playing a part, but that, while in the sight of men they may and do seem to be righteous, in the sight of God they are not. That is, the distinction may not be so much between what they want other people to think about them and what in fact they are; but between what they think of themselves and what God thinks of them.

If Matthew placed the Woes at the beginning of this last section of teaching in order to balance the blessings at the beginning of the first section of teaching, it may be that he went even further in his love of chiasmic arrangement, and put the Woes in such an order that each one paired off with one of the blessings, taken in the reverse order: i.e. first Woe with last Beatitude, second Woe with seventh Beatitude, etc. Thus:

THE WOES	THE BLESSINGS
1. *you shut the kingdom of heaven*	8. *theirs is the kingdom of heaven*
2. *child of hell (huion geennēs)*	7. *sons of God (huioi theou)*
3. *blind . . . blind . . . blind*	6. *they shall see God*
4. *mercy*	5. *mercy . . . merciful*
5. *the outside of the cup and of the plate*	4. *hunger and thirst*
6. *tombs . . . dead men's bones*	3. *those who mourn*
7. *that upon you may come all the righteous blood shed on earth*	2. *they shall inherit the earth*

Some of these indications of conscious arrangement in pairs are extremely slight, and may be purely fortuitous; but there is perhaps enough to show that Matthew had the order of the Beatitudes in mind here.

23¹³   THE FIRST WOE: SHUTTING THE KINGDOM
Luke 11⁵²

¹³'*But woe to you, scribes and Pharisees, hypocrites! because you shut the kingdom of heaven against men; for you neither enter yourselves, nor allow those who would enter to go in.*'ᵃ

> *a* Other authorities add here (or after verse 12) verse 14, *Woe to you, scribes and Pharisees, hypocrites! for you devour widows' houses and for a pretence you make long prayers; therefore you will receive the greater condemnation*

The first Woe accuses the scribes and Pharisees of shutting men out of the kingdom, and of not entering it themselves. The reference is, in the first place, to the *heavy burdens* which they place on *men's shoulders* (23⁴), i.e. their many regulations; though to Matthew and his readers their persecution of the Christians will also be in mind (cf. the last Beatitude, *Blessed are those who are persecuted for righteousness' sake* 5¹⁰; 10¹⁷ *... they will deliver you up to councils, and flog you in their synagogues*).

ॐ

Instead of Matthew's *you have shut the kingdom of heaven against men*, Luke has *you have taken away the key of knowledge*, and it is disputed which is the more original version.

13
For the idea of the *gate* or *door* into the kingdom of heaven, see 7⁷ᶠ·, 13ᶠ·, 25¹⁰.

[Verse 14 is omitted in many of the manuscripts and versions, and is probably an interpolation from Mark 12⁴⁰.]

THE SECOND WOE: PROSELYTIZING

¹⁵'*Woe to you, scribes and Pharisees, hypocrites! for you traverse sea and land to make a single proselyte, and when he becomes a proselyte, you make him twice as much a child of hell^a as yourselves.*'

a Greek *Gehenna*

The first Woe accused the scribes and Pharisees of shutting men out from the kingdom; the second accuses them of making converts: because their converts are, like themselves, outside the kingdom, and on the way *to destruction* (7¹³).

ന്ന

15
There was disagreement among the rabbis at the time of Jesus over the mission to the Gentiles: Shammai was sceptical, but Hillel was favourable; and the attitude of Hillel prevailed.

a single proselyte: Probably the Greek is a translation of an Aramaic expression which means no more than 'a proselyte'; the indefinite article should not be stressed; cf. note on 12¹¹.

a child of hell: Another semitism, meaning one who deserved, and would receive, the punishment of Gehenna.

twice as much . . . as yourselves: If this is the correct text, then it means that the convert becomes twice as zealous as his converter; but there is some evidence for the omission of the word translated *as yourselves*, and in that case the meaning will be 'twice as much a child of Gehenna as he was before'.

23^{16–22}   THE THIRD WOE: OATHS

¹⁶'*Woe to you, blind guides, who say, "If any one swears by the temple, it is nothing; but if any one swears by the gold of the temple, he is bound by his*

oath." ¹⁷*You blind fools! For which is greater, the gold or the temple that has made the gold sacred?* ¹⁸*And you say, "If any one swears by the altar, it is nothing; but if any one swears by the gift that is on the altar, he is bound by his oath."* ¹⁹*You blind men! For which is greater, the gift or the altar that makes the gift sacred?* ²⁰*So he who swears by the altar, swears by it and by everything on it;* ²¹*and he who swears by the temple, swears by it and by him who dwells in it;* ²²*and he who swears by heaven, swears by the throne of God and by him who sits upon it.'*

The first two Woes have been general charges against the scribes and Pharisees: the third and the fourth give particular instances, to support the earlier statements. In this Woe, the example is taken from the rabbinic teaching about oaths: the purpose of the oath was to bind the taker of the oath; but the rabbis taught that certain kinds of oath (oaths by *the temple* or *the altar*) were not binding; the oath must be taken by *the gold of the temple* or *the gift that is on the altar*. However, the function of an oath is to swear by something that is greater than oneself (cf. Heb. 6¹⁶ff.); and since *the temple* is greater than *the gold of the temple*, and *the altar* than *the gift that is on the altar*, oaths taken by *the temple* and *the altar* are in themselves binding. (There is no evidence for these particular distinctions from the rabbinic sources.) The passage is an interesting example of chiasmic arrangement; there are two chiasmuses, followed by a third which includes within itself the first two; thus: I (*a*) *temple*, (*b*) *gold*: (*b*) *gold*, (*a*) *temple*; II (*c*) *altar*, (*d*) *gift*: (*d*) *gift*, (*c*) *altar*; III (*c*) *altar*, (*a*) *temple*.

∞

16
blind guides: Cf. 15¹⁴ where Jesus says of the Pharisees, *let them alone; they are blind guides*. For blindness as a symbol of the state of man in his need of salvation, see also 9²⁷ff., 11⁵, 12²², 15³⁰f., 20³⁰, 21¹⁴, 23¹⁷, ¹⁹, ²⁴, ²⁶.

it is nothing . . . he is bound by his oath are technical terms, meaning that the oath commits him or does not commit him.

17
Since *the temple* is greater than *the gold*, an oath by *the temple* is more binding than an oath by *the gold of the temple*.

18, 19
The same argument is repeated with different examples.

20

and by everything on it may be a mistake for 'and by him that is above it', i.e. God; this would make this verse fit the pattern of the next two verses, where *the temple* and *heaven* are shown to be circumlocutions for God.

21

For *the temple* as the dwelling-place of God, cf. 5³⁵ *Jerusalem . . . the city of the great King.*

22

For *heaven* as *the throne of God,* cf. 5³⁴.

(In view of the suggestion made on p. 368 that this third Woe is the pair of the sixth Beatitude in 5⁸, it is worth noticing that Matthew is here repeating phrases and ideas which he had used in 5³³f., where, we suggested, he was giving examples of the meaning of the same sixth Beatitude.)

23²³, ²⁴   THE FOURTH WOE: cf. Luke 11⁴²
WEIGHTY AND LIGHT

²³'*Woe to you, scribes and Pharisees, hypocrites! for you tithe mint and dill and cummin, and have neglected the weightier matters of the law, justice and mercy and faith; these you ought to have done, without neglecting the others. ²⁴You blind guides, straining out a gnat and swallowing a camel!*'

Another example of the regulations of the rabbis which prevent them and others from entering the kingdom of heaven, and make their converts into children of hell: they do not distinguish between the great commandments and the lesser, but pay so much attention to the lesser that they pass over the greater. There was a rabbinic saying: 'Be heedful of a light precept as of a weighty one, for thou knowest not the recompense of reward of each precept.' The terms are again arranged chiasmically: (*a*) mint, etc. (*b*) justice, etc.; (*b*) these, (*a*) the others; (*a*) gnat (*b*) camel.

ॐ

There is a similar saying to v. 23 in Luke 11⁴²: *Woe to you Pharisees! for you tithe mint and rue and every herb, and neglect justice and the love of God; these you ought to have done, without neglecting the others*; Luke's version may well be later than Matthew's.

23

Apparently mint was not liable to tithe, but dill and cummin were.

Justice and mercy and faith: Cf. Mic. 6⁸ . . . *what does the Lord require of you but to do justice, and to love kindness* [*eleos*, the same word as in Matthew], *and to walk humbly with your God?*

these you ought to have done without neglecting the others: This saying, like 23³, implies that Jesus commanded his disciples to keep the whole of the Law, and the rabbinic regulations; it is by no means certain that the saying is authentic.

24

straining out a gnat: In view of Lev. 11⁴¹ᶠᶠ·, which forbade the eating of things that swarmed or crept on the earth, the Jews strained their wine before drinking it.

swallowing a camel: The saying is an example of hyperbole in the teaching of Jesus; cf. 7³ (*the log that is in your own eye*), 19²⁴ (*it is easier for a camel to go through the eye of a needle . . .*).

23²⁵, ²⁶	THE FIFTH WOE: OUTSIDE AND INSIDE	cf. Luke 11³⁹⁻⁴¹

²⁵'*Woe to you, scribes and Pharisees, hypocrites! for you cleanse the outside of the cup and of the plate, but inside they are full of extortion and rapacity.* ²⁶*You blind Pharisee! first cleanse the inside of the cup and of the plate, that the outside also may be clean.*'

The fifth Woe is similar to the fourth: the scribes and Pharisees pay more attention to their outward appearance than to their inward reality, that is, to what they are in the sight of men than to what they are in the sight of God. Cf. the teaching in 6¹ᶠᶠ· concerning not practising *piety before men to be seen by them*, and in 15¹⁻²⁰ concerning the defilement which comes from *out of the heart* in contrast with the defilement which comes from outside (eating *with unwashed hands*).

The terms are again arranged chiasmically: (a) *outside*, (b) *inside; (b)
inside,* (a) *outside.*

ဢ

The Lucan parallel, Luke 11³⁹⁻⁴¹, may be from a different source, or an
adaptation of this passage.

25

The saying uses a symbol (the ceremonial washings of the Pharisees) to
describe their religious attitude (externality), and the thing symbolized
has affected the way in which the symbol is described – i.e. *you cleanse
the outside of the cup and of the plate*; no doubt in fact they washed both
the inside and the outside of cups and plates.

extortion and rapacity: Literally, 'robbery and lack of self-control'.
Cf. 7¹⁵, *Beware of false prophets, who come to you in sheep's clothing,
but inwardly are ravenous wolves,* where the words for *inwardly* and
ravenous are the same as here.

23²⁷, ²⁸   THE SIXTH WOE: cf. Luke 11⁴⁴
                OUTWARD AND INWARD

²⁷'*Woe to you, scribes and Pharisees, hypocrites! for you are like whitewashed tombs, which outwardly appear beautiful, but within they are full of
dead men's bones and all uncleanness.* ²⁸*So you also outwardly appear
righteous to men, but within you are full of hypocrisy and iniquity.*'

The same point is repeated in this Woe: the contrast between outward appearance and inward reality. In this Woe the terms are not
arranged chiasmically.

ဢ

The Lucan version, which omits the whitewashing of the tombs and is
much shorter, may be an abbreviation of Matthew.

27

tombs, it was believed, could defile anyone who touched them and
make him unclean. They were therefore whitewashed, so that they

could be more easily seen. Hence the contrast between the outward whiteness and beauty of them, and their inward contents.

28

Similarly, the scribes and Pharisees have the appearance of righteousness, but not the inward reality of it.

23²⁹⁻³⁶   THE SEVENTH WOE: cf. Luke 11⁴⁷⁻⁵¹
                  THE PAST AND THE PRESENT

²⁹‘*Woe to you, scribes and Pharisees, hypocrites! for you build the tombs of the prophets and adorn the monuments of the righteous,* ³⁰*saying, "If we had lived in the days of our fathers, we would not have taken part with them in shedding the blood of the prophets."* ³¹*Thus you witness against yourselves, that you are sons of those who murdered the prophets.* ³²*Fill up, then, the measure of your fathers.* ³³*You serpents, you brood of vipers, how are you to escape being sentenced to hell?ᵃ* ³⁴*Therefore I send you prophets and wise men and scribes, some of whom you will kill and crucify, and some you will scourge in your synagogues and persecute from town to town,* ³⁵*that upon you may come all the righteous blood shed on earth, from the blood of innocent Abel to the blood of Zechari'ah the son of Barachi'ah, whom you murdered between the sanctuary and the altar.* ³⁶*Truly, I say to you, all this will come upon this generation.*’

   a Greek *Gehenna*

The seventh and last Woe makes a different distinction from the two previous Woes: in them, it was the contrast between appearance and reality; now, between the past and the present. The scribes and Pharisees pay lip-service to the prophets and condemn those who killed them; in fact, Jesus says, they are the descendants of the murderers of the prophets, and they continue their activities and will continue them. They will always be against God's messengers, and they will receive from God their due punishment.

The Lucan parallel, 11⁴⁷⁻⁵¹, contains all these verses, except 30, 32, 33, in a slightly different form. Verse 33 is a repetition of 3⁷.

29

The reference is probably not merely metaphoric: the Jews did venerate the prophets at their graves, or at the traditional sites of their graves.

adorn the monuments of the righteous is not in Luke 11⁴⁷; Matthew couples *the prophets* and *the righteous* together in 10⁴¹, 13¹⁷, and may have done so here also; and to prepare for the mention of *innocent* (literally, 'righteous') *Abel* in v. 35.

30

They condemn their *fathers* for killing the prophets, and pride themselves on being better.

31

By saying *our fathers*, they admit that they themselves are *sons* of the murderers of the prophets. In semitic languages, to be the son of somebody means to be like him. Thus they give evidence against themselves: they too are murderers of prophets.

32

This sentence is ironical: 'Be like your fathers; complete the work that they began.'

33

The end of their disobedience to God will be condemnation to Gehenna at the judgement.

34

In Luke 11⁴⁹ this saying is ascribed to *the Wisdom of God*. Here, Jesus speaks of his own future sending of *prophets and wise men and scribes* (cf. 5¹² for *prophets*, and 13⁵² for Christian *scribes*).

crucify: Crucifixion was a Roman, not a Jewish, method of execution. Possibly the meaning is, Hand over to the Romans for execution, as in the case of Jesus himself.

some you will scourge in your synagogues: See 10¹⁷; *they will ... flog you in their synagogues* (the same verb is used in the Greek in both passages).

persecute you from town to town: See 10²³, *When they persecute you in one town, flee to the next.*

35f.

This generation will thus *fill up the measure of their fathers*, and be liable for all the *righteous blood* (i.e. innocent lives) which has been shed on the earth, from the first martyr *Abel* to the last martyr recorded in the Old Testament (2 Chron. 24²⁰ff.), *Zechariah*, who was not, in fact, *the son of Barachiah* (this was the other Zechariah, Zech. 1¹) but the son of Jehoiada.

between the sanctuary and the altar: See 2 Chron. 24²¹, they stoned him with stones in the court of the house of the Lord.

all this will come upon this generation: Cf. 24³⁴, *this generation will not pass away till all these things take place*; that is, the tribulation which is described in the next chapter, leading up to the coming of the Son of man in glory, will come upon this generation, and their condemnation in the last judgement will be their punishment for their rejection of the prophets.

23³⁷⁻³⁹   JESUS FORETELLS THE   Luke 13³⁴, ³⁵
             DESTRUCTION OF JERUSALEM

³⁷'O Jerusalem, Jerusalem, killing the prophets and stoning those who are sent to you! How often would I have gathered your children together as a hen gathers her brood under her wings, and you would not! ³⁸Behold, your house is forsaken and desolate.ᵃ ³⁹For I tell you, you will not see me again, until you say, "Blessed be he who comes in the name of the Lord." '

   a Other ancient authorities omit *and desolate*

These verses are the last words of Jesus to *the crowds* in this Gospel: Jesus warns Jerusalem of the fate which is coming to it, and tells them the reason why it will be so. Jerusalem has always rejected the prophets whom God sent. Jesus speaks of himself as the one who had often wished to gather the people of Jerusalem into the kingdom: but they refused. So judgement will come upon them; Jesus himself will not be seen again by the crowds until he comes in glory, and then it will be too late for them to repent.

✵

These verses are almost identical with Luke 13^{34f.}, where, however, they are placed in an entirely different context. In Matthew, they round off and summarize what has gone before.

37

killing the prophets picks up the phrase in v. 34, *I send you prophets . . . some of whom you will kill.*

stoning those who are sent to you is suggested by the reference to Zechariah in v. 35, who was stoned.

as a hen gathers her brood under her wings: For the image of God's *wings*, see Deut. 32¹¹, Pss. 17⁸, 36⁷.

and you would not: Cf. the refusals in the parables, 21^{29f.}, 22³.

38

your house: May mean either the temple, or the city of Jerusalem, or the commonwealth of Israel.

39

These words look forward to the second coming: Jesus will not be seen by Jerusalem again before he comes in judgement, and then they will greet him, but with mourning; see 24³⁰ *then all the tribes of the earth will mourn, when they see the Son of man coming in the clouds of heaven with power and great glory.* See note on 21⁹.

24, 25: The End of the World

The main part of these chapters (24⁴–25^{end}) is a long speech of Jesus, which he gives in answer to the question of the disciples about the date of the destruction of the temple, and the sign of Jesus' coming and of the end of the world. The prophecy of the destruction of the temple, and the question of the disciples, are recorded in 24^{1–3}: as Jesus leaves the temple, he tells his disciples that the whole building will be destroyed, and on the Mount of Olives they ask him, privately, when this will be. We may compare 13³⁶ and 18²¹ for the interruption of teaching sections by a change of scene, and by a disciple's question.

The speech which starts in 24⁴ begins with the warning that there will be first a period of distress, *the beginning of the sufferings*, during which the Church will experience apostasy and internal discord

(24^{4-14}); this will be followed by a second stage, *the great tribulation*, when the temple will be desecrated (24^{15-28}); after that, there will be disorder in the heavens, and this will immediately precede the coming of the Son of man and the gathering of the elect into the kingdom (24^{29-31}).

This has answered the question of the disciples in 24^3; but Jesus goes on to say that the signs which he has given are certain and will be fulfilled during the lifetime of *this generation* (24^{32-35}); and that the coming of the Son of man will be sudden, *at an hour when you do not expect* (24^{36-44}). So his disciples are to be ready for him; three parables teach the necessity of being ready on the part of the disciples (24^{45-} 25^{30}); and a final parable shows what this readiness is – a life of charity towards those who are in need (25^{31-46}).

About half of the material in these two chapters has been taken from Mark: Matthew 24^{1-44} is mainly a reproduction of Mark 13^{1-35}, though even here Matthew has supplemented Mark from other sources. From 24^{45} to the end of 25, Matthew draws almost entirely on non-Marcan sources, with only occasional echoes from the rest of Mark 13. Some of this non-Marcan material is found also in Luke, and may therefore have come from a written source; the rest is found only in this Gospel.

What is the twentieth-century reader to make of these two chapters? As they stand, they are a prediction of future events made by Jesus. Some of these events had happened when Matthew wrote his Gospel: e.g. the temple had been destroyed in A.D. 70, and there had been a famine *c.* A.D. 46 and earthquakes *c.* A.D. 61. But the other events foretold in these chapters have not taken place: e.g. the disordering of the sun, moon, and stars, the coming of the Son of man in glory, and the gathering together of the elect. What are we to say about this?

It is tempting to lay great emphasis on the saying in 24^{36}, *Of that day or hour no one knows, not even the angels of heaven, nor the Son, but the Father only*, and to 'save' the predictions in this way. However, Matthew certainly thought that this saying was compatible with the saying in the previous verse but one, *Truly, I say to you, this generation will not pass away till all these things take place* (24^{34}). Matthew believed that Jesus had taught that he would return in glory sometime within the years A.D. 30–110, although Jesus himself had not known the exact date of his coming; and Matthew was probably right in thinking that Jesus had taught this. Nevertheless, the second coming did not happen within that period.

Does it follow that Matthew 24 and 25 are of no value for the present-day reader? If that were the case, a great deal of the New Testament would have to be set aside also, because much of it was written in the belief that the end of the world was coming soon.

Some would say that we do not in fact know whether our generation will be the last in the history of the world, and we must live as if it were. The difficulty about this is that it becomes more and more impossible to make this 'as if' real, as generation continues to follow generation. To Matthew and to the other early Christians, the nearness of the end was not a hypothesis, but a fact.

If we are therefore to find something valuable for ourselves in these chapters, we must go deeper than this: we must first recover from the study of them the sense which the writers had of living in the last days, and see what this involved for them; then we must inquire whether the kind of life which is expressed in these terms cannot also be expressed in terms which do not demand a belief in the nearness of the end of the world. We shall therefore begin by studying these chapters and seeing what they meant to Matthew and his first readers, and then consider whether there is anything in them that can be valuable for us today. (See pp. 402ff.)

24$^{1, 2}$ JESUS FORETELLS THE   Mark 13$^{1, 2}$
                     DESTRUCTION OF THE TEMPLE

24 *Jesus left the temple and was going away, when his disciples came to point out to him the buildings of the temple.* [2]*But he answered them, 'You see all these, do you not? Truly, I say to you, there will not be left here one stone upon another, that will not be thrown down.'*

Jesus had entered the temple as far back as 21^{23}, and all that was recorded between that point and the end of Chapter 23 should be thought of as taking place in the temple: this is Matthew's meaning, whether in fact he has placed the events and teaching correctly, or not. Jesus' last words to the crowds in the temple foretold its desolation (23³⁸); and now, as he goes out of the buildings and the courts, his disciples come to show him their magnificence. But Jesus says that these things will be completely destroyed.

ະəɑ

Matthew has slightly changed Mark's words here; notice in particular the direct speech in Mark, *Look, Teacher, what wonderful stones and what wonderful buildings!*

1

Josephus describes the magnificence of Herod's temple in his *Antiquities*, XV, II.

It is not clear how Matthew intends his readers to understand the sentence, *his disciples came to point out to him the buildings of the temple*; does he mean that Jesus had not seen them before? or is it merely a peg on which to hang the prediction of the temple's destruction?

2

that will not be thrown down: The Greek word here (*kataluein*) is used twice later in the Gospel, in the charge against Jesus that he had said he was able to *destroy the temple of God* (26⁶¹), and in the mocking at the crucifixion (27⁴⁰); and the same word was used earlier of not abolishing the Law and the prophets, but fulfilling them (5¹⁷). The Christians believed that although the temple at Jerusalem had been destroyed, yet the intention of God to dwell among men, of which the temple had been a temporary symbol, had been now fulfilled, and they themselves were the new temple (e.g. 1 Cor. 3¹⁶).

24³⁻⁸   THE BEGINNING OF THE   Mark 13³⁻⁸
                          SUFFERINGS

³*As he sat on the Mount of Olives, the disciples came to him privately, saying, 'Tell us, when will this be, and what will be the sign of your coming and of the close of the age?'* ⁴*And Jesus answered them, 'Take heed that no one leads you astray.* ⁵*For many will come in my name, saying, "I am the Christ," and they will lead many astray.* ⁶*And you will hear of wars*

*and rumours of wars; see that you are not alarmed; for this must take place,
but the end is not yet. ⁷For nation will rise against nation, and kingdom
against kingdom, and there will be famines and earthquakes in various
places: ⁸all this is but the beginning of the sufferings.'*

Jesus and the disciples go from the temple to the Mount of Olives,
on the east side of the city, and there they ask him privately when
the temple will be destroyed, and what will be the sign of his return
and of the end of this age. Jesus begins to answer this question – and
the answer runs on to the end of the next chapter.

First of all, the disciples must not be led astray by many who will
claim to be Messiah, and who will have considerable followings. Nor
must they think that wars, famines, and earthquakes mean that the
end has come. These things are only the beginning of the birthpains
of the new world.

᙭

In Mark 13³⁻⁸, the question was asked by only four of the disciples,
Peter, James, John, and Andrew, and the answer was given to them
alone; Matthew does not specify how many disciples were present,
and the reader must assume that they were all there. In Mark, again,
the question seems to relate mainly to the destruction of the temple:
at least, that is assumed to be one of the signs of the end; but here,
because by the time Matthew was writing the temple had been destroyed and the end had not come, the scope of the question is enlarged.

3
For Jesus sitting to teach in this Gospel, see 5¹, 13¹, ², 26⁵⁵.

on the Mount of Olives: The Mount of Olives was mentioned in Zech. 14⁴,
On that day his feet shall stand on the Mount of Olives . . . and this may
have been understood by the Christians as a prophecy of the second
coming; it would therefore be a suitable place for the discourse about
the parousia; cf. Acts 1¹¹f., where the ascension and the return of Jesus
are both located here.

Matthew has changed Mark's *When will this be, and what will be the
sign when these things are all to be accomplished?* to make room for an
interval between the destruction of the temple and the Lord's return.

of your coming, and of the close of the age: The word translated *coming*
(*parousia*) is used only by Matthew of all the Gospel-writers (see

24^{27, 37, 39}); and *the close of the age* is another purely Matthean phrase
(see 13^{39, 40, 49}, 28²⁰).

4

Take heed that no one leads you astray: This chapter contains a number of
warnings against being deceived – vv. 5–8, 11, 23–28. We know from
other sources that there were Messianic claimants in the first century; see,
for example, Acts 5^{36f.}. The disciples are not to be misled by false
pretenders.

5

many will come in my name: See 18⁵; here it seems to mean 'claiming to
have my authority', i.e., as Matthew explains by the words which he has
added, *saying, I am the Christ*; see also v. 24.

they will lead many astray because there will always be many who will
prefer the assurance and 'certainty' that the end is near and Christ has
returned to the insecure position of the disciples who are to go on
waiting.

6

wars and rumours of wars are a regular feature in Jewish belief about
the end of the world; they are within the divinely ordained plan, but
they are not an indication that the end is near.

for this must take place is a quotation from Dan. 2²⁸: *God . . . has made
known to king Nebuchadnezzar what will be* (or, 'what must take place')
in the latter days; the word *must* implies divine preordination.

7

nation will rise against nation, and kingdom against kingdom is an echo of two
Old Testament passages, Isa. 19² and 2 Chron. 15⁶.

8

the beginning of the sufferings: Literally, 'the beginning of the birth-
pangs'; the word is almost a technical term in this literature for the
sufferings and tribulations that lead up to the age to come.

The emphasis throughout this paragraph is on not getting over-
excited, and on not thinking that the end is already near; there is more
to happen before the end comes. We know from 2 Thess. that Christians sometimes gave up their normal work and life, in the mistaken
belief that the end was just coming. This paragraph may have been
compiled to answer a situation similar to that for which 2 Thess. was
written.

⁹'*Then they will deliver you up to tribulation, and put you to death; and you will be hated by all nations for my name's sake.* ¹⁰*And then many will fall away,ᵃ and betray one another, and hate one another.* ¹¹*And many false prophets will arise and lead many astray.* ¹²*And because wickedness is multiplied, most men's love will grow cold.* ¹³*But he who endures to the end will be saved.* ¹⁴*And this gospel of the kingdom will be preached throughout the whole world, as a testimony to all nations; and then the end will come.*'

  a Or *stumble*

This paragraph describes the sufferings which will come upon the Christians: they will be persecuted, martyred, and hated by everyone. There will be those who leave the Church, those who betray Christians to their enemies, and those who hate one another within the Church. Moreover, there will be false prophets who lead Christians astray by their teaching; there will be wickedness and a cooling-off of charity. The disciples are promised that those who continue in hope, waiting for the end to come, will enter the kingdom. Furthermore (and this may be the reason for the delay in the coming of the end) they are told that the good news about the kingdom will be proclaimed everywhere in the world, so that all the nations may hear it: *then the end will come.*

ॐ

Matthew had already used the corresponding paragraph in Mark (Mark 13⁹⁻¹³ᵃ) in his second teaching section (Matt. 10¹⁷⁻²¹); he therefore fills in the gap at this point with other sayings, though with echoes from Mark.

9
Matthew has here summarized Mark 13⁹ᵃ, ¹³ᵃ.

10
many will fall away (margin, *stumble*), that is, give up living by faith and waiting for the return of the Lord and his vindication of them. Cf. 13²¹, *he has no root in himself, but endures for a while, and when*

tribulation or persecution arises on account of the word, immediately he falls away (margin, *stumbles*).

and betray one another is from Mark 13^{12} where, however, the reference is probably to unbelievers betraying believers; here, on the other hand, it may be to divisions within the Church.

11

This verse seems to be an abbreviation of Mark 13$^{21f.}$ which Matthew reproduces at the parallel point (24$^{23f.}$). By introducing it into this paragraph, which deals with the situation within the Church in the last days, he may be pointing to false teachers who have already arisen among the faithful; cf. Acts 20^{30}, *From among your own selves will arise men speaking perverse things, to draw away the disciples after them;* and 1 John 2$^{18f.}$, *many antichrists have come ... They went out from us, but they were not of us ...*

12

The *wickedness* which will be *multiplied* will be both within the Church and outside it, and it will strain the *love* of Christians for one another: see Rev. 2^4, 3$^{15f.}$.

13

This verse is from Mark 13^{13b}. Endurance, or hope, formed a triad (with faith and love) which was frequently used in the earliest Christian teaching; see, for example, 1 Cor. 13^7, *love ... believes all things, hopes all things, endures all things.*

14

This verse is an expansion of Mark 13^{10}. The apostles will be sent to *all nations* (28^{19}) to proclaim the good news of the coming kingdom, and to make disciples through faith and repentance. *Then the end* of this age *will come*, and the elect will be gathered into the kingdom (24^{31}).

24$^{15-28}$ THE GREAT TRIBULATION   Mark 13$^{14-23}$
                                                     Luke 17$^{23f.,37}$

^{15}'*So when you see the desolating sacrilege spoken of by the prophet Daniel, standing in the holy place* (*let the reader understand*), ^{16}*then let those who are in Judea flee to the mountains;* ¹⁷*let him who is on the housetop not go down to take what is in his house;* ¹⁸*and let him who is in the field not turn back to take his mantle.* ¹⁹*And alas for those who are with child and for those who give suck in those days!* ²⁰*Pray that your flight may not be in winter or on a sabbath.* ²¹*For then there will be great tribulation, such as has not been from the beginning of the world until now, no, and never will be.* ²²*And if those days had not been shortened, no human being would be saved; but for the sake of the elect those days will be shortened.* ²³*Then if any one says to you, "Lo, here is the Christ!" or "There he is!" do not believe it.* ²⁴*For false Christs and false prophets will arise and show great signs and wonders, so as to lead astray, if possible, even the elect.* ²⁵*Lo, I have told you beforehand.* ²⁶*So, if they say to you, "Lo, he is in the wilderness," do not go out; if they say, "Lo, he is in the inner rooms," do not believe it.* ²⁷*For as the lightning comes from the east and shines as far as the west, so will be the coming of the Son of man.* ²⁸*Wherever the body is, there the eagles^a will be gathered together.'*

a Or *vultures*

A new stage in the development of the time leading up to the end and the coming of the Son of man will begin when Daniel's prophecy of the desolation of the temple is fulfilled; there will be even greater sufferings than before, greater than the world has ever known. The Christians in Judea are to flee to the mountains, to escape the tribulation which is coming upon the Jews. Once more there will be those who falsely claim that the Messiah or his prophet has come, and there will be false pretenders. The disciples are not to believe them. When the Son of man does come, there will be no doubt about it: his coming will be evident to all (like lightning), and sudden (like the appearance of vultures after a death in the desert).

৵৵

Matthew has taken vv. 15–25 from Mark 13^{14–23}, and made some slight alterations in them; vv. 26–28 are parallel to Luke 17^{23f., 37} and may therefore be from another written source.

15

the desolating sacrilege is a phrase used in Daniel (9²⁷, 12¹¹) where it referred to the desecration of the temple at the command of Antiochus

Epiphanes in 168 B.C.; but the book of Daniel was regarded as a pro-phecy of future events, and so the passage in Daniel was looked upon as not yet fulfilled.

Matthew changes Mark's *set up where it ought not to be* to *standing in the holy place* by which he probably means the temple; and he also adds the words *spoken of by the prophet Daniel* to make the reference to the prophecy more clear. For a similar expectation, see 2 Thess. 2³f., *Let no one deceive you in any way; for that day will not come, unless the rebellion* [or, apostasy] *comes first, and the man of lawlessness is revealed, the son of perdition, who opposes and exalts himself against every so-called god or object of worship, so that he takes his seat in the temple of God, proclaiming himself to be God.*

Wickedness, to the Christians, is idolatry, i.e. the worship of a creature in the place of God (Rom. 1²⁵); if wickedness is to be multiplied (v. 12), then, they believed, there could be a complete and final manifestation of evil, wrongly claiming to be God. For another expression of this expectation, see Rev. 13, and note specially v. 4, *Men worshipped the dragon* [i.e. the devil], *for he had given his authority to the beast* [i.e. anti-christ] *and they worshipped the beast . . .*

let the reader understand is similar to the injunction in Rev. 13¹⁸, *let him who has understanding reckon the number of the beast*; it means, Look more deeply into this, because what is said is less than what is meant.

16
When this happens, the Christians *who are in Judea* and thus nearest to the centre of the trouble are to flee to the uninhabited mountains for safety.

17f.
They are to flee in haste, not going from the roof into the house (the staircase would be on the outside of it), or going back in the field to collect an outer garment left off for work.

19
Expectant and nursing mothers will find it difficult to make haste in this time of flight.

20
in winter there would be greater difficulty in travelling fast, because of the rivers and the state of the roads. Matthew has added the words *or on a sabbath*: the Law forbade travelling further than just over half a mile on the sabbath. Apparently Matthew expected his readers to keep this law.

21

The suffering at this time will be unprecedented. The words used in describing it recall Dan. 12¹, *And there shall be a time of trouble, such as never has been since there was a nation till that time.*

22

The passive tenses in this verse, *had not been shortened, would be saved, will be shortened*, refer to divine action: God will shorten the days of the tribulation; God will save the elect.

23f.

The sufferings of this time will lead some to anticipate the arrival of the Christ and announce his coming before he arrives. In Rev. 13, the beast from the sea is the false Christ, and the beast from the earth is the false prophet.

25

The warnings of Jesus are to arm the disciples for the life of endurance which will be necessary at this time.

26

The disciples are to turn a deaf ear to those who say that Jesus has returned: cf. 2 Thess. 2¹ᶠ., *Now concerning the coming of our Lord Jesus Christ and our assembling to meet him, we beg you, brethren, not to be quickly shaken in mind or excited, either by spirit or by word, or by letter purporting to be from us, to the effect that the day of the Lord has come.*

27

The coming of the Son of man will not happen unnoticed, but will be obvious for all to see, like the *lightning* which lights up the whole of the sky.

28

This saying is probably proverbial (cf. Job 39³⁰), and it means here that just as the vultures gather immediately a corpse appears, so the Son of man will come to earth suddenly.

24²⁹⁻³¹   THE COMING OF THE   Mark 13²⁴⁻²⁷
                      SON OF MAN

²⁹'*Immediately after the tribulation of those days the sun will be darkened, and the moon will not give its light, and the stars will fall from heaven, and*

the powers of the heavens will be shaken; ³⁰*then will appear the sign of the Son of man in heaven, and then all the tribes of the earth will mourn, and they will see the Son of man coming on the clouds of heaven with power and great glory;* ³¹*and he will send out his angels with a loud trumpet call, and they will gather his elect from the four winds, from one end of heaven to the other.'*

The disciples had asked, *what will be the sign of your coming and of the close of the age?* (v. 3), and the answer of Jesus began with warnings that they were not to have premature expectations of his return: there would be much suffering, and many temptations to think that the end was near. Even the *great tribulation* which he has just described is not the final sign of the end: there will still be disorder in the heavens before he comes; but then he will come in glory and gather the elect into the kingdom, while the others will be sent to punishment in Gehenna.

৩৫১

Matthew has here copied Mark 13²⁴⁻²⁷ making a few changes and additions; notice particularly the additions in vv. 30f.

29

the tribulations of those days refers to the whole paragraph 24¹⁵⁻²⁸.

the sun will be darkened . . . is a free quotation from Isa. 13¹⁰, 34⁴. The heavenly bodies were thought of as the seat of angelic forces which controlled the history of the world. Their power would have to be taken away before God reigned in his kingdom on earth and in heaven (see note on 6¹⁰).

30

then will appear the sign of the Son of man in heaven is a Matthean addition, and answers the question in v. 3, *what will be the sign of your coming?* It is not clear what this sign will be, or whether Matthew intended his readers to understand something other than the Son of man himself.

all the tribes of the earth will mourn is another Matthean addition, from Zech. 12¹²ff. where *the tribes of the earth* are explained as the families of *David, Nathan, Levi, and all the families that are left.* It seems likely, therefore, that Matthew understood, by *all the tribes of the earth,* the unbelieving Jews.

the Son of man coming on the clouds of heaven is a phrase from Dan. 7¹³, where it refers to the coming of the Son of man to God; here, however, it means his coming from God to the earth for judgement; cf. 26^{64}, *hereafter you will see the Son of man seated at the right hand of Power, and coming on the clouds of heaven.*

31

he will send out his angels: For the angels of Christ as the harvesters of the kingdom, cf. 13^{41}, *The Son of man will send his angels,* and 13^{49}, *The angels will come out and separate the evil from the righteous.*

with a loud trumpet call is another Matthean addition, taken from Isa. 27^{13}, *In that day a great trumpet will be blown . . .* For similar references to the trumpet, see 1 Cor. 15^{52}, 1 Thess. 4^{16}, Rev. 8.

and they will gather his elect from the four winds, from one end of heaven to the other is an echo of Zech. 2^6 and Deut. 30^4.

24$^{32-35}$ THE LESSON OF THE FIG TREE   Mark 13$^{28-31}$

^{32}'From the fig tree learn its lesson: as soon as its branch becomes tender and puts forth its leaves, you know that summer is near. ^{33}So also, when you see all these things, you know that he is near, at the very gates. ^{34}Truly, I say to you, this generation will not pass away till all these things take place. ^{35}Heaven and earth will pass away, but my words will not pass away.*

Although the question of the disciples has been answered, Jesus continues his teaching about the last days. Just as the appearance of leaves on the fig tree is evidence of the coming of summer, so the signs of which he has told them will certainly precede his return. And this will happen during the lifetime of his contemporaries. The present form of the world will be changed, and God will bring in a new order: but the disciples can trust Jesus and his words, which will certainly be fulfilled.

තිස

Matthew has copied Mark 13$^{28-31}$ with little significant alteration.

32f.

its lesson (*tēn parabolēn*): Literally 'the parable'.

the fig tree is almost the only tree in Palestine that loses its leaves; therefore, the appearance of the leaves of the fig is a sign of the coming of *summer*. *Summer* is used as a symbol of the end of the world, because in Palestine the harvest takes place in summer and not in autumn; and the gathering of the elect is thought of as a harvest (e.g. v. 31). So, what the leaves of the fig are to summer, the words of Jesus (i.e. the signs which he has just given) are to his coming. It is possible that the original context of this parable was not the final coming of Jesus at the end of the world, but his ministry in Palestine; and that the leaves stood for his words and deeds, which were the signs of the immediate coming of the kingdom; cf. 12²⁸, *If it is by the Spirit of God that I cast out demons, then the kingdom of God has come upon you.*

34
Although attempts have been made to interpret *this generation* as the Jews, or as the human race in general, it is more likely that originally it meant the generation living at the time of Jesus. For the same belief in the imminent end of the world, see also 10²³, 16²⁸.

35
Cf. 5¹⁸, *Till Heaven and earth pass away, not an iota, not a dot, will pass away from the law until all is accomplished.* The words of Jesus, unlike the Law, will not pass away: they will be in force in the age to come, because he is the King in the kingdom of heaven.

| 24³⁶⁻⁴⁴ | THE COMMAND TO WATCH AND BE READY | Mark 13³², ³⁵ Luke 17²⁶f., ³⁵, 12³⁹f. |

³⁶'But of that day and hour no one knows, not even the angels of heaven, nor the Son,ᵃ but the Father only. ³⁷As were the days of Noah, so will be the coming of the Son of man. ³⁸For as in those days before the flood they were eating and drinking, marrying and giving in marriage, until the day when Noah entered the ark, ³⁹and they did not know until the flood came and swept them all away, so will be the coming of the Son of man. ⁴⁰Then two men will be in the field; one is taken and one is left. ⁴¹Two women will be grinding at the mill; one is taken and one is left. ⁴²Watch therefore, for you do not know on what day your Lord is coming. ⁴³But know this, that if the house-*

*holder had known in what part of the night the thief was coming, he would
have watched and would not have let his house be broken into.* [44] *Therefore
you also must be ready; for the Son of man is coming at an hour you do not
expect.'*

a Other ancient authorities omit *nor the Son*

Although Jesus is certain of the imminence of his return, he does not
claim to know the exact time when it will happen; such knowledge
is the Father's only. And so, because he cannot tell his disciples when
it will happen, he commands them to *watch*, and to be ready, lest he
come when they do not expect him. If they do this, they will not be
overtaken by events as those were who lived before the flood, or
as a man whose house was burgled while he was asleep.

This section counterbalances what was said earlier in this chapter,
and prepares for the teaching in the three parables that follow: in the
former, the warnings were directed against those who concluded
too hastily that the end had come; here and in what follows they are
directed against those who live a life of carelessness and unreadiness,
as though the judgement were not coming.

ဘာ

As in 24^{23-28}, Matthew has inserted non-Marcan material, which is
similar to parts of Luke's Gospel. Verse 36 repeats Mark 13^{32}, but
Matthew omits Mark $13^{33f.}$ and in its place he puts Matt. 24^{37-41}
which is parallel to Luke $17^{26f.}$, [35], and Matt. 24^{43-44} which is
parallel to Luke $12^{39f.}$. Matt. 24^{42} is from Mark 13^{35}. The omission
of Mark $13^{33f.}$ may be due to its similarity to the parable in Matt.
25^{14-30}.

36
Jesus cannot be more explicit concerning the date of the end than he
has been in v. 34, because the exact time is known only by *the Father*.
Notice how *that day and hour* is used as a refrain, repeated in vv. 42,
day, and 44, *hour*, 50, *day* and *hour*, 25^{13} *day* and *hour*.

37–39
Notice the *inclusio*, formed by repeating the words *so will be the coming
of the Son of man*, v. 37, in v. 39. On Matthew's use of the word *coming*
(*parousia*), see note on v. 3.

For the story of *Noah* and the *flood*, see Gen. 6ff.; and for Christian use of this story see Heb. 11⁷, 1 Pet. 3²⁰, 2 Pet. 2⁵. Noah is an example for the Christians of a man who lived by faith, and who was preserved from destruction because of his obedience to God.

40f.
The coming of the Son of man will divide men (see e.g. the parables in Chapter 25), and the division will cut across visible and apparent distinctions, because it will be the judgement of God, not of man. *Taken* means taken into the kingdom; *left* means left for destruction – by the angels or by God.

42
Because they do not know when the end will be, and because their own attitude to it (their readiness for it) determines their fate, Jesus tells them, *Watch therefore*, that is, 'Be on the alert'. This positive attitude to the coming of the Lord will involve a negative attitude to the world.

43f.
The parable of the householder and the thief. The meaning of the parable in this context is, Be ready, and then you will not suffer loss in the coming judgement. But it may be that the original context was warnings to the crowd (not to the disciples) to listen to his teaching while there was still time. For the coming of the end as a thief, see also 1 Thess. 5²ff., 2 Pet. 3¹⁰, Rev. 3³, 16¹⁵.

24⁴⁵⁻⁵¹   **THE SERVANT SET OVER**   Luke 12⁴²⁻⁴⁶
THE HOUSEHOLD

⁴⁵'*Who then is the faithful and wise servant, whom his master has set over his household, to give them their food at the proper time?* ⁴⁶*Blessed is that servant whom his master when he comes will find so doing.* ⁴⁷*Truly, I say to you, he will set him over all his possessions.* ⁴⁸*But if that wicked servant says to himself, "My master is delayed,"* ⁴⁹*and begins to beat his fellow servants, and eats and drinks with the drunken,* ⁵⁰*the master of that servant will come on a day when he does not expect him and at an hour he does not know,* ⁵¹*and will punish^a him, and put him with the hypocrites; there men will weep and gnash their teeth.*'

  a Or *cut him in pieces*

The disciples are to be like a servant who is put in charge of the other servants during his master's absence. His work is to distribute provisions to them at the right time. If he does so, he will win the approval of his master on his return and be rewarded. If he does not do so, but indulges in terrorizing, or in licentiousness, he will be caught out and punished. These alternatives, reward or punishment, lie before the Christians during their time of waiting for the end; and their conduct during this time will determine their final fate.

ॐ

This paragraph is another addition to the Marcan material, with a parallel in Luke 12⁴²⁻⁴⁶.

The parable may originally have been used by Jesus in a different context: i.e. the condemnation of the scribes, who had been *set over* Israel (God's *household*) to teach the Law, and had misused their responsibility. Matthew uses it of the return of Christ, *the master* (or 'Lord', *ho kyrios*), who seems to be *delayed* in his return, but will come on *a day* when they do not expect him, and at an unknown *hour*, and punish those who are not ready for him.

The parable, in its present form, fits the context so well that it must have been considerably edited by Matthew: for *faithful and wise*, compare the *wise* maidens (25²), and the *faithful servant* (25²¹, ²³); for the coming of the Lord, compare 25¹⁰; for *set him over all his possessions* compare, *I will set you over much* (25²¹, ²³); for *that wicked servant*, compare *You wicked and slothful servant* (25²⁶); for *My master is delayed* compare *the bridegroom was delayed* (25⁵); for *eats and drinks* compare *eating and drinking* (24³⁸); for *on a day when he does not expect him and at an hour he does not know* compare *of that day and hour no one knows* (24³⁶), *you do not know on what day your Lord is coming* (24⁴²), *at an hour you do not expect* (24⁴⁴), and *you know neither the day nor the hour* (25¹³); for *there men will weep and gnash their teeth* compare the same phrase (which is characteristic of Matthew) in 25³⁰. The fact that it is both full of Matthean language and also used by Luke almost word for word is a strong argument for Luke's knowledge of Matthew's Gospel at this point.

45

The question invites the disciples to choose between two possible lives: Will you watch and be ready, or will you misuse your time and be punished for it? The same alternatives are set before the disciples in each of the parables in Chapter 25.

46

Blessed (makarios): See 5$^{3-11}$.

47

he will set him over all his possessions: The reward which Christ will give to his disciples is to share with him in the reign of God over the world; cf. 5$^{3, 5}$ ... *theirs is the kingdom of heaven ... they shall inherit the earth.*

48

We know from 2 Pet. 3^4 that there were those who said, *Where is the promise of his coming?*

51

and will punish him (Greek *dichotomēsei,* literally, 'divide', 'cut in two'): There may be a mistranslation here of an Aramaic word which means either 'give him blows' or 'assign him his portion'.

there men will weep and gnash their teeth: See 8^{12}, 22^{13}, 25^{30}.

25$^{1-13}$ FOOLISH AND WISE BRIDESMAIDS

25 'Then the kingdom of heaven shall be compared to ten maidens who took their lamps and went to meet the bridegroom.^{a} ^{2}Five of them were foolish, and five were wise. ^{3}For when the foolish took their lamps, they took no oil with them; ^{4}but the wise took flasks of oil with their lamps. ^{5}As the bridegroom was delayed, they all slumbered and slept. ^{6}But at midnight there was a cry, "Behold, the bridegroom! Come out to meet him." ^{7}Then all those maidens rose and trimmed their lamps. ^{8}And the foolish said to the wise, "Give us some of your oil, for our lamps are going out." ^{9}But the wise replied, "Perhaps there will not be enough for us and for you; go rather to the dealers and buy for yourselves." ^{10}And while they went to buy, the bridegroom came, and those who were ready went in with him to the marriage feast; and the door was shut. ^{11}Afterward the other maidens came also, saying, "Lord, lord, open to us." ^{12}But he replied, "Truly, I say to you, I do not know you." ^{13}Watch therefore, for you know neither the day nor the hour.'

a Other ancient authorities add *and the bride*

The idea of the separation which will be made at the last judgement was first introduced into this section of teaching at $24^{37ff.}$: *Noah* and the rest; *the two men* and the *two women*; the *faithful and wise servant* and the *wicked servant*. This distinction dominates the remainder of the discourse – the parables of the bridesmaids, the servants, and the sheep and the goats. (Cf. the similar contrasts at the end of the first section of teaching, 7^{13-27}.)

The bridesmaids are waiting at night for the bridegroom to come so that they can go with him to the bride's house, and then go with them both to his house, where the ceremony will take place. Five are ready when he comes, but five are not ready and so they miss the marriage feast. The point of the parable, in its present context, is that the disciples are to be prepared, and be ready when the Lord comes and thus enter the kingdom.

છપ્ત

The parable as it stands has no parallel in the other Gospels, but there are sayings in Luke $12^{35ff.}$, $13^{23ff.}$ which are similar.

Matthew has certainly adapted the parable for its present context: the statement in v. 5, that they all *slumbered and slept*, does not go well with the conclusion of the parable, *Watch therefore* . . . , v. 13. It may be that as in the case of other parables, the original reference was to the crisis caused by the ministry of Jesus, and the Church or the Evangelist has applied it to the second coming.

I

Then (*tote*) refers to the last judgement, as also in 24^{40}, 25^{31}.

the kingdom of heaven shall be compared to ten maidens does not mean that the kingdom is like the bridesmaids, but that the situation at the last judgement will be like the situation in which these *maidens* found themselves: some ready for it, some not ready.

to meet the bridegroom at his house, and accompany him to fetch the bride from her home. The addition of the words *and the bride* (margin) in some of the authorities may reflect the influence of a passage such as Rev. 21^2, *And I saw the holy city, new Jerusalem, coming down out of heaven from God, prepared as a bride adorned for her husband.*

2

For the distinction *wise* and *foolish* here, compare the end of the first teaching section, the parable of the *wise man* and the *foolish man* who each built a house, $7^{24ff.}$.

3f.
In the original parable, the emphasis may have been on those who had *oil*, and those who had none; and *oil* is a symbol for repentance: cf. 6¹⁷, *anoint your head*, i.e. repent of your sins.

5
See 24⁴⁸.

10·
those who were ready: Cf. 24⁴⁴, *you also must be ready.*

to the marriage feast: Cf. 22²ᶠᶠ·, where the kingdom is also likened to a marriage feast, and Rev. 19⁷, *the marriage of the Lamb has come, and his Bride has made herself ready.*

the door was shut: Cf. 7⁷ᶠ·, ¹³ᶠ·

11
Lord, Lord: Cf. 7²¹· ²², and notice specially, *On that day many will say to me, Lord, Lord . . .*

12
I do not know you is an Aramaic formula meaning 'I will have nothing to do with you'; cf. 7²³, *I never knew you.*

13
Repeats the refrain of 24³⁶· ⁴²· ⁴⁴· ⁵⁰.

25^{14-30} FAITHFUL AND WICKED   Luke 19¹²⁻²⁷
                                  SERVANT

¹⁴'*For it will be as when a man going on a journey called his servants and entrusted to them his property;* ¹⁵*to one he gave five talents,ᵃ to another two, to another one, to each according to his ability. Then he went away.* ¹⁶*He who had received the five talents went at once and traded with them; and he made five talents more.* ¹⁷*So too, he who had the two talents made two talents more.* ¹⁸*But he who had received the one talent, went and dug in the ground and hid his master's money.* ¹⁹*Now after a long time the master of those servants came and settled accounts with them.* ²⁰*And he who had received the five talents came forward, bringing five talents more, saying, "Master, you delivered to me five talents; here I have made five talents more."* ²¹*His master said to him, "Well done, good and faithful servant; you have been*

faithful over a little, I will set you over much; enter into the joy of your master." 22*And he also who had the two talents came forward, saying, "Master, you delivered to me two talents; here I have made two talents more."* 23*His master said to him, "Well done, good and faithful servant; you have been faithful over a little, I will set you over much; enter into the joy of your master."* 24*He also who had received the one talent came forward, saying, "Master, I knew you to be a hard man, reaping where you did not sow, and gathering where you did not winnow;* 25*so I was afraid, and I went and hid your talent in the ground. Here you have what is yours."* 26*But his master answered him, "You wicked and slothful servant! You knew that I reap where I have not sowed, and gather where I have not winnowed?* 27*Then you ought to have invested my money with the bankers, and at my coming I should have received what was my own with interest.* 28*So take the talent from him, and give it to him who has the ten talents.* 29*For to every one who has will more be given, and he will have abundance; but from him who has not, even what he has will be taken away.* 30*And cast the worthless servant into the outer darkness; there men will weep and gnash their teeth."'*

   a This talent was probably worth about £300

This parable continues the theme of rewards and punishments; and it also explains more fully what is meant by watchfulness or readiness. It is not an inactive condition, but involves work – trading. There are again two classes of servant: those who use their lord's property, and those who do not. When the lord returns to settle accounts with them, one group will be rewarded, the other punished. So it will be when the Son of man comes at the last day: those who have used his gifts faithfully will enter the life of the age to come and reign with him; those who have not done so will be cast into hell.

≈≈≈

This parable is preserved in three forms: Matthew's version, Luke's (Luke 19^{12}ff.), and the version in the later non-canonical *Gospel of the Hebrews*. Matthew's is probably nearest to the original, though Luke's may contain some less-developed features than Matthew's, together with some elaborations and additions of his own.

   The original context may have been the crisis produced by the ministry of Jesus rather than the future parousia; the parable may have been part of Jesus' denunciation of the scribes, who had 'buried' the Law under the mass of their traditions and regulations.

14

the day and *the hour* of the last judgement (v. 13) will be like a day of reckoning (v. 19).

a man going on a journey will mean, in Matthew's allegorical understanding of the parable, the ascension of Jesus to heaven; *his servants* will mean the Christians (cf. $24^{45ff.}$ where also the Christians are spoken of as *servants*); and *his property* may be the gifts of the Holy Spirit.

15

The *talent* was originally a measure of weight, then a unit of coinage; it was the highest currency denomination; cf. 18^{24}. It should be strongly emphasized that, to Matthew and his readers, the word would not carry any of the associations which it has for us (natural endowments, or abilities).

16f.

made (ekerdēsen) five talents more . . . made two talents more: Is it possible that Matthew understood this to mean *made* converts for the Church? The same word is used in this sense, in 18^{15}, *You have gained your brother*, and in 1 Cor. 9^{19-22}, when R.S.V. translates it as *win*.

18

Hiding money or treasure in the ground was a common method of preserving it in first-century Palestine; cf. 13^{44}.

19

after a long time will refer to the delay in the return of Christ; see also 24^{48}, 25^5.

settled accounts with them: The last judgement is likened to a day of reckoning in 18^{23}, *Therefore the kingdom of heaven may be compared to a king who wished to settle accounts with his servants.*

21ff.

I will set you over much: See note on 24^{47}. *Joy* may mean a festive dinner or banquet; cf. 8^{11}, $22^{2ff.}$, 25^{10}, where the kingdom is compared to a feast.

29f.

These verses are probably Matthew's own additions to the parable. Verse 29 repeats 13^{12}; *cast the worthless servant into outer darkness* is a typically Matthean sentence (cf. 8^{12}, 22^{13}); for *there men will weep and gnash their teeth* see 8^{12}, 22^{13}, 24^{51}.

³¹'*When the Son of man comes in his glory, and all the angels with him, then he will sit on his glorious throne.* ³²*Before him will be gathered all the nations, and he will separate them one from another as a shepherd separates the sheep from the goats,* ³³*and he will place the sheep at his right hand, but the goats at the left.* ³⁴*Then the King will say to those at his right hand, "Come, O blessed of my Father, inherit the kingdom prepared for you from the foundation of the world;* ³⁵*for I was hungry and you gave me food, I was thirsty and you gave me drink, I was a stranger and you welcomed me,* ³⁶*I was naked and you clothed me, I was sick and you visited me, I was in prison and you came to me."* ³⁷*Then the righteous will answer him, "Lord, when did we see thee hungry and feed thee, or thirsty and give thee drink?* ³⁸*And when did we see thee a stranger and welcome thee, or naked and clothe thee?* ³⁹*And when did we see thee sick or in prison and visit thee?"* ⁴⁰*And the King will answer them, "Truly, I say to you, as you did it to one of the least of these my brethren, you did it to me."* ⁴¹*Then he will say to those at his left hand, "Depart from me, you cursed, into the eternal fire prepared for the devil and his angels;* ⁴²*for I was hungry and you gave me no food, I was thirsty and you gave me no drink,* ⁴³*I was a stranger and you did not welcome me, naked and you did not clothe me, sick and in prison and you did not visit me."* ⁴⁴*Then they also will answer, "Lord, when did we see thee hungry or thirsty or a stranger or naked or sick or in prison, and did not minister to thee?"* ⁴⁵*Then he will answer them, "Truly, I say to you, as you did it not to one of the least of these, you did it not to me."* ⁴⁶*And they will go away into eternal punishment, but the righteous into eternal life.'*

The last parable elaborates on this question of watching and being ready for the second coming. It is another parable of division into two groups, and of reward and punishment; but now, for the first time in this section of teaching, we are told explicitly what kind of life will be rewarded, and what kind of life will be punished. The distinction is made according to whether a man has, or has not, shown mercy to the oppressed.

It is possible to trace a train of thought going through the Gospel which builds up to this conclusion. Jesus had said to the disciples that unless their righteousness exceeded the righteousness of the scribes and Pharisees they would never enter the kingdom of heaven, 5²⁰; and that this righteousness consisted of deeds, not words, 7²⁰; because the Son of man would repay everyone for his deeds, 16²⁷. Moreover, these deeds are not the sacrifices of the Law, but mercy, 9¹³, 12⁷; and this mercy must be shown to those who are weak and like children, and in this way shown to Jesus himself, 18⁵.

The parable forms the most fitting conclusion to the whole of the discourse which began in 23: one of the faults of the scribes and Pharisees was that they talked but did not do anything, they laid burdens on men but did *not move them with their finger*, 23³ᶠ. And we have seen how the answer to the disciples' question in 24³ about the time of the end moves into a series of warnings about being ready: now we are told how to be ready – namely, by practising mercy to the poor and suffering, and thus to Christ. Moreover, this parable is also the last section before the account of the Passion in Matthew's Gospel, and there we shall see how *the King*, to whom mercy is shown by those who minister to the oppressed, identifies himself with them voluntarily by his crucifixion and death.

∞

There is no parallel in the other Gospels.

31ff.
Cf., for these expressions, 13⁴¹, ⁴⁹, 16²⁷, 19²⁸, 24³⁰ᶠ.

For *all the nations*, cf. 24¹⁴, 28¹⁹; for the separation, see 13⁴⁹. It may be that these introductory verses are the work of the Evangelist.

Mixed flocks of *sheep* and *goats* are usual in Palestine, and they must be separated in the evening because goats have to be kept warm at night. The sheep are more valuable than the goats, and this is why, in the parable, the sheep are placed on the right hand, the place of honour (cf. 22⁴⁴, 26⁶⁴).

34
the King here refers to Jesus, as also in 2², 21⁵, 27¹¹, ²⁹, ³⁷, ⁴².

inherit the kingdom: Cf. the first two Beatitudes, 5³, ⁵, *theirs is the kingdom of heaven . . . they shall inherit the earth.*

35f.

The word *I* is emphatic in Greek.

37ff.

the righteous are unaware that they have ministered to *the King: thee*
is emphatic, and is repeated four times.

40

one of the least of these my brethren: Cf. 10^{42} *Whoever gives to one
of these little ones even a cup of cold water because he is a disciple.* ...
Matthew probably thought of the *brethren* here as the disciples of
Jesus; but in the original parable it may have referred to anyone who
was in distress.

41

Depart from me, you cursed: Cf. 7^{23} (though it is not identical in the
Greek), *Depart from me, you evildoers.*

into the eternal fire: See $13^{40, \ 42, \ 50}$, 18^{8}.

prepared for the devil and his angels: As *the kingdom* was *prepared for* the
blessed, so the fire is prepared for the devil, his angels, and the cursed.
The Jews believed that when Satan, who had been created as an angel,
disobeyed God other angels joined with him; these are *his angels*.

46

The last verse changes the order, putting first the punishment of the
cursed and second the reward of the righteous: the Jews preferred to
end a book, or a section of a book, on a happy note, and not with a
message of doom.

NOTE. We must return to the question which was raised at the beginning of Chapters 24, 25 – What is the twentieth-century reader to
make of this material?

First of all, the earliest Christians believed that the world would end
soon, and they were wrong.

Second, there was a considerable emphasis in 24^{4-28} on not being led
astray, not being alarmed, not believing that the end had come. Thus,
although they believed that history must end soon, they were on their
guard against allowing this belief to produce the wrong results, alarm
and excitement.

Third, in the section $24^{36}-25^{13}$, the emphasis was on not knowing the
day or the hour when the end would come – 24^{36} is repeated like a
refrain in $24^{42, \ 44, \ 50}$, 25^{13}. This does, to some extent, qualify the
expectation that the end will be soon, though not completely. At least
it provided an escape-route, when Christ's return was seen to be

delayed; and this seems to have happened already, by the time Matthew is writing; see 24⁴⁸, *My Master is delayed*, and 25⁵, ¹⁹.

Fourth, in this section (24³⁶–25¹³), the argument runs, Because we do not know the time of the end, therefore we must be ready, we must watch. And in the next parable (25¹⁴ff.) this readiness is interpreted in terms of work, the use of money to gain more money being an image of some activity in which the Christian must engage; though we are not told what this is until the final parable.

The last paragraph (25³¹ff.) shows that the kind of life which will receive the approval of Christ on his return is a life of mercy to the oppressed, and the life which will not be approved is that in which there has been no charity.

Thus the expectation of the imminent end is used, in Matthew, to urge men to charity; but the command to love one another is not dependent upon a belief that the world is coming to an end soon. It is possible, therefore, to find, in what may have been the real and ultimate intention of the Evangelist, a meaning that is independent of the form in which he held it. And it is interesting to notice that somewhere else, about the same time that Matthew was writing his Gospel, another Christian or group of Christians were producing the fourth Gospel and letters of John, in which the idea of the end of the world plays very little part at all, but charity is one of the keywords. *We know*, they say, *that we have passed out of death into life, because we love the brethren* (1 John 3¹⁴): for them, too, the date of the end does not matter; the question which is all-important is, Have we, who have this world's goods and see our brother in need, yet closed our hearts against him? (1 John 3¹⁷).

Matthew 26-28

The Passion and Resurrection

The greater part of these three chapters describes events which happened on a Wednesday (26^{1-16}), Thursday (26^{17-75}), Friday (27^{1-61}), Saturday (27^{62-66}), and Sunday (28^{1-15}); this is followed by another scene which is not dated (28^{16-20}). The Evangelists provide us with precise dating of the events here, in contrast to the earlier parts of their Gospels. The matters, especially those which happened on the Friday and the Sunday, were for them of the greatest significance, and had been so from the dawn of Christianity; compare one of the earliest accounts of the apostles' preaching, *I delivered to you as of first importance what I also received, that Christ died for our sins in accordance with the scriptures, that he was buried, that he was raised on the third day in accordance with the scriptures, and that he appeared to Cephas, then to the twelve* (1 Cor. $15^{3\text{ff.}}$).

This last section of the Gospel begins and ends with words of Jesus; and his words form a commentary upon the narrative, explaining for the reader the meaning of what is happening.

At the beginning, Jesus says to his disciples: *You know that after two days the Passover is coming, and the Son of man will be delivered up to be crucified* (26^2). Jesus is here reminding the disciples (and thereby the reader of the Gospel also) of his predictions of his Passion in 16^{21}, $17^{22\text{f.}}$, $20^{18\text{f.}}$. They are not to forget that he is *the Son of man*, who is now undergoing suffering, but who will come again in glory. He is to die at the time of the Jewish *Passover* – that is, the time when the Jews give thanks for the deliverance of the nation from its oppressors. He foresees his death, and willingly accepts it because it is the will of God and *in accordance with the scriptures*.

At the end of the section, Jesus says: *All authority in heaven and on earth has been given to me. Go therefore and make disciples of all nations, baptizing them in the name of the Father and of the Son and of the Holy Spirit, teaching them to observe all that I have commanded you; and lo, I am with you always, to the close of the age* (28^{18-20}). That is to say, he claims that because of his obedience to death he has received *all authority* from the Father: the right to command them what to do, and the power to enable them to do what he commands. He sends them to *all nations*, whereas before he had confined their mission and his to *Israel* (10⁵ᶠ·, 15²⁴); he commands them to *make disciples* by *baptizing*, and by *teaching* their converts what he had taught them: there had been no command to teach when he sent them out before in 10⁵ᶠᶠ·. And he will be *with* them *always*, guiding, directing, and empowering them, until *the close of the age* when he will return in glory to judge and to reward.

These two sayings of Jesus, at the beginning and end of this section of the Gospel, are both Matthean compositions, the Evangelist apparently thinking it right to preface and conclude the narrative with comments spoken by the chief actor.

There are also twelve other occasions during these chapters on which Jesus speaks; they become more infrequent as the story proceeds; but their purpose, also, is in every case to explain the significance of the events – this is the will of God, the scriptures are being fulfilled, God is making a new *covenant* with man.

The R.S.V. divides the section into twenty-seven paragraphs: the first nine describe the events leading up to and including the prayer of Jesus in Gethsemane (during which time Jesus is with his disciples); the next nine describe his arrest and trials, Peter's denial, and the release of Barabbas; the last nine relate the crucifixion, death, and resurrection, and the events which followed.

The suggestion has already been made that Matthew intended these chapters to balance Chapters 1–4 at the beginning of the book: the trials by the Jews pair off with the temptations by the devil; the death pairs with the baptism; with his going from Jerusalem to Galilee after the resurrection, compare his withdrawal into Galilee in Chapter 2; and his last word in the Gospel, *I am with you always*, is a fulfilment of the prophecy in Chapter 1, *Emmanuel (which means, God with us)*.

Matthew is almost entirely dependent on Mark in these chapters, though he feels himself free to omit, to add, and to change details when he wishes. Nevertheless his alterations do not suggest that he had access to any account of the Passion and resurrection other than Mark's – except for the Old Testament, which, as we have already seen, Matthew regarded as a better authority than the earlier Gospel.

26 *When Jesus had finished all these sayings, he said to his disciples,*
^{2}*'You know that after two days the Passover is coming, and the Son of man
will be delivered up to be crucified.'*

The fifth discourse, finishing at 25^{46}, completes the teaching of Jesus.
The time has come for him to turn from teaching to action; and
by this action to become more than a teacher – the Lord of the Church,
the one who has all authority in heaven and on earth. But we have
already been told that the Son of man will not come to power in the
way that the rulers of the Gentiles do, but by an act of service, giving
his life as a ransom for many (20^{25}ff.). In these two verses, the reader is
instructed to prepare for this event, which follows the teaching of
Jesus in this Gospel, and in which Jesus put his teaching into practice.

ɷ

Matthew has combined his formula for transition from speech to
narrative (see 7^{28}, 11^1, 13^{53}, 19^1) with the statement in Mark 14^{1a} *it
was now two days before the Passover . . .*, and turned the Marcan note of
time into a final prediction in the mouth of Jesus.

1
all these sayings: Matthew adds the word *all* here, because this is to be
his last use of the formula, and the teaching of Jesus is now complete.

2
after two days the Passover is coming probably means that Jesus is speaking
on the Wednesday, Nisan 13th.

Passover and the delivering up of Jesus to be crucified are linked together
in this verse; and Christians at an early date saw a providential significance in this. The Passover was the annual commemoration of God's
deliverance of Israel from her enemies, and it looked forward to the final
deliverance in the last days, when the Messiah, the greater Moses,
would lead them into the promised land of the kingdom of heaven.

will be delivered (*paradidotai*): Here in the present tense, literally, 'is being delivered', whereas in 17^{22}, 20^{18} the tense was future. The passive voice may indicate God's action; cf. Rom. 8^{32}, God *did not spare his own Son but gave him up* (the same word as here) *for us all*; in and through the actions of Judas, the Jews, and the Romans, God is carrying out his purpose.

26^{3-5} THE DECISION OF THE   Mark $14^{1b, \, 2}$
                        SANHEDRIN

³ *Then the chief priests and the elders of the people gathered in the palace of the high priest, who was called Ca'iaphas,* ⁴*and took counsel together in order to arrest Jesus by stealth and kill him.* ⁵*But they said, 'Not during the feast, lest there be a tumult among the people.'*

Jesus' prediction of his crucifixion immediately begins to be fulfilled: the Jewish council, the Sanhedrin, meets in the high priest's palace, and they plan *to arrest Jesus by stealth*, and privately, in order to avoid a public disturbance among the Jews. Matthew has written this paragraph in such a way that his readers will see here not only the fulfilment of Jesus' prophecy, but also the fulfilment of a scriptural passage, namely, Ps. 2^2, *The rulers take counsel together against the Lord and his anointed* (in Greek, 'his Christ').

೧೪

Matthew's changes in Mark $14^{1b, \, 2}$ emphasize that the decision to kill Jesus was taken by the official leaders of the Jews, and fulfilled the Old Testament, i.e. Ps. 2.

3
Matthew puts *elders of the people* instead of Mark's *the scribes*; and says that the meeting took place *in the palace of the high priest, who was called Caiaphas*; he is emphasizing the official nature of the meeting.

gathered (*synēchthēsan*) from Ps. 2^2: see also 2^4, 22^{34}, 26^{57}, and Acts 4^{25}ff. where the Psalm is quoted and interpreted of the decision of the Jews to kill Jesus.

Caiaphas was not mentioned by name in Mark; he was high priest from A.D. 18–36 (Josephus, *Antiquities*, XVIII, 2, 2).

4

by stealth: Cf. 21^{46} *when they tried to arrest him, they feared the multitudes, because they held him to be a prophet*; this explains why they decide to arrest him *by stealth.*

5

Not during the feast: If this is the right translation, then their plan was not fulfilled, because Jesus was arrested on the night of the feast, 26^{47}ff. Some scholars however think that it means 'not in the festival crowd', i.e. not publicly, but *by stealth.*

26$^{6-13}$ JESUS IS ANOINTED FOR BURIAL   Mark 14$^{3-9}$

^{6}*Now when Jesus was at Bethany in the house of Simon the leper, ^{7}a woman came up to him with an alabaster jar of very expensive ointment, and she poured it on his head, as he sat at table. ^{8}But when the disciples saw it, they were indignant, saying, 'Why this waste? ^{9}For this ointment might have been sold for a large sum, and given to the poor.' ^{10}But Jesus, aware of this, said to them, 'Why do you trouble the woman? For she has done a beautiful thing to me. ^{11}For you always have the poor with you, but you will not always have me. ^{12}In pouring this ointment on my body she has done it to prepare me for burial. ^{13}Truly, I say to you, wherever this gospel is preached in the whole world, what she has done will be told in memory of her.'*

Matthew brings us back from the high priest's palace in Jerusalem to the house of Simon the leper at Bethany, a few miles east of the city. Jesus and his disciples are at supper, when a woman anoints his *head* with expensive ointment, and his disciples complain of the waste. Jesus says that she has anointed his *body, for burial,* and that her deed will be recalled wherever the gospel is preached. Here again Jesus is shown as knowing beforehand what is to happen to him: he is to die, and to be buried without the customary rite of anointing the body. There may also be a suggestion that, though kings were anointed on the *head* and so entered into their authority, he will receive his power by the death and burial of his *body*.

ဢ

Matthew has copied this from Mark 14^{3-9} without significant alteration.

6

For *Bethany*, see 21^{17}; *Simon the leper* is not mentioned elsewhere.

7

For anointing kings on the head, see, e.g., 2 Kings 9^6, *The young man poured the oil on his head, saying to him, Thus says the Lord the God of Israel, I anoint you king over the people of the Lord, over Israel.*

as he sat at table: Literally, 'as he reclined' – see also 9^{10}, 26^{20}.

8f.

The disciples see only the waste of the ointment; they fail to see either of the two possible interpretations: the anointing of a king, or the anointing of the dead.

10f.

Jesus defends the woman's good deed: he will not always be present with them in the flesh, but the poor will be; the woman has made the most of an opportunity that will not be presented again.

12

According to Mark 16^1, three women went to anoint the body of Jesus on the day after the sabbath, but arrived too late, because he was already risen from the tomb. (Matthew omits this, 28^1.) Jesus claims that the woman's anointing of his *head* has taken the place of the anointing of his *body for burial*.

13

Jesus looks beyond his death and burial to the preaching of the gospel *in the whole world* (cf. 24^{14}), when her deed will be recalled. It has been suggested that the saying in this verse originally meant, 'Amen, I say unto you: when God's angel announces the victory of God to the whole world, this also that she hath done, shall be spoken of (before God's throne, in the last judgement) that God may mercifully remember her.'

JUDAS RECEIVES MONEY   Mark $14^{10f.}$
                    FROM THE CHIEF PRIESTS

14 *Then one of the twelve, who was called Judas Iscariot, went to the chief priests* 15*and said, 'What will you give me if I deliver him to you?' And they paid him thirty pieces of silver.* 16*And from that moment he sought an opportunity to betray him.*

In sharp contrast with the gift of the woman in the previous paragraph, Matthew tells now of the money paid to Judas by the chief priests, for delivering Jesus to them. The amount which they pay is *thirty pieces of silver*, and Matthew sees in this a fulfilment of a prophecy in Zechariah, so that even here, in the disloyalty and treachery of Judas, the plan of God is being carried out, and the things that had been written by the prophets about the Son of man are being fulfilled.

꧇

Matthew adds in the question of Judas, and the quotation from Zechariah in v. 15.

14
For *Judas Iscariot* see 10⁴ where he was mentioned last in the list of the twelve apostles. Cf. Gen. 37²⁶ff. where Judah (= Judas in Greek) suggested the sale of Joseph to the Ishmaelites for *twenty shekels of silver*; it may be that Matthew had this in mind here, but see next verse.

15
Matthew has changed Mark's: *they promised to give him money* to *they paid him thirty pieces of silver*; but it is unlikely that Matthew had historical information about this point, since the words are a quotation from Zech. 11¹², *They weighed out as my wages thirty shekels of silver.* There are also allusions to the last chapters of Zechariah in 21⁵, 24³, ³⁰, ³¹, 26²⁸, 27⁹ (where the same passage is quoted in full). Matthew has read this detail out of the Old Testament.

THE DISCIPLES ARE SENT TO Mark 14¹²⁻¹⁶
PREPARE THE PASSOVER

¹⁷*Now on the first day of Unleavened Bread the disciples came to Jesus,
saying, 'Where will you have us prepare for you to eat the passover?'* ¹⁸*He
said, 'Go into the city to such a one, and say to him, "The Teacher says,
My time is at hand; I will keep the passover at your house with my disciples."'*
¹⁹*And the disciples did as Jesus had directed them, and they prepared the
passover.*

The prediction of Jesus at the beginning of the chapter mentioned
(*a*) Passover, (*b*) the delivering up of the Son of man to be crucified.
Matthew, in his characteristic way has dealt with (*b*) first and now he
comes to (*a*), the Passover. The day is probably Thursday, Nisan 14th;
on that day the Passover lambs were killed in Jerusalem, and the feast
had to be eaten that evening, in the city.

The disciples therefore ask Jesus where he wants them to prepare
the meal, and Jesus sends them to Jerusalem with a message to a
particular man who has a house there. The message includes the further
prediction of Jesus, *My time is at hand*, which Matthew has added in
order to show that Jesus is aware of the plans and arrangements of
the Sanhedrin and Judas Iscariot.

తస

Matthew has abbreviated Mark, omitting some of his details; notice in
particular that in Mark only two disciples are sent, and the change in
the message to the man in Jerusalem.

17
the first day of the Unleavened Bread would be Nisan 15th, the day after
the Passover; see Num. 28^{16f.}. But Matthew obviously means the day
before the Passover, and there is some evidence that this could be
referred to as *the first day of Unleavened Bread*. The Passover could be
eaten only in Jerusalem.

18
My time is at hand is a Matthean addition to Mark.

I will keep the passover at your house with my disciples: Matthew puts this as a statement, instead of the question in Mark, *Where is my guest room, where I am to eat the passover with my disciples?*

This paragraph is clear evidence that Matthew (like Mark) thought that the Last Supper was the Passover meal. In the fourth Gospel, on the other hand, the Passover is to be eaten on the evening after the death of Jesus (John 18^{28}). The majority of scholars at the moment think that the Marcan and Matthean date is right, and that John changed it for theological reasons.

26^{20-25}	JESUS PREDICTS HIS BETRAYAL BY JUDAS	Mark 14^{17-21}

^{20}*When it was evening, he sat at table with the twelve disciples;^{a} ^{21}and as they were eating, he said, 'Truly, I say to you, one of you will betray me.' ^{22}And they were very sorrowful, and began to say to him one after another, 'Is it I, Lord?' ^{23}He answered, 'He who has dipped his hand in the dish with me, will betray me. ^{24}The Son of man goes as it is written of him, but woe to that man by whom the Son of man is betrayed! It would have been better for that man if he had not been born.' ^{25}Judas, who betrayed him, said, 'Is it I, Master?'^{b} He said to him, 'You have said so.'*

  a Other authorities omit *disciples*
  b Or *Rabbi*

Jesus joins the disciples for the Passover meal in Jerusalem, and during it he tells them that one of them will betray him. They all ask, Is it I, Lord? and Jesus says that it is one who has shared food with him; he is going to his death in accordance with the scriptures and the will of God, but even so the man who hands him over to the Jews is responsible for his action and will be severely punished by God. Judas then asks, Is it I, Rabbi? and Jesus, who knows all that is to happen, says that it is.

৩৩

Matthew's alterations to Mark are slight; he has omitted *one who is eating with me*, from Mark 14^{18}, and this is strange, since it is possibly an allusion to Ps. 41⁹ (quoted in John 13¹⁸), and Matthew does not usually miss a point where the fulfilment of the Old Testament is concerned; but some of the commentators on Mark think that these words were not in Mark when Matthew used it and were added later. Matthew has added *Lord* in v. 22 and the whole of v. 25 in which Judas is declared to be the betrayer.

20f.

For the regulations for the Passover meal, see Exod. 12¹ᶠᶠ·: it had to be eaten at night; originally it was eaten standing, but later this was changed to reclining; *he sat at table* is literally, 'he reclined', cf. 9¹⁰, 26⁷.

22

one after another: Literally, 'each one'. *Is it I . . . ?* should perhaps be translated, 'Surely not I?' *Lord* which Matthew adds, perhaps contrasts with Judas' *Rabbi* in v. 25 (see note).

23

He who has dipped his hand in the dish with me: At the Passover meal, they all dipped their hands into a dish; at the other meals, they dipped bread into the dish.

24

The Son of man goes as it is written of him: i.e. written in the Old Testament; see, for example, v. 31 where Zech. 13⁷ is quoted.

but woe to that man by whom the Son of man is betrayed: Divine predestination does not abolish human responsibility. Judas will therefore be judged for what he has done, and his punishment will be such that it would have been better for him never to have existed. The words *It would have been better for that man if he had not been born* come in 1 Enoch 38², and may perhaps be a proverbial expression.

25

This verse is added by Matthew, and as so often in other parts of the Gospel Matthew builds it up from phrases which he uses elsewhere: for *Judas who betrayed him*, see 10⁴; for *Is it I*, see v. 22; for Jesus addressed by Judas as *Rabbi*, see 26⁴⁹; for *You have said so*, see 26⁶⁴. By the addition of this verse, Matthew shows Jesus as the one who goes to his Passion knowing what will happen, in every detail.

JESUS INTERPRETS HIS   Mark 14²²⁻²⁵
                         DEATH TO HIS DISCIPLES

²⁶*Now as they were eating, Jesus took bread, and blessed, and broke it, and gave it to the disciples and said, 'Take, eat; this is my body.' ²⁷And he took a cup, and when he had given thanks he gave it to them, saying, 'Drink of it, all of you; ²⁸for this is my blood of the^a covenant, which is poured out for many for the forgiveness of sins. ²⁹I tell you I shall not drink again of this fruit of the vine until the day when I drink it new with you in my Father's kingdom.'*

a Other ancient authorities insert *new*

Jesus has said that he is going to his death in fulfilment of the scriptures; he now explains to his disciples how his death can be within the purpose of God, and what it will effect. He does this by means of a twofold prophetic action (cf. the double parables in 7²⁴⁻²⁷, 13⁴⁴⁻⁴⁶): he compares the *bread* to his *body*, and the *cup* of wine to his *blood*. The separation between *body* and *blood* suggests sacrifice, because in the Old Testament sacrifices the blood was separated from the body; and here also Jesus says that his blood is *blood of the covenant, which is poured out for many for the forgiveness of sins*. Therefore by these words concerning the bread and the wine, Jesus is saying that his coming death will be a sacrifice offered to God, by which a new *covenant* between God and man will be established; and in telling the disciples to *eat* the bread and to *drink* the cup, he is saying that they will be the beneficiaries of his sacrifice – and not only they, but the *many*, that is, the whole world. Moreover he looks forward to the fulfilment of what he will inaugurate by his death – namely, his *Father's kingdom*, the messianic banquet, when he and they will again feast together.

ಐಐ

Matthew makes some small alterations in Mark 14²²⁻²⁵ to bring out the meaning of the passage.

26

Jesus took bread, and blessed, and broke it, and gave it to the disciples: This was the normal way of saying grace among the Jews; cf. 14^{19}, 15^{36}. *Blessed* means blessed God, gave thanks to God – not blessed the bread. The word *eat* has been added by Matthew.

this is my body: Jesus compares the bread which he has broken to his body which is soon to be put to death; and by commanding the disciples to eat the bread, he is offering them a part in the situation which his death will effect, i.e. a place in the kingdom.

27f.
The same actions are performed with the cup: Jesus gives thanks to God; and commands the disciples to drink it (Matthew has changed Mark's *and they all drank of it* to a command, *Drink of it, all of you*); and he interprets the cup as his *blood of the covenant*: the words are from the Old Testament (Exod. 24^8, Jer. 31^{31}, Zech. 9^{11}), and recall both the covenant which God gave after the exodus from Egypt, and the new covenant of the last days which the prophets had foretold. *which is poured out* is a prophetic present tense, and means, 'which is about to be poured out'. *for many* is a semitic way of saying 'for everybody'; it does not mean for some and not for others, but that Jesus is dying for the rest of the world; cf. 20^{28}, *to give his life as a ransom for many*.

for the forgiveness of sins has been added by Matthew: he probably has Jeremiah's description of the new covenant in mind, e.g. Jer. 31^{34}, *I will remember their sin no more*.

29
This saying was probably a vow of abstinence from wine until the kingdom should come; among the Jews such vows accompanied and strengthened prayer. Jesus is saying, May my death be the way in which God will begin his kingly rule in the world; then, as at a banquet, I shall drink *new* wine *with you*, in *the new world* (19^{28}).

26^{30-35} JESUS PREDICTS THE   Mark 14^{26-31}
FAILURE OF THE DISCIPLES

^{30}*And when they had sung a hymn, they went out to the Mount of Olives.* ^{31}*Then Jesus said to them, 'You will all fall away because of me this night; for it is written, "I will strike the shepherd, and the sheep of the flock will be scattered." * ^{32}*But after I am raised up, I will go before you to Galilee.'*

³³*Peter declared to him, 'Though they all fall away because of you, I will never fall away.' *³⁴*Jesus said to him, 'Truly, I say to you, this very night, before the cock crows, you will deny me three times.' *³⁵*Peter said to him, 'Even if I must die with you, I will not deny you.' And so said all the disciples.*

Those who kept the Passover in Jerusalem must remain there all night; but because there were so many pilgrims, the area of Jerusalem for this purpose was extended to include the west side of the Mount of Olives. Jesus and his disciples go there from the house in Jerusalem, and Jesus tells them that Zechariah's prophecy, *I will strike the shepherd, and the sheep of the flock will be scattered*, will be fulfilled during that night: he will be arrested; they will leave him. But he assures them that after his resurrection, he will lead them to Galilee – the land of the Gentiles, where the gospel will be preached and disciples will be made. Peter declares that he will remain faithful to Jesus, but Jesus says that, on the contrary, Peter will deny him three times before cock-crow. Peter continues to protest: he will be faithful unto death; and the other disciples say the same.

∞

Matthew's alterations to Mark 14^{26-31} are again very slight, and are usually small additions.

30

when they had sung a hymn: If, as Mark and Matthew believed, the supper was the Passover meal, then *a hymn* means Pss. 114–118, which were always sung as part of the feast.

the Mount of Olives: In the note on the previous reference in Matthew to *the Mount of Olives* (24^{3}ff.) we referred to the fact that it is mentioned in Zech. 14^{4}. It is worth noticing that here, where *the Mount* is again the scene of the words of Jesus, he quotes from Zechariah. In Chapter 24 he predicted the falling away of many disciples before the end, 24^{10}; here he predicts the falling away of all of them before his Passion.

31

you will all fall away because of me this night: Matthew has added here *because of me this night*; for *fall away*, see 13^{21}, 24^{10}.

The quotation is from Zech. 13⁷. For Jesus as *the shepherd*, and Israel as *the sheep*, see 9³⁶, 25³².

32

This is the first prediction of the resurrection in this chapter.

For *Galilee* and the mission to the Gentiles, see 4¹²ff., 28⁷, ¹⁶ff.. *I will go before you* may mean 'will lead you forth, like a shepherd'; cf. John 10⁴ of the shepherd, *he goes before them, and the sheep follow him, for they know his voice* (but a different word is used in the Greek).

33

Matthew has again added the words *because of you* (cf. v. 31 above), and the second *fall away*. Cf. 14²⁸ff. for Peter's failure to follow Jesus, and 16²²f. for his refusal to believe that Jesus must be killed.

34

Jesus' prediction of Peter's denials is fulfilled in 26⁶⁹⁻⁷⁵.

35

Peter's statement, *Even if I must die with you . . .* shows that he has still not accepted the inevitability of the death of Jesus, and of anyone who will not deny him; cf. 10³⁸, *he who does not take his cross and follow me is not worthy of me.*

And so said all the disciples: In his failure to believe and understand, Peter is only the spokesman of the others.

26³⁶⁻⁴⁶   JESUS ACCEPTS THE WILL   Mark 14³²⁻⁴²
                      OF HIS FATHER

³⁶ *Then Jesus went with them to a place called Gethsem'ane, and he said to his disciples, 'Sit here, while I go yonder and pray.'* ³⁷ *And taking with him Peter and the two sons of Zeb'edee, he began to be sorrowful and troubled.* ³⁸ *Then he said to them, 'My soul is very sorrowful, even to death; remain here, and watch*ᵃ *with me.'* ³⁹ *And going a little farther he fell on his face and prayed, 'My Father, if it be possible, let this cup pass from me; nevertheless, not as I will, but as thou wilt.'* ⁴⁰ *And he came to the disciples and found them sleeping; and he said to Peter, 'So, could you not watch*ᵃ *with me one hour?* ⁴¹ *Watch*ᵃ *and pray that you may not enter into temptation;*

the spirit indeed is willing, but the flesh is weak.' ⁴²*Again, for the second time, he went away and prayed, 'My Father, if this cannot pass unless I drink it, thy will be done.'* ⁴³*And again he came and found them sleeping, for their eyes were heavy.* ⁴⁴*So, leaving them again, he went away and prayed for the third time, saying the same words.* ⁴⁵*Then he came to the disciples and said to them, 'Are you still sleeping and taking your rest? Behold, the hour is at hand, and the Son of man is betrayed into the hands of sinners.* ⁴⁶*Rise, let us be going; see, my betrayer is at hand.'*

a Or *keep awake*

This is the last paragraph in which Jesus is with his disciples: at the end of the paragraph that follows it, *all the disciples forsook him and fled* (26⁵⁶); and they are not reunited until 28¹⁶ff. Here, however, Jesus commands three of them to watch with him; and we are shown how they did not obey him, and thus how it came about that they were separated from him. Their disobedience to his command, and to the will of God, is the cause of their separation from Jesus. He himself accepts God's will: he says to the Father, *thy will be done.* But they sleep, and so, when the moment comes, they fail.

The first Christians used to contrast the disobedience of Adam, which was the cause and origin of all the evil in the world, with the obedience of Christ, the cause and origin of all good: *as one man's trespass led to condemnation for all men, so one man's act of righteousness leads to acquittal and life for all men. For as by one man's disobedience many were made sinners, so by one man's obedience many will be made righteous,* Rom. 5¹⁸f. In the story of Jesus in Gethsemane, the reader is shown the obedience of Jesus to the Father, which is the 'essence' or significance of the crucifixion.

For Jesus, and for the three disciples, there is a conflict between *the spirit* and *the flesh*, and this conflict causes him great sorrow and trouble. For him there is a victory of the spirit over the flesh: he accepts *the cup*, or destiny, which the Father is holding out to him. But in them there is a victory of the flesh over the spirit: they sleep, and thus are faced by the temptation or trial to which they will not be able to stand up. Jesus' prediction, *You will all fall away because of me this night*, will therefore be fulfilled.

൧൧

Matthew's main alteration to Mark here is the insertion of the words of the second prayer of Jesus, in v. 42.

36
Gethsemane was either on the side of the Mount of Olives or at the foot of it. In this Gospel we are twice told that Jesus prayed, here and at 14²³.

37
Peter and the two sons of Zebedee (Mark: *Peter and James and John*): See 4²¹, 10², 20²⁰, 27⁵⁶. These three are alone with Jesus during the transfiguration, 17¹: there, they see his glory; here, his obedience, because of which he will be crowned with glory. For sorrow as the result of a conflict, cf. 14⁹ (Herod's promise, and his fear of John) and 19²² (the young man's love of his possessions, and the command of Jesus); here the conflict is between *the spirit* and *the flesh* (v. 41).

38
My soul is very sorrowful: A quotation from Ps. 42⁵.

even unto death: A quotation from Jonah 4⁹, meaning *enough to die*: i.e. his sorrow is so great that it seems to be engulfing him.

watch with me: Matthew has added *with me*: Jesus commands the three disciples to join with him, but they fail to do so. The word translated *watch* means literally *Keep awake* (margin), and it is used in the double sense of being awake from sleep and of being on the look-out for the day of the Lord and avoiding the temptations of Satan, in the hortatory passages in the letters of the New Testament, e.g. *Be sober, be watchful. Your adversary the devil prowls around like a roaring lion, seeking some one to devour* (1 Pet. 5⁸).

39
My Father (Mark: *Abba, Father*; as elsewhere, Matthew has omitted Mark's Aramaic word.): Cf. the Lord's prayer: *Our Father* 6⁹.

if it be possible: Mark had, *all things are possible to thee*, but Matthew changes this, possibly because he thought it inappropriate in the circumstances, i.e. because the prayer of Jesus was not answered.

let this cup pass from me: Matthew has made some re-arrangements in Mark's account, but has retained the word *pass from* (*parelthatō*), perhaps because it was used in the Old Testament in connexion with the Passover (Exod. 12²³). For *cup* see 20²², 26²⁷; 'In the Old Testament *potērion* [= cup] is an expression for destiny in both good and bad senses. On the concept of drinking a cup of suffering cf. Isa. 51$^{17, 22}$, Lam. 4^{21}, Ps. 11^6, (*Lexicon*).

nevertheless, not as I will, but as thou wilt: These words, together with *My Father* above, may have suggested the Lord's Prayer to Matthew, and thus given him the words for the prayer in v. 42 below.

40

For sleep contrasted with watch, cf. for example 1 Thess. 5^6, *So then let us not sleep, as others do, but let us keep awake and be sober*; 'sleeping' is used in Christian literature for being unaware of the critical time before the end and living a life of sin. Matthew again adds *with me* – see v. 38. Because they do not *watch with* him, they cannot *die with* him, v. 35.

41

They will be kept from the attacks of Satan – i.e. *temptation* – by watching and prayer. Cf. another phrase in the Lord's Prayer, *Lead us not into temptation*, 6^{13}.

42

The words of this prayer have been added by Matthew, and he builds it up from v. 39 and from the Lord's Prayer, 6^{10}, together with the idea of drinking the cup, for which see 20^{22}.

44

Matthew has composed this verse, using Mark 14^{39}, Mark's description of Jesus' second prayer.

45f.

The *hour* for Jesus to be handed over to the power of *sinners* (possibly = Gentiles) has now come, because Judas, their agent (26$^{14-16}$) has come. Jesus wakes the disciples up: *Rise* (from sleep); *let us be going* to meet him, and to do the will of God.

26$^{47-56}$ JESUS IS ARRESTED   Mark 14$^{43-50}$

^{47}*While he was still speaking, Judas came, one of the twelve, and with him a great crowd with swords and clubs, from the chief priests and the elders of the people.* ^{48}*Now the betrayer had given them a sign, saying, 'The one I shall kiss is the man; seize him.'* ^{49}*And he came up to Jesus at once and said,*

'Hail, Master!'ᵃ And he kissed him. ⁵⁰Jesus said to him, 'Friend, why are you here?'ᵇ Then they came up and laid hands on Jesus and seized him. ⁵¹And behold, one of those who were with Jesus stretched out his hand and drew his sword, and struck the slave of the high priest, and cut off his ear. ⁵²Then Jesus said to him, 'Put your sword back into its place; for all who take the sword will perish by the sword. ⁵³Do you think that I cannot appeal to my Father, and he will at once send me more than twelve legions of angels? ⁵⁴But how then should the scriptures be fulfilled, that it must be so?' ⁵⁵At that hour Jesus said to the crowds, 'Have you come out as against a robber, with swords and clubs to capture me? Day after day I sat in the temple teaching, and you did not seize me. ⁵⁶But all this has taken place, that the scriptures of the prophets might be fulfilled.' Then all the disciples forsook him and fled.

a Or Rabbi
b Or do that for which you have come

Matthew does not tell us when Judas left the disciples of Jesus; but at some point between the Supper (26²⁵) and the present moment he had gone to the Sanhedrin, collected a great crowd of armed men, and arranged a signal with them: they are to arrest the man whom he kisses. He arrives with this party, greets Jesus and kisses him, and Jesus is arrested. One of the disciples attempts to defend Jesus with force, but Jesus rebukes him and warns all who resort to force of its self-destructiveness. In any case, he has other powers upon which he could call if he wished; but the will of God does not lie in that direction. He rebukes the crowds for coming to arrest him as one would apprehend a robber, when he had been teaching in the temple daily and they could have arrested him openly. But this is the will of God, foretold by the prophets. The disciples then leave Jesus, as he had predicted: *the sheep of the flock will be scattered.*

෴

Matthew's main changes to Mark are additions – vv. 50a, 52–54.

47
Matthew emphasizes the size of the *crowd* by adding *great*: such a crowd was unnecessary, because Jesus had accepted the will of God; see vv. 55f.

48

The *kiss*, which should be the sign of love (in Greek the same word means 'to love' or 'to kiss'), is chosen by Judas to indicate the one whom he is betraying.

49

Master: Cf. 26²⁵; these are the only places where Jesus is addressed as 'Rabbi' in this Gospel, on both occasions by Judas.

And he kissed him: A different word is used from that used in v. 48; it may mean, 'kissed him repeatedly'.

50

Matthew has added *Jesus said to him, Friend, why are you here?* The word translated *Friend* (*hetaire*) is used in the New Testament by Matthew only, and always in situations in which the person so addressed is in the wrong; see 20¹³, 22¹². The meaning of *Why are you here?* is not certain: it may mean *do that for which you have come* (margin) or '(do you kiss me) for the purpose for which you have come?'

51

Matthew changes Mark's *one of those who stood by* to *one of those who were with Jesus* – i.e. one of the disciples. In John 18¹⁰ this is said to have been Simon Peter.

52–54

These verses have been added by Matthew, and have no parallel in Mark or Luke.

52

All who take the sword shall perish by the sword may have been a proverb: see Gen. 9⁶, Rev. 13¹⁰. Jesus had taught his disciples not to resist evil in 5³⁹ff.

53f.

Jesus could appeal to the Father for angelic power to deliver him, but to do so would be to disobey the purpose of God which had been declared in the Old Testament – e.g. Zech. 13⁷, quoted at 26³¹.

55

For their decision to arrest Jesus in secret, see 26⁴. Matthew adds the word *sat*, see 5¹, 13¹, ², 24³.

56

Matthew adds the words *all this has taken place* to clarify the sense of Mark; and he has also added *of the prophets*, possibly because he has

Zechariah's prophecy in mind; though it may be that he is thinking of another particular prophecy: Jesus has been arrested as a *robber* (v. 55), and Isaiah had said that the servant *was numbered with the transgressors*; Isa. 53¹² which is quoted in Luke 22³⁷.

The flight of the disciples fulfils the prediction of Jesus in v. 31.

Matthew has omitted Mark's story of the young man who ran away naked, Mark 14⁵¹ᶠ.

26⁵⁷⁻⁶⁸   JESUS IS CONDEMNED BY   Mark 14⁵³⁻⁶⁵
                      THE SANHEDRIN

⁵⁷*Then those who had seized Jesus led him to Ca'iaphas the high priest, where the scribes and the elders had gathered.* ⁵⁸*But Peter followed him at a distance, as far as the courtyard of the high priest, and going inside he sat with the guards to see the end.* ⁵⁹*Now the chief priests and the whole council sought false testimony against Jesus that they might put him to death,* ⁶⁰*but they found none, though many false witnesses came forward. At last two came forward* ⁶¹*and said, 'This fellow said, "I am able to destroy the temple of God, and to build it in three days."'* ⁶²*And the high priest stood up and said, 'Have you no answer to make? What is it that these men testify against you?'* ⁶³*But Jesus was silent. And the high priest said to him, 'I adjure you by the living God, tell us if you are the Christ, the Son of God.'* ⁶⁴*Jesus said to him, 'You have said so. But I tell you, hereafter you will see the Son of man seated at the right hand of Power, and coming on the clouds of heaven.'* ⁶⁵*Then the high priest tore his robes, and said, 'He has uttered blasphemy. Why do we still need witnesses? You have now heard his blasphemy.* ⁶⁶*What is your judgement?' They answered, 'He deserves death.'* ⁶⁷*Then they spat in his face, and struck him; and some slapped him,* ⁶⁸*saying, 'Prophesy to us, you Christ! Who is it that struck you?'*

The crowd takes Jesus to the palace of the high priest in Jerusalem, where the Sanhedrin is waiting to try him and condemn him to death. For this purpose they need at least two witnesses, to fulfil the regulation in Deut. 19¹⁵, *A single witness shall not prevail against a man . . . only on the evidence of two witnesses, or of three witnesses, shall a charge be sustained.* The only two who agree report Jesus' prediction that he would destroy the temple and rebuild it in three days. Jesus is silent during this part of the trial: *like a sheep that before its shearers is dumb, so he opened not his mouth* (Isa. 53^7). The high priest then puts Jesus on oath to say whether he is the Christ, the Son of God. Jesus says that he is, and predicts in scriptural words his enthronement as the Son of man and his return in judgement. The high priest asks the Sanhedrin if this is not blasphemy, and they condemn him to death, and spit on him, and hit him, and mock him. Matthew describes this in words which echo Old Testament prophecy, so that the reader knows that even here, where Israel has rejected its King, the will of God is being fulfilled.

෴

Matthew has slightly abbreviated Mark 14$^{53-65}$, but added the oath of the high priest in v. 63 and part of the words of mockery in v. 68.

57
Here, as in v. 3, Matthew has inserted the name of the high priest; and replaced Mark's *were assembled* by *had gathered* (*synēchthēsan*), an allusion to Ps. 2^2; see 26^3.

58
Peter's denial will be described in the next paragraph. Matthew changes Mark's *warming himself at the fire* to *to see the end*, perhaps intending this ironically: Peter thinks that the condemnation and death of Jesus will be *the end* of him, because he does not yet believe in the resurrection which Jesus had promised in v. 32.

59
Matthew changes Mark's *sought testimony* to *sought false testimony*.

60
Matthew has abbreviated Mark here: Mark says that the witnesses did not agree, and that is why *they found none*; they had to have two or three who agreed, before they could proceed.

61f.
For Jesus' prediction of the destruction of the temple, see 23^{38}, 24^2, and its repetition at 27^{40}. No action is taken on this evidence; perhaps it is mentioned here because, to the Christian reader, it provides a true interpretation of the death and resurrection of Jesus; cf. John 2^{21}, *But he spoke of the temple of his body.*

63

The high priest makes a further effort to secure a conviction, by the oath; this has been added by Matthew.

64

You have said so: Cf. Jesus' answer to Judas in v. 25; Matthew has changed Mark's *I am.*

hereafter may mean 'soon'.

seated at the right hand of Power: Power is a periphrasis for God, and the words are a quotation from Ps. 110¹. *the Son of man . . . coming on the clouds of heaven* is a quotation from Dan. 7¹³.

65

It was laid down by the rabbis that when anyone heard a person speak blasphemy, he must tear his robes.

67

In Greek there is an allusion here to the Greek version of Isa. 50⁶, *I gave my back to the smiters, and my cheeks to those who pulled out the beard; I hid not my face from shame and spitting.*

68

Matthew adds this verse, to show how the Jews, like the soldiers later, 27²⁷⁻³¹, mocked Jesus for claiming to be what in fact he was.

PETER DENIES JESUS
                   THREE TIMES

⁶⁹*Now Peter was sitting outside in the courtyard. And a maid came up to him, and said, 'You also were with Jesus the Galilean.'* ⁷⁰*But he denied it before them all, saying, 'I do not know what you mean.'* ⁷¹*And when he went out to the porch, another maid saw him, and she said to the bystanders, 'This man was with Jesus of Nazareth.'* ⁷²*And again he denied it with an oath, 'I do not know the man.'* ⁷³*After a little while the bystanders came up and said to Peter, 'Certainly you are also one of them, for your accent betrays you.'* ⁷⁴*Then he began to invoke a curse on himself and to swear, 'I do not know the man.' And immediately the cock crowed.* ⁷⁵*And Peter remembered the*

saying of Jesus, 'Before the cock crows, you will deny me three times.' And he went out and wept bitterly.

Matthew goes back to Peter, sitting in the courtyard: two female servants and the other bystanders say that Peter is a disciple: a first girl says it to Peter himself; then, a second girl says it of Peter to the bystanders; finally, they accuse him. Each time, Peter denies it; and after the third, the cock crows. So Jesus' prediction is fulfilled, *Truly, I say to you, this very night, before the cock crows, you will deny me three times* (26³⁴).

⁂

Matthew has made slight changes in Mark which are of no great importance.

70
Matthew has added *before them all* (emprosthen pantōn), perhaps because he has the saying of Jesus in 10³³ in his mind here, *Whoever denies me before men* (emprosthen tōn anthrōpōn), *I also will deny before my Father who is in heaven.*

74
to invoke a curse on himself: e.g. 'God smite me if I am not telling the truth.'

75
Refers to v. 34.

And he went out and wept bitterly replaces two words in Mark, the meaning of which is not certain.

It may be that we are meant to contrast the penitence of Peter with the despair of Judas (27⁴ᶠ.). Paul similarly speaks of two kinds of grief: *godly grief produces a repentance that leads to salvation and brings no regret, but worldly grief produces death* (2 Cor. 7¹⁰).

How are we to reconcile Peter's denial of Jesus with the saying of Jesus in 10³³ that he will deny before the Father those who deny him before men? Only by seeing that the mercy of God and the forgiveness of sins, which Jesus' death brings to the world, are greater than anything man does; and that even the words of Jesus must not be used to limit God's grace.

27 *When morning came, all the chief priests and the elders of the people took counsel against Jesus to put him to death;* [2]*and they bound him and led him away and delivered him to Pilate the governor.*

Matthew now records another meeting of the Sanhedrin in the morning, and their decision to put Jesus to death. They bind him, and hand him over to Pilate. First, Judas had delivered Jesus to the Sanhedrin; now, the Sanhedrin delivers him to the Romans. These two actions had been foretold in the second prediction of the Passion and resurrection (20[18f.]), *The Son of man will be delivered to the chief priests and scribes, and they will condemn him to death, and deliver him to the Gentiles.*

જ્જ

Matthew takes this paragraph from Mark 15[1].

1

Matthew adds *against Jesus to put him to death*, repeating what he had said in 26[59]. The reason for this second meeting is not clear, either in Mark or here, but it may have been that rabbinic regulations demanded two trials before a death sentence could be imposed; but see D. E. Nincham, *The Gospel of St Mark*, pp. 400ff.

2

Matthew adds *the governor*, to explain who Pilate was. (This is the first time he is mentioned in Matthew.) He was procurator of Judea from A.D. 26 to A.D. 36, when he was recalled because of his cruelty (Josephus, *Antiquities*, XVIII, 4, 1f.).

27[3-10]   THE DEATH OF JUDAS AND THE
THIRTY PIECES OF SILVER

[3]*When Judas, his betrayer, saw that he was condemned, he repented and brought back the thirty pieces of silver to the chief priests and the elders,*

[4]*saying, 'I have sinned in betraying innocent blood.' They said, 'What is that to us? See to it yourself.'* [5]*And throwing down the pieces of silver in the temple, he departed; and he went and hanged himself.* [6]*But the chief priests, taking the pieces of silver, said, 'It is not lawful to put them into the treasury, since they are blood money.'* [7]*So they took counsel, and bought with them the potter's field, to bury strangers in.* [8]*Therefore that field has been called the Field of Blood to this day.* [9]*Then was fulfilled what had been spoken by the prophet Jeremiah, saying, 'And they took the thirty pieces of silver, the price of him on whom a price had been set by some of the sons of Israel,* [10]*and they gave them for the potter's field, as the Lord directed me.'*

Matthew uses the interval between the decision of the Sanhedrin and the trial before Pilate to tell his readers about the end of Judas. At this point, Matthew is not following Mark: there was no further mention of Judas in Mark, after the arrest of Jesus. Matthew's intention here is not to satisfy the curiosity of those who asked, 'What happened to Judas?' but to show once more how even here the scriptures were being fulfilled.

Judas, he says, changed his mind when he saw that Jesus had been condemned, took the money back to the Sanhedrin, and confessed his sin to them. They have achieved their purpose in the arrest and condemnation of Jesus, and so they have nothing to say to Judas: he must do whatever seems best to himself. He puts the money in the temple-treasury, and goes out to hang himself. The chief priests say that since this is money which has bought a life, it may not be put into the temple-treasury; so they use it to buy a plot of land for a cemetery. This fulfils a prophecy, which Matthew ascribes to Jeremiah, but was in fact from the book of Zechariah which has already played an important part in Matthew's narrative.

৯৩

The death of Judas is recorded by Luke in Acts $1^{18f.}$, which partly agrees with Matthew's account, and partly differs from it: Judas himself buys the field in Luke, and dies there; and that is why it is called *Field of Blood*. Either Matthew and Luke had independent access to similar stories about Judas, or Luke has abbreviated Matthew's account and made alterations to it.

3

he repented (*metamelētheis*): This word may have a weaker sense than *metanoein*, which is Matthew's other word for 'repent'; it may mean, regret, change one's mind.

4

innocent blood: Possibly (the manuscripts are divided here) 'righteous blood'; cf. 27¹⁹ *that righteous man* and 27²⁴ margin.

blood here means a living person; see also vv. 8, 24f.

See to it yourself: See 27²⁴ where Pilate uses the same words, also in a non-Marcan passage.

5

throwing down the pieces of silver in the temple: This may mean that Judas put the money into the temple-treasury; cf. Zech. 11¹³, *I took the thirty shekels of silver and cast them into the treasury in the house of the Lord.*

6

The chief priests say that, according to the Law, money which has been gained in this way may not be used for the temple; they may have based this on Deut. 23¹⁸.

7

For *the potter's field* see v. 10.

8

the Field of Blood: Because it was bought with the *blood money*, vv. 4, 6.

9f.

The quotation is from Zech. 11^{12f.}, and not from *Jeremiah*; possibly the confusion is due to the fact that Jeremiah bought a field and visited a potter, Jer. 32⁶⁻¹⁵, 18^{2ff.}. The quotation from Zechariah existed in different forms, and this accounts for the alternative interpretations of it given in v. 5 and here.

27¹¹⁻¹⁴   JESUS IS ACCUSED BEFORE   Mark 15²⁻⁵
                              PILATE

¹¹*Now Jesus stood before the governor; and the governor asked him, 'Are you the King of the Jews?' Jesus said to him, 'You have said so.' ¹²But when he was accused by the chief priests and elders, he made no answer.*

^{13} Then Pilate said to him, 'Do you not hear how many things they testify against you?' ^{14} But he gave him no answer, not even to a single charge; so that the governor wondered greatly.

The death of Judas had been a digression: Matthew returns to Jesus and *Pilate the governor*. Jesus had told the Sanhedrin that he was *the Christ*, and they have, presumably, brought that before Pilate as the charge against Jesus, explaining the technical term *Christ* as *King*. Pilate therefore asks Jesus, *Are you the King of the Jews?* Jesus' reply, as Matthew understands it, is almost certainly an affirmative; but to other accusations by the Jews he makes no reply, even when Pilate urges him to do so.

ॐ

The insertion of the paragraph about the death of Judas has made it necessary for Matthew to add an introductory sentence, 27^{11a}; otherwise Matthew has not changed Mark very much.

11
For *the King of the Jews* as the equivalent of *the Christ*, see 2$^{2,\ 4}$; in both cases, the former is the term used by Gentiles, the latter by Jews, because the Jews did not speak of themselves as Jews, but as Israel; so they would say, *the King of Israel*, as in 27^{42}.

You have said so (*su legeis*): Cf. the similar *su eipas* in 26$^{25,\ 64}$. In Matthew (though perhaps not in Mark) both expressions seem to be plain affirmatives.

12
Cf. the silence of Jesus before the Sanhedrin, 26$^{62f.}$.

14
not even to a single charge may be a mistranslation; the meaning may be, 'not even one word' (*Lexicon*).

27$^{15-23}$ **THE JEWS CHOOSE BARABBAS**   Mark 15$^{6-14}$
                        INSTEAD OF JESUS

^{15} Now at the feast the governor was accustomed to release for the crowd any one prisoner whom they wanted. ^{16} And they had then a notorious prisoner, *called Barab'bas.ª* ¹⁷*So when they had gathered, Pilate said to them, 'Whom do you want me to release for you, Barab'basª or Jesus who is called Christ?'* ¹⁸*For he knew that it was out of envy that they had delivered him up.* ¹⁹*Besides, while he was sitting on the judgement seat, his wife sent word to him, 'Have nothing to do with that righteous man, for I have suffered much over him today in a dream.'* ²⁰*Now the chief priests and the elders persuaded the people to ask for Barab'bas and destroy Jesus.* ²¹*The governor again said to them, 'Which of the two do you want me to release for you?' And they said, 'Barab'bas.'* ²²*Pilate said to them, 'Then what shall I do with Jesus who is called Christ?' They all said, 'Let him be crucified.'* ²³*And he said, 'Why what evil has he done?' But they shouted all the more, 'Let him be crucified.'*

a Other ancient authorities read *Jesus Barabbas*

The Evangelists tell us that Pilate used to release a prisoner chosen by the people at Passover, and that there was at that time a well-known prisoner whose name (according to some of the manuscripts of Matthew) was *Jesus Barabbas*. Pilate gives them the alternatives: *Jesus Barabbas*, or *Jesus who is called Christ*. He hopes that they will choose Christ, partly because he knows that the Sanhedrin has acted out of envy of Jesus, rather than for any just reason; partly because his wife has told him of a dream she has had, which informed her of the innocence of Jesus. The crowd has the choice, but they are persuaded by the Sanhedrin to choose Barabbas. Pilate asks them what he is to do with *Jesus who is called Christ*, and they demand his crucifixion. Pilate asks on what charge; but they merely repeat their demand more urgently.

Matthew's aim in this paragraph is to show that the responsibility for the crucifixion lay with the Sanhedrin and not with the Romans.

છ૭

Matthew has added to Mark the story of Pilate's wife and her dream, v. 19, and the detail that Barabbas was also called *Jesus* (if that is the original reading). He has omitted Mark's description of Barabbas: *among the rebels in prison, who had committed murder in the insurrection, there was a man called Barabbas* (Mark 15⁷).

15
There is no evidence for this custom, apart from the Gospels of Mark, Matthew, and John.

16

The reading *Jesus Barabbas* is found in Greek manuscripts, Syriac and other versions, and in one of the ancient Christian writers, Origen. It is more likely to be original than not: as time went on, the name *Jesus* was treated as a sacred name, and so the tendency would be to omit it, rather than to insert it; and Matthew has rewritten vv. 17 and 21f. because both the prisoners are called *Jesus*. The name Barabbas means Son of Abba, i.e. Son of the Father.

17

Mark had here *Do you want me to release for you the King of the Jews?* In Matthew, Pilate asks them to choose between *Jesus Barabbas* and *Jesus who is called Christ*.

18

For the *envy* of the Jewish leaders, see $21^{15f.}$, 45.

19

This addition is written in the Evangelist's own style, and its purpose is to explain why Pilate did not wish to order the crucifixion, and thus underline the responsibility of the Jewish leaders.

20

the people (*tous ochlous*) should be translated 'the crowds'. Matthew has added *and destroy Jesus*, emphasizing the guilt of the Jewish leaders.

21

Pilate's second question has been added by Matthew, and so has the answer to the crowds. He says *Jesus who is called Christ*, here and in the next verse, to distinguish him from *Jesus Barabbas*.

22f.

Matthew changes Mark's *crucify him* to *let him be crucified* in these two verses, to put the weight of responsibility on the Jews, and not on Pilate.

27^{24-26} PILATE AND THE PEOPLE;   Mark 15^{15}
BARABBAS AND JESUS

[24] *So when Pilate saw that he was gaining nothing, but rather that a riot was beginning, he took water and washed his hands before the crowd, saying, 'I am innocent of this man's blood;[a] see to it yourselves.'* [25] *And all the people*

answered, 'His blood be on us and on our children!' ²⁶ *Then he released for them Barab'bas, and having scourged Jesus, delivered him to be crucified.*

a Other authorities read *this righteous blood* or *this righteous man's blood*

Pilate has gone as far as he is prepared to go: he is prepared to declare Jesus innocent, but he is not prepared to risk the peace of Judea. He therefore publicly disclaims all responsibility for the execution: he releases Barabbas, and scourges Jesus and hands him over to the soldiers for crucifixion. Meanwhile, the Jewish people accept the responsibility for themselves and for their descendants.

Here again Matthew's intention is very clear: the Roman procurator is responsible only in that he allows the Jews to have their own way; apart from that the guilt lies entirely upon the Jews.

৵৶

Mark says only: *So Pilate, wishing to satisfy the crowd, released for them Barabbas; and having scourged Jesus, he delivered him to be crucified* (Mark 15¹⁵). Matthew adds both the action and the words of Pilate, in which Pilate dissociates himself from the death of Jesus. He also adds the words of *the people.*

24

The action of washing hands as a sign of innocence is Jewish rather than Roman; see Deut. 21¹ff. and note *all the elders of that city nearest to the slain man shall wash their hands . . . and they shall testify, Our hands did not shed this blood . . .* It is very unlikely that Pilate would have done this.

this man's blood means 'life', as in 27⁴ff. If *righteous* should be added, as in some of the manuscripts, it would then be a repetition of v. 19 (and possibly v. 4).

see to it yourselves: Cf. 27⁴.

25

all the people (pas ho laos): i.e. the Jewish nation. Matthew has not used the word 'crowd' (*ochlos*) as in vv. 15, 20, 24, because he means the words to be spoken by the Jews as *the people* of God.

26

Scourging was a regular Roman practice before the execution of a criminal; Jesus had predicted it in 20¹⁹.

THE SOLDIERS MOCK JESUS AS Mark 15^{16-20}
KING OF THE JEWS

27 *Then the soldiers of the governor took Jesus into the praetorium, and they
gathered the whole battalion before him.* 28 *And they stripped him and put a
scarlet robe upon him,* 29 *and plaiting a crown of thorns they put it on his
head, and put a reed in his right hand. And kneeling before him they mocked
him, saying, 'Hail, King of the Jews!'* 30 *And they spat upon him, and took
the reed and struck him on the head.* 31 *And when they had mocked him, they
stripped him of the robe, and put his own clothes on him, and led him away to
crucify him.*

The Roman soldiers mock Jesus for claiming to be what the readers
know him to be, *the King of the Jews*. They dress him in a soldier's
cloak as a substitute for the emperor's purple robe; they make him a
crown of thorns to parody the crown which the emperor wore, and
give him a reed for a sceptre; they kneel to him and address him as
one would address Caesar. But they also spit on him and strike him
with his sceptre. Then they restore his own clothes to him, and take
him off for crucifixion. The power of this passage lies in the combina-
tion of truth with ignorance: Jesus is what he is mocked for claiming
to be.

❧

Matthew has made several small alterations in Mark 15^{16-20}: he has
changed Mark's *purple cloak* into a *scarlet robe*, added the *reed in his right
hand*, and changed the order so that the reference to kneeling comes
earlier in the passage.

27
the praetorium: The Roman procurator's official residence in Jerusalem.

the whole battalion, or cohort – i.e. the tenth of a legion; normally 600
men.

28
they stripped him (*ekdysantes*): Some manuscripts have the very similar
word in Greek, *endysantes*, i.e. 'they clothed him'; he would have been
stripped for the scourging, v. 26.

437

a scarlet robe: Mark had *a purple cloak.* The emperor's colour was *purple* but the soldiers would use one of their own cloaks (*chlamys*) for the purpose, and these were *scarlet.*

29

plaiting a crown of thorns: The emperor is shown on coins of the period wearing a crown with radiant spikes. The soldiers imitate this with thorns; their intention is to mock Jesus, rather than to inflict pain upon him.

reed, or staff: the emperor is also shown holding a sceptre in his right hand as the symbol of his power to rule.

Hail, King, corresponds to the Latin greeting to the emperor, *Ave Caesar.*

31

The Evangelists say that the clothes were restored to Jesus, because they will be mentioned again, in v. 35, when Ps. 22 is fulfilled in the soldiers' dividing them by casting lots.

The next paragraph will describe the crucifixion, thus fulfilling Jesus' prediction in 20¹⁸ᶠ·, *The Son of man will be delivered to the chief priests and scribes, and they will condemn him to death, and deliver him to the Gentiles to be mocked and scourged and crucified, and he will be raised on the third day.*

27³²⁻⁴⁴	JESUS IS CRUCIFIED, AND MOCKED AGAIN	Mark 15²¹⁻³²

³²*As they were marching out, they came upon a man of Cyre'ne, Simon by name; this man they compelled to carry his cross.* ³³*And when they came to a place called Gol'gotha (which means the place of a skull),* ³⁴*they offered him wine to drink, mingled with gall; but when he tasted it, he would not drink it.* ³⁵*And when they had crucified him, they divided his garments among them by casting lots;* ³⁶*then they sat down and kept watch over him there.* ³⁷*And over his head they put the charge against him, which read, 'This is Jesus the King of the Jews.'* ³⁸*Then two robbers were crucified with him, one on the right and one on the left.* ³⁹*And those who passed by derided him, wagging their heads* ⁴⁰*and saying, 'You who would destroy the temple and build it in*

three days, save yourself! If you are the Son of God, come down from the cross.' 41*So also the chief priests, with the scribes and elders, mocked him, saying,* 42*'He saved others; he cannot save himself. He is the King of Israel; let him come down now from the cross, and we will believe in him.* 43*He trusts in God; let God deliver him now, if he desires him; for he said, "I am the Son of God." '* 44*And the robbers who were crucified with him also reviled him in the same way.*

Matthew describes the crucifixion in words which are full of Old Testament associations: the wine mingled with gall, the dividing of Jesus' garments by casting lots, the passers-by wagging their heads, the last words of the mocking Sanhedrin, the reviling by the robbers – are all echoes from Pss. 22 and 69. Matthew has, as we shall see, underlined the fulfilment of scripture: the idea was there in Mark, and indeed from the beginning (I Cor. 15³, *Christ died for our sins in accordance with the scriptures*); but Matthew brings out more fulfilments than Mark.

There is another aspect of Matthew's account of the crucifixion, and this also he has taken over from Mark: the passers-by and the Sanhedrin mock Jesus, repeating the false evidence about destroying the temple and building it in three days, and calling on him to come down from the cross; the Christian reader knows that Jesus is bringing the old order, of which the temple was the focus, to an end; and that Jesus could, if he wished, come down from the cross – he could appeal to the Father who would send *more than twelve legions of angels*. Thus the mocking is partly ironical (this is what Matthew has taken from Mark); but it is also a repetition of the temptation of the devil – *If you are the Son of God, throw yourself down; for it is written, He will give his angels charge of you* (4⁶). The Jews are therefore the mouthpiece of the devil; and Jesus withstands them here, as he withstood Satan before.

∞

Matthew uses Mark 15²¹⁻³², picking up the allusions to the Psalms and clarifying them; bringing in a reference back to the temptations in Matthew 4; but otherwise making only small changes in his source.

32
As they were marching out (exerchomenoi): Literally, 'as they came out' (i.e. of the city); the crucifixion outside Jerusalem had been predicted

in the parable in 21³⁹, in Matthew's version of it: *they took him and cast him out of the vineyard, and killed him.*

Simon by name: His name may have been mentioned because it was the same name as Peter's, and Jesus had said to Peter and the disciples, *If any man would come after me, let him deny himself* [Peter had denied Jesus] *and take up his cross* [in Greek the same word as *carry* here] *and follow me* (16²⁴).

compelled: See note on 5⁴¹.

33
Golgotha: The place may have been a hill shaped like a skull, or an unclean place used for executions; and at some time there was a legend that Adam's skull was buried there.

34
they offered him wine to drink, mingled with gall (Mark . . . *mingled with myrrh):* An allusion to Ps. 69²¹ *they gave me poison* [Greek, gall] *for food;* see v. 48 below for another reference to this verse of Ps. 69.

Mark had, *but he did not take it;* Matthew changes this, to *but when he tasted it, he would not drink it:* the purpose of the drink was to dull the pain, and this may be why the Evangelists record that Jesus did not drink it.

35
they divided his garments among them by casting lots: The soldiers had a right to the clothing of the criminal; but the Evangelists see also a fulfilment of Ps. 22¹⁸, *they divide my garments among them, and for my raiment they cast lots.*

36
Mark's next sentence is: *And it was the third hour, when they crucified him,* but Matthew changes this to *then they sat down and kept watch over him there.* Notice also the addition of the words *keeping watch over Jesus* in v. 54. The reason why Matthew adds these references to the guarding of Jesus during the crucifixion and after (see vv. 62–66, 28⁴, ¹¹⁻¹⁵) may be that there were people who said that Jesus had been removed from the cross before he was dead; one of the gnostic sects of the second century said that Simon of Cyrene was crucified instead of Jesus. Matthew may be countering these suggestions.

37
It was customary to display the charge for which a criminal was executed. See 26⁶³, 27¹¹. Matthew has added the words *This is Jesus;* cf. the voice at the baptism: *This is my beloved Son . . . , 3¹⁷.*

38

The two robbers may have been mentioned to recall Isa. 53¹², *he . . . was numbered with the transgressors*; certainly a later scribe of Mark's Gospel thought this appropriate (see Mark 15²⁸).

39

Cf. Ps. 22⁷, *All who see me mock at me, they make mouths at me, they wag their heads.*

40

For the destruction and rebuilding of the temple, see 26⁶¹.

Matthew adds the words, *If you are the Son of God*, repeating the devil's words in 4³, ⁶.

41f.

The Sanhedrin say *King of Israel*, not *King of the Jews*; see note on 27¹¹. They demand a miracle in order that they may believe; cf. 4⁵ᶠ.

43

The whole verse has been added by Matthew, using Ps. 22⁸: *He committed his cause to the Lord; let him deliver him, let him rescue him, for he delights in him!* . . .

for he said, I am the Son of God – cf. again the temptations, 4³, ⁶.

44

reviled him (ōneidizon): Cf. Ps. 69⁹, *the insults of those who insulted thee have fallen on me*, where the same word is used in the Greek.

27^{45-50} JESUS DIES   Mark 15³³⁻⁴¹

⁴⁵Now from the sixth hour there was darkness over all the land*a* until the ninth hour. ⁴⁶And about the ninth hour Jesus cried with a loud voice, 'Eli, Eli, la'ma sabach-tha'ni?' that is, 'My God, my God, why hast thou forsaken me?' ⁴⁷And some of the bystanders hearing it said, 'This man is calling Eli'jah.' ⁴⁸And one of them at once ran and took a sponge, filled it with vinegar, and put it on a reed, and gave it to him to drink. ⁴⁹But the others said, 'Wait, let us see whether Eli'jah will come to save him.'*b* ⁵⁰And Jesus cried again with a loud voice and yielded up his spirit.

  a Or *earth*
  b Other ancient authorities insert *And another took a spear and pierced his side, and out came water and blood*

The Evangelists do not stress the suffering of Jesus during the time of his crucifixion; they have other ways of understanding the meaning of the Lord's death, and of bringing it home to their readers; and they do this mainly by allusions to the Old Testament. Thus the darkness over all the land from noon till 3 p.m. fulfils prophecy, and may also have recalled the darkness which was one of the last plagues before the Exodus. The only words of Jesus from the cross in this Gospel are the opening line of Ps. 22, the Psalm which has already been referred to in the previous paragraph; and the vinegar given to Jesus is an allusion to Ps. 69, the other Psalm that was used in those verses. The bystanders misunderstand Jesus' *Eli, Eli*, and think that he is calling for Elijah to save him; but their misunderstanding drives home the point which the Evangelists have made so frequently, that Jesus has renounced his miraculous powers, in order that he may save others.

ɶ

Matthew makes no major changes in Mark 15³³⁻³⁶; some of his minor alterations are noted below.

45

Mark had *over the whole world* (eph' holēn tēn gēn) and Matthew changes this to *over all the land* (epi pasan tēn gēn); this apparently unimportant alteration may be due to his recollection of Exod. 10²², *there was thick darkness in all the land* (epi pasan gēn) *of Egypt three days*. This darkness was the last plague in Egypt before the death of the first born: Jesus' death is parallel to the last plague, so it may be that Matthew saw this three-hour darkness as the fulfilment of the three-day darkness in Egypt. The Jewish expectation that the last days would be like the days of Egypt would predispose him to think so. But we may also compare Amos 8⁹, *And on that day, says the Lord God, I will make the sun go down at noon, and darken the earth in broad daylight.*

46

The manuscripts of both Mark and Matthew give the words of Jesus in different forms, but it is probable that Mark wrote *Eloi, Eloi*, which is the Aramaic, and that Matthew wrote *Eli, Eli*, which is the Hebrew version of Ps. 22¹. For previous references to this Psalm, see 27³⁵, ³⁹, ⁴³. In 26³⁶⁻⁴⁶ we were shown that Jesus accepted the will of God for him; that this involved a *cup* of suffering; and that it had been foretold in *the scriptures*. Then in 27³²⁻⁴⁴ we were shown that one of these scriptures was Ps. 22. It was therefore appropriate that the one saying of Jesus during the crucifixion should be the opening words of that Psalm. They express the sense of being abandoned by God in the face of hostility. Jesus has accepted this as the cost of rescuing men from the devil's power.

47
According to the Old Testament legend, Elijah did not die, but was taken up to heaven alive, 2 Kings 2$^{9-12}$; and it was believed that he would return to help those in distress. The bystanders misunderstand *Eli* as 'Elijah'.

48
Cf. Ps. 69^{21}, *and for my thirst they gave me vinegar to drink*; see 27^{34} for use of the earlier part of this verse.

49
The distinction between the one who gave Jesus the vinegar and the other who said, *Wait* . . . is due to Matthew: in Mark, the same man gives him the vinegar and says these words. In Matthew, *the others* address the man who has given him the vinegar: *aphes* (*wait*) is in the singular; whereas in Mark it is plural (*aphete*), and is addressed to the bystanders.

50
Matthew has slightly rewritten Mark here, possibly in order to imply that Jesus' death was a voluntary and active surrender of his life to God; *yielded up his spirit*, instead of Mark's *breathed his last*.

27$^{51-54}$ THE SIGNS AFTER THE   Mark 15$^{38, 39}$
                        DEATH OF JESUS

^{51}*And behold, the curtain of the temple was torn in two, from top to bottom; and the earth shook, and the rocks were split;* ^{52}*the tombs also were opened, and many bodies of the saints who had fallen asleep were raised,* ^{53}*and coming out of the tombs after his resurrection they went into the holy city and appeared to many.* ^{54}*When the centurion and those who were with him, keeping watch over Jesus, saw the earthquake and what took place, they were filled with awe, and said, 'Truly this was a son of God!'*

Matthew has been generally content with Mark's narrative of the crucifixion up to this point; but from here on he begins to add considerably. Mark had recorded two signs which followed the death of Jesus and explained its meaning for those with eyes to see; namely, the tearing of the curtain in the temple, and the words of the centurion. The former showed that Jesus had brought the old order to an end, and the latter expressed what Christians believed about Jesus: he was the Son of God. Matthew adds further signs: an earthquake, the opening of the tombs, the resurrection of the saints and their appearing to many in Jerusalem after the resurrection of Jesus. These legendary events are included by Matthew to show that the death of Jesus was an act of God, which God endorsed by the earthquake and by splitting the rocks; and that the effect of this act will be life for the dead: Jesus is *the first fruits of those who have fallen asleep* (1 Cor. 15^{20}).

୨୦୧

Matthew has used Mark 15^{38} for 27^{51a}, and Mark 15^{39} for 27^{54}; so far as we know, he had no written source for vv. 51b–53.

51
There were two curtains in the temple: an outer curtain, and a second curtain before the Holy of Holies (see, for example, Heb. 9$^{1ff.}$); probably the Evangelists mean here the second curtain; and the point which they wish to make is that Jesus has made it possible for man to approach God in a new way. This is how this sign seems to have been interpreted in Heb. 10$^{19f.}$, *Therefore, brethren, since we have confidence to enter the sanctuary* [i.e. the presence of God] *by the blood of Jesus, by the new and living way which he opened for us through the curtain, that is, through his flesh. . . .*

the earth shook, and the rocks were split: For earthquakes as evidence of God at work, see e.g. Judges 5^4, 2 Sam. 22^8, Ps. 68^8. An earthquake and the breaking of the rocks are mentioned in 1 Kings 19^{11}.

Josephus records similar signs before the destruction of the temple in A.D. 70, *The Jewish War*, VI, 5, 3 (Penguin ed., pp. 326f.).

52f.
the saints: i.e. the holy men of Israel's past. They appear *after his resurrection*, because Jesus is *the first fruits*. The legend is an extrapolation of Christian faith in the form of a story.

54

Matthew adds the words, *and those who were with him, keeping watch over Jesus* – see note on v. 36 above; and he changes Mark's *saw that he breathed his last,* to *saw the earthquake and what took place, they were filled with awe.*

Truly this was a son of God! The Greek can be translated, 'The Son of God'; the centurion and his soldiers act as mouthpieces for the Christians, and confess their faith in Jesus.

^{55}*There were also many women there, looking on from afar, who had followed Jesus from Galilee, ministering to him;* ^{56}*among whom were Mary Mag'dalene, and Mary the mother of James and Joseph, and the mother of the sons of Zeb'edee.*

The disciples had fled when Jesus was arrested, and though Peter had followed as far as the high priest's courtyard, we do not hear any more of him after his denials of Jesus. Mark, Matthew, and Luke tell us that the witnesses of the crucifixion were women who had come with Jesus from Galilee to Jerusalem. They see his burial, they find the tomb empty on the Sunday morning, and they meet Jesus, 27^{61}, 28$^{1, 9}$. Matthew may have had two reasons for mentioning them: they link up the crucifixion and burial with the resurrection; and they fulfil another Psalm, 38.

≈≈≈

For Matthew's changes in Mark 15$^{40f.}$, see the notes.

55

looking on from afar (apo makrothen): Cf. Ps. 38^{11} *my kinsmen stand afar off (apo makrothen)*; Luke brings out the reference to the Psalm more clearly, *And all his acquaintance . . . stood at a distance* (Luke 23^{49}).

56

Mary Magdalene, and Mary the mother of James and Joseph: They are mentioned again at 27^{61} and 28^{1}. Mark had *of James the younger and of*

Joses; and although Matthew says in 13^{55} that two of Jesus' brothers were called *James and Joseph*, he can hardly mean by his second *Mary*, Mary the mother of Jesus.

The mother of the sons of Zebedee, mentioned before at 20^{20}. Mark had *Salome* here.

^{57}*When it was evening, there came a rich man from Arimathe'a, named Joseph, who also was a disciple of Jesus.* ^{58}*He went to Pilate and asked for the body of Jesus. Then Pilate ordered it to be given to him.* ^{59}*And Joseph took the body, and wrapped it in a clean linen shroud,* ^{60}*and laid it in his own new tomb, which he had hewn in the rock; and he rolled a great stone to the door of the tomb, and departed.* ^{61}*Mary Mag'dalene and the other Mary were there, sitting opposite the sepulchre.*

The Jews believed that corpses were unclean, and that this was especially so with the corpses of those who had been crucified; the law said: *If a man has committed a crime punishable by death and he is put to death, and you hang him on a tree, his body shall not remain all night upon the tree, but you shall bury him the same day, for a hanged man is accursed by God* (Deut. 21^{22ff}). It was important to the Jews, therefore, that the body of Jesus should be removed before night; and this was done by an otherwise unknown disciple, Joseph of Arimathea. He obtains permission from Pilate, wraps the body in a clean shroud, and lays it in his own unused tomb, closing the doorway with a great stone. Matthew says that the two Marys were sitting opposite the sepulchre: they will therefore be able to identify the right tomb two days later, and thus bear witness to the resurrection.

જી

Matthew has abbreviated Mark 15$^{42-47}$, but also added a few details of his own.

57
When it was evening: Presumably Matthew means before sunset, since

the sabbath would begin at sunset, and no work would then be allowed. Josephus says, 'The Jews pay so much regard to obsequies that even those found guilty and crucified are taken down and buried before sunset,' *The Jewish War*, IV, 5, 2 (Penguin ed., p. 238).

a rich man: Matthew has changed Mark's *a respected member of the council* to *a rich man* (*anthrōpos plousios*), presumably because he wanted to allude to Isaiah's account of the burial of the servant of the Lord: *and they made his grave with the wicked and with a rich man in his death* (Isa. 53⁹).

58
Matthew has omitted Mark 15⁴⁴, Pilate's inquiry of the centurion into the death of Jesus.

59f.
Matthew adds here the words *clean*, *his own new*, and *great*.

61
Mark had *saw where he was laid*; Matthew says, *were there, sitting opposite the sepulchre*; like the guards sitting at the crucifixion, 27³⁶, the women make certain for the reader that there was no mistake about the identity of the place: it is the Jesus who was crucified, dead, and buried, who was raised up on the third day.

27^{62-66}   THE TOMB IS GUARDED

⁶²*Next day, that is, after the day of Preparation, the chief priests and the Pharisees gathered before Pilate* ⁶³*and said, 'Sir, we remember how that impostor said, while he was still alive, "After three days I will rise again."* ⁶⁴*Therefore order the sepulchre to be made secure until the third day, lest his disciples go and steal him away, and tell the people, "He has risen from the dead," and the last fraud will be worse than the first.'* ⁶⁵*Pilate said to them, 'You have a guard*ᵃ *of soldiers; go, make it as secure as you can.'*ᵇ ⁶⁶*So they went and made the sepulchre secure by sealing the stone and setting a guard.*

    a Or *take a guard*
    b Greek *know*

Matthew has already shown his concern that people should not be able to say that there had been any deception: no one could have removed Jesus from the cross during the crucifixion, because the Roman soldiers were there guarding him (vv. 36, 54). He now adds an entirely new paragraph, explaining how the watch on the tomb was kept up during the sabbath, and the reason why this was done: the Jewish leaders explained to Pilate that Jesus had said that he would be raised up after three days; his disciples may remove him from the tomb and say that he has been raised; this can be prevented by precautions taken at the tomb until the third day. The arrangements are made; the stone is sealed and a guard is set. But in the event this only serves to bear witness to the action of God, by proving that Jesus was raised by God, and not removed by the disciples.

അ

There is no parallel in the other Gospels.

62

Next day, that is, after the day of Preparation, i.e. on the sabbath. The expression is strange; it may, however, be an example of Matthew fitting in a word of Mark's which he had omitted earlier – at 27[57] he had left out *the day of Preparation* in Mark 15[42].

63f.

The words *impostor* and *fraud* are from the same root in Greek (*planos, planē*); therefore when the Jews say, *the last fraud will be worse than the first*, they mean by *the first*, belief in Jesus as Messiah; and by *the last*, belief in his resurrection.

65

The margin translation is better, *Take a guard*: they would be a guard of Roman soldiers, not Jewish.

66

sealing the stone: Cf. Dan. 6[17], *A stone was brought and laid upon the mouth of the den, and the king sealed it with his own signet and with the signet of his lords, that nothing might be changed concerning Daniel*. Daniel's escape from the den of lions was a type or parable of Jesus' resurrection, in the early Church.

THE RESURRECTION   Mark 16¹⁻⁸

28 *Now after the sabbath, toward the dawn of the first day of the week,
Mary Mag'dalene and the other Mary went to see the sepulchre.* ²*And
behold, there was a great earthquake; for an angel of the Lord descended
from heaven and came and rolled back the stone, and sat upon it.* ³*His
appearance was like lightning, and his raiment white as snow.* ⁴*And for
fear of him the guards trembled and became like dead men.* ⁵*But the angel
said to the women, 'Do not be afraid; for I know that you seek Jesus who was
crucified.* ⁶*He is not here; for he has risen, as he said. Come, see the place
where heᵃ lay.* ⁷*Then go quickly and tell his disciples that he has risen from
the dead, and behold, he is going before you to Galilee; there you will see him.
Lo, I have told you.'* ⁸*So they departed quickly from the tomb with fear and
great joy, and ran to tell his disciples.* ⁹*And behold, Jesus met them and said,
'Hail!' And they came up and took hold of his feet and worshipped him.*
¹⁰*Then Jesus said to them, 'Do not be afraid; go and tell my brethren to go to
Galilee, and there they will see me.'*

a Other ancient authorities read *the Lord*

Matthew comes now to the morning of the first day of the week; the
resurrection and empty tomb which he will describe will not surprise
the reader: he had heard of it first in this Gospel at 12⁴⁰, and he had
been reminded of it as recently as 27⁶³. The two Marys, who had sat
opposite the sepulchre on Friday evening now return to see it; but
there is another earthquake, and an angel rolls back the stone, to
reveal the emptiness of the tomb, and to give the women a command
to the disciples to go to Galilee. Then, as they go from the tomb,
they meet Jesus, and he repeats the message. In Matthew, this
paragraph is not the climax of the story as it is in Mark, but a transition
passage, preparing for the last scene in Galilee, which is the climax
in this Gospel.

 споре

Matthew has been radical in his treatment of Mark 16¹⁻⁸. As far as we
know, the Gospel according to Mark, as Matthew had it, ended at
Mark 16⁸; so the appearance of Jesus to the women in Matthew 28⁹ᶠ· has
been added by Matthew. Similarly, the earthquake, the angel descending

from heaven and rolling back the stone, and the fear of the guards (vv. 2–4) are all Matthean additions, for which Matthew has 'made room' by omitting Mark 16$^{3-5}$. Thus Matthew 28$^{1, 5-8}$ are from Mark 16$^{1, 2, 6-8}$, but the 'atmosphere' of these, and of the whole passage, has been changed: Mark gives the impression of the women's terror in the presence of an act of God; in Matthew, fear is still mentioned, but it has been swallowed up by the *great joy* of the women, who obey the angel and see and worship their Lord.

1

Matthew has omitted *Salome* again (see above 27^{56}), and has changed Mark's statement that the women bought spices so *that they might go and anoint him* to *to see the sepulchre*. Presumably, since Matthew has introduced the sealing of the stone (27^{66}), he had to make this adjustment here.

2–4

Matthew has to avoid the women's question in Mark, *Who will roll away the stone for us from the door of the tomb?* because he has introduced the guard in 27^{66} who are there to prevent any tampering with the stone by the disciples. For *earthquake*, cf. 27^{51}. For the description of the angel, cf. 17^{2}.

5–7

Matthew omits Mark's specific reference to Peter, *Tell his disciples and Peter*, and this is strange, in view of the interest in Peter shown elsewhere in this Gospel, e.g. 10^{2}, 16$^{17ff.}$.

8

In Mark, the women do not obey the message, but in Matthew they do; in Mark they flee in *trembling and astonishment*, but in Matthew they run in *fear and great joy*. Matthew is reading the Easter joy of the Church back into his account of the resurrection.

9, 10

Mark's Gospel, as far as we know, contained no account of the appearance of the risen Lord – though some scholars have suggested that there was originally more of Mark than has been preserved, or than what was known to Matthew and Luke and used by them. Matthew adds two appearances of Jesus after the resurrection, here and in the final paragraph, and in both places he says that Jesus was *worshipped*.

For the *great joy* in v. 8 and the worshipping of Jesus here, cf. the Magi in 2$^{10f.}$; Matthew is bringing the end of the Gospel into line with the beginning of it.

THE GUARD, THE CHIEF PRIESTS,
AND THE JEWS

[11]*While they were going, behold, some of the guard went into the city and
told the chief priests all that had taken place.* [12]*And when they had assembled
with the elders and taken counsel, they gave a sum of money to the soldiers*
[13]*and said, 'Tell people, "His disciples came by night and stole him away
while we were asleep." * [14]*And if this comes to the governor's ears, we will
satisfy him and keep you out of trouble.' * [15]*So they took the money and did
as they were directed; and this story has been spread among the Jews to
this day.*

The guard report back to the chief priests, and there is a final assembly
with the elders, which proposes a financial arrangement with the
guard: the soldiers are to say that the disciples stole the body by
night while the guard was asleep, and the priests will see that there
is no trouble with Pilate. Matthew says that this is the story which
has been current among the Jews ever since, and he thus explains
how it was that they did not believe in the resurrection of Jesus.

೧೪೨

Matthew no longer has Mark as his source; he probably composed this
paragraph and the last himself, as the evidence of vocabulary and
style show.

11
As Pilate had commanded the chief priests to set the guard at the
sepulchre (27[65]), some of the guard now report back to *the chief priests*.

12
Cf. 26[14f.] for a previous use of money by the chief priests.

13f.
The chief priests now make use of the fraud which they had expected
the disciples to perpetrate, 27[64].

JESUS SENDS HIS DISCIPLES
TO ALL NATIONS

¹⁶*Now the eleven disciples went to Galilee, to the mountain to which Jesus had directed them.* ¹⁷*And when they saw him they worshipped him; but some doubted.* ¹⁸*And Jesus came and said to them, 'All authority in heaven and on earth has been given to me.* ¹⁹*Go therefore and make disciples of all nations, baptizing them in the name of the Father and of the Son and of the Holy Spirit,* ²⁰*teaching them to observe all that I have commanded you; and lo, I am with you always, to the close of the age.'*

Matthew's final paragraph picks up the loose ends in the Gospel, and prepares for the life and work of the Church. The promise of Jesus to go before them to Galilee, and the words of the angel at the tomb, are now fulfilled. So also the various hints throughout the Gospel that Jesus would eventually send his disciples to the Gentiles are now endorsed by the explicit command to go to *all nations*. The disciples are at last told to *teach* what Jesus had commanded them; and he promises to be with them until the end of the age, when he will come in glory to judge and to reward.

※

16
the eleven disciples: See 27⁵ for the death of Judas.

Galilee: In Chapter 2 Joseph was directed to Galilee because of the unbelief of Herod and Archelaus in Judea; that situation has now been repeated in the unbelief of the Jews in Jerusalem, and the mission to the Gentiles from Galilee. Notice also the prophecy in 4¹⁵ᶠ· of *a great light* for the people in *Galilee of the Gentiles*. It is almost certain that in fact the Church began in Jerusalem, not in Galilee; and that is what Luke says: *stay in the city, until you are clothed with power from on high* (Luke 24⁴⁹). Matthew's placing of this final scene in Galilee is due partly to his following hints in Mark 14²⁸, 16⁷, partly to his use of Galilee as the symbol for the Gentile world; but it is probably not historical.

to the mountain to which Jesus had directed them: This is probably the right translation, rather than 'to the mountain where Jesus had appointed them'. But Matthew has not recorded the direction of Jesus to a particular mountain; possibly he means the mountain mentioned at 5^1.

17

they worshipped him: See note on 28^9.

but some doubted: Presumably some of *the eleven disciples*. It is not at all clear why Matthew says this, though we may compare the resurrection stories in Luke and John, which in each case contain references to doubt and unbelief (Luke $24^{22\text{ff.}}$, $36^{\text{ff.}}$, John $20^{8\text{ff.}}$, $11^{\text{ff.}}$, $24^{\text{ff.}}$).

18

Cf. what is said of *the Son of man* in Dan. 7^{14}, *To him was given dominion and glory and kingdom, that all peoples, nations, and languages should serve him.* Contrast Jesus' limited mission, to Israel only, 15^{24}. Jesus' saying here fulfils his promise in 26^{64}, *You will see the Son of man seated at the right hand of Power.*

has been given to me = 'God has given to me'.

19

Go therefore and make disciples of all nations: Contrast the limited mission of the disciples, to Israel alone, in 10^6. It is improbable that Jesus said this, in view of the hesitation of the first disciples over preaching to Gentiles, as this is recorded in Acts (N.B. Acts. Acts $11^{1\text{ff.}}$ and 11^{19}).

baptizing them in the name of the Father and of the Son and of the Holy Spirit: This is the only explicit command of Jesus to baptize. The first disciples baptized *in the name of Jesus Christ*, and not in the threefold name – e.g. Acts 2^{38}.

20

teaching them: The work of Jesus was described as *teaching, preaching, and healing* in 4^{23}, 9^{35}; he commanded the disciples to *heal* in $10^{9,\ 8}$ and to *preach* in 10^7; the command to *teach* has been reserved till the end of the Gospel, perhaps because Matthew regarded the teacher's office as the highest in the Church.

all that I have commanded you: Matthew thinks of Jesus as the second Moses, giving the final laws of God; see, for example, 5^{17-48}.

I am with you always: Cf. 1^{23}, *Emmanuel ... God with us*; 18^{20}, *there am I in the midst of them.*

the close of the age is Matthew's characteristic expression for the end; see $13^{39\text{f.}}$, 49, 24^3.

453

Indexes

Index of References

THE BIBLE
Old Testament

New Testament

NON-BIBLICAL AUTHORS

MODERN AUTHORS

Index of Biblical Proper Names

Index of Subjects

Israel, 19, 46, 94, 95, 125, 128, 137,
146, 149f., 156f., 159, 160, 161,
172f., 174, 178, 190, 193ff., 196f.,
199, 203, 205ff., 217, 218f., 237,
250, 252, 254, 255, 256f., 305, 307,
317, 336, 340, 341, 348, 378, 394,
407, 408, 409, 420, 427, 433, 436,
441, 453; the New, 15, 44, 151,
160, 193ff., 206, 236, 265f., 269,
297f., 317, 341

Jews, 11, 15, 19, 21, 22, 24, 26, 34,
43, 44, 46, 53, 55, 56, 76, 80, 84,
85, 102, 109, 122, 123, 124, 125,
129, 134, 137, 140, 145, 151, 156,
161, 165, 179, 180, 181f., 198f.,
204, 212, 225, 226, 230, 236, 249,
254ff., 259, 268, 270, 276, 279f.,
281, 284, 308, 317, 332, 336, 339,
343, 347, 350, 352, 354, 357, 365,
386, 389, 391, 402, 407, 408, 410,
415, 433ff., 436, 439, 441, 442, 446,
448, 451, 452
John, Gospel of, 162, 186, 229, 242,
266, 268, 403, 415, 425, 427, 434,
453
Joy, 47, 227, 283, 314, 399, 450
Judaism, 140, 197ff., 213
Judgement, 22, 23, 26, 51, 52, 56, 57f.,
72, 80, 87, 88, 101, 103, 107ff., 114,
133, 150, 155, 157, 158, 159, 161,
164, 166, 171f., 177, 178, 182f.,
184, 199, 200f., 202, 204f., 220,
225, 226, 229, 270, 274, 276, 290,
292f., 296, 300ff., 314, 317, 319f.,
322, 324, 336, 344f., 350, 364, 368,
376, 377f., 389, 392, 393, 396, 399,
407, 412, 416, 427, 429, 433, 452

Keys, 264ff., 269f., 369
Kill, 86
King, Jesus as, 23, 33, 34, 36, 38, 40,
45, 46, 47, 53, 57, 78, 128, 157, 184,
226, 227, 268, 274, 275f., 284f.,
305, 317, 324f., 328f., 331, 333ff.,

348, 391, 395, 401f., 411f., 427,
433, 437f., 441
Kingdom, coming of, 21, 57, 72, 74,
76, 78, 81, 101, 102, 107, 108, 120,
126, 139, 141, 146, 149, 152, 156f.,
159, 163, 172, 176, 178, 179, 183,
184, 185, 190, 196, 198f., 202f.,
214, 215ff., 218f., 221f., 223, 224,
226, 231, 242, 244, 262, 269, 273,
290, 342, 366, 384f., 389, 391, 396,
409, 417; divided, 196ff.
Kingdom of heaven, 14ff., 23, 24,
25, 51, 52, 53, 54, 55, 67, 71, 73,
76, 79, 80, 81, 82, 83, 85, 101, 105,
110, 112, 124, 125, 137, 138, 140,
157, 172, 177, 179, 185, 198f., 211,
221f., 223, 226, 227, 228, 230, 243,
265, 267, 269f., 289, 290f., 305, 308,
310, 311f., 312ff., 316f., 319ff.,
323ff., 336, 340, 345, 349, 350f.,
355, 368ff., 372, 377, 389, 393, 396,
398, 401, 417f.
Kings. See Rulers
Kiss, 424ff.
Kneel, 121, 122f., 142, 281, 324,
437
Know. See Acknowledge

Labour, 172, 187
Labourers, 25f., 71, 149ff., 318ff.
Laden, heavy, 172, 187
Lame, 176, 257, 290, 333f.
Lament over Jerusalem, 363f.
Lamp, 84, 106, 109
Landlord, 340ff.
Last, 80, 82, 204f., 289, 318, 319,
321f., 323ff.
Last Supper, 54, 267, 291, 415f., 419,
424
Law, 43, 56, 77, 84f., 90f., 92, 95, 96,
121f., 135, 137f., 139, 140, 142,
152, 185f., 187, 188ff., 191ff., 227,
230f., 236, 248ff., 251f., 254, 259,
278, 284, 308, 314, 321, 334, 352,
354, 356, 366, 369, 372f., 387, 391,
394, 398, 401, 432, 446, 453

Index of Greek Words

MORE ABOUT PENGUINS

Penguinews, which appears every month, contains details of all the new books issued by Penguins as they are published. From time to time it is supplemented by *Penguins in Print*, which is a complete list of all books published by Penguins which are in print. (There are well over four thousand of these.)

A specimen copy of *Penguinews* will be sent to you free on request, and you can become a subscriber for the price of the postage. For a year's issues (including the complete lists) please send 30p if you live in the United Kingdom, or 60p if you live elsewhere. Just write to Dept EP, Penguin Books Ltd, Harmondsworth, Middlesex, enclosing a cheque or postal order, and your name will be added to the mailing list.

Some other books published by Penguins are described on the following pages.

Note: *Penguinews* and *Penguins in Print* are not available in the U.S.A. or Canada

PAUL'S FIRST LETTER TO CORINTH

John Ruef

The Pelican New Testament Commentaries mark a new departure in Bible criticism. Former commentaries have usually been of two kinds – either abstruse and academic, or over-simplified and out of date. These new paragraph-by-paragraph commentaries have been written by modern scholars who are in touch with contemporary Biblical theology and also with the needs of the average layman. They interpret the words of the New Testament for the twentieth century, in the light of the latest archaeological, historical and linguistic research.

John Ruef, Professor of Theology at Berkeley Divinity School in Connecticut, is well acquainted with the most recent trends in theology. He brings to his examination of Paul's first letter to Corinth a particular understanding of the confusing pattern of religious borrowing and syncretism which prevailed when the epistle was written. His commentary sets out very clearly what Paul, in the excitement of the times, was trying to say about the Resurrection and about possession by the Spirit – doctrines which had been misunderstood by the young Church at Corinth, with its gnostic bias.

PAUL'S LETTERS FROM PRISON

PHILLIPIANS, COLOSSIANS, PHILEMON AND EPHESIANS

J. H. Houlden

Paul was a Jew of the dispersion, familiar with Greek ideas and culture. An exotic style, the corruption of texts handed down to us, and a thick layer of pietistic interpretation produced by 2,000 years of Christianity, have obscured his work for us. The purpose of this book, which includes Paul's letters to the Phillipians, Colossians, Ephesians, and to Philemon, is to let Paul speak for himself, without the assumptions imposed by many modern readers.

Paul's main concern was to reconcile the two dominant principles of his work: the omnipotence of God as Lord of the Universe, and the alienation of man. This reconciliation Paul saw typified in the person of Jesus; but in one very clear direction, the direction which landed him in jail. Man's alienation could be cured not merely by coming to a better 'moral state', but by coming into a new status, a new pattern of social relationships.

The 'captivity epistles' are of dubious authorship and from different times, but together they form a valuable introduction to the apostle's work.

METHODISM

Rupert E. Davies

The prodigious horseback ministry of John Wesley in the eighteenth century ranks as a saga of Christian faith. By his exertions Wesley inspired, organized, and welded 'the people called Methodists' into a church which has today grown into the greatest force in the Protestant world.

The Vice-Principal of Didsbury College, Bristol, outlines in this new book the history of the Methodist Church since Wesley's day and discusses its present condition. He shows how Methodism has, in fact, been a recurrent brand of Christianity since the earliest times. Describing John Wesley's personal religious development, his proclamation of the orthodox doctrines of the Christian Church with his own particular emphases, and his extraordinary power over men's minds, as well as the importance of Charles Wesley's poetry, he succeeds in correcting many false images of Methodism.

With the tide set in the direction of Christian unity, his estimate of the contribution which world-wide Methodism can make to the 'coming great Church' necessarily commands both interest and respect.

THE ORTHODOX CHURCH

Timothy Ware

This book is a clear, detailed introduction to the Orthodox Church, written for the non-orthodox, as well as for Orthodox Christians who wish to know more about their own tradition. Part One describes the history of the Eastern Church over the last 2,000 years and particularly its problems in twentieth-century Russia. Part Two explains the beliefs and worship of the Orthodox today. Finally the author considers the possibilities of reunion between East and West.

The former Pope, John XXIII, was noted for his sympathy and friendship towards the Orthodox, yet this is but one symptom of a rapidly growing interest in the West. Timothy Ware believes that an understanding of Orthodoxy is necessary before the Roman Catholic and Protestant Churches can be reunited, and here he explains the Orthodox views on such widely ranging matters as Ecumenical Councils, Sacraments, Freewill, Purgatory, Icons, the Papacy, Protestantism, and the relation between the different Orthodox Churches.

More than ten per cent of Russia's 208,000,000 people attend church regularly, even after forty-five years of active hostility and persecution by the state. This book answers the questions most often asked about their faith.

MYSTICISM

A STUDY AND AN ANTHOLOGY

F. C. Happold

Mysticism is concerned with spiritual knowledge – the knowledge of truths we cannot understand with our minds. Most books on mysticism are difficult to follow without acquaintance with the writings of the mystics themselves, and the latter are hard to come by and too extensive for the ordinary reader.

This new book offers an original and effective solution of the difficulty. In it the author has combined both a study of mysticism, which makes its own contribution to the literature of the subject, and an anthology of mystical writings. Covering a wider field than previous selections, this anthology has been compiled to illustrate and complement the study. Its twenty-seven sections (each with an introductory note) are taken from the work not only of Christian mystics, but also from the *Upanishads* and the *Baghavad Gita*, from Plato and Plotinus, and from the Sufi mystics of Islam.

In effect this forms a very simple and complete introduction to the vast range of mystical thought and speculation.